CLIVE OF IND

Books by the same author

The remarkable Irish
Palaces of the Raj

Fiction

All a nonsense
Paradise escaped
Nothing in the city

CLIVE OF INDIA

Mark Bence-Jones

Constable London

First published in Great Britain 1974
by Constable and Company Limited
10 Orange Street, London WC2H 7EG

ISBN 0 09 467820 0

Printed in Great Britain by
St Edmundsbury Press Limited
Bury St Edmunds, Suffolk

To Gill

Contents

Illustrations

MAPS

Immediately prior to the index there are maps of India in the 18th century, the Carnatic and Bengal. The reader is strongly advised to refer to these.

Preface

Having spent the greater part of my childhood in India, I was familiar with the name of Clive from a very early age. It was for me synonymous with the remote past; since my father, and no doubt others too, used to say of anything particularly antiquated, whether it was a car, a chair or a camera, 'It must have come out with Clive!' Clive has always, therefore, held a special fascination for me; but he remained a shadowy figure until I started work on this book. As the founder of British India, everybody had heard of him. They knew he had won the battle of Plassey, that he was afterwards badly treated, and that he had spoken of being astonished at his own moderation; some believed him to have committed suicide. But the picture of Clive which they derived from these various scraps of knowledge was really no clearer than my own childhood vision of him coming to India from England in the Dark Ages, bringing a cargo of outmoded merchandise.

In trying to learn more about him, I discovered why Clive was the most elusive of the great Englishmen of the eighteenth century; and in the answer lay my reason for embarking on this book. No satisfactory biography of him had as yet been written. Such biographies as existed numbered no more than about half-a-dozen in all, of which the first, Sir John Malcolm's three-volume work, published in 1836 with the approval of Clive's son, was probably still the best.

But if there was a shortage of printed books about Clive, there was certainly no lack of contemporary manuscript material, much of which appeared to have been disregarded by previous writers, or had not yet come to light in their day. Clive kept almost every letter he received, and a copy of almost every letter he wrote, and all of these were preserved in the Powis and Clive Collections. Then there were the papers of his three closest friends and associates, John Walsh, Henry Strachey and General John Carnac, in the Ormathwaite and Sutton Court Collections, which included many fascinating and hitherto undiscovered letters from his wife, Margaret. There was a host of minor sources, many of them new, including a small but valuable collection of the papers of Clive's great enemy, Laurence Sulivan, about whom previous writers had been able to find out so little. And then, of course, there were the East India Company records and the immense collection of manuscripts accumulated by Clive's sometime friend Robert Orme, the first chronicler of his battles. In quoting from eighteenth-century sources, I have used modern spelling; and I have tried to adhere to the most recent usage in the rendering of Indian words and names.

In thanking those who allowed me to quote from unpublished manuscripts, enabled me to see, and perhaps reproduce, pictures, or helped me in other ways – and in many cases, gave me encouragement and hospitality as well – I must first of all mention the following representatives of the Clive family: the Earl and Countess of Powis; the Earl and Countess of Plymouth; Viscount and Viscountess Bridgeman; Lady Mary Clive; Mr George Clive; the late Mr Christopher Hussey, CBE; and Mrs Derek Schreiber. To Lord Powis, who kindly gave me permission to quote from manuscripts in the Powis and Clive Collections, I am particularly indebted.

For permission to quote from manuscripts in the Ormathwaite and Sutton Court Collections, I am grateful to Lord Ormathwaite, to the late Lord Strachie and his great-nephew, Lord O'Hagan – who also kindly allowed me to quote from Jane Latham's diary – and to the Rev. Sir Nicholas Rivett-Carnac, Bt. Unpublished Crown copyright material in the India Office Library or India Office Records transcribed or reproduced in this book appears by permission of the Controller of Her Majesty's Stationery Office. Other unpublished manuscript material is transcribed by courtesy of the British Library (British Museum); the Bodleian Library; the National Maritime Museum; the Ames Library of South Asia, University of Minnesota, Minneapolis; the Henry E. Huntington Library and Art Gallery, San Marino, California; and of the following: Lord Kenyon; Colonel Sir John Carew Pole, Bt, DSO, TD; Sir Francis Sykes, Bt; Mr Nigel Arnold-Forster; Mr John Arundell; Mrs David Babington-Smith; Mr Charles Bradshaw; Miss Margaret Dickinson; Mr Richard Howard-Vyse; Mr J. R. Johnstone; Mr E. G. M. Leycester-Roxby; and Mr P. S. Palmer. As well as expressing my gratitude to the owners of the copyright of these sources, I must thank the staffs of the libraries and archives where most of them are housed; particularly Miss Joan C. Lancaster, Dr Richard Bingle and the other members of the staff of the India Office Library; the Shropshire County Archivist, Miss Mary C. Hill; the staffs of the British Library (British Museum); of the

National Library of Wales; of the Bodleian Library; of Gloucestershire County Records Office; and of the East Riding of Yorkshire County Record Office.

Among those who gave me the benefit of their expert knowledge, Dr C. Collin Davies must certainly have pride of place. He suggested lines of research in the book's early stages; he read my script when it was finished; and for most of the long intervening period, he was trusting and unselfish enough to allow me to borrow his precious Indian Records Series volumes. Dame Lucy Sutherland and Dr Peter Marshall were always cheerfully willing to answer my questions. Mr Brinsley Ford very generously gave me access to his notes, on which my account of Clive's Italian tour is mostly based; he also enlightened me on various aspects of Clive's picture collection, as did Sir Anthony Blunt. Miss Dorothy Stroud provided information on the building of Claremont. Dr John Creightmore made suggestions as to the nature of Clive's illness. Mr John Gurney, Mrs E. Norman-Butler, Mr J. B. Owen and the Hon. Guy Strutt each advised me on one or more points. Madame Yvonne Robert Gaebelé, talking to me in her delightful old house in Pondicherry, helped me to understand the character of Clive's great French adversary, Dupleix.

When, in 1967, my research took me back to India, my ways were made smooth by many kind people, in England as well as in India itself, most of whom did not confine their kindness to the business of the book, but helped to give my wife and myself a highly enjoyable two months. Of them, I must mention the following: Lord and Lady Tanlaw; the late Sir A. L. Mudaliar; the late Lieutenant-General Sir Archibald Nye, GCSI, GCMG, GCIE, KCB, KBE, MC; Sir John and Lady Jardine Paterson; Professor Arokiaswami, of Madras University; Mr Philip Astley, of the British Council; Mr Billimoria, of the Great Eastern Hotel, Calcutta; Mr Philip Crosland; Mr Amiya Krishna Deb; Mr Gupta, Curator of the Victoria Memorial, Calcutta; Mr and Mrs A. Hayward; Mr and Mrs W. C. F. Hindmarsh; Mr and Mrs Peter Joy; Professor and Madame Labarre, of the Alliance Française; Mr and Mrs David Lancashire; Mr and Mrs McCall, of the Trichinopoly Club; Mr Philip Mason, CIE, OBE; Mrs A. Oakly; Mr and Mrs John Robson; Mr Pearson Surita; Mr and Mrs Govind Swaminadhan; and Mr and Mrs R. Wright.

In the often frustrating task of collecting illustrations, I received much help from Mrs M. Archer and Miss P. M. Harrold of the India Office Library Prints and Drawings Department. In this respect, I would also like to thank Mr Hugh Brigstocke of the National Gallery of Scotland; Mr

W. Y. Carman of the National Army Museum; Lieutenant-Commander E. F. P. Cooper; my cousin, Mr W. R. Price-Jones; Mr Francis Russell; and Mr Reg Thompson, Art Editor of *Country Life*.

I have already remarked on how so many of the people whose help I have acknowledged were hospitable as well as helpful; yet I feel I must say a special word of thanks for the hospitality of Mr and the Hon. Mrs Michael Parish, of Mr Peter Dawnay and of the Rev. James Forbes, OSB, Master of St Benet's Hall, Oxford. Mr Dawnay had me to stay throughout my lengthy researches in London; and whenever my work took me to Oxford, I was entertained splendidly by Father James, from whom, as a schoolboy, I had received my first introduction to eighteenth-century politics. It is to him and to two other Ampleforth masters, Mr Thomas Charles-Edwards and the late Abbot William Price, more than to anybody else, that I owe my interest in history.

CHAPTER I

So Hare-brained Fools

So hare-brained fools to Indian Climates rove
With a vain hope their fortune to improve;
They spend their slender cargo and become
Worse slaves abroad than e'er they were at home.

ANONYMOUS, about 1750

I

The part of Shropshire north of Shrewsbury still has the feeling of being sleepy and off the beaten track, a country of narrow lanes and gently rolling fields. Along some of the narrowest and most winding of these lanes, so that it seems remote even though it is only a couple of miles from the town of Market Drayton, is the little village of Moreton Say. Yet another couple of miles of lanes and fields separate the village from its big house, Styche Hall. The house can be seen plainly from some way off, standing on a hill; a typical small country house of the eighteenth century.

That it was built to replace the older timbered house of the family who had owned the surrounding land for many generations is something one could easily guess. But one would not guess that the Georgian squire who rebuilt the home of his ancestors in this modest way was Robert, first Lord Clive, Clive of India, who was born in the older house on September 29, 1725. Considering the size of his fortune, he was not generous to his ancestral home; so that Styche still recalls the Clives as what they were before being transformed by Indian wealth: small country gentry.

As country gentry went, their ancestry was highly respectable. They held land in Shropshire as far back as the reign of Henry II; their name has a territorial origin—always regarded as the best origin for an English surname – coming, as it seems, from the village of Clive north of Shrewsbury.[1] In Tudor days, the family produced a successful government official, Sir George Clive, and in the next century the formidable Cromwellian Colonel Robert Clive caused the Royalists of Shropshire to pray:

> From Wem and from Wyche
> And from Clive of the Styche,
> Good Lord, deliver us.[2]

By 1725, when the third Robert Clive, the future Clive of India, was born, the eldest son of Richard Clive of Styche and Rebecca, his wife, there were many living descendants of the Cromwellian Robert Clive. From such portraits of them as exist, there seems to have been a distinct Clive face: solid and reliable, the nose large and a little bulbous, the eyebrows dark and thick. Richard Clive of Styche was definitely of this type. Like others of the cousinhood, he had a firm mouth, which in his case did not denote strength of character, for he seems to have been ineffective if amiable. Under his management, Styche became heavily mortgaged. To supplement his meagre rent-roll of £500 a year he practised as a lawyer in London, but without much success.[3]

Rebecca Clive's family, the Gaskells, were from Manchester, and it was there that her eldest son was sent when less than three years old to live with her sister and brother-in-law, Elizabeth and Daniel Bayley, whose house was called Hope Hall. He was a delicate child and Manchester was a healthier and more countrified place than London, being still an overgrown village – though it was even then described as 'the largest, most rich, populous and busy village in England'[4] – rather than a city. One might have attributed the insecurity in Clive's difficult and contradictory nature to this early separation from his parents, if one did not know that his uncle and aunt were devoted to him, and he to them, and that his childhood was consequently happy. They both seem to have given up all their time to nursing him through a dangerous bout of fever soon after his third birthday; and when he had begun to recover and the patience he had shown at death's door had given place to 'as eminent a degree of crossness',[5] as his uncle remarked in a letter to another of the child's uncles, they rightly took this as a good sign and treated him indulgently. When he was well enough to come down to the parlour, where he ran about and chattered, asking many questions, 'very merry and good as it is possible', his uncle and aunt let him rule them. 'This afternoon Bob, with some reluctance, suffered his Aunt Bay to go to chapel', her husband wrote on a Sunday evening.[6]

Far from suffering deprivation through being parted from his parents, it is possible that he was overspoilt by his uncle and aunt, and that this was a cause of his egoism in later life, as well as of his tendency to self-pity and dissatisfaction. And yet his uncle and aunt appear to have been firm as well as kind; thus they took care to give him nothing but plain and simple food, while admitting that they would have liked to have treated him to more delicacies.[7] And in June 1732, when he was nearly seven, his uncle showed some concern about his character:

> I hope I have made a little farther conquest over Bob, and that he regards me in some degree as well as his Aunt Bay. He has just had a suit of new clothes, and promises by his reformation to deserve them. I am satisfied that his fighting (to which he is out of measure addicted) gives his temper a fierceness and imperiousness, that he flies out upon every trifling occasion: for this reason I do what I can to suppress the hero, that I may help forward the more valuable qualities of meekness, benevolence and patience.[8]

If one can read future character in this account of an ordinary high-spirited and self-willed little boy of six, one can recognize, at this early age, Clive's love of fighting and his hot temper. Indeed, his military successes owed more to the pluck and resource of the schoolboy than to the calculating mind of the adult strategist. As to his temper, he was never really cured of his habit of flying out upon every trifling occasion, often with unfortunate consequences to himself. Of the qualities which his uncle hoped to instil into him, meekness was something that passed him by; but he could show benevolence and if the ability to write and rewrite many hundreds and thousands of letters, speeches, minutes and memoranda and to wade through or listen to as great a number can be called patience, he certainly had that too.

One can also perhaps see an early manifestation of his love of clothes in the fact that the new suit constituted so great a reward. Though knowing how he was never extravagant or ostentatious, one wonders if his dandyism was not merely another facet of his insecurity, an attempt to disguise his rather unprepossessing appearance. If this is so, one could trace its origin to the occasion when—according to a story which may be apocryphal—King George II stopped his coach to laugh at the little Clive who was wearing a man-sized wig. To have been made to feel a fool by the passing monarch in front of all the crowds could have had a lasting effect on a self-conscious and highly-strung boy of nine, which would have been his most likely age at the time of the incident, if it actually happened. For when Clive was this age, his Aunt Bay died; so it is very possible that he went to stay with his parents in London. To the shock and sense of loss occasioned by the death of his aunt, who was then more like his mother, would have been added the traumatic experience of exchanging the rural peace of Manchester for the noise, the jostling crowds and the smells of the London of Hogarth; a large city even by present-day standards.

His dislike of London in later life may well have stemmed from this first visit. It is clear, too, that he regarded Hope Hall as more of a home than his parents' house; yet this is only to be expected, since he spent his most impressionable years there, and does not necessarily denote that he was in any way unhappy when living with his parents. He was somewhat in awe of his father, but so were most boys in those days; his subsequent generosity to him would indicate that he did not suffer any undue harshness from him in his childhood or boyhood, for he was never quick to forgive a past injury. Like most of the Clives, his father was short-tempered; but his mother, who was the stronger character, is said to have been good at smoothing him down.[9] Indeed, the influence of Clive's parents' house is likely to have been predominantly feminine; for while five of the seven daughters borne by his mother lived to be grown up, only two of her six sons survived, apart from himself; and of these two, one was about fifteen and the other twenty years his junior. It is, of course, possible that Clive had a brother closer to him in age whose death may have been a factor in transforming the cheerful if pugnacious little boy of Hope Hall into the reserved and at times melancholy youth; but more probably his three other brothers died in infancy, so that for most of the time which he spent in his parents' house he would have been the only boy among a bevy of girls. His sisters doubtless hero-worshipped him, which may not have been good for him as he already tended to be arrogant. And perhaps it was through this feminine influence that his character developed its strangely feminine twist, making him impulsive and irrational yet at the same time giving him the intuition that was frequently to stand him in good stead.

It would be wrong, however, to suppose that Clive lacked the companionship of other boys. In Manchester he had a cousin with whom he was very close; and from an early age he experienced the rough-and-tumble of school – first at Dr Eaton's at Lostock in Cheshire,[10] then, after the death of his aunt, at the grammar school at Market Drayton in his native Shropshire. The stories of his wildness at Market Drayton, how he climbed on to a gargoyle at the top of the church tower, and how he led a gang who terrorized the local shopkeepers, though unreliable in detail, since they are not based on contemporary sources, can at least be taken to indicate that as a schoolboy he was still the extrovert he had been as a child of six.[11]

Macaulay built on these stories the image of Clive as a madcap delinquent, and assumed, because he went to four different schools, that he was 'a dunce, if not a reprobate'. But as a twentieth-century biographer of Clive rightly points out, his progress from private school to grammar school, then to public school – Merchant Taylors' – and finally to a sort of business school, kept by a Mr Sterling at Hemel Hempstead in Hertfordshire, was perfectly normal and does not necessarily mean that he was at any time expelled.[12]

Without being either a dunce or a reprobate, Clive may not have been much of a scholar.[13] Nevertheless, he was to show, in later life, a knowledge of the classics and a talent for writing and speaking excellent English, as well as an immense capacity for hard work. It seems only fair to allow Merchant Taylors' and the other establishments a little of the credit. One can, moreover, assume that Clive's schooldays were relatively happy from the fact that he sent his own sons to school, instead of educating them privately, which would then have been quite normal for the sons of someone as rich as he had become. And whatever may be said about the brutalizing effects of boys' schools in the old days, Clive's schooling does not seem to have had any such effect on him. On the contrary, he was surprisingly humane, given the age in which he lived, the circumstances of his career and his own autocratic and neurotic temperament.

From the legend of Clive's wildness, it has naturally been assumed that his father shipped him out to India because he was good for nothing else. Far more likely he was sent there because it seemed the best opportunity. He had to make his way in the world, even though he was the eldest son; and of the limited choice of careers open to an impoverished young gentleman in those days, the East India Company service would have been one of the most attractive. For it would be hard to exaggerate the importance of the East India Company in mid-eighteenth-century England. Since its foundation in 1600, and its reconstitution in 1709, it had grown into far and away the largest and most complex trading company in the land; its annual sales of East Indian goods amounted to some

£2m. sterling, at a time when the total annual imports of Great Britain were not worth much more than £10m. As well as trading, it had territorial powers over the settlements in India; the Governors of its three Presidencies of Madras, Calcutta and Bombay held more lucrative posts than did the Governor of any Crown colony. It was the first of the few joint-stock companies then in existence; its stock was pre-eminent on the London market, the nearest thing in those days to a gilt-edged security. As a supporter of the public credit, both by lending money directly to the State, and by helping in the arrangement of State loans, the Company occupied a position in the City comparable only to that of the Bank of England; and, like the Bank, it was in close alliance with the Government.

It was fortunate for Clive that his father knew one of the Directors of this mighty organization. On December 15, 1742, he was summoned to East India House in Leadenhall Street, the Company's City headquarters, where he was formally admitted to the juniormost rank of 'writer', and assigned to Fort St George, Madras. Before being ushered into the presence of the Honourable Chairman, he was kept waiting for an hour or two in a lobby full of other young candidates. One wonders if any of them noticed him. We have no picture or description of him at seventeen, but from what we know of his appearance later in life—he was regarded by smart society in general as of 'very mean appearance', and by the critical Horace Walpole as 'a remarkably ill-looking man'[14] – he cannot have been very prepossessing, though he was on the tall side of middle height. Even at this age he may have had some of the fullness of flesh above the eyelids,[15] which made his brow seem heavy and gave him an unattractive expression, 'gloomy, sullen and forbidding' as his enemies were later to describe it.[16] In him, the characteristic Clive features, large and broad nose, determined eyes and mouth, thick, dark eyebrows, were arranged a little lopsidedly, as though to illustrate his own candid admission later in life, 'irregular was in my very nature'.[17] They were also crowded together, making his face seem pinched, ample though it was – like a terrestrial globe with eyes, nose and mouth forming a compact archipelago in the southern hemisphere.

Now that Clive was virtually a man, he can no longer have been the extrovert he was as a child and boy. Already that reserve, which made him seem 'awkward and unmannerly',[18] would have hindered him from striking up casual acquaintances. Yet one at least of the young men in the lobby was no stranger to him, his cousin, William Smyth King. And he may have brought himself to converse with two of the others, John Walsh and John Pybus, who were to become his close friends.

To Walsh, India was a second home; he had friends and relatives there, and had himself spent his early childhood with his parents at Madras. They were now dead, and he had inherited his patrimony of £2000 – great riches for a youth of sixteen. It may have been on account of his wealth that Walsh established an ascendancy over Clive, which he was to maintain even after the roles had been reversed and Clive was far and away the richer and more important of the two. Clive would listen to Walsh when he listened to nobody else, so that Walsh, whose principles were more clear-cut than were his own, became, in a manner of speaking, his conscience. Walsh's orderly and logical mind – which seemed to match his spare frame and ferret face – served as a sheet anchor for Clive's wayward temperament. Unfortunately he was inclined to be quarrelsome, so that under his influence Clive was more than ever ready to take offence.

On March 10, 1743, Clive sailed from the Thames in the East India Company's vessel *Winchester*. To his homesickness at leaving England, parents and family, were added the terrors of the voyage, and the uncertainties of life in a strange and distant land. Yet we are apt to regard a passage to India in the mid-eighteenth century through our own rather than through contemporary eyes. We think of how the unhealthiness of India in those days cut short the lives of so many young hopefuls; forgetting that the not-so-very-much-better sanitary conditions at home meant that a young man of Clive's generation was far more inured to the likelihood of an early death than his twentieth-century counterpart – just as he grew up with a much stronger resistance to disease.[19] Again, the India to which Clive set sail may seem to us infinitely remote; but even before he met Walsh, he must have known people who had been there, having spent so much of his boyhood in the upper-middle-class world of London where the East India trade loomed large. Such apprehensions as he may have had were offset by the feeling of adventure. He was going to regain the family fortunes; that he might just as likely have ended in a far-away grave or, more likely still, returned home poorer than he had left, having failed to shake the proverbial 'pagoda tree', probably did not occur to him as he boarded the great East Indiaman, as fine a ship as any afloat, of 500 tons and only on her third voyage; with the red and white striped ensign of the Honourable Company flying proudly from her stern.[20]

Clive did not suffer from seasickness; but he had to resign himself to many weeks of cramped conditions, of stink from the bilge, of cold on deck and heat below, as the *Winchester* made her slow, creaking passage across the Atlantic.* And while the captains of some East Indiamen fed and wined their passengers surprisingly well, it is unlikely that Captain Gabriel Steward of the *Winchester* did; for he was inconsiderate and grasping. The prices of his goods were exorbitant, and when Clive was obliged to ask for credit, he charged him a high rate of interest.[21]†

Clive must have particularly resented paying, having run short of clothes and money simply because the voyage took more than fourteen months, instead of six. Having seen one of her companion vessels wrecked on a shoal in the Cape Verde Islands, with, as it was supposed at the time, the loss of all hands, the *Winchester* herself ran aground on the eastern tip of Brazil. Boats reached her from the shore, and efforts were made to lighten ship. In the confusion that followed, Clive lost some of his possessions.[22]

It took a week to refloat the ship and owing to gales she had to lie at anchor off the coast for four months before she could be got into the nearby port of Pernambuco for repairs. One day during these months when the ship was rolling at anchor in a particularly heavy sea, Clive, who was standing on the poop, fell overboard. He was saved by the captain, who threw him a bucket on a rope which happened to be handy. Clive grabbed the bucket and was hauled back on board, having lost his hat and wig and also his shoes on which were a pair of silver buckles, a present from a family friend.[23]

Having gone aground in May, the ship made harbour in September and the repairs took till February of the following year. During those nine months Clive learnt Portuguese,[24] which was to make it easy for him to speak the debased Portuguese *lingua franca* of the Indian coast. When at long last the *Winchester* resumed her voyage, she met a storm and was obliged to put in at the Cape of Good Hope for eleven days. This, for Clive and his fellow passengers, meant another expensive stay ashore; although Cape Town, with its neat, straight, tree-lined streets at the foot of steep hills, its Botanical Gardens, its fruit and its Constantia wine, was a pleasant enough place. After the Cape came the most uncertain part of the voyage, with the danger of storms and uncharted rocks. But the

* It was necessary to sail as far as the coast of Brazil in order to pick up the south-east trade wind for the passage round the Cape of Good Hope.

† East India captains acted as general suppliers of European goods—clothes, furniture, delicacies and so on—selling both to their passengers and to the inhabitants at their destination.

Winchester suffered no further mishap, and two months later, on June 1, 1744, Clive had his first sight of India, the long, low line of the Coromandel Coast.[25]

At seven in the evening, after the sun had set in a blaze of orange and scarlet beyond the shore, the *Winchester* dropped anchor in Madras Roads. Lights flickered on shore and in the darkness could be felt the drift of warm air off the land, with a whiff of the unforgettable smell of India, that mixture of hot dust and burnt dung. Next morning, Clive was woken at sunrise by the guns of the ship firing the customary salutes.[26] Coming on deck he felt the hot land breeze and saw beyond the white of the surf, the battlemented wall of Fort St George, from behind which rose houses and the steeple of St Mary's Church. The latter could have come straight out of a corner of London, except for its brilliant whiteness; for like the houses and the walls, it was covered with *chunam*, a cement made of burnt sea-shells, which glowed as the sun rose peach-coloured above the horizon to the east. Immediately to the right of the Fort were the huddled houses of the native or 'Black' Town; and some way to the left, a village with another church tower which was the old Portuguese settlement of St Thomé. On either side, yellow sand and green palm trees stretched away into the haze.

Then followed the adventure of landing. Clive had to cross the surf in a flimsy *masula* boat, while the boatmen shouted '*ya-li, ya-li*' in unison, and ride up the beach on the wet and slippery back of a fisherman. At the Sea Gate of the Fort, he found himself in the midst of a noisy crowd, Indian and European, while many people clamoured to be appointed as his *dubash*.*

At the time of Clive's arrival, the English settlement of Fort St George, Madras, had been in existence for just over one hundred years, and had grown during that period into the most important and prosperous town on the Coast of Coromandel, with a European population of 400 and a native population of 40,000. It was the chief English possession in India, more of a colony than a mere trading settlement, though officially no more than the latter. The jurisdiction which the Governor exercised in and around the Fort was in theory only that of a *zemindar* or tenant-in-chief of the Nawab of the Carnatic, who was himself a deputy of the Nizam of the Deccan, the southern *Subadar* or Viceroy of the Mogul Emperor. But just as the Emperor had now become a cipher, and his

* Literally, interpreter; but in effect a general factotum or steward, like the *banyan* in Bengal.

viceroys and their deputies more or less independent princes, so did the lower members of this shaky pyramid, including the Governor of Fort St George, become to all intents and purposes independent.

Most of the European inhabitants of Madras lived in the Fort itself, which was more like a miniature walled town than a fortress; the wall being of little defensive use except to keep out marauders. The smallness of the area inside the wall, four hundred yards by a hundred, meant that the houses were close together; but they were lofty and spacious, rather Italian-looking with big, shuttered windows and colonnades.[27] As well as private houses, there was the Governor's house, larger and grander than the rest; there were the offices and warehouses of the East India Company, the hostel for the younger servants, the barracks for the three hundred inferior troops who made up the garrison and accounted for three-quarters of the European population. There were the two churches, the Englishness of St Mary's contrasting with the simplified baroque of the Portuguese Catholic Church.

Immediately beyond the wall of the Fort on the north side was Black Town, a typical eastern town of the more cosmopolitan sort; its population included Portuguese, Armenians and Jews as well as Indians in the narrower sense. The streets were crowded with humanity and had more than their fair share of beggars, some deformed and diseased; there were all the smells of India, joss-sticks burning in the shops, overripe fruit, stale jasmine, the spicy aroma of cooking food, the smell of the smoke which came curling out of cracks in the houses, the smell of burnt dung.

Outside the Fort and Black Town was as empty as it was crowded within. To the west, the Choultry Plain stretched away into the great open spaces of the Carnatic; much of it almost a desert, particularly in the dry, scorching month of June: bare, reddish earth or grey-green scrub. This wilderness was relieved by patches of cultivation, where there were ponds, known there as tanks, by lines of palms, by clumps of spiky aloes and cactus; by villages in the shade of dusty and wide-spreading banyan trees; by pagodas of fawn-coloured stone, encrusted with ornament. Close to the Fort were the trees and walls of the 'garden houses' of the Governor and the richer European merchants. There were a few more garden houses at the foot of St Thomas's Mount, an odd-shaped little hill of bare, reddish earth some ten miles to the south-west, the traditional place of the Apostle's martyrdom.

What impact this land and its people made on Clive, we do not know. He recorded no such impressions in his first letter home to his father; just as, in all the numerous letters that survive from him, written in the course of his career, there is not a mention of the wonders that must have been constantly before his eyes. One would suspect him of having been totally blind to his surroundings, had he not shown himself to have had an eye for landscape after his return to England. There is also evidence that he was impressed by at least one of the scenic wonders which he saw during the course of his travels, the Peak of Teneriffe;[28] as well as one masterpiece of Indian architecture, the mosque at Sasaram, near Benares.[29] On the whole, however, his interest in India, when it was not political and commercial, seems to have been zoological and scientific.

Whether or not he marvelled at the beasts and temples, the sunsets and the gaily clad throng, Clive may have felt something of the hopelessness and the sinister vein which is never very far from the attractive side of India. In this respect, India matched his own temperament; for even now, at nineteen, he may have been feeling the manic-depressive tendencies which were evident in him a few years later. The letter he wrote to his cousin in February 1745, on which the traditional view of him as a miserable, friendless outcast is mostly based, may well have been written during one of his fits of depression, made worse by the climate and the sense of hopelessness already mentioned.

> I have not enjoyed one happy day since I left my native country. I am not acquainted with any one family in the place, and have not assurance enough to introduce myself without being asked. If the state I am now in will admit of any happiness it must be when I am writing to my friends. Letters were surely first invented for the comfort of such solitary wretches as myself.[30]

On the other hand, when he wrote to his father in the previous September, he could well have been enjoying one of his periods of cheerful energy:

> I can assure you my stay in this place is in every respect pleasant, and satisfactory to me, as it is backed with the hopes (if it please God to preserve my life), of being able to provide for myself, and also of being of service to my relations.[31]

Unless it can be attributed to a passing mood, Clive's lament that he had not yet got to know a single family does suggest a somewhat grim state of affairs, for society and hospitality were always a great feature of

English life in India, an antidote to the monotony and the homesickness. There is the oft-repeated story of how Clive arrived in Madras with a solitary letter of introduction, only to find that the person to whom it was addressed had just left for England. In fact, the letter of introduction was to no less a personage than the previous Governor, and would have brought Clive to the notice of his successor, Nicholas Morse.

Governor Morse asked him to dine on his arrival, and also allowed him to use the library of the Governor's House.[32] It seems unlikely that Mr and Mrs Morse – towards whom Clive showed considerable affection in later years – should have seen the young man coming in and out of the library without offering him further hospitality, particularly as it was the habit of Governors always to have some guests at their table. It must be remembered, too, that as a Company servant, Clive belonged to an élite. He would have been counted superior to the military officers, who were mostly ex-rankers, to the 'free merchants' not in the Company's employ,[33] to the seafaring men and hangers-on. Unless human nature was very different in those days, a young man fresh from England would always have been welcome among those merchant families who were permanently settled in Madras and had Indian or Portuguese-Indian blood, families like the Powneys and the Carvalhos. Thirty years later, Clive's widow was to speak with gratitude of Mrs Powney's 'partiality' to Clive when he was a young man, and her 'maternal pleasing behaviour to the young people of Madras'.[34]

Then he had the companionship of his fellow-writers. Walsh, King and Pybus became his close friends. There is no reason why he should have stood aloof from them, or they from him, in these early months, though the fact that he arrived after the others owing to the mishaps of his voyage may have made him like the new boy at school who arrives in the middle of term.

If Clive's description of himself as a solitary wretch was not just occasioned by depression, or by his tendency to exaggeration and self-pity, it can be explained by another facet of his character. While he found little satisfaction in the company of casual acquaintances, the company of close friends – as was his cousin – was to him so great a necessity that he was never content unless one or more of them was present, even after he was happily married. Having been in Madras only eight months, he might not yet have got to know anyone well enough to regard them as friends according to his own high standards of friendship, of which we learn something in the letter he wrote to his cousin:

If there is any such thing which may properly be called happiness here below, I am persuaded it is in the union of two friends who each love each other without the least guile or deceit, who are united by a real inclination, and satisfied with each others merits . . . when you write me, I beg it may be carelessly and without study, for I had much rather read the dictates of the heart than those of the understanding.

This passage also shows a thoughtfulness and a gift for expression that would have been unlikely in the dunce or reprobate depicted by Macaulay, who is as responsible as anyone for the legend of Clive's early unhappiness; giving as further reasons for this the fact that he was 'wretchedly lodged' and in debt. All Clive says about his quarters is that they were unfurnished, which was to be expected, and that he had them cleaned out and whitewashed before moving in, the normal practice in India down to the present day. If we can rely on the tradition that Clive had rooms in the building in Fort St George which now bears his name, he must have been housed quite reasonably. It is high, three-storeyed and imposing, with many large windows facing the sea. Inside, there are lofty beamed ceilings and massive pillars. A bit barn-like, but well suited to the climate.

As for being in debt, Clive was short of money like all young writers, except for those few, such as Walsh, who had some capital. The Company paid purely nominal salaries, rewarding its servants by enabling them to trade under more favourable conditions than those enjoyed by the free merchants. Clive's salary as a writer was £5 a year, together with free quarters, and an allowance of eight pagodas twenty-three fanams* a month to pay for laundry and candles and the wages of at least three servants. On arrival, he had to furnish his quarters and buy extra clothes. Until his trading started to show returns, he would certainly have been hard up. But he took care to avoid being in debt to anyone but his father. When he found that the £54 16*s.* 6*d.* in cash which he had brought out with him was not enough, he got what he needed from Captain Steward, to be paid for by his father on the Captain's return to England. As he explained to his father, it was better to pay Steward's prices and the fifty per cent which he charged for credit, rather than run up debts in Madras, which would have incurred the Company's displeasure and even led to dismissal, or suspension.[35]

* The pagoda was a gold coin current in south India until the beginning of last century, worth about seven shillings. The fanam was a small coin worth about twopence.

Clive took pains to assure his father that he was not being extravagant; which could be an early instance of his habit of over-justifying himself, rather than an indication of meanness on his father's part. 'I hope you'll be so kind as not to take exception at the wine as there are no other sort of drinkables here but that, and punch,[36] and as I always shall drink it with water, intend to make it serve me a whole year.' As for the large quantity of linen, one had to change every day in this sweltering climate, preferably twice a day. As well as linen, he needed a new suit, having only two coats left after the voyage, one of them woollen and uncomfortable. His laced waistcoat needed altering, for it would no longer button: a sign that he was already beginning to acquire the spread which is noticeable in his portraits.[37]

The youthful Clive has been depicted as an angry young man, resentful towards his father for having been exiled. His letters home from Madras, unless they were written with his tongue in his cheek, show him as the reverse: an affectionate, dutiful son, expressing gratitude rather than resentment, anxious to do the right thing to the point of priggishness. 'I think myself not only very happy, but infinitely obliged to you for my education, and as it has rendered me in a fair way of improving my talent, I flatter myself with the hopes of enlarging tenfold.' 'I shall let no opportunity slip of improving myself in everything where I can have the least view of profit.' 'I shall always make it my duty to behave worthy and deserving of your confidence and esteem, and am willing to give up all pretensions to your favour in case I don't behave with that sobriety and diligence which is expected.'[38]

His requests were all to help his career: letters of recommendation, for by getting to know people he would become 'better acquainted and more fully instructed of the customs and advantages of this country'; books, because reading was 'one of those diversions which may be of service to me'. He offered to invest any money his father cared to send him and promised good returns. He asked his father to try to get him transferred to Bengal, where living was cheaper and trade more profitable, and to pull strings to get him promoted to the higher rank of Factor. On this point, he moralized: 'The world seems to be vastly debased of late, and interest carries it entirely before merit, especially in this service, though I should think myself very undeserving of any favour were I only to build my foundation on the strength of the former.' At the same time, he noted approvingly that the Company servants at Madras were 'a set of very prudent and industrious people, some few excepted'.[39]

Industry, prudence, self-improvement. It is all rather Victorian and far from the picture of Clive as a wild remittance man. He even pleaded in an avuncular way on behalf of a certain young man of the latter sort, apparently known to his family, who had reformed and was returning to England 'well persuaded of the bad consequences that attend a debauched and extravagant life'.[40]

One is therefore inclined to doubt the story of how his behaviour towards the Secretary at Fort St George was so indisciplined that the Governor made him apologize to that official.[41] No less dubious is the story of how he attempted suicide, twice firing a pistol at his own head and exclaiming 'I am reserved for something!' when it failed to go off.[42] It smacks of having been invented in the knowledge that Clive did eventually end his life by suicide – then, he was tortured by illness, whereas in these early years he spoke of enjoying good health. However, he may have been suffering from one of his fits of depression, or felt unusually low after a fever which killed twelve of his colleagues. Or he may have been driven suicidal by the heat, the discomfort and the monotony of his life at Fort St George. Day after day, in his working clothes of cotton shirt, nankeen breeches and white cap, he checked bales of cloth, argued with Indians and tried to make figures add, while he itched with prickly heat and the sweat ran off his face and mingled with the ink on the pages of his ledger.

Each morning he scanned the intense blue of the sea, looking for the sail of a ship from home that was never there. And when at last a sail *did* appear, or rather the several sails of a convoy, there were letters for everyone except Clive.

> I had for a long time kept up hope with the pleasing pleasure of what was to come, and I do declare never in my life did I enjoy such real happiness, as upon sight of the five above-mentioned ships, not all the riches of the Indies could have satisfied my desires more fully than news from my native country, but it seems fortune had elevated me to this high summit of expectation that I might in a greater degree experience so heavy a disappointment, in short I was the only sorrowful person in Madras.[43]

He would have felt the nostalgia which he expressed some time before to his Uncle Bayley:

> The pleasant and delightful days I have spent with my kind relations and

> friends in Lancashire, refreshes and entertains my mind with very agreeable ideas. I must confess at intervals when I think of my dear native England it affects me in a very particular manner, however knowing it to be for my own welfare rest content and patient, wishing the views for which my father sent me here may in all respects be fully accomplished.[44]

As well as the homesickness and monotony, there was the discomfort of India, all the lesser plagues ranging from boils to diarrhoea, from mosquitos which no net could entirely keep out, to sudden invasions of giant ants, covering the floor, the furniture and everything with their seething blackness. Later in the year there were violent hurricanes, tearing the roofs off houses, uprooting trees, lifting the more flimsy huts bodily into the air. Great seas broke over the wall of the Fort and the inhabitants sat in darkened rooms, the shutters rattling frenziedly, the flames of the lamps and candles doing a wild dance in their glass shades if indeed they could be kept alight at all. And everywhere there was a coating of dust, from the great swirling column that rose against the sky, turning day into night.

Yet until the advent of electricity, piped water, refrigeration and air conditioning, which had not reached some of the more remote places even by the very end of the Raj, India would have been only marginally less uncomfortable than it was in Clive's time. If Clive wanted a bath, the water had to be brought in skins by the *bhisti*: but this would also have been the case in many parts of India right down to the present.[45] And with all its discomforts, India had its charms. The cheerful and willing Madrassi servants always eager to do what Master wanted.[46] The cool of the evening sea breeze which in Madras blows as regularly as the morning land breeze. There were walks along the beach before sunset, and early morning rides through country sweet with herbs and wild jasmine. Then, when Clive made a few more friends, he must have taken part in gaieties like those described by Walsh's sister, Eliza, who followed her brother to India: balls, moonlight suppers, childish games played about the streets. Eliza Walsh found it 'just like living in a country town in England but in a much grander manner'.[47]

In fact it would have been a mixture of English and Oriental: a society that included people with Indian blood, Portuguese, Armenians and Jews. Many of them would have been as dark as the Indians whom Clive, in common with most of his contemporaries – Warren Hastings being a notable exception – referred to as 'blacks';[48] but because they belonged to the settlement, he regarded them as Europeans, showing that, despite his use of a term repugnant to modern ears, he had no colour prejudice.[49] However much this society may have been insulated from the vast land that lay beyond the bounds of the settlement, it is certain that by living in it, Clive must have absorbed some Indian ideas, just as, like everybody else, he acquired Indian habits such as smoking a hookah and chewing betel-nut; though he never seems to have had the slightest interest in Indian customs and culture.

Alongside an Eastern grandeur – the Governor processing in state attended by mace-bearers – went a pioneering, evangelical simplicity. Councillors often had to sort cloth themselves. There was compulsory church service twice daily for the juniors, which may have given Clive his lifelong distaste for public worship. One doubts, however, if he had much private religion either, from the almost total absence of pious sentiments in his letters; though his mention of 'here below' and 'if it please God to preserve my life' might suggest that he was a believer, at any rate as a young man. He is said never to have spoken irreverently of sacred matters, nor suffered others to do so;[50] but this may have been after he had married a wife who was herself deeply religious. If he lacked the puritan zeal of some of his colleagues, he was also free from their bigotry; showing kindness to the somewhat persecuted Catholic priest at Madras, Father Severini.[51]

The strongly religious atmosphere of Fort St George was reflected in the Governor's library, which contained numerous Bibles, sermons and spiritual works of all kinds. But there was also plenty to interest someone as secular-minded as Clive on the evenings which he spent there; for it was a well-stocked library by any standards.[52] There was a good run of the classics, both Latin and Greek; there were authors such as Bacon, Descartes, Confucius, Erasmus, Grotius, Hobbes, Locke, Josephus, Machiavelli and Shakespeare. There was Hakluyt's *Voyages*, Ralegh's *History of the World*, Vitruvius's *De Architectura*, the *Art of Speaking*, and Webster on witchcraft.[53] The one notable lacuna lay in books on military science; nor was there much about India and the East. Perhaps Machiavelli helped him to understand the tortuous politics of Bengal, and he may have acquired his skill as an orator from the *Art of Speaking*. In any case, self-improvement in Clive's day did not merely consist in learning one's trade; he is said to have benefited chiefly from his evenings in the library by perfecting his Latin.

But what of the less improving recreations of a young writer – cards drinking in the punch houses, exploring the brothels of Black Town? Clive's fondness for cards in later life (though he was never a gambler) would indicate that he took time off from his Latin to join some of the other writers in a game. By the standards of eighteenth-century India, he was abstemious: but his subsequent wine bills suggest that he drank more than was good for him in the climate. We know, too, that he went whoring, though this may not have been until he had left the cloistral atmosphere of Fort St George and was sharing a house with a rather wild young Marine officer.

2

When, with the departure of the peace-loving Sir Robert Walpole from the premiership in 1742, and the advent of the reckless and German-minded Lord Carteret, England, having been fighting Spain on account of the popular clamour over Captain Jenkins's ear, became embroiled in the current European conflict in support of Maria Theresa's claim to the Austrian throne, nobody would have imagined that this was to set in movement a chain of events leading to a British empire in India. The fact, however, that France was on the opposite side of the conflict made it inevitable that the battles being fought in Germany and the Low Countries by Marshal Saxe and Frederick of Prussia, by Cumberland and Charles of Lorraine, should have had repercussions in remote corners of the globe. Since the Dutch had given up the navy which, in the previous century, had enabled them to eclipse the declining colonial powers of Spain and Portugal, the English and French had been left as the two great European rivals for the trade and territorial prizes of the world beyond the seas. This rivalry, which had first been evident during the reign of Louis XIV, continued in a latent form after the Regent Orleans's minister, Dubois, had brought about an Anglo-French alliance. Now that the two nations were once again at war, it was bound to erupt into a conflict in the colonial field; though this was more likely to happen in the Western Hemisphere, with the slave trade and the territory of North America as the two main bones of contention, rather than in India, where the English and French had managed to trade peacefully side by side; even though the gentlemen of Fort St George may have watched with apprehension as the chief French settlement of Pondicherry, only ninety miles away from them along the coast, grew into an up-to-date European town.

However, also in 1742, Joseph François Dupleix had become Governor-General of the French Indian possessions. For all that is known about him, Dupleix remains an enigma. One can see him as an intensely patriotic Frenchman who loved *la gloire* and regarded himself as the instrument of Providence in establishing French power in India. One can also see him merely as a merchant pursuing a vigorous and forward policy on behalf of his Company. While being, like so many Frenchmen, exceedingly practical, a disciplinarian and an organizer with a tremendous capacity for work, his chief weakness lay in refusing to face up to the realities of a situation. This, to some degree, was due to optimism. And yet his cold, taciturn aloofness, the rather worried look in his portraits, and the fact that while he was generally philosophical in the face of a disaster, seeking a remedy rather than indulging in reproaches, there were times when he gave way to anger and despondency, would all suggest that this optimism was not so much in his nature, but stemmed from a pathological need to believe that success was near at hand, though every indication may have been to the contrary.

The character of Dupleix has been further obscured by misconceptions on the part of the English. Thus the pomp and circumstance with which he surrounded himself—the salutes, the fireworks, the kettle-drums, the state elephants, the palace which he built at Pondicherry—was taken as a sign of his vanity, whereas it was more a show put on to impress the Indians, and thus further his policies. He has also become shrouded in the legend that grew up around his wife Johanna Begum, known as Madame. This remarkable woman, a beauty with the eyes of a lemur and the head of a politician, who had Indian blood through her Portuguese mother, has been depicted as her husband's evil genius; a sort of Catherine the Great, an adulteress, an arch-intriguer, a poisoner.[54] The real Madame seems to have been brave and intelligent, kind to the poor and loyal to her husband, who, while he benefited from her knowlegde of the country and her tireless efforts on his behalf, did not accept her judgement uncritically, much as he admired her.

When he heard that his country and England had commenced hostilities, Dupleix's first inclination was to revert to the custom which had prevailed during earlier Anglo-French wars, whereby the two nations maintained a neutrality in India so that trade might not be affected. It was only when such an arrangement had been precluded by the arrival in Indian waters of an English naval squadron bent on the destruction of French shipping that Dupleix decided to attack Madras; and even then, his object was to damage the trade of a rival rather than to gain territory. He was encouraged in his decision by reports of the weakness of the English defences—his spies included Madame's daughter by her first marriage, who actually lived in Fort St George. A wave of gay chauvinism swept over Pondicherry in that summer of 1746; particularly after the arrival of a garbled account of the previous year's Jacobite rising, according to which the Pretender had ousted the Hanoverian monarch from the British throne.[55] Early in September, the French troops sailed for Madras in a naval squadron from the French Islands, commanded by a tough and able Breton sailor, Bernard La Bourdonnais. They landed unopposed, the English naval squadron having fled, and bombarded Fort St George from two sides. The English garrison, outnumbered three to one by the French, and consisting of indisciplined men under the command of a seventy-year-old veteran of Louis XIV's wars, surrendered after two days of this bombardment, though it killed no more than six people. La Bourdonnais allowed the English very favourable terms, in return for a ransom which was to be largely for his own benefit.

In Pondicherry, church bells rang and salutes were fired.[56] Then La Bourdonnais and Dupleix proceeded to quarrel over the spoils, and the argument dragged on until the breaking of the October Monsoon, when a hurricane wrought havoc in the French fleet. La Bourdonnais and his remaining ships retired from the scene, leaving Madras and most of his troops in the hands of Dupleix, who cancelled the terms of surrender which had been previously agreed with the English. Governor Morse and his Council were taken as prisoners to Pondicherry, where Madame was kind to Mrs Morse and helped her to retrieve some of her possessions.[57] The rest of the English were made to give their parole that they would not bear arms against the French until they were exchanged, and then expelled from the town.

Many refused to give this parole and escaped. Among them were Clive and his friends Walsh, King, Pybus and a pleasant if somewhat irresponsible young cousin of Walsh's named Edmund Maskelyne, and known as Mun. They put on Indian clothes, blackened their faces and wore black stockings to simulate bare Indian legs. Clive himself was in the garb of a *dubash*.[58] Thus disguised, they started out at dusk. Crossing the bridge outside the town, they ran into trouble, for the Indians saw through their disguise 'from their not being able to jabber in their language'.[59] But they managed to get by and made their way southward through the country to the English settlement of Fort St David, a few miles south of Pondicherry.

CHAPTER II

The Two Goddesses

The people . . . assert that the Goddess of Fortune has departed from Madras to take up her residence at Pondicherry, and that the Goddess of Misfortune has gone in her stead from here to dwell at Madras.

ANANDA RANGA PILLAI, 1746

I

For Clive, the fertile, thickly wooded country round Fort St David was a change after the dry plain of the Carnatic. The Fort itself was smaller than Fort St George, but of a more professional, Vaubanesque shape; situated on rising ground near the sea, south of the River Ponnaiyar. A mile to the southward was Cuddalore, the settlement's 'Black Town', surrounded by its own very decrepit wall. The whole settlement extended three miles along the coast and four inland. It was protected on the landward side by a thick hedge of aloes and cactus; the villainous spines of the plants constituting a most effective barrier against barefooted marauders.

Outside the Fort, but within the 'Bounds Hedge', were the pleasant houses of the more well-to-do Company servants, with gardens full of pineapples, pomegranates and other fruit, and shaded by rows of the evergreen tulip tree, which also formed the avenue leading to the Palladian portico of the Governor's Garden House.[1] Governor Hinde, who lived here when not in the Fort, was well prepared to meet a French attack.[2] He had hired *peons** to supplement his meagre garrison of 200

* Untrained Indian soldiers.

Europeans and 100 *topasses*;* he had laid in provisions for a six-months' siege – including wine supplied by Dupleix himself, for Pondicherry was only twelve miles away, close enough for guns fired in one settlement to be heard in the other.

Soon after coming to Fort St David, Clive, with Maskelyne and another friend, volunteered for military service. It would be idle to suggest he took this step for any more significant reason than that soldiering seemed a preferable alternative to being unemployed, or joining the Fort St David civil establishment as a temporary writer – particularly if he still had his childhood love of fighting. He would have been able to trade just as well in the military employ of the Company as in the civil.

During the weeks of inactivity that followed, Clive once again courted death and was spared, if we believe another story.[3] Having fired and missed in a duel with an officer whom he had accused of cheating at cards, he exclaimed, when ordered at pistol point to take back his accusation: 'Fire and be damned, I said you cheated, I say so still, and I will never pay you!'[4] As well as showing how he led a charmed life – for the officer did not fire, declaring him to be mad – the story is meant as an example of Clive's moral courage (or obstinacy) in that he alone among his companions refused to be bullied into paying up, even though all were agreed that the officer and another had cheated. It also depicts him as magnanimous – which we know to have been by no means invariably the case throughout his life – in that he afterwards declined to make any public complaint against the cheating officer.

Clive had his baptism of fire when the French attempted to capture Fort St David in December 1746 and again in the following March. Both attempts failed, the first because the French allowed themselves to be surprised while preparing themselves a meal in the grounds of the Governor's Garden House; the second on account of the unexpected return of the English naval squadron. In the earlier action, the English had the support of an army sent by the Nawab of the Carnatic, who was friendly towards them despite the intrigues of Dupleix. The commander of the army, the Nawab's younger son, Mohammed Ali, sat, a bearded and conspicuously fair-skinned figure, on his elephant, from which he refused to dismount even though the French were pointing their guns in his direction. It was Clive's first sight of what he and his friends would have called a 'Nabob', little realizing that this corruption of a Mogul rank would come to be applied to themselves.

* Half-caste Portuguese, so called because they wore a *topi*, or European-style hat.

Governor Hinde was sufficiently impressed by the part Clive played in these actions to give him an ensign's commission, and to mention his 'martial disposition' when writing to the Directors.[5] Clive's next encouragement came with the arrival from England, in January 1748, of Major Stringer Lawrence. A bluff, portly John Bull, loved by his men to whom he was known as 'The Old Cock', Lawrence had virtues such as appealed to eighteenth- and nineteenth-century English historians, causing them to exaggerate his abilities as a commander, and to overlook his no less characteristic faults; for he was vain, susceptible to flattery, narrow-minded, not very literate, and, as his portraits betray, touchy. But his portraits also make it clear that he was a fighter: the small, tight mouth, the firm, if double, chin. More important, he was an efficient professional soldier, a veteran of Fontenoy and Culloden, very different from the military misfits who had hitherto officered the Company's forces. While at fifty he was old for someone facing the Indian climate for the first time, he nevertheless showed great energy, organizing the motley troops of Fort St David into a proper force, the germ of the great Indian Army of which he has been called the father. He also became Clive's military father and mentor. If he recognized talent in the young man, he would also have been inclined to favour him, coming as he did from the same part of England.[6] Himself of obscure birth, he would have been flattered to take under his wing a sprig of the local squirearchy.

Since the previous March, the English naval squadron had kept the French inactive, apart from the machinations of Madame, who employed the former Governor Morse's *dubash* as a spy – until he was discovered and hanged – and also, according to legend, used Mrs Morse to work on the commander of the squadron, who was her lover.[7] During the months following Lawrence's arrival, this lull was interrupted by two further French attempts on Fort St David, occasioned by the squadron's temporary absence. The first proved abortive, while in defeating the second, a night attack on the 'Black Town' of Cuddalore, Lawrence taught Clive the ruse of ostentatiously withdrawing one's troops and cannon by day, so as to make the place seem undefended, and then returning them after dark. To be ready for such attacks, the English troops remained in the field for some time. Clive was with them, but military preoccupations did not make him forget his trade, which was still on a small scale and had suffered owing to the fall of Madras. In January, when Dupleix was in the offing, he was writing about the disposal of a box of gold thread worth £113 10*s*. and a box of sewing thread worth £56 10*s*. which he hoped would sell to 'the ladies at Calcutta'. The proceeds were to be invested in 'handkerchiefs' and 'mens' and womens' ruffles'.[8]

When the news of the fall of Madras reached England, the East India Company asked for help from the Government. A powerful squadron was fitted out, and twelve independent companies of troops were raised; though half of these were under strength and had to be made up with deserters, highwaymen and riff-raff. The squadron, commanded by Admiral Edward Boscawen, arrived off Fort St David in August 1748. Boscawen's troops added to Lawrence's garrison made an army of 4000 Europeans and 2000 native foot; outnumbering Dupleix's garrison at Pondicherry, which consisted of 1800 Europeans and *topasses* and 3000 sepoys. With these superior numbers, the English expedition against Pondicherry, which began on August 8/19, should have been successful; but it was a fiasco from start to finish. 'How very ignorant we were of the art of war in those days,' wrote Clive, when looking back on the affair fourteen years later.[9]

The first mistake was to waste eleven days in reducing a small fort on the way, which taught Clive the lesson that such obstacles need only be given a wide berth. It was not just time that was lost. Lawrence was taken prisoner and the one officer who knew anything about siege warfare mortally wounded. With nobody to advise him, Boscawen chose to encamp in a position 'fraught with every disadvantage which could attend a siege', as Clive afterwards described it.[10] This amateurishness was particularly unfortunate in that Pondicherry was defended on efficient and up-to-date lines. While Boscawen's engineers bungled the placing of their batteries, Dupleix walked the ramparts encouraging his men and showed great personal bravery. Madame is said to have walked with him, as careless of danger as he was; but a modern French historian paints a less heroic picture of her sheltering in the church of Les Missions Etrangères, surrounded by her daughter, mother, sisters, servants, furniture and valuables, yet still managing to run her spy service.[11]

The French suffered a real misfortune in the death of the brilliant engineer Paradis, who fell leading a sortie against the English trenches. During this action, Clive performed his first recorded act of valour. The French grenadier company and some sepoys attacked an English trench containing three platoons, one of them under the command of Clive. The other two platoons fled, leaving Clive and his thirty men holding the trench. The French approached under cover of some huts to within ten yards, fired on the trench for three or four minutes and then attempted to take it by force; but Clive's platoon gave them such heavy fire in return that they retreated.[12]

This may have been the occasion when Clive is said to have received a shot in his hat and another in his coat. There is also the story of how, in the heat of battle, he ran back to get more ammunition, which led to his being subsequently accused of cowardice. Such insinuations were certainly made by an officer named Allen, who was obliged to ask Clive's pardon in the presence of two thousand men.[13]

By the time the English batteries were ready, the October Monsoon was about to break, and sickness was taking its toll. After his ships had bombarded the town with little effect – though Madame was shaken by a near miss – Boscawen raised the siege. In Pondicherry, there were Te Deums and parties; Dupleix, Madame and their guests drank champagne and played hazard at little tables, in the manner of Versailles under Le Grand Monarque.[14]

A couple of months later, news reached India that preliminaries of peace had been signed in Europe. According to the Treaty of Aix-la-Chapelle, Madras was handed back to the English. Lawrence was released, having been well treated as a prisoner. For the time being the Governor, or President, Charles Floyer, who had taken over Morse's powers in 1747, remained at Fort St David. So did most of the English, including Clive, who shared a house at Bandlipollam on the hilly ground to the west of the settlement with his new friend John Dalton, a handsome and rumbustious lieutenant of Marines, now soldiering for the Company.

It was a small Indian house, for the place was overcrowded and many of the English houses had been demolished for military reasons. 'You'd be surprised to see what strange holes people are forced to put up with', wrote John Walsh's sister, Eliza, who had a house of this sort 'exactly like an English barn', with a little bedroom divided off at each end, and the space in the middle used as a parlour.[15]

Some years later, Dalton contrasted Clive's grand establishment at Madras with 'our Bandlipollam economy'.[16] One feels that he, and Clive too, must have looked back wistfully to when they enjoyed the carefree life of two young bachelors sharing a ramshackle Indian bungalow, a set-up in which one can see Kipling's India before its time. They may have been poor, but they could afford a chaise. If they wanted feminine company, they could dine with Mrs Prince, wife of one of the senior officials, who provided sixteen dishes and had as many servants as an English duchess.[17] There were other girls who had come out on the same ship as Eliza Walsh;

there was Eliza herself, going around in her palanquin carried by five bearers, a soldier marching in front sword in hand and a boy running by her side to keep her petticoats down.[18]

But girls like her had come to India in hopes of matrimony, for which neither Clive nor Dalton had the means, nor yet probably the inclination. They contented themselves with the wenches of the country. Dalton was an inveterate womanizer, and Clive at this time was by no means chaste; they paid for it by being more than once, in Dalton's words, 'clapped'.[19] No doubt they drank too, but they kept a sense of the fitness of things. Clive refused to do duty with a certain officer because he had met him reeling drunk in the streets of Cuddalore, arm-in-arm with a sergeant.[20]

Early in 1749, Clive was involved in a more serious row, with the Chaplain of Fort St David, the Reverend Francis Fordyce. The East India Company settlements had to make do with pretty poor material for their pastors, but the Reverend Francis Fordyce was a disgrace even by the standards of the time; he had been obliged to leave his previous chaplaincy at St Helena to escape the vengeance of a planter whose daughter he had debauched.[21] At Fort St David, as well as neglecting his pastoral duties,[22] he slandered the Governor and every member of the Council, threatening to thrash one of them and to slit the nose of another.[23] Soon after the Pondicherry expedition, reports went around that he was casting aspersions on the behaviour of the Company's troops during the siege. Fordyce blamed Clive for spreading these reports. 'He would break every bone in his skin and half a dozen more of them', he told an officer, who thought this outburst rather 'ill timed' as he had just performed Divine Service.[24]

For some weeks, Fordyce 'scandalized' Clive's character,[25] until Clive, meeting him in the street in Cuddalore, declared that he could stand it no longer and hit him two or three times with his cane. After hesitating a moment, Fordyce hit back and 'closed in' with Clive.[26] One can imagine the Indian bystanders laughing at the sight of the two Masters 'cudgelling each other in the street'.[27] Fortunately, there was another officer present who managed to separate them, just as Dalton and a friend drove up in their chaise and helped to put a stop to the fight.

Fordyce gave notice that he would complain to the Council about Clive's 'violence and riot',[28] then, realizing that a local investigation would only rebound on himself, he decided to make his complaint in England where his character was not so well known. Clive, however, insisted on the matter being heard at Fort St David. Fordyce was summoned, and spoke insultingly to the Governor and Council, who promptly dismissed him from the Company's service. Reporting the affair to the Directors, they stated that Clive was 'generally esteemed a very quiet person and no ways guilty of disturbances'.[29]*

The affair tells us a thing or two about Clive at this time. That he was regarded as 'a very quiet person' would indicate that even if there is any truth in the stories of his wildness as a schoolboy, he did not grow into a rowdy or a swashbuckler; though for all his reserve and his periods of depression, he must have had a considerable store of high spirits to become the boon companion of the gay extrovert, Dalton. That he alone, of all those whom Fordyce slandered, actually tackled the obnoxious clergyman, shows that, however quiet he may have been, he was not the sort of man to take things lying down. Again, the fact that Fordyce chose to slander him, at the same time as he slandered the Governor and Council, shows that Clive was already a somebody, though only twenty-three and still very junior.

2

Macaulay compares the state of India following the death of the Emperor Aurungzeb in 1707 with that of Europe after the death of Charlemagne. Charles the Bald, Charles the Fat and Charles the Simple have their counterpart in the later Mogul Emperors 'sunk in indolence and debauchery' who 'sauntered away life in secluded palaces, chewing *bang*, fondling concubines and listening to buffoons'. Just as the Count of Flanders and the Duke of Burgundy became independent, yet still 'acknowledged the superiority of the most helpless driveller among the later Carlovingians', so did the Nizams and Nawabs of India make themselves into independent sovereigns while still sending presents to, and obtaining charters from, the Mogul. And in the same way as Europe suffered from

* Clive's statement at the inquiry was slightly at variance with those of Dalton and two more of his friends. This would indicate that he had a bad memory for detail, for he had no reason for contradicting Dalton and the other two, who were wholly in his favour. At various times in later life, Clive seemed not to have a strict regard for the truth; it could have been carelessness and forgetfulness, as on this occasion.

the invasions of Vikings, Magyars and Saracens, so was India, in the first half of the eighteenth century, invaded by Persians and Afghans.[30] The sack of Delhi by Nadir Shah in 1739, when, symbolically, the celebrated Peacock Throne of the Moguls was carried off as a prize, marked the end of effective Mogul rule.

Eighteenth-century India was also at the mercy of plunderers from within: the Marathas. This once-peaceful people from the hill country behind Bombay had, towards the end of the century before, turned into a race of warriors, of fierce freebooting horsemen. They established kingdoms at Poona, at Gwalior, in Berar, even in Tanjore in the far south; no part of India was safe from their raids. Nawabs and even the Emperor himself paid them an annual tribute as protection-money; while the English at Calcutta dug what was long afterwards known as the Maratha Ditch as a defence against them. As well as freebooting, the Marathas acted as soldiers of fortune, hiring themselves to one side or the other in the wars between potentates and rival claimants to provinces which were the natural result of 'the political decay that had eaten into the heart of the Indian state system'.[31]

At the time when the Treaty of Aix-la-Chapelle put an end to open warfare between the English and the French, there were rival candidates for the thrones of both the Deccan and the Carnatic. The Nawab of the Carnatic was in theory subordinate to the Nizam of the Deccan, but by this time he was as independent of his overlord as the Nizam himself was independent of the Emperor. In the Deccan, following the death of the powerful Nizam-ul-Mulk in June 1748, there was rivalry between the late Nizam's second son, Nasir Jang, and his grandson, Muzaffar Jang. In the Carnatic, the Nawab, Anwar-ud-din, the father of Mohammed Ali, was in fact a usurper; his position was threatened by a relative of the previous ruling family, Chanda Sahib,[32] a chivalrous and colourful adventurer.

The story of these rival princes is remarkable in that to the normal Oriental confusion of wars, murders, bribery and intrigue was added a new factor, the intervention of the French and the English. There were various reasons for this fishing in troubled Indian waters. The recent war had left both nations with more troops than were necessary to defend their settlements in peacetime. By putting troops at the disposal of one or other Indian potentate, it not only meant that the expenses of these troops would be paid, but there was also the chance of large gains, both for private individuals and for the Company concerned, should their side win.

The next stage was for the French and English to use the wars between the rival Indian princes as a cloak for carrying on a war between themselves, even though they were officially at peace. Thus the French supported Chanda Sahib, the English supported Anwar-ud-din and after his death, Mohammed Ali; the French supported Muzaffar Jang, the English supported Nasir Jang. The principals in these conflicts became little more than puppets in a struggle as to whether the French or the English should enjoy the lion's share of Indian trade.

How far the ambitions of Dupleix went beyond trade to empire-building is uncertain. According to a distinguished French historian,[33] there is no evidence of a systematic attempt on his part to establish a French empire in India; although as early as 1749 the English suspected him of such designs. Clive believed that Dupleix originally aimed at no more than the control of a district round Pondicherry, but that once engaged in the politics of the country his successes opened a scene of great power to him.[34]

It was in fact the English who first played the game of intervention in the smaller sphere of Tanjore, a kingdom of rich fields studded with pagodas some thirty miles south of Fort St David. The former ruler of Tanjore, who had been driven out in 1739, wanted help to regain his kingdom. The English agreed to send him troops in return for their expenses and a grant of Devikottai, a fort at the mouth of the Coleroon river.

The first Tanjore expedition, which set out in March 1749 under the command of Captain James Cope, was a fiasco. When, after being held up on the way by a storm, the English troops reached Tanjore, they failed to make contact with the reinforcements which had been sent by sea, though separated from them by a distance of only four miles. There was nothing for it but to retreat, and as a final mishap they lost most of their baggage and 400 of their coolies were drowned when crossing a deep *nullah** under fire. Clive, recently promoted to lieutenant, went with the expedition in charge of a company. He afterwards recalled how he and his comrades were 'a little staggered, when the hostile Tanjore army suddenly appeared in full view; it was the first time most of them had been confronted by so vast a host.[35]

To redeem this failure, the whole of the Company's forces at Fort St David, under the command of Stringer Lawrence, were shipped to the mouth of the Coleroon and landed, together with heavy artillery, on an island close to Devikottai. When it came to storming the Fort, Clive asked if he could lead the assault party. Lawrence agreed, and gave him a platoon

* Watercourse.

of thirty Europeans and 700 sepoys. Clive led this force across a *nullah*, losing four or five of his Europeans by enemy fire. He then advanced towards the flank of the enemy's entrenchment, without first making sure that all his sepoys had crossed the *nullah*. In fact only some of them had got across, and these failed to keep close to the platoon and protect its rear. Thus unprotected, the platoon came close to the enemy and was about to open fire, when it was attacked in the rear by a body of enemy cavalry, who charged from only forty yards away, having been hidden between the projecting towers of the fort. In an instant all but the front three or four men of Clive's platoon had been cut to pieces. Clive himself narrowly escaped death by stepping aside as one of the horsemen came at him, his sword raised ready to cut him down.[36]

He ran back to the *nullah*, where he found his sepoys drawn up in good order. Lawrence then led his whole army against the Fort, which the enemy quickly abandoned. There is some uncertainty as to whether Clive had first checked the Tanjore cavalry with his sepoys or whether Lawrence saw him in difficulties and came to his rescue. If the latter, Clive's attempts to storm the fort would have done nothing to facilitate its eventual capture. One cannot help feeling that it was his youthful impetuosity which caused the loss of most of his platoon.

Fortunately for Clive, Lawrence thought otherwise. 'This young man's early genius surprised and engaged my attention', he wrote later, 'as well before as at the siege of Devikottai, where he behaved in courage and judgement much beyond what could be expected from his years.'[37] Whatever his judgement on this occasion, Clive certainly showed courage; and it was courage that was needed to rout Indian armies. When, from the ramparts of the fort, he saw the Tanjore army of fifteen or twenty thousand retreating across the plain, it was impressed upon his mind how easily a small but determined European force could put an Indian host to flight.

The English made peace with the actual ruler of Tanjore, who ceded Devikottai to them, paid the cost of the expedition and pensioned off the pretender. Lawrence's next job was to act as one of the English Commissioners for the handing back of Madras by the French. He took Clive with him as his quartermaster. They went in August 1749 to Pondicherry. At last Clive saw the place from within and was able to admire and perhaps envy its broad streets and handsome buildings: the Tour de l'Horloge with its fluted pilasters, the baroque churches and Dupleix's still unfinished palace, its colonnades reminiscent of the Louvre, rising above the walls of the fort. He may have had the pleasure of meeting Dupleix himself, and perhaps Madame as well. After the splendours of Pondicherry, Madras must have seemed very primitive, particularly as it was handed over in a sorry state.

That autumn, Clive decided to return to civilian employ. He had failed to get command of a company; the Governor and Council were bent on reducing military expenses, being 'entirely attached to mercantile ideas'.[38] The fact that he could afford to lose his military pay shows that he was better off than Mun Maskelyne, who preferred to remain in the army even though there now seemed no future in soldiering.

With notable assurance, Clive wrote to the Directors asking for promotion. He spoke of his own 'great courage and bravery' in several 'desperate' actions.[39] He did not have to wait for an answer, for on November 30 he was appointed Steward. This was a profitable post: the Steward was responsible for provisioning the settlement and the garrison, receiving a commission on his purchases. So for the next few months he was immersed in 'Europe beef', Bengal beef, Tranquebar pork, turmeric, arrack, tobacco and lamp-oil. He also had to list and check all the Company's furniture and equipment in Fort St George and Fort St David: the chairs, tables, cots and *almiras*, the remarkably fine collection of silver plate, together with objects ranging from a birdcage to a state palanquin.[40]

Clive's good fortune in being appointed Steward was quickly followed by a severe bout of fever. To recuperate he went early in the New Year of 1750 to Calcutta,* where after the more spartan conditions of the Coast, he would have been struck by the grandeur and luxury, the great mansions like Italian *palazzi* along the river front, and round the Park with its central tank; the elegant Factory House rising above the walls of Fort William. It was more like a large European city than Madras, with houses and public buildings in streets outside the Fort, rather than all crowded into its confines. But it also lacked the spruceness of Fort St George. Unless they had been very recently given a coat of white, even the grandest façades in Calcutta looked stained and dilapidated on account of the damp. Similarly, for all the champagne and silver lace, Calcutta society would have seemed a little frowsty compared with the more pioneering Madras life.

* A winter in Bengal was a recognized health cure; for though the surrounding swamp and jungle made Calcutta very unhealthy in hot weather, it did enjoy a couple of cool months whereas the Coromandel Coast was hot all the year round.

On this first visit to Calcutta, Clive met Robert Orme, a Company servant three years younger than himself whose literary talents had earned for him the nickname 'Cicero'. After Clive returned to the Coromandel Coast, he and Orme traded in partnership; Orme visited Madras in 1751 and the two became close friends. It is through this friendship, although it had its ups and downs, that many of Clive's military exploits are recorded for posterity, in the pages of Orme's *magnum opus*, the *History of the Military Transactions of the British Nation in Indostan*. How far Orme exaggerated Clive's feats of daring is open to argument. Orme himself claimed to have given Clive the best possible write-up; but Orme was an unreliable person, vain, touchy and snobbish,[41] as his fine-drawn, oversensitive features betray.

After visiting Calcutta, Clive once again hoped to be transferred there;[42] which shows how, at the age of twenty-four, he had no thought of resuming his military career. He would have regarded his amateur soldiering as merely an episode; the real business of his life in India was to make money, and it still seemed that the best way to make money was by trade. In this year, 1750, his exploits at Pondicherry and Devikottai would have mattered less to him than the fact that he and his Bengal associates now dealt in whole shiploads.

His idea of being transferred to Calcutta is also a sign of his impulsiveness. By now, he had built up a position for himself on the Coast. He was Steward, he enjoyed the favour of both Lawrence and Governor Floyer, he had a number of friends. Yet he was ready to throw all this up and move to a strange settlement simply because he had seen a rather fly-blown show of wealth and heard Orme and his other Bengal acquaintances talk big. But while we know that he was inclined to concentrate so much on his favourite object as to be blinded to all else, we cannot accuse him of short-sightedness in planning to leave the Coast just as it was about to become the scene of momentous happenings. In fact, he may have been longer-sighted than Governor Floyer and the Council, who imagined that they could now concentrate peacefully on their 'mercantile ideas', even though Dupleix was still there; his very prescience may have urged him to leave. Momentous happenings are not good for trade; his few small military laurels were not enough to tell him that in such happenings lay his great chance.

None the less, he stayed on the Coast, and we hear nothing more of him during 1750, except that he was 'chin deep in merchandize'.[43] Early in the following year, the former Eliza Walsh, now Mrs Joseph Fowke, wrote to her aunts in England, telling them that her cousin, Mun Maskelyne, had 'laid out a husband for Peggy if she chooses to take so long a voyage for one, that I approve of extremely, but then she must make haste, as he is in such a marrying mood that I believe the first comer will carry him'.[44]

Peggy was Mun's sister Margaret, then aged fifteen, who eventually became Clive's wife. We know that Mun arranged the marriage, so the prospective husband mentioned by Eliza must almost certainly be Clive. That he was 'in such a marrying mood' and regarded as a good match by both Mun and Eliza would suggest that his trade and a year as Steward were bringing substantial returns. Eliza's approval of him as a husband for her young cousin would also indicate that he was steady-going, rather than dissolute.

There is a romantic tradition that Clive saw and admired a miniature of a young girl in Mun's room and on being told that she was his sister, begged him to invite her to Madras. It is also said that Clive fell for Margaret by hearing Mun read aloud her letters to him. Certainly Margaret's letters show a personality full of sweetness and humour, and a lively and enquiring mind.

She was just the sort of girl who would have gone to India in search of a husband, having neither parents nor money. Her father had been a minor civil servant and came of a family that had once been of some importance in Wiltshire, where she lived with aunts. She attended Mrs Saintsbury's school at Cirencester and, for a girl of her time, was well educated; she had inherited a taste for poetry and astronomy from her mother, and her French was so good that when she wrote to Eliza in that language, her older cousin felt unequal to composing a worthy reply. Eliza offered to pay for her to go for a year to a 'good day school' in London, to perfect her French and also her dancing.[45]

CHAPTER III

Arcot

> Anyone might have thought of it; it was the strategy of the march to Blenheim, of Jackson's march to Mannassas Junction, of the expeditions to the Dardanelles and Gallipoli.
>
> PHILIP WOODRUFF

In the summer of 1749, not long after the English had tried their luck in Tanjore, Dupleix began his policy of adventure by giving military help to the two pretenders, Muzaffar Jang and Chanda Sahib, who had joined forces and invaded the Carnatic. With their combined army they defeated and killed the Nawab, Anwar-ud-din, and took his elder son prisoner; the younger son, Mohammed Ali, fled to Trichinopoly in the south. Dupleix received the two pretenders with salutes, fireworks and dancing-girls.[1] As though he were already Nizam, Muzaffar Jang conferred the government of the Carnatic on Chanda Sahib, who showed his gratitude to Dupleix by granting various territories to the French, including forty-two villages in the neighbourhood of Fort St David. From the very ramparts of the Fort, the English could see the white flags going up to mark the new French territory. It seemed as if the French were trying to cut off their trade and communications with the rest of the country.

The English tried to play the same game as Dupleix and gave military help to the two *de facto* princes, Mohammed Ali and Nasir Jang, but Dupleix continued to win all the points. His greatest triumph came with the murder of Nasir Jang in December 1750. Muzaffar Jang became Nizam, and not only granted still more territory to the French, but made Dupleix his deputy for the South. Chanda Sahib was confirmed as Nawab of Arcot under the suzerainty of Dupleix.

A French army commanded by Dupleix's best general, Charles, Marquis de Bussy, escorted Muzaffar Jang back to Hyderabad, his capital. On the way, Muzaffar Jang was killed in a skirmish, but Bussy quickly replaced him with his uncle, Salabat Jang, who confirmed all Muzaffar Jang's grants. Dupleix was now at the height of his power, theoretically the ruler of the whole of the southern part of the peninsula, the autocrat of thirty million souls; with his lieutenant, Bussy, as the real master of the Deccan. Mohammed Ali still held court as a *roi fainéant* in his fortress town of Trichinopoly, but it seemed only a matter of time before the weak English force which kept him there would yield to French superiority: in terms of European troops alone Dupleix had 1800 compared with the English 800. Without the pretence of a Nawab to fight for, the English 'would have nothing to do but submit to the mercy of Dupleix'.[2]

'The French are setting up one Nawab and we another and their design is to drive us off the Coast', wrote Eliza Fowke to her aunts in September 1750.[3] But she wrote mainly of picnics and balls, of the Misses Rous getting engaged and a certain clergyman siring a bastard, showing how casually the inhabitants of Madras and Fort St David regarded the situation.[4] In this very month, however, the ineffective, card-playing Floyer was replaced as Governor by Thomas Saunders, a man of ability, judgement and common-sense, who was determined to resist Dupleix to the last.[5] Orme wrote of him a few yars later: 'Had I anything on earth to expect, or anything to fear, he is the man on earth I should dread as an enemy.'[6]

It would be tempting to ascribe Clive's decision to stay on the Coast to the advent of Saunders, but it is most unlikely that Clive, who was not a particularly good judge of character, would have recognized him as his man of destiny. Cold, silent and unresponsive, the new Governor would not have been inclined to encourage a young hopeful of 'martial disposition' until he had proved himself. At present, all he knew of Clive was that Lawrence favoured him – scant commendation in that he did not much care for the 'Old Cock'. In any case, Lawrence had little time to push his favourite, since he sailed for England soon after Saunders's arrival, the Directors having decreed to cut his salary.

Saunders gave increased military aid to Mohammed Ali, but without Lawrence he lacked a commander of any worth. In May 1751 a force under Captain Rudolph de Gingens, a brave but incompetent Swiss, was sent to intercept Chanda Sahib who, it was reported, was about to march with a large army to besiege Mohammed Ali in Trichinopoly. Being Steward, Clive accompanied this force as Commissary. His allowance of half a rupee a day for every European soldier he fed left him a comfortable profit, for the cost was only about two-thirds of this sum. Nevertheless, his job was no sinecure. It took great organizing powers to keep a moving army supplied with food and forage in a country devastated by successive invaders. He had to obtain cattle and sheep, together with rice, ghee and curry-stuffs for the sepoys; he had to find oxen, camels and elephants to carry guns and stores over rough country and across many rivers. He had to keep the peace among the camp-followers and negotiate *ad hoc* loans from Indian merchants with which to pay the troops. Clive profited from his work as Commissary not just in terms of cash, but in knowledge and experience—how to deal with Indians of different types and castes and win their trust. From leading drivers and coolies, he learnt how to lead Indian troops into battle.

As well as doing his Commissary's work, Clive fought as a volunteer.[7] It was an inglorious campaign. The English missed an opportunity of routing Chanda Sahib's army through panicking at a cannonade which turned out to be harmless, and were obliged to retire into Trichinopoly, while Chanda Sahib encamped before the town. Clive returned to Fort St David and volunteered for military service without pay, provided he was given captain's rank. His offer was gladly accepted. Now that most of the army was cooped up at Trichinopoly, there was such a shortage of officers that a detachment had to be sent out under the command of a young civilian member of Council, the tough and genial George Pigot. Clive went with this detachment and he and Pigot had a narrow escape when they were surprised by the horsemen of a hostile *poligar*, or robber-baron; fortunately for them, their own mounts were swifter.*

Soon after he was made a captain, Clive took a small detachment to Trichinopoly by way of Tanjore. The expedition was uneventful, but it is of historic importance in that while he was at Trichinopoly, Mohammed Ali probably won him over to his favourite military plan. This was to make an attack on Arcot, a town some sixty miles inland from Madras which was the capital of the Carnatic and the seat of Chanda Sahib's government, but which had been left without a strong enough garrison owing to most of the enemy forces being gathered at Trichinopoly. Mohammed Ali was convinced that such an attack would draw off some of the enemy forces,[8] and he also hoped that if the attack were successful, it would be possible to replenish his depleted military chest with the

* Pigot subsequently rode his to hounds; even in those days, the English in India hunted the jackal.

revenues of the rich Arcot country. Such was the idea behind Arcot, a name immortal in military history. It was a daring feat of arms rather than a great battle, yet it was a decisive event both in the history of British India and in Clive's own life.*

While Clive was still away, Saunders decided to adopt the plan, writing to ask Gingens to lead part of his force into the Arcot country. Just as Saunders heard from Gingens that this was impossible, Clive arrived back at Fort St David. Gingens's negative answer was his chance, and he persuaded Saunders to give him the command of the expedition.

Having decided on the expedition and put Clive in charge of it, Saunders and his Council staked everything on its success. They gave Clive all the troops they could possibly spare, amounting to 130 Europeans and some sepoys, leaving themselves with only 100 men to defend Fort St David. On August 22† the party sailed in a ship suitably named the *Wager* to Madras, where the Deputy Governor, Richard Prince, provided a further eighty Europeans, reducing his own garrison to a mere fifty. On August 26, the expedition began its march.

Clive's force consisted of some 200 Europeans and rather more than that number of sepoys.[9] He had eight officers under him, including his friends Pybus and Bulkley,[10] and a surgeon, Doctor James Wilson. Of the officers, only Clive himself, Bulkley and perhaps one other had been in action before; the rest were young civilian volunteers. The European troops, if not actually 'the scum and refuse' of England, as Clive was afterwards to describe the Company's army in those early days,[11] were none the less badly disciplined, while the sepoys, compared with the trained and seasoned Indian troops of twenty years later, were little more than peons. As for artillery, the force had only three small field-pieces.

They must have been a strange mixture of East and West, the European soldiers in red, the sepoys in ordinary Indian shirts with bare legs and marching to the beat of tom-toms. They marched through the dust of the Choultry Plain, a vast expanse of orange-coloured sand dotted with scrub and tall cactus, with distant grey hillocks to the left. Every now and then there was a village of straw huts, smelling of smoke, surrounded by scattered palm trees and inhabited not only by humans and cattle but also by grey monkeys with pink faces. After a while the ground became paler and more like desert. They had sixty-four miles to go and the heat was

* Writers down to the present time have followed Orme in attributing the idea to Clive himself, whereas the credit for it must go to Mohammed Ali.

† All dates in this chapter are Old Style.

intense. But they marched quickly. By the third day they had travelled forty miles and were in sight of the great pagoda of Conjeveram, which rose out of the plain flanked by two smaller pagodas.

They entered the town that clustered around the high walls of the group of temples, one of the major shrines of Hinduism, overshadowed by the vast and heavily carved pagodas of golden-brown stone. Here they learnt that the garrison of Arcot was stronger than they had anticipated, so Clive wrote back to Madras for two eighteen-pounder guns to be sent after them. Prince answered Clive on the very same day—one admires the speed of the couriers—promising twelve-pounders at least.[12] Throughout the expedition, Clive was in constant touch with Madras and Fort St David. Prince wrote to him almost daily, giving him the benefit of his experience, as well as organizing the expedition's supplies, its intelligence service and its liaison with the notables of the country.

Saunders, too, wrote frequently. The expedition was in fact a remarkable piece of co-ordination between Clive at Arcot, Prince at Madras and Saunders at Fort St David; each situated at a different point of a triangle and separated from the others by sixty to a hundred miles of hostile country. Clive's youth—he was not yet twenty-six—helped in that he cheerfully took the corrections of his seniors; and for their part, Prince and Saunders left final decisions to Clive, however much they guided him. It was always a case of 'you are the best judge'.[13] The atmosphere of friendship and trust in which the three of them worked must have greatly contributed to their success; it was very different from the jealousies and bickerings that seemed to blight so many enterprises in India, and to which the affairs of Dupleix were particularly prone.

Clive did not wait at Conjeveram for the arrival of the heavy guns, but pushed on. Distant hills drew closer, and turned from grey to pink. On the 31st the weather broke and there was a terrific storm of thunder, lightning and rain. Clive and his followers did not look for shelter, but marched on through the storm though they were soaked to the skin and the dust had turned to a sea of mud. They did not pause till that evening, when they camped for the night ten miles from their goal.

Early next morning they approached Arcot. They were now among the hills; beyond the city was a further and more impressive range, with sharp and blunt peaks half hidden in the mist. They reached the gate and found, to their astonishment, that they were able to enter unmolested. The garrison, 1100 strong, had fled during the night, having heard from their spies of how the English had marched unconcernedly through the storm, heedless of the omens of heaven. This to them denoted superhuman courage, so they reckoned it was no good trying to resist such a foe.[14]

An advance party hoisted Mohammed Ali's colours of white and green on the Nawab's palace, which stood next to the fort. At ten that morning the main part of Clive's force marched in, complete with field-pieces, ammunition and – as a French agent noted – two chests of liquor.[15] As they made their way along the narrow streets to the fort, they were watched by the city's hundred thousand inhabitants.

By such gestures as returning valuable merchandise left in the fort for safe keeping to its owners, Clive won many of the inhabitants over to his side.[16] This was in accordance with Saunders's injunction 'not in any shape to molest or distress the inhabitants'[17] – words dictated as much by policy as by humanitarianism, for he asked for special care to be taken of the houses of bankers.

Clive learnt the lesson that it pays to treat the populace well. He might so easily have lost his head at finding himself the master of a rich and teeming city. Saunders did his best to bring him down to earth: 'It is with pleasure I observe the reception you met with, but when you consider that those people were entirely in your power, 'tis nothing extraordinary.' And: 'If the merchants have a mind to make you a present I have nothing to say to the contrary, but take care there be no compulsion.'[18] Clive was never to use compulsion – despite what his enemies may have insinuated to the contrary – in order to get 'presents' from those in his power.

Saunders also took care to instil in Clive the importance of legitimacy, of maintaining the pretence that the English were only acting as auxiliaries. He reminded him to hoist the Mogul's and Mohammed Ali's colours and to proclaim, by beat of tom-tom, that the place had been taken in the name of the Mogul, who in theory was Mohammed Ali's overlord.[19] Clive, who in a burst of patriotism had asked Prince to send him a Union Jack,[20] heeded Saunders's words so well as to abide by the fiction of Mogul legitimacy for the rest of his life.

Having hoisted the flags and beat the tom-toms, Clive was faced with the task of raising revenues for Mohammed Ali. He brought pressure to bear on two or three *killedars*,* but could never stay long enough to produce any effect. No less urgent was the question of what to do when

* Commandants of forts or garrisons.

the enemy recovered from their surprise and attempted to regain the city.

At first, Clive was uncertain whether to make a stand at Arcot, whether to retire to the neighbouring fort of Timiri or divide his troops among a number of different forts, or whether even to go back to Madras. He was not alone in his ignorance of the political value of holding the capital; even the knowledgeable Prince advised him to withdraw when it was reported that Chanda Sahib's son, Raza Sahib, was coming with 2000 horse.[21] Saunders, however, urged him to hold Arcot if it was in any way tenable. Pigot, who never lacked courage, added his word: 'There is a good deal in the name of the place, and I like the sound of Arcot.' He expressed his faith in Clive's 'noddle', and jokingly called him a Nawab – pointing out that to retire to Timiri would demote him to being merely '*Faujdar** Clive'.[22]

Clive had 'noddle' enough to stay at Arcot, and set to work preparing the fort to stand a siege.[23] Provisions had to be got in, and paid for by bills on the Company. There was the need for a safe water supply. It was all very well for Clive to report cheerfully that the water tasted good; it might still have given his men fluxes, as Prince pointed out.[24] Attempts were made to burn down some of the houses overlooking the walls, but with no success, for they contained little that would burn. Being closely surrounded by houses was not the only disadvantage of the Arcot fort. The walls were a mile in circumference, too long to be comfortably held by a force as small as Clive's; the towers were so tumbledown that few of them could carry cannon; the moat was dry or fordable in many places.

After two unsuccessful attempts to dislodge the former garrison of Arcot, which was encamped a few miles away and impeding the bringing-in of provisions, Clive refrained from any more sallies while putting the fort to rights. The enemy, who had grown in number to 3000, took this as a sign of fear and moved up close to the city. Clive waited until two hours after midnight on September 14, then marched silently with most of his force and attacked them while they were asleep. They fled in confusion, hardly troubling to fire a shot while the English force went right through their camp firing continuously. The English then retired, having lost not a single man. Terrible shrieks and groans from the camp told of the havoc they had wrought. Next morning, none of the enemy remained

* Local governor.

in sight.[25] This action taught Clive how deadly a night attack on an Indian camp could be. When nearly every horseman had his family and all his possessions with him, when tents, horses, bullocks, camels and elephants were jumbled together in what was more like 'a great confused town than a body of military men encamped',[26] a determined attack by night could cause instant chaos.

By September 16, the two eighteen-pounders which Clive had asked for were on their way, escorted by only a few sepoys. There was a strong enemy force in the neighbourhood of Conjeveram waiting to intercept the convoy, so Clive sent almost his entire garrison to make sure it reached Arcot safely. Realizing the situation, the enemy changed their plan and returned quickly to Arcot.

The party left to hold the fort was so small that there were not even enough sentries; they had to keep moving from post to post. But when, at two in the morning, the enemy attacked the main gate, hoping to distract the garrison by their shouts and their blaring music, they were routed by a few grenades. An hour later they went round and attacked the back gate of the fort, but they gave the garrison ample warning 'by the hideous shouts and noise they made'.[27] Once again, they were driven off. Next morning, the main force under Bulkley returned—complete with the eighteen-pounders and 300 head of cattle—and the enemy fled.

As their numbers increased, the enemy took to entering the city at odd times and attacking Clive's soldiers as they walked about off duty. But as long as Raza Sahib and his French allies failed to arrive, the English at Arcot were comparatively safe. For this breathing-space, Clive had largely to thank Dupleix, who had at first been inclined to dismiss the news of his exploit as a bazaar rumour. Even later, when he realized the seriousness of the situation,[28] and was so angry at the prospect of losing the Arcot revenues that his factor, Ananda Ranga Pillai, dared not go into his presence,[29] he still thought that Clive intended to 'escape' back to Madras.[30] Meanwhile, Raza Sahib refused to march on the day that Dupleix had appointed, for like many orientals he believed some days to be luckier than others.[31] At last, however, a propitious day came along and he marched with 4000 Indians and 150 French under the command of an officer named Du Saussay.

As Raza Sahib's army approached, Clive and his men shut themselves up in the fort. The enemy troops entered the city on the night of September 23, and next day, Clive made a desperate attempt to drive them out. He sallied forth with most of his troops and there was a fierce cannonade between his artillery and that of the French along the street separating the fort from the Nawab's palace. Most of the French gunners were killed, and Clive hoped to fetch away their guns; but a murderous musket fire from the windows of the palace and the adjoining houses obliged him to retire into the fort. It was hard enough to get his own guns back without too much loss of life: typically resourceful, he made his gunners dodge in and out of a *choultry** which ran along one side of the street, firing and loading so that the guns moved back by their own recoil.

The action cost Clive fifteen of his Europeans. He himself had a narrow escape when an enemy sepoy aimed at him from a window; he was pulled aside just in time by Lieutenant Trenwith, who received the fatal shot. According to the accepted rules of warfare, he should never have attempted a sally of this kind in his situation. He was greatly outnumbered, he could not afford to lose a single man, his men were exposed and the enemy were safely under cover in the houses. But if it achieved nothing else, the action gave his men confidence and made the enemy respect them.

In fact Clive was breaking the rules by trying to hold out at all. As a reckless young man, encouraged by civilians who were playing a desperate game, he took a chance where an experienced soldier would have been put off by the impossible size and dilapidation of the fort, and by the enormous disadvantage in numbers. Raza Sahib's army, together with the former garrison of Arcot and a force from the nearby fortress of Vellore, made a total enemy strength of 10,000. Clive's force was reduced to 120 Europeans and 200 sepoys. This was not just on account of casualties, but because he had sent part of his force back to Madras, so as not to leave that settlement too short of men.

From now on, Clive and his men were closely besieged. The weather was hot and humid; the fort, shut in by houses, airless. In their heavy red uniforms, the European soldiers never ceased to stream with sweat. Disease quickly made its appearance.

The enemy cut the water supply from outside, so the garrison had to make do with water from an unwholesome reservoir in the fort. Prince was sympathetic: 'It's hard indeed to be obliged to drink bad water, and no wine to qualify it!'[32] They might have had no water at all, but for an Indian mason who knew of an underground channel by which the enemy could have drained the reservoir, and blocked it before this could happen.[33]

* Open shelter for travellers.

One thing they did not suffer was hunger, even though the siege lasted fifty days; Clive having laid in provisions for more than three months.*

The garrison's chief hardship, as Clive himself said, was fatigue.[34] To man such lengthy walls with such small numbers meant that nobody had enough sleep. The enemy kept up a continual musket fire from the houses, which were so close that people were actually hurt by stones thrown from them; and in the words of Doctor Wilson, 'a man could not show a nose over the parapet without being shot'.[35] Yet some of the garrison had always to be patrolling the ramparts, to make sure that there was not a surprise attack. On three occasions Clive had a sergeant shot dead beside him while going his rounds.[36] One night, Lieutenant Glass and a couple of men were let down over the wall by ropes and tried to blow up the houses from which the fire was most troublesome; but their attempt failed, and as Glass was being hauled back again the rope broke and he fell and was injured.

Meanwhile, Saunders and Prince were trying to get a relief force to Clive. There was the hope of Gingens coming, of Mohammed Ali sending a force, of help from the Regent of Mysore. But neither Gingens nor Mohammed Ali was willing to reduce the garrison at Trichinopoly; the Mysoreans were too much intimidated by the French to do anything. Prince was continually being promised troops by this *poligar* and that *zemindar*. Some of Raza Sahib's allies—one of them, nicknamed 'the Dog', was supposed to have attempted to poison Raza Sahib—started to intrigue with Clive, who trusted them no more than Prince did, but spun out the correspondence in the hope that it would keep them inactive.[37]

Saunders scraped together a force of 130 Europeans and 100 sepoys, his position having been slightly improved by the arrival of some recruits from Europe. He promised this force at the beginning of October, but it was another three weeks before it actually set out from Madras on the road to Arcot, under the command of Lieutenant Innes. Having waited all this time, the weary garrison must have expected it from day to day,

* The well-known story of the sepoys offering to let the Europeans have all the rice, and saying that they themselves would be content with the water in which it had been boiled, must be regarded as a myth. It was first told by Sir John Malcolm, *Life of Robert, Lord Clive* (London 1836), and made into an epic by Macaulay, who ends with the peroration: 'History contains no more touching instance of military fidelity, or of the influence of a commanding mind.'

hour to hour. And then the news came that Innes's force had been intercepted by the enemy and obliged to retire.

In any case, Clive reckoned the enemy were now so strong that it would take no less than 1000 Indians and 200 Europeans to relieve him.[38] But the constant talk of English reinforcements kept Du Saussay, the commander of the French force with Raza Sahib, in a state of alarm. Dupleix had no faith in Du Saussay,[39] and replaced him with another officer, Goupil, who was himself about to be replaced at the time when the siege ended. These changes did not give the Indians a high opinion of the French commanders. As for their own general, Raza Sahib, his incapacity was notorious.

Clive held out hopes to Saunders that he could defend a breach should the enemy make one. It was now the middle of October and the French heavy artillery had arrived from Pondicherry. A battery was opened to the north-west of the fort. The first few shots disabled one of the English eighteen-pounders and dismounted the other; which was afterwards only used where it was not exposed to heavy metal. The French cannon continued their bombardment for six days, by which time the entire wall between two towers had fallen. But the garrison quickly made an inner defence of trenches, pallisades and rubble, the officers working side by side with the men.[40]

To show Raza Sahib that they were not all that hard pressed, Clive indulged in a schoolboy prank. The fort contained a huge old cannon, said to have been sent by the Emperor Aurungzeb, complete with its seventy-two-pound iron balls. This ancient gun was hoisted on to a mound of earth built on top of the tallest tower of the fort, and fired so that its shot went through the palace, which was Raza Sahib's headquarters. Once a day for three days, Clive saluted Raza Sahib in this manner, at the hour when he knew all his officers would be with him – but on the fourth day, the old gun burst. The enemy, as though to retaliate, built a mound on top of a house so as to be able to fire on to all parts of the fort. The English waited till it was finished and the cannon duly perched on it, together with a crew of fifty. They then toppled the mound over with the remaining eighteen-pounder.

These diversions did not stop the enemy from setting up a battery to the south-west of the fort, and although their gunners were frequently driven away by English musketry, they made a breach even larger than the first. Once again the garrison toiled at digging a trench and throwing up a breastwork.

'Our people sickly and not above 80 military fit for duty,' wrote a British sergeant early in November.[41]* But now, after forty days of siege, a new hope came from the rugged pink hills to the west, where an army of 6000 Marathas, under a famous commander, Morari Rao, was encamped. They had been hired by the Regent of Mysore[42] to help Mohammed Ali, but reckoning his cause to be hopeless, bided their time, not wanting to come in on the losing side. In the middle of October, Morari Rao assured Clive's messenger that he would send help without a moment's delay, being now convinced that the English could fight.[43] However, he put off marching until he had settled the finances of his campaign with the Mysore Regent and Mohammed Ali. These hagglings dragged on into November, although Prince heard an optimistic report that Morari Rao would be ready to march if he were given 'a little dog, some birds and a pair of fine pistols'.[44]

When Raza Sahib heard that Morari Rao was being won over by English diplomacy, he sent a messenger to the fort, offering Clive an honourable surrender and a large present. If these terms were not accepted, he threatened to storm the fort immediately and put every man to death. Clive treated both the offer and the threat with contempt, and by taking the messenger all over the fort, managed to give him the impression that his ammunition was still plentiful, whereas in fact it was running low.[45] He was determined to hold out to the last, and told Saunders and Prince that he 'was not under the least apprehension' unless the enemy breached more than half the fort.[46] He doubtless took courage from the news that the Marathas were coming, and that the reinforcement from Madras, now increased in numbers and under the command of Captain James Killpatrick, was once again on its way.

Faced by the double threat of the relief force and the Marathas, Raza Sahib decided to storm the fort. In the evening of November 13, a spy brought news to the garrison that the attack was to be next day. Clive snatched a little sleep and was awakened half an hour before dawn. They were coming.

It was the tenth day of Mohurrum, the climax of the fast and mourning for the death of Hassan and Hussein, the two grandsons of the Prophet. The Shiah Muslim soldiers of Raza Sahib worked themselves into a religious frenzy, certain that if they died fighting the infidel they would go straight to Heaven. 'Ya Hassan, ya Hussein!' they cried, as they rushed

* By 'military' he meant Europeans; with sepoys, the active strength of the garrison amounted to over 200.

CLIVE

A portrait attributed to Thomas Gainsborough

CLIVE

Mezzotint by J. McArdell after a missing portrait by Gainsborough

CLIVE

by Nathaniel Dance

up. A great multitude carried ladders to different parts of the walls; a crowd attacked each gate, driving elephants in front of them with iron fixed to their foreheads. Before the beasts could batter down the high old wooden doors, their hides were stung by bullets as the garrison opened fire. Maddened, they turned and stampeded, trampling over the men who were urging them on.[47]

Meanwhile, other parties attacked the two breaches. At the breach to the north-west, the moat was fordable. The attackers swarmed into the breach and as many as could pass through it came over, 'with a mad kind of intrepidity'. Some of them had even crossed the first trench before the garrison gave them a deadly and prolonged fire, each man when he had discharged his musket being handed another one already loaded. Wave after wave of men came through the breach and were driven off in the same way; those beyond the wall awaiting their turn were forced back across the moat by bombs.[48] The commander of the enemy sepoys, Abdul Codah Khan, led this attack with great bravery, mounting the breach himself and planting a flag in it. Next moment, a bullet threw him into the moat below, mortally wounded.[49]

Abdul Codah Khan's was the only party which really attacked. The others behaved feebly. At the south-west breach seventy men tried to cross the moat on a raft, only to panic and upset when a few shots were fired at them from a field-piece directed by Clive himself.[50] 'The French were worse than the rest.'[51] Their commander, Goupil, had been against the idea of storming the fort, so had made no plans. He did not even think it necessary to put a French platoon at the head of each of the attacking parties, but stationed his men in a safe place, from which they just looked on. A French sergeant was reported to have been shot by one of the sepoys under him, as he abandoned his party during an attack.[52]

At the death of Abdul Codah Khan the enemy lost heart, and they retired on the pretext that daylight made a further attack impracticable. Before going, they tried to carry off their dead, who lay thick in the breaches and in the moat, imagining that the garrison would allow them to perform this duty. The English continued to fire on them, showing an ignorance of Eastern chivalry which may have been deliberate, though pardonable in the desperate circumstances. One of the enemy sepoys braved the fire of forty muskets to carry off the body of Abdul Codah Khan.[53]

Clive and his men were left 'to gaze at each other in the first garish brilliance of the suddenly uplifted sun'.[54] The fighting had lasted no more than an hour, during which time they had suffered six casualties, four Europeans killed and two Indians wounded.[55]

Two hours later the enemy began to fire at the fort with muskets from the houses, and with cannon. At two in the afternoon they asked for a truce so as to be able to bury their dead. This was granted, and while the dead were carried off by the enemy, their weapons were collected by the English. At four the truce ended and the firing began again, continuing until two the following morning, when it suddenly ceased. At dawn the garrison heard that Raza Sahib's army had fled from the city, leaving behind most of their guns. The siege was over.[56] Later that day, Kill-patrick arrived with his relieving force.

It was not just the bravery of the garrison which won Arcot, for this alone would not have been enough against such odds. It was also luck. Had Abdul Codah Khan not been killed, the outcome might have been different. In those days, an Indian army, however great its numbers, invariably lost heart if its commander fell – a lesson Clive was to learn again and again. There was also the ineptitude of both Raza Sahib and Goupil.

Dupleix was angry at the raising of the siege. 'You would never believe that four or five hundred beggarly Marathas would make M. Goupil determine to raise the siege,' he wrote, but he had no idea of its full significance.* For Arcot was the turning of the tide. It may have been luck, it may have been bungling on the part of the enemy, but it created the legend of English courage and invincibility which was to carry English arms in India from one success to another. And no one person helped to create this legend as much as Clive, who was now known to the Indians as Sabit Jang – 'steady in war', a name given him by Mohammed Ali.[57] The *mullahs* wrote the tale of the siege, which was told far and wide and became part of South Indian folklore.[58]

But while it greatly helped the English cause for Clive to become a hero, it had an unfortunate effect on his character. Arcot created a false concept of him as a military genius, a concept to which he himself was to cling for the rest of his life, though he was far too intelligent to be wholly taken in by it. This led to a growing sense of insecurity as none of his subsequent successes quite came up to his first as a daring exploit that fired men's imagination; and he made desperate and often arrogant attempts to

* So little was thought of Arcot in Pondicherry that the diary of Ananda Ranga Pillai, Dupleix's Indian factor, makes no mention of it from the time when Raza Sahib's army set out in the middle of September.

justify the military image so dear to him. He was only twenty-six at the time of Arcot; as far as his military career was concerned, he suffered the classic misfortune of success coming too early. Yet he would have been none the worse for this had he only been willing to see his first great success in its true light, as the foundation of the personal ascendancy which he was able to build up over the Indians by other means than war.

CHAPTER IV

Kaveripak and Trichinopoly

You are a very great Bahadur being always victorious over your enemies . . . you are a well-known invincible . . . you are a complete prudent.

REGENT OF MYSORE to CLIVE, 1752

Though the siege of Arcot was over, Clive had still to drive the enemy out of the surrounding country. Raza Sahib was 'entrenched . . . up to the eyes'[1] under the protection of the great fortress of Vellore, a few miles to the west; before he could be attacked, it was necessary to 'unharbour the young gentleman'.[2] Clive also waited for Maratha help. Morari Rao had moved on to join Mohammed Ali with the main body of his troops, but he had left behind a thousand horse under the command of his brother, Buzangara. Like most Marathas, Buzangara was a slippery customer, more interested in plunder than in helping Clive with his campaign. However, the French foolishly attacked his camp, which drove him for the time being on to the English side.

So Clive set off with those fierce and outlandish warriors, naked but for turbans, shorts and plaids, riding long-legged horses said to be sustained with opium. His object was to stop a French reinforcement on its way to Raza Sahib from Pondicherry. He then heard that Raza Sahib had left Vellore with his whole force and had joined the French reinforcement. Clive marched rapidly by night, so as to engage the enemy before they returned to Vellore.

The two armies met on the morning of the following day, December 3,* near the town of Arni, some twenty miles south of Arcot. Clive showed a

* The dates in this chapter are Old Style. The English adopted the New Style calendar in September 1752.

natural ability for choosing his ground. He placed his European troops and artillery on an eminence, facing the enemy across swampy paddy fields. In a village to the right he put his sepoys, and the Maratha horse—now reduced to 600, the others having gone off to plunder—moved up into a palm grove on the left.

The enemy advanced at noon and began to cannonade, but their shot buried itself harmlessly in the paddy fields. The English cannon, however, firing down the slope, had great effect. Owing to the swampiness of the fields, the enemy could not advance their artillery except along a narrow causeway to the right, which ran past the village. They brought their guns this way, together with part of their army, only to be enfiladed by Clive's sepoys and prevented from going any further.

In the palm grove to the left, the Marathas charged five times, but were driven back by musket fire. Clive sent a party under Bulkley with a couple of field pieces to support them. For some unknown reason they forgot to take any ammunition, so he ordered them back, telling them to march slowly as though on parade. This was so as not to look as if they were retreating, and it appeared to the enemy that the English were making a concentrated attack against their artillery which was stranded on the causeway to the right. Their sepoys began to move over to that side, leaving their horse to the mercy of the Marathas and of Bulkley who duly returned with his field pieces, this time with ammunition also.

Clive had sent a platoon of Europeans to join the sepoys in the village. He noticed the French troops, who were with the artillery, advancing under cover of a nearby *choultry*, and ordered the sepoys and this platoon to attack them. The French panicked and scattered, causing the enemy sepoys and horse alike to retire. The Marathas chased the horse and Clive advanced with his infantry and field pieces along the causeway in pursuit of the main body of the enemy. They made a stand in three different *choultries*, but were beaten out of each, and at nightfall the pursuit ceased.[3] The enemy fled during the night, leaving most of their baggage. Two hundred of them were killed or wounded, including fifty French, whereas the English lost no Europeans and only eight sepoys. Raza Sahib's army scattered in groups of twenty or thirty. The French did not stop until they reached the fortress of Gingee, half-way to Pondicherry.

Arni was Clive's first victory in the field; he won it through his skill in placing his men and artillery, and also on account of the poor behaviour of the French.[4] Many of the enemy sepoys were so disgusted with their leaders that they determined to go over to his rising star, and offered him their services on the day after the battle; but he was only able to take on the 600 of them who had arms. There was no means of arming the others – Fort St George contained no more than fifty spare weapons – so they had to be turned away.[5]

Clive's success at Arni seems to have convinced him that all was over, and he planned to return to Madras – one of those sudden, rather feminine impulses which from time to time influenced his actions. Saunders and his Council told him not to be 'too hasty',[6] and urged him to attack Conjeveram, now held by a detachment of French who were disrupting communications between Madras and Arcot. They had also captured a party of English sick and wounded returning after the siege, subjecting them to great cruelties.[7]

Clive agreed to move against Conjeveram and arrived there about December 15. The enemy held the great temple, which was surrounded by inner and outer walls and had various fortifications. Their commander, a hunchbacked Portuguese soldier of fortune known as La Volonté, refused to surrender, threatening, if the English did not withdraw, to hang the two officers in the captured party, Lieutenant Robert Revell and Lieutenant Glass, who had been injured during the siege by falling from a rope.[8] Clive ignored this threat and his cannon began to batter the massive temple walls on December 16.[9]

'Captain Clive is very busy and I could wish he exposed himself less,' wrote Doctor Wilson to Orme that day.[10] The doctor's fears were justified, for although the enemy had no cannon, they kept up a fierce musket fire which killed several men. When Clive and Bulkley were reconnoitring the temple over an adjoining garden wall, Bulkley was shot through the head at Clive's side.[11] Once again Clive narrowly escaped death. It must have been a bitter moment for him; Bulkley was one of his oldest friends, and they had soldiered together since the early days at Fort St David.

After two days of bombardment, the wall began to crumble. Revell was forced by La Volonté to mount the breach in the hope that his presence there would stop the English fire; but he was quickly brought down again by the intervention of Moden Sahib, Chanda Sahib's governor of Conjeveram, who seems to have been humane as well as secretly in league with the English and Mohammed Ali. To humour La Volonté, Moden Sahib made Revell write a letter to Clive, repeating that he and Glass would be hanged if the English did not withdraw; and then made sure it was never sent.[12] Clive had probably already heard from Moden Sahib and knew he would protect Revell and Glass against the threats of La Volonté, hence his apparent indifference to the fate of his two brother-officers.

La Volonté and his garrison fled in the night, leaving the two officers behind alive. Having taken possession of the great temple, the English destroyed its defences and then abandoned it. Two days later, it was re-occupied by the French, though it was now useless as a fort. This was typical of the ups and downs of the campaign. Clive's victories had been psychological rather than productive of any solid territorial gains for Mohammed Ali.[13] Raza Sahib's army was scattered, but there was the danger of its remnants coming together. Clive would then have been at a great disadvantage, unless he could have counted on Maratha help. Buzangara, however, having removed everything of value from Conjeveram, was threatening to leave for Trichinopoly. Prince tried to bribe him to stay with 'two or three fine guns, some pocket spying glasses and birds',[14] but Buzangara demanded an elephant – an impossible gift in that Prince and Clive were not empowered to confer the honour which it would have implied. Without the Marathas, there was little Clive could do; so he sent most of his force to support Killpatrick at Arcot and himself returned to Madras, going on to Fort St David where he gave Saunders an account of his campaign. At both Madras and Fort St David, he was welcomed as a hero – he even had the scars of battle on his face, though how and when he was wounded, we do not know. His superiors now listened to him on strategy; he and Saunders together considered the next move.

Meanwhile, Raza Sahib 'took fresh spirits',[15] and collected his scattered army. Just as Clive had reduced the pressure on Trichinopoly by his march to Arcot, so did the enemy now try to prevent the English from relieving the garrison of Mohammed Ali and Gingens by threatening Madras itself. They ravaged the country to the west of the settlement; and burnt and plundered the fashionable garden houses at the foot of St Thomas's Mount, carrying off the furniture to Pondicherry.

The Madras gentlemen appealed to Fort St David for help. Saunders and his Council sent Clive to Madras to build up a force and then, when it was strong enough, to command it against the enemy. Clive quickly raised 500 sepoys; there was once again the problem of arms, which seem to have been supplied from Fort St David – possibly bought from the Dutch.

As luck would have it, a party of 100 European soldiers from Bengal arrived about this time. Clive was also joined by a detachment from the

Arcot garrison under Killpatrick. So by the middle of February 1752, his army 'made no dispicable figure',[16] consisting as it did of 400 Europeans and 1300 sepoys. It was a larger command than he had ever held, and seems to have aroused the jealousy of a more senior officer at Madras.[17] In numbers, Clive was now much closer to the enemy than he had been in the previous campaign. According to the information which he received of their strength, he greatly outnumbered them in Europeans, of whom they only had thirty, and he equalled them in sepoys. Their superiority was in horse, of which they had 1400 to his 120.[18]

Clive at first hesitated to attack Raza Sahib, who was entrenched in a very strong camp. Saunders urged him to do so, though he recommended rather than ordered.[19] In the end, it was Raza Sahib who turned the situation in Clive's favour by suddenly abandoning his strong camp, and dispersing his troops. They regrouped at Conjeveram, and Clive hurried off in pursuit of them along the now familiar Arcot road.[20]

Ten years later, in an account written for Orme's *History*, Clive spoke of having decided to attack Raza Sahib's camp from the rear – he had, he said, been told it was weaker on that side. But he made no mention of this in his report to Saunders at the time; in fact, after Raza Sahib had withdrawn from the camp, he repeated his conviction that the enemy could never have been attacked had they remained there.[21] One suspects him of embroidering the account he wrote for Orme, lest it should seem that he had lacked courage; whereas it would have been common prudence not to attack a fortified camp. It was an unfortunate side of Clive's character that made him sometimes disregard the truth in attempting to justify himself, when no justification was necessary.

When the English reached Conjeveram they found that Raza Sahib's army had moved on. At dusk on February 28, the English army approached the village of Kaveripak, close to where, on Clive's first march to Arcot, there had been the providential storm. And now, all of a sudden, the air was once again rent with thunder; this time not from the heavens but from Raza Sahib's cannon. Clive had stumbled unknowingly into the enemy camp and was trapped.

At first there was confusion. Night was falling, Clive's troops were tired after their march, nobody expected a battle. But Clive kept calm and ordered all his men into a dry watercourse to the left of the road, sending his baggage some distance beyond it. The enemy artillery was firing from a mango grove to the right of the road, where the French were stationed.

Raza Sahib's main body of troops advanced towards the English from the open ground to the left of the road, but were kept at a distance by the English musketry and by two field pieces firing across the watercourse. Clive's other field pieces fired at the mango grove from the road, but the French fire was much superior. As well as the French in the grove, there were French sepoys in the watercourse.

For two hours, under the bright Indian moon, the firing continued, in three directions, on two levels; neither side advancing or giving way. As the English casualties mounted, Clive sent a Portuguese half-caste *subadar** named Shawlum to find a side road by which his army could escape. Shawlum came back from his reconnaissance with the idea that the French could be surprised from their rear, having discovered that the bank and ditch which protected the mango grove did not surround it completely. Clive 'rejoiced at such an opportunity' and immediately ordered a detachment of 200 Europeans and several companies of sepoys to go round, guided by the trusty Shawlum.[22] He put Ensign William Keene in charge of this detachment, and himself accompanied it for part of its way.[23] He then returned, only to find that his absence had caused the rest of his troops to lose heart: they had left the watercourse and were retreating. Such was the magic of Clive's presence that he rallied them, which the other officers had failed to do.

Meanwhile, Keene's detachment marched silently by a roundabout way through the night and eventually halted three hundred yards from the rear of the French. Ensign Symmonds was sent on alone to have a closer look and stumbled on a trench full of enemy sepoys, who pointed their guns at him. With great resourcefulness, he spoke French to them and pretended to be a Frenchman. He went on to within a few yards of the French, and satisfied himself that they were all facing the other way, firing their muskets and cannon at the watercourse. He then returned safely to the detachment, and led it to the grove, giving the sepoys in the trench a wide berth. What with the darkness, and the noise of the firing, the French had no idea that Keene's detachment was so close to them until they received a volley from a distance of less than fifty yards. Clive, who had been waiting in agonized suspense for more than an hour, heard the volley and knew that Keene had reached his objective.[24]

No sooner had Keene's detachment fired, than the French commander

* This word denotes the chief native officer of a company of sepoys, as well as a Mogul viceroy.

cried: 'Every man for himself!' and was the first to run.[25] The rest of his party followed suit, though one or two of them must have put up a fight, for Keene was wounded. There was the inevitable *choultry* close at hand into which about forty of the French crowded; so tightly packed they could not use their weapons. The English could have massacred them but preferred to offer them quarter which was gladly accepted.

As soon as the French guns had been silenced, Clive set out with the rest of his force to join Keene. Some of Raza Sahib's infantry continued to fire, not realizing what had happened. But when the fugitives from the grove told them of the disaster, they joined in the general flight. Clive was certain that not a single man would have escaped, had it not been 'late in the evening' – by which he must have meant after the moon had gone down.[26]

Day broke on a field strewn with dead, and with all the artillery and baggage of the defeated army. The dead included the commander of Raza Sahib's horse, whose death much discouraged his men, for they did nothing throughout the action. Clive, in his report, described the English losses – forty Europeans and thirty sepoys killed – as 'pretty considerable', which shows how light the casualties usually were in the Indian wars of those days.

Kaveripak was won by a single daring move, for which Clive was at the most only partly responsible. But it was also won by Clive's ability to bring out the best in his Indian troops. He was able to rally the sepoys who fled from the watercourse. He trusted Shawlum, to good effect. It is significant that he afterwards gave credit for the plan to the half-caste *subadar*, rather than to Keene. The English in those days were all too often inclined to regard Indian soldiers as generally worthless, like the sergeant at Arcot who patronizingly wrote of the men who swarmed into the breach as showing 'bravery uncommon to blacks'.[27] Clive, on the other hand, saw that the Indians could make just as good soldiers as the English.

A daring move, mutual trust between the Indians and their commander, these were the classic ingredients of Clive's success, and together they made the victory at Kaveripak. But there was probably also a third and less savoury ingredient, an ingredient that was present in most of the Indian victories of those days, among which Clive's were no exception. This ingredient was treachery in the enemy ranks.

Orme says nothing about it, but Dupleix, writing soon after the battle, accused the commander of Raza Sahib's sepoys of having treacherously abandoned an important post to enable Keene's detachment to reach its objective unhindered.[28] Shawlum may have made contact with this commander; Clive may have accompanied the detachment for part of the way – an otherwise pointless procedure – in order to have a secret meeting with him. If this is so, it would explain why Keene's services went apparently unacknowledged.[29] It is also surprising how Shawlum managed to lead the detachment to its objective by night, through strange country which while being flat was broken up with ditches and mounds, and without stumbling on to the enemy. More likely the detachment was guided by someone from Raza Sahib's army.

But, by whatever means it was achieved, Kaveripak was a decisive victory, destroying the army built up by Dupleix and Raza Sahib in the previous autumn, which now finally disbanded. And, unlike Clive's earlier successes, it brought territorial gains. The 'Arcot Country', that area of sixty miles by thirty over which the fighting had taken place, was now clear of the enemy and acknowledged Mohammed Ali, giving him a potential annual revenue of 400,000 pagodas.

Psychologically, the victory greatly enhanced the reputation of the English and it made Clive seem more than ever invincible, with an uninterrupted course of success. Only Pondicherry remained unaware that the tide had turned. Dupleix was almost alone in regarding the situation as serious; but he attributed it to treachery and to the hopelessness of his own troops rather than to any superiority on the other side. 'A few shots more,' he wrote, 'and all would have been over with the English . . . their commandant, Mr Clive, hid throughout the combat'[30] – an allusion, no doubt, to the time he spent in the watercourse.

Having settled who would collect the Arcot revenues on behalf of Mohammed Ali – his first venture in Indian politics – Clive marched southward with his whole army. As they approached Fort St David, they passed the place where, fifteen months earlier, Nasir Jang had been murdered. Dupleix had built a village here in commemoration of that event, and had named it Dupleixfatehabad, 'the town of Dupleix's victory'. There was a column at Pondicherry awaiting erection in the middle of the village square; its plinth 'with a pompous Latin inscription'[31] was already standing. Clive took it on himself to destroy this 'monument of villainy', as he called it,[32] and he burnt the surrounding village.[33]

No sooner had Clive and his troops reached Fort St David than they set out for Trichinopoly, under the command of Stringer Lawrence, who had returned unexpectedly from England, having obtained satisfaction as to his pay.[34] It was necessary to attack as quickly as possible, before the French were reinforced from Europe, or obtained help from Salabat Jang. At present the enemy forces were outnumbered by those of Mohammed Ali, who had been joined by armies from Tanjore and Mysore as well as by Morari Rao and his Marathas.[35]

With this strength, Gingens could have achieved something already, but he preferred to remain inactive. The Marathas had abused the English to their face, comparing their conduct most unfavourably with that of Clive's men at Arcot.[36] However, the leadership on the other side was no better. The gouty D'Auteuil (whose wife was a sister of Madame) had been replaced by Jacques Law, the timid and vacillating scion of a distinguished Lowland Scots family.* When Dupleix heard that Lawrence's army was heading for Trichinopoly, he sent Law every soldier he could spare as a reinforcement, urging him to crush the relieving column before it arrived: 'Tout dépend de ce coup. Ne négligez rien pour réussir. Je vous laisse carte blanche.'[37] But this injection of *la gloire* had no effect on Law, to whom *carte blanche* was merely an encouragement to do nothing.

The army of Law and Chanda Sahib was encamped to the east of Trichinopoly, south of the Cauvery river. The city itself, held by Gingens and Mohammed Ali, was also south of the river, surrounded by four miles of fortified wall. From inside this enclosure rose the great orange and white striped rock, its two humps crowned with a citadel and a temple.

Law should have opposed Lawrence's troops as they approached from the east on the morning of March 29. Instead, he allowed them to join up with a force of 200 Europeans and 400 sepoys which had slipped out during the previous night. It was a great moment for Clive when he saw his old friend John Dalton at the head of this force. By now it was noon and the heat so intense that Lawrence ordered a halt for breakfast. Hardly had they sat down when scouts came running back to say that the enemy were approaching. The army of Mohammed Ali's allies, including the Maratha horse, next appeared, having been put to flight by Chanda Sahib's cannon. They fell in behind Lawrence's troops, and the whole host advanced across the plain, drums beating and colours flying. When the enemy came in sight, the country for miles around seemed to swarm with 'horse, foot, elephants and camels'; while 'a surprising number of silk colours and standards of different sorts, afforded a very extraordinary prospect'.[38]

* He was a nephew of the Scottish financier, John Law of Lauriston, who became adviser to the Regent Orleans and produced the disastrous Mississippi scheme.

Clive went off reconnoitring on horseback and saw a group of buildings including a *choultry* which would afford cover for most of the army. On his return, Lawrence ordered him to lead a detachment to take this *choultry*. He did so, in the face of enemy fire, quickly opening fire with his own guns. The main troops then moved up and also opened fire, and there followed 'the hottest cannonade that was ever seen in the East Indies'.[39] Lawrence's men were protected by the buildings, the enemy were completely exposed and at point-blank range. Very soon the French wavered and drew off their guns. Chanda Sahib's horse kept their ground longer than any of the other enemy troops, owing to the courage of their commander, Allam Khan. Then a cannon ball took off his head and his men joined in the retreat.

By now the sun was so hot that seven of Lawrence's men had dropped dead. These seven made up a third of his total casualties, whereas large numbers of the enemy had been killed. The way to Trichinopoly was open, the morale of Mohammed Ali's Indian allies greatly improved. The Regent of Mysore had been growing tired of Gingens's delays, and threatening to withdraw his great army of 20,000 horse and 80,000 foot. When he heard that Lawrence and Clive were coming, he decided to stay. The potentates of the allied camp presented Clive and Dalton with ceremonial dresses, horses and elephants. Dalton tried to turn these presents into hard cash, but elephants were at a discount – it was expected that the plundering of Chanda Sahib's camp would cause a glut.[40]

Soon after Lawrence's troops entered Trichinopoly, Law committed his crowning blunder of retreating into the so-called island of Srirangam, a peninsula several miles long and about two miles wide between the Cauvery and another river further north, the Coleroon. Here, opposite the city, stood two great temples, their pagodas towering above the surrounding trees. That to the west, the larger of the two, attracted pilgrims from all over India. Seven enclosures protected the innermost bejewelled sanctuary. With their walls twenty-five feet high, these enclosures provided Law with a citadel in which he could feel really secure.

The English accordingly took steps to besiege him. It was planned to send half the army across to the north side of the Coleroon, to cut off Law's communications with Pondicherry. With any other enemy but Law, it would have been a dangerous gamble to separate the two halves of the army by two broad rivers.[41]

Clive was put in command of the force which crossed the two rivers, consisting of 400 Europeans, 1200 sepoys, 700 Marathas and most of the

Tanjore army.* He established his force at Samiaveram, a village nine miles north of Trichinopoly on the road to Pondicherry, where there were two walled pagodas, one on each side of the road. A few earthworks made it into an excellent position, commanding the road along which Law's supplies would have to pass, and close enough for the two halves of the army to reunite by a forced march in the event of an attack by the whole enemy strength.

When Clive had been a few days at Samiaveram, the enemy showed signs of movement. A convoy with vital stores and seven lakhs† of rupees was on its way from Pondicherry. It was led by the ageing D'Auteuil, who, for want of a better officer, had been reinstated by Dupleix as commander of the French forces. Dupleix had been disgusted at Law's retreat into Srirangam and in writing to recall him remarked: 'Je suis persuadé que cet arrangement va faire plaisir à madame votre femme, qui ne désire que le moment de vous tenir dans ses bras.'[42]

It was essential for the English to prevent D'Auteuil from reaching Srirangam, and the safest way of doing so was to intercept him when he was marching through the narrow pass of Utatur, about fifteen miles from Samiaveram. Clive did not feel strong enough to deal with D'Auteuil and at the same time leave enough troops to defend Samiaveram against a possible attack by Law. He asked Lawrence for an additional force – he had his eye on Dalton's company – but Lawrence replied that it would be 'as full of bad consequences for me to divide my force as you yours', while adding: 'I leave it to your discretion as you won't be so far from your post.'[43]

* This may have caused resentment among some of the more senior Trichinopoly captains; but the anonymous letter they were supposed to have addressed to Lawrence, objecting to the appointment of 'a man who till lately has emerged from the obscurity of a counting-house into the field of honour' and complaining of Clive's 'unbecoming haughtiness', is almost certainly a later fabrication, displaying, on the part of its author, a complete ignorance as to the true status of a Writer in the East India Company service. It was first printed in the *Life of Robert, Lord Clive*, an extraordinary publication which appeared within a couple of years of Clive's death, under the alleged authorship of Charles Carraccioli, a literary hack who had no apparent connection with Indian affairs. In fact, the book is not a consecutive biography, but a compendium of unrelated material from different pens, mostly to Clive's detriment, but some of it having nothing to do with him and lifted bodily from contemporary works on India. Though much of the book is scurrilous and wildly inaccurate, it gives us an idea of what Clive's enemies thought of him. It also contains some material which is clearly first-hand, written by army officers who were in India at the time.

† A lakh is a hundred thousand rupees, worth between £8000 and £10,000.

At his discretion, Clive took a gamble. Instead of dividing his troops, he preferred to make sure of D'Auteuil by leading his whole force against him on the night when he was by way of setting out from Utatur. By marching silently at dusk and leaving the camp all standing, he hoped Law would not know they had left. They made a forced march of fourteen miles only to learn that D'Auteuil did not intend to move that night. There was no question of attacking him when he was shut up in the Utatur fort, so they hurried back to Samiaveram, arriving exhausted at about eleven.

As it happened, Law got wind of Clive's departure from Samiaveram, and sent a force of eighty Europeans and five hundred of his best sepoys to seize the camp while it was undefended. Having done so, they were to signal to the rest of Law's army to join them. When these troops were on their way, an Indian deserter from Samiaveram came to tell them that Clive had returned. The French commander, named Calquier, thought this was a blind,[44] and forced the Indian to lead his party to the camp at pistol-point.

Some twenty of the Europeans in Calquier's force were English deserters, led by one Kelsey, a former sergeant at Madras who had since been made an officer by Dupleix. When they reached the camp at about four in the morning, and were challenged by the sepoy guard, Kelsey was able to tell the *subadar* in English that they were a party sent by Lawrence – thus unknowingly paying back the French-speaking Ensign Symmonds. The *subadar* was convinced, and not only omitted to ask for the password, but detailed one of his men to lead the party to headquarters, where Clive slept. This was a *choultry* near the smaller of the two walled pagodas. Inside the pagoda wall were the sepoys who acted as Clive's bodyguard, together with the baggage and stores; the rest of the sepoys and Europeans were within the enclosure of the other and larger temple. When challenged by the sentry at the entrance to Clive's *choultry*, the deserters again answered in English. But this man was not so easily deceived, and fired to give the alarm. The enemy party then opened fire at both the *choultry* and the pagoda, and pandemonium broke out.

Clive jumped up from his sleep and ran out of the *choultry* in his nightshirt. He had no idea the enemy troops were in the middle of the camp, but thought it was being attacked from outside. He was confirmed in this belief when he saw Calquier's sepoys firing in the direction from which the enemy would have been most likely to come. Knowing that sepoys were liable to lose their heads in night attacks and fire at random, Clive went among them and 'began to abuse them in as much of the country language as he knew',[45] striking several of them. An enemy *subadar* made a cut at him with his sword: Clive dodged the worst of the blow by coming to grips with the Indian, who was himself cut down a moment later by another English officer. Clive next found himself in the midst of six Frenchmen, but had the presence of mind to tell them that they were 'surrounded and would certainly be cut to pieces if they did not surrender immediately', at which three of them surrendered, and the other three ran to join their comrades who had managed to seize the smaller pagoda.[46]

Bleeding from wounds on his forehead and chest, caused by the *subadar*'s sword, Clive hurried across the road in search of the main body of his troops, whom he found already under arms. He then led them back to besiege the French in the smaller pagoda. The French put up a spirited defence, firing through the gateway and throwing grenades over the walls.

Then the sun in all its blaze of scarlet appeared on the eastern horizon. Clive feared that more of the enemy would attack the camp from outside as soon as it was daylight, and that his own troops would be at a great disadvantage with this party of Frenchmen holding out in their midst. So he decided to storm the enclosure. Lieutenant Wight, who like Clive was in his nightshirt and slippers, called for volunteers to follow him and rushed at the gate sword in hand, but perished with several of his men on the French bayonets. Calquier, who led a no less gallant attempt to rush out, suffered a similar fate. Now is supposed to have occurred the celebrated episode when a bullet fired at Clive by the English deserter Kelsey missed him but went through the bodies of two soldiers on whom he leant, being weak from loss of blood.*

* The explanation of this 'miracle', as Clive's chief enemy of later years was to call it (Orme MSS, Vol. J, Speech of George Johnstone in General Court), was that Clive and the two soldiers were standing sideways-on to the opening of the gate, and that as he was taller than they were, he was stooping as he leant on their shoulders, causing his body to be out of line with theirs (*Biographia Britannica*). It could thus have been yet another of those strange pieces of luck which gave Clive the name for leading a charmed life. But what makes one doubt the story is that it is based on the sole authority of Clive himself. The two other accounts of the Samiaveram affair, by Lawrence and Dalton, make no mention of it, although if it had happened it would have been observed by many. Clive's account was written as material for Orme, eight or nine years after the other two, at a time when he was concerned with his public image. It also—perhaps significantly—features another hairbreadth escape over which Lawrence and Dalton are equally silent: how when he was sleeping in the *choultry* the enemy bullets killed a servant who lay on

OLD STYCHE HALL

FORT ST GEORGE, MADRAS

Engraving by Jan Van Ryne

Not long after daybreak, the French in the pagoda called for quarter. The enemy sepoys had already slipped away, only to be overtaken by galloping Marathas who cut every one of them to pieces. Clive regretted this, although from a military point of view it made the affair into an English success, depriving Law of many of his best troops. As a further sign of his humanitarianism, he prevented Mohammed Ali's representative—his theoretical superior, according to the fiction of the English being 'auxiliaries'—from putting to death the English deserters, though he afterwards, on Lawrence's orders, hanged Kelsey, together with the unfortunate Indian who had guided Calquier at pistol-point.[47]

'I rejoice at your success, as your wounds are not dangerous, and if they spoil the beauty of your face they raise your fame,' wrote Lawrence to Clive on the day following the Samiaveram affair.[48] The Old Cock was almost as jubilant as Mohammed Ali and the Regent of Mysore; he reported to Saunders that half the enemy force had been destroyed and 'the rest so cooped up that they cannot escape'.[49] Clive took a more cautious view of the situation, pointing out that the rivers were rising and that the enemy were making rafts. As soon as the Coleroon became unfordable they would cross it with their whole force. He would then have to face them alone, for Lawrence would be unable to cross to his help. For this reason, he urged that most of Lawrence's troops should cross to his side of the rivers before they rose much more.[50]

Lawrence disagreed, pointing out that if the whole army were north of the rivers, the enemy would then be able to cross the Cauvery and escape south-eastward to the minor French settlement of Karikal, on the coast. He reckoned Clive's half of the army to be 'more than a match' for the enemy, who could be easily stopped if they tried crossing the river when it was in flood.[51] Clive continued to argue and finally went to see Lawrence and managed to persuade him to send a force under Dalton to deal with D'Auteuil. By the time Dalton's troops had dislodged D'Auteuil from Utatur, the Coleroon was too high for them to cross back

the ground beside him and penetrated a portable writing-desk at the foot of the palanquin which served as his bed. Without actually inventing these incidents, Clive could have made them seem more exciting. The servant may have been killed, the desk riddled, but neither may have been quite so perilously close to where he was sleeping. And perhaps the two soldiers on whom he leant *were* both shot—but with more than one bullet and not fatally. Clive, in fact, does not specify whether or not they were killed; it is Orme—always ready to add an extra touch of drama—who makes them both fall 'mortally wounded' (*History*, Vol. I, p. 225).

to Trichinopoly; so they joined Clive who thus, thanks to the river, got his way and increased his force at the expense of Lawrence's.[52]

The net was closing around Law and Chanda Sahib, even though the rising of the rivers made their stronghold more impregnable. Chanda Sahib's troops began to desert and come over to the English; there was an acute food shortage in his camp. Clive and Dalton now moved up to attack Pitchanda, the remaining enemy stronghold on the north bank of the Coleroon, where there was yet another walled pagoda. Before attacking the pagoda itself, they decided to cannonade Chanda Sahib's Indian camp, which lay immediately across the river from here.

The guns were positioned during the night and at daybreak opened fire on the unsuspecting enemy. There was immediate confusion in the camp, which was more like a great fair than a military encampment, a seething multitude of tradesmen, servants, women and children, elephants, camels and oxen.* The inhabitants all seized what was most valuable to them and ran; in less than two hours not a tent remained standing. The camp was eventually set up again near the smaller of the two temples;[53] but its bombardment destroyed all popular confidence in Chanda Sahib. This was particularly serious in that everything depended on credit from the merchants who followed the army.

Next day, the guns were turned on the Pitchanda pagoda. The houses of a nearby village provided cover for Clive's sepoys to fire their muskets, which prevented the garrison of the pagoda from using their cannon. By about four in the afternoon, the wall had tumbled and the French commander decided to surrender. A white flag was hung on the breach and a drummer stood beside it beating the *chamade*. Clive's sepoys mistook this for defiance, and rushed into the breach, killing the dummer and several of the garrison and causing such terror that fifteen Frenchmen jumped into the river and were drowned.[54] The three French officers who survived the action later alleged that Clive himself had led the sepoys into the breach, regardless of the flag of truce; but according to Clive's account, he was, at the time, having a cup of tea on the far side of the village. For all their complaints against him, the French officers, when given the choice, preferred to be detained in his camp than in Lawrence's. Despite

*Writers have depicted Clive looking down on this seething multitude from a height across the river, and deciding, in a rather cruel fit of schoolboy devilment, to bombard it. But as the river would have been something between half a mile and a mile wide, and the ground equally flat on both sides of it, Clive could have seen little more than the bare line of tents.

his natural reserve, he ended by fraternizing with them overmuch, for he told them that the Regent of Mysore was going to pay the English sixty lakhs.[55] 'Mr Clive is a little indiscreet,'[56] wrote Dupleix, who took up this disclosure as a sign that the English were exceeding their *soi-disant* role as 'auxiliaries'.

Having taken Pitchanda, Clive resumed his bombardment of the enemy camp across the river. The desertions from Chanda Sahib's army increased, and soon most of his officers and allies decided to leave him. Chivalrous to the end, he bade them a warm farewell, promising to pay what he owed them if ever he enjoyed better fortune.[57] Fifteen hundred of his horse and a large number of his sepoys joined Clive. By May 18, not a tent remained on Srirangam. Chanda Sahib and the loyal remnant of his army occupied the larger temple; Law and the French were in the smaller one. Lawrence moved into Srirangam and encamped to the east of the French.

Clive's next task was to go north once again and finally dispose of D'Auteuil, who, outnumbered as well as hungry—the provisions which Madame Duplans had sent him from Pondicherry had gone astray[58]—quickly surrendered. In the first flush of victory, he agreed to give the French the terms they asked for, then remembered that he was not empowered to grant any terms and was consequently accused by D'Auteuil of breaking his word.[59] The action yielded a certain amount of booty, including Raza Sahib's elephant, the finest Dalton had ever seen, which Clive and his officers presented to Lawrence—a rather dubious gift, if elephants were still as hard to dispose of as they were in April. D'Auteuil's seven lakhs had, however, dwindled to a mere half lakh—either he managed to smuggle the balance back to Pondicherry in his baggage, or else it was embezzled by the soldiers of both sides.

Lawrence's battering cannon arrived on May 31, the day after Clive returned to Srirangam. Before the English opened fire on the temple, Law was summoned to surrender, but refused to do so unless he could march out with all his troops. That same evening, Chanda Sahib was made a prisoner, the Tanjore general having enticed him into his camp by offering to help him escape to Karikal.

Next day, in the face of a threat of no quarter from Mohammed Ali, Law began peace talks with Lawrence in the presence of Clive and Dalton. He argued at great length and with true Scottish tenacity that the French and English were at peace and that therefore his troops should be allowed to return to Pondicherry. Lawrence maintained that he was acting on behalf of Mohammed Ali, who would not allow such terms. Eventually it was agreed that the officers should be released on parole and the men be made prisoner.

During these talks, Lawrence kept retiring into 'a closet contrived in his tent' to confer with Clive. Law regarded Clive as the evil genius who influenced Lawrence to refuse various French requests, as well as 'the oracle he consulted for the pretended intentions of the Nawab'.[60] More likely, Clive was just enabling Lawrence to pass the buck.

A few hours after the French flung down their arms, Chanda Sahib was no more. The once colourful adventurer, now old and broken, was stabbed and beheaded by a Pathan on the orders of the Tanjore general.[61] Lawrence knew that Mohammed Ali and his Indian allies were determined to put Chanda Sahib to death, and he did nothing to restrain them. As such, he might have been guilty of complicity in the murder, though he certainly did not order it, as Dupleix accused him of having done. Clive, too, can be blamed for not taking advantage of the favour in which he stood with Mohammed Ali and the other potentates to persuade them to spare the life of their vanquished foe.

'Mr Dupleix is a good man, a generous man, and it is not to him we owe our misfortunes but to his wife whose violent spirit leads him to do things against his nature and will always involve us in endless difficulties,' Law had blurted to Lawrence.[62] Dupleix had indeed involved his Company in difficulties, in a highly expensive policy which they had never sanctioned and which had failed completely. Chanda Sahib was dead; Mohammed Ali, the English protégé, was now the undisputed Nawab; Pondicherry had lost all its garrison except for a few recruits. When Dupleix heard the news of Chanda Sahib's death he was so upset he could neither eat his dinner nor go to Mass.[63]

But he and Madame soon consoled themselves by moving into their magnificent new *Gouvernement* in the fort, which was just finished; with its colonnades reminiscent of the Louvre, its *grand vestibule* adorned with marble figures of Justice, Truth, Prudence and Commerce; its *salle des fêtes* glittering with silver leaf and hung with green velvet; its lustres and its bibelots. 'Such a palace is but worthy of you,' said Ananda Ranga Pillai, Dupleix's Indian factor, and Dupleix was duly gratified.[64] Little did he know that he would only be there for a few months, that the news of Trichinopoly, when it reached France, would lead to his recall.

He was about to pay for his mistake of underestimating the ability of the English leaders, whom he persisted in regarding as 'contemptible riff-raff'. Saunders he thought 'a madman, an *enragé*'; Lawrence he believed to be highly venal and of ungovernable temper. As for Clive, who more than either of these two was responsible for his downfall, he 'scarcely entered into Dupleix's mental horizon. He was to Dupleix merely a secondary figure reported dead or wounded times without number . . . a coward who had remained hidden behind a tree during one engagement . . . an arrogant fellow given to much boasting.'[65]

Despite the failure of Dupleix, India was to be the scene of further conflict between the English and French. But while the French could still at times be a grave menace to their rivals, the overall advantage henceforth lay with the English; not only on account of the prestige which they had won in the eyes of the Indians, but also because they were backed by a nation where the prevailing mood was one of confidence – it was now more than ten years since people had started singing *Rule Britannia*. France, on the other hand, had already entered the period of decline and disillusionment that was to last until the Revolution; discredited as a European power by the Treaty of Aix-la-Chapelle, financially bankrupt, her government in the control of Madame de Pompadour and her aristocracy more interested in the ideas of the *philosophes* than in dreams of empire.

CHAPTER V

The Angels

Guard your heart well against these.

CHARLES BODDAM to CLIVE, 1752

Just before Law's surrender, Clive's friend Charles Boddam wrote to him of the impending arrival of some ships from England, which were bringing out eleven young women: 'after such a campaign as you had,' he told him, 'these beauties will have a wonderful effect upon you'.[1] The 'beauties', who arrived towards the end of June, included Margaret Maskelyne. India, to her, was a mixture of the strange and the familiar, for though this was her first sight of the country, she had been brought up on its lore, having had an uncle here as well as two aunts. She stayed with Mun at his house in the suburb of Veperi, west of the Fort; he was still on parole, having been taken prisoner shortly before Arcot, so had plenty of time to entertain her. Not that she needed such brotherly attentions, for there would have been young men eager to make her acquaintance from the moment she was lifted from her *masula* boat and put down by the Sea Gate; she would quickly have been swept off her feet in a whirl of balls, concerts and picnics. Years later, she referred to this time in Madras as 'my happy days'.[2]

The name of Clive would have been on everybody's lips. It must have been a great thrill for her to find that Mun's friend and candidate for her hand was now the hero of the settlement. Clive himself returned to Madras from Trichinopoly soon after her arrival. We have no record of their first meeting. He would have seen a small and slender girl of seventeen with dark hair and large eyes that gave the impression of being dark but were in fact grey – a face that might have already been familiar to him from her portraits. She was prevented from being beautiful by her too large nose and too thick eyebrows; yet the liveliness of her eyes, her smile, her expression which was a mixture of sweetness, intelligence and humour, made her face more attractive and memorable than mere perfection of features could have done. This is apparent in her portraits, and would have been infinitely more so when her face was animated by her flow of bright and amusing chatter. How far Clive shared her interests – music, poetry, astronomy – is doubtful. But she was the sort of girl who is interested in most things, and he would have found it gratifying to be admired by someone of such obvious intellect; while he liked adulation, he was too clever to be taken in by brainless flatterers.

For her part, she would have found in Clive a young man who could not be called handsome. Dalton nicknamed him Beauty, which was presumably ironic, unless it referred to his success. But though his features were pinched, crowded together and a little lopsided, though he may already have acquired something of the spread which appears in his portraits, his eyes – determined, yet wistful – would have been attractive. And his physical imperfections would have been disguised by fine clothes. His wardrobe was now very different from what it had been when he first arrived in India eight years before – coats of blue and brown trimmed with silver lace, fifteen pairs of silk breeches and three of velvet, twenty shirts with lace ruffles and forty pairs of stockings.[3]

He also had an Indian dress, gold coat, gold turban and silk pantaloons. Thus attired, he must certainly have looked like Sabit Jang Bahadur, the hero who in less than a year had restored a Nawab to his dominions, humbled the proud Dupleix, given lustre to English arms, raised troops, endured hardships, frequently escaped death – at any rate to a girl of seventeen whose world had up to now been bounded by her aunt's house at Purton Stoke, her uncle's house at Purton Down and Mrs Saintsbury's establishment in Cirencester.

Success seems to have broken down some of Clive's reserve; and though the long campaign had undermined his health, the inevitable mental reaction to the exertions of the past few months had not yet set in; in fact his energy continued, and made him join wholeheartedly in the gaieties of that Madras summer. He himself entertained lavishly at the house he had rented in Charles Street, within the Fort; a house spacious enough to be subsequently used by the Governor. 'I hear that you keep one of the best houses in Madras,' wrote Dalton, who was still at Trichinopoly and thinking wistfully of Clive 'gallanting the ladies'.[4] 'By God,' he remarked in another letter, 'it would be a good joke if your countenance was to smite one of them, and you were to commit matrimony. I should however be concerned at it as it would put me out of all hopes of the pleasure I propose myself in ******* [the asterisks are Dalton's] in company with you in Covent Garden, etc.'[5] This mention of Covent Garden and its pleasures, with the delicate omission of the operative word, would suggest that he and Clive had already planned to go back to England in the near future. Clive's profits as Commissary made him rich enough to return home. As for Dalton, he doubtless counted on the generosity of his friend, for which he was full of gratitude. This is the first time we hear of one of Clive's chief virtues, his open-handedness which increased with his wealth and was all the better in that he knew the value of money and was never extravagant.

Clive had other business than 'gallanting the ladies'. There was his work as Commissary. He had to settle the accounts of the recent campaign and deal with such problems as disposing of the stud of elephants which he had accumulated through the misplaced generosity of various potentates, and which were eating their heads off.[6] He also had to continue feeding the army. This sometimes just took the form of remitting money to people like Dalton, or Lieutenant James Repington, who were with the troops; at other times he himself had to wrestle with turmeric, salt fish, rice, ghee and firewood. Nor was it only the nourishment of the ordinary soldiers that concerned him. Madeira, 'tea of the best sort' and other luxuries had to be procured for the officers, in particular for Lawrence, who 'cut no small figure at table'.[7] According to Repington, however, the fact that Clive was 'beloved' by the Indians enabled him to get his provisions at a reasonable price, which was how he managed to make so large a profit.[8]

The army was still in the field, peace negotiations having broken down when Dupleix insisted on the French prisoners being released before he would treat; which would have given him back his military strength before he had bound himself to any terms. So the war went on and Dupleix for once acknowledged the importance of Clive by capturing a convoy of *masula* boats in which, according to a false report, he was travelling from Madras to Fort St David; though this was not so much in order to deprive the English of their best commander as on account of his value as a hostage.[9] In September, Clive was sent to reduce the two French-held forts of Covelong and Chingleput, some thirty miles south of Madras and close enough to be of annoyance. He was handicapped by being given newly-raised sepoys and raw recruits from England, who panicked when they came under fire for the first time – one of the sentries was found hiding at the bottom of a well – though by standing himself in the thick of the fire he was able to shame them into behaving like soldiers. This was hardly necessary, for the commandants of both forts seem to have been of English origin and potential traitors – one of them surrendered on condition he was allowed to take away his stock of turkeys and snuff.[10] Saunders afterwards referred to this expedition as Clive's 'glorious campaign'.[11] But it was little more than an epilogue – though it may have helped his courtship, showing Margaret that he was more than just a hero of past glories.

Soon after the capture of Chingleput, Clive fell ill – the first appearance of the illness that was to plague him for the rest of his life. From the symptoms – agonizing spasms of abdominal pain, accompanied by acute biliousness – it would seem that he suffered from gallstones, which were possibly induced or exacerbated by chronic malaria. The attacks seldom lasted very long, but during a bad period they recurred at intervals of a few hours or days. Thus, on this first occasion, they started in October, or earlier, and he was still having them at the end of November. Eventually, the attacks would cease altogether and he would be free of them for several months, or even years.

It is hard to know whether these abdominal attacks were responsible for the bouts of nervous prostration from which, henceforth, Clive was to suffer; or whether the latter resulted from his manic-depressive tendencies. The fact that his breakdowns were apt to follow periods of great activity, and that during them, his mood would alternate between cheerfulness and black depression, suggests the latter; on the other hand, from now on, they seldom occurred without being accompanied by abdominal attacks. Having been prescribed opium – then the recognized palliative for gallstones – as a pain-killer, Clive took to using the drug when suffering only from depression. But contrary to popular belief, he was never an opium addict.

One wonders if, during this first attack of his illness, he was nursed by Margaret. If so, it may have speeded his recovery, as well as speeding him along the road to marriage. But he still hesitated over the final step. 'The swarthy world here had spread a report that you were on the point of committing matrimony,' wrote Dalton to him on October 21. 'But Maskelyne has undeceived me in that particular, he says you f—k as usual.'[12] Clive's illness at this juncture cannot have been so bad as to prohibit his normal amorous pursuits.

Dalton still promised himself 'a Covent Garden exploit' in the company of Clive, who as late as February 15 of the following year intended to return home as a bachelor, for he applied on that day for single accommodation in the ship *Admiral Vernon*. Three days later, with characteristic impulsiveness, he married Margaret, the ceremony being performed by a Danish missionary, the Reverend John Philip Fabricius, to whom he gave a particularly handsome offering. From a remark made by his friend Repington, it seems that the indecision was his rather than hers. We know from her letters that the marriage was a love match as far as Margaret was concerned, and that she worshipped Clive for the rest of his life with a devotion that seems to belong more to the Victorian age than to the eighteenth century. For his part, the fact that he married her after deciding to go home would indicate that he loved her or at any rate was much attracted to her. There is every sign that he was an affectionate and faithful husband; and while he could be all too frequently thoughtless in his dealings with others, he always showed consideration for her; thus when he later returned to India by himself and was plagued by a particularly unpleasant female fellow passenger, he was grateful that at any rate Margaret had been spared this infliction.[13]

Clive did not share Margaret's interests, and though she closely followed his career, and he told her all about it, he never seems to have consulted her, nor did she in any way influence his policies. It was not a marriage of companionship in the modern sense; he and she were seldom alone together, except in bed. But while he could never do without the society of other men, he was happiest when she was present also. And though he was generally engrossed in more serious discussions, it seems that he was quite capable of chattering lightheartedly with her, if we go by a remark which she made some years later: 'I would not give a pin for a man without a tongue, as I think it as necessary he should chatter as a magpie or a woman.'[14]

As well as needing to escape from the Indian climate, Clive may have been glad to get out of range of the 'snarlers' – as Lawrence called them – who envied the £40,000 he had made as Commissary. They attributed his success to mere good luck; Lawrence countered them by speaking of his 'undaunted resolution', 'cool temper' and 'quickness of thought',[15] and told Clive: 'Let them snarl on since they can't bite, you are right in making it a subject of mirth.'[16] Clive's mirth may have been only affected; his skin was then not so thick as it was later to become.

The atmosphere at Madras and Fort St David was poisoned that autumn and the following winter by a quarrel between Saunders and Lawrence.

At first Clive managed to keep in with both of them; but by the time he left for England he was in the Governor's bad books, thanks largely to the mischief-making of Orme, who was himself engaged in taking away Saunders's character. Saunders never even wrote Clive the customary letter of thanks for his services. For his part, Clive was at a loss to know why he had incurred the Governor's displeasure, and was rather hurt: 'I think in justice to the military in general I cannot leave this coast without leaving a paper behind me representing the little notice taken of people of our profession,' he told Lawrence. 'I hope the world will not accuse me of vanity or be of opinion that I think too highly of my own successes as I seldom or ever opened my lips upon this subject.'[17] Unless his character changed drastically as he grew older, Clive showed a considerable vanity in thus claiming to be modest, for we know how inclined he was, later in life, to self-advertisement.

Orme's growing unpopularity was doubtless a reason why he now decided to accompany Clive and Margaret to England. He waited until they were safely aboard the *Bombay Castle* and then, before boarding the ship himself, went to Saunders and 'in the most abject mean manner' begged his pardon for having slandered him.[18] That he should have postponed this interview until it was too late for Saunders to have a subsequent conversation with Clive is evidence of his treachery; he must have made further mischief between the Governor and his unsuspecting friend in order to save his own skin.

CHAPTER VI

The Hero

The proof is now beyond all doubt
Since about Clive they keep such rout,
Where'er he goes 'tis holiday,
The tradesmen throw their work away,
All run in crowds unto the windows
To see the Conqu'ror of the Indies.

VERSES ADDRESSED TO CLIVE

The *Bombay Castle* was uncomfortable, and the food ran short. At the Cape, however, Clive, Margaret and Orme were able to transfer to a better ship, the *Pelham*. Orme was already writing his *History*, so we can be sure that he and Clive spent long hours discussing battles, which must have been a little hard on Margaret. The voyage was, after all, her honeymoon, but from a remark Clive made later, he did not find being cooped up with her for several months in an Indiaman exactly conducive to romance.[1]

On October 10 they were in the Thames. After ten years, Clive was reunited with his family. His father and mother were now living in a large house in Swithin's Lane in the City of London, together with four of his five surviving sisters; the rest of the family being away at school. Ever since the news of his successes had reached England, his father had looked after his public relations. Writers have depicted the elder Clive bustling in and out of the anterooms of the Great in a clownish manner, and it has been suggested that Clive was embarrassed by the activities of this 'old rustic' as Horace Walpole called him. But while he may have been of mediocre ability, Richard Clive had practised in the Court of Chancery for thirty years and so would have known his way about London and been quite equal to the task of bringing his son's achievements to the notice of the right people, a perfectly honourable ploy for the father of an up-and-coming young man in the eighteenth century when 'interest' and patronage were all-important.

Soon after arriving in London, Clive went to pay his formal respects to the Directors. He must have felt very different from when he last went to East India House, as a young hopeful of seventeen. This time he was congratulated by the Chairman and it was resolved to make him 'a proper present',[2] a gold-hilted sword set with diamonds. Clive refused to accept it unless Lawrence were similarly honoured. So the Directors agreed to give swords to both of them, Lawrence's being worth £750 and Clive's £500. England at that time was short of military glory: Clive found that he was something of a national hero, and was compared with Marshal Saxe and other great generals.

Clive and Margaret set up house in Queen Square, Ormond Street. Their two Indian servants, Robert May and Tom, would have given a suitably exotic touch to the trim, red-brick house. 'Black Robin' was the favourite, though he was 'a little thick-headed and not quite sober'. They arranged for him to be baptised, and stood as his sponsors.[3]

There is no evidence to support the popular belief that Clive lived extravagantly during his first stay in England.* If he was short of money, it was due neither to horses and fine clothes, nor to his generosity to his family—which at present was limited to reducing the £8500 mortgage on Styche by £6000[4]—but to the difficulty of remitting his fortune from India. Part of it was sent in diamonds which failed to clear and had to be sold in Holland, where they made less than their value; other jewels had to be sold as far afield as Constantinople.[5]

With the myth of Clive's extravagance goes the belief that he was obliged to return to India because his fortune was exhausted. In fact, he intended to return regardless of his financial position. Mun and others in Madras expected him back as early as 1754. After he had been in London a few months, the Directors invited him to go out in a senior capacity with the right of succession to Pigot, who was himself about to become Governor of Madras in place of Saunders. He refused this offer on account of his health, but asked if he would be allowed to go out under the same

* To add to this legend, writers have confused Clive's address with the more fashionable Queen Square in St James's. There is another legend that Clive was financially crippled by his father, who as soon as he heard of his son's success started to live beyond his means. This seems to be based solely on his mother's reference to Swithin's Lane as 'a large house'.

terms in the following year, to which the Directors agreed.[6] So when, a year later, he did return to India under these terms, it was not a snap decision due to shortage of money or disillusionment with English life, but something he had planned all along. He told Walsh in 1755 that had he been offered the actual post of Governor in the previous year, rather than just the succession to it, he would have set out immediately, 'from death's door'.[7]

He had to work to get his new appointment – showing maps of his battles to anyone of influence, preparing a long memorandum on the revenues of the Arcot province to impress the Directors.[8] 'I find *by experience* that a man is not the farther from preferment by paying a visit to his native country,' he wrote to a friend in Madras.[9] He was actually speaking of Orme, who had also come to England for the sake of preferment, and by impressing the Duke of Cumberland and other great men with a draft of his *History* had been sent back to Madras as a Councillor. Clive, who had been put wise to his treachery by Mun, hastened to assure Pigot that he had taken no hand in his promotion.[10] But he took a philosophic view of Orme's self-interest – 'you will allow that dear self gets the better of every other consideration'[11] – and declared that he personally would continue to esteem him, 'in spite of his oddities'. Cynics would attribute this steadfastness to Orme's good write-up of Clive in the draft of his *History*, yet Clive does seem to have had a genuine affection for 'Cicero', with all his faults. He was not always a good judge of character, but when writing to Pigot he showed that he really did understand the character of his unreliable friend: 'Orme is proud and overbearing and must be kept at a distance; at the same time his capacity may with a little management be made serviceable to yourself and the Company.'[12]

One hopes Clive found time to enjoy life in London, at any rate for Margaret's sake. Unfortunately, there is no record of any entertaining at Queen Square – except that Margaret used sometimes to ask the twelve-year-old musical prodigy, Miss Thompson, daughter of a musical instrument maker near Swithin's Lane, to dinner.[13] Nor is there any mention of the Clives being seen in Society. One would like to have heard the reactions of a Walpole or a Lady Mary Coke to Margaret as she was at this time, a lively and graceful girl of eighteen.

Her London life, such as it was, would have been interrupted in March 1754, when she gave birth to a son, whom they called Edward after Clive's influential cousin, Sir Edward Clive, Judge of the Court of Common Pleas.[14] There was a further interruption when Clive went to Bath for the sake of his health. But knowing how Margaret was never really taken up by aristocratic English society, not even when her husband was very rich and a peer, one doubts if she received many smart invitations at this time. Otherwise she would surely have made some aristocratic women friends of her own age. New friendships came easily to her, and she kept most of her friends for life; but her large circle was drawn almost entirely from India, from the professional classes and the lesser gentry. It is a striking instance of the exclusiveness of the aristocracy in eighteenth-century England.

Clive's enemies, after his death, suggested that he was rebuffed by the Great World, quoting an alleged remark by the brilliant but unstable Charles Townshend that 'the fellow was right to transplant himself, he could not thrive in his native soil'.* Writers of a later generation give a different, but equally false, picture of Clive being taken up by some of the more raffish members of the political aristocracy – doubtless on account of his reputed high living. Much is made of his friendship with the cynical Henry Fox and the Earl of Sandwich, the notorious though probably maligned 'Jemmy Twitcher', who are thought to have given him his first – and a rather unsavoury – introduction to politics. In fact Clive's acquaintance with Fox and Sandwich was a result of his Parliamentary attempt, rather than the other way round. His first patrons among the Great World were two more respectable, if less colourful, figures, both self-made men of solid, middle-class background: Thomas Herring, Archbishop of Canterbury, a friend of his father; and the Lord Chancellor, the Earl of Hardwicke, a friend of his cousin, the Judge.

It was through the Judge that Clive stood as Parliamentary candidate for the Cornish borough of Mitchell in the general election of April 1754. The Judge had himself represented the borough from 1741 to 1745, under the patronage of a local magnate, Thomas Scawen;[15] it was natural that he should make over his interest there to his famous young cousin from India. Mitchell was complicated even by the standards of eighteenth-century boroughs; the fifty-odd voters being controlled by no less than six patrons. Scawen's interest was traditionally joined to that of Charles Courtenay, a minor and a nephew of Sandwich, who acted on his behalf.

Since the Scawen–Courtenay interest could only be sure of about half the voters, the election was contested – and, as was often the case with

* Townshend was notorious for 'abusing and ridiculing every mortal in different companies'. (Lady Mary Coke, quoted in Namier and Brooke, *History of Parliament*, London 1964, Vol. III, p. 546.)

contested elections in the eighteenth century, expensive, costing Clive about £5000. It seemed at first to have been money well spent, for he and his fellow-candidate* won, polling 30 out of the 55 votes. Then their opponents raised an objection, and petitioned for them to be unseated.

The contest thus shifted to the House of Commons itself, and became a long and bitter struggle between the major political factions of the country in which the candidates and even the patrons were of little moment. The borough-mongering Duke of Newcastle, all-powerful as Prime Minister, supported Clive's opponents because he mistrusted Sandwich. Sandwich enlisted the support of Hardwicke in the Lords and Fox in the Commons. Although Fox managed to keep a foot in the Government camp, the dispute developed into a contest between him and Newcastle for the control of the House. In the end, Newcastle prevailed and Clive found himself unseated. His £5000 had, however, bought him a certain amount of political credit, which he could draw on at a later date.

On the day after his unseating, Clive signed an agreement to serve the East India Company for five years as Deputy-Governor of Fort St David with the right of succession to the Government of Madras. This gives the impression that his return to India was the direct result of his political defeat; in fact his appointment to Fort St David was settled before the final division in Parliament—the signing was a mere formality.[16] And while the Parliamentary issue was still pending, the Directors applied for a Lieutenant-Colonel's commission on his behalf, which would have caused his seat in Parliament to be automatically vacated as soon as the commission was signed—a circumstance of which he appears to have been unaware.[17] It might seem strange that Clive should have tried to get into Parliament when he was planning to return to India so soon afterwards; but it must be remembered that, apart from the technicality over the Lieutenant-Colonel's commission, there was nothing to prevent him from going back to India while keeping his seat, as a means of furthering his career.

Clive's military commission—Lieutenant-Colonel of Foot 'in the East Indies only'—was part of a plan for striking a further blow at French power in India. Although Dupleix had been dismissed in August 1754,† his most able commander, Charles de Bussy, was building up a strong

* The borough returned two members.

† He had, as would be imagined, taken his dismissal with an appearance of *sang-froid*, and accepted it for the good of France. He and Madame then said goodbye for ever to their world and sailed for Europe, where poverty and recriminations awaited them.

French influence in the Deccan, having obtained a grant of the territory known as the Northern Sarkars along the coast between the Carnatic and Bengal. The English therefore planned to assist the Marathas in attacking Salabat Jang and scaring him into breaking with the French. It was the time-honoured game of acting as 'auxiliaries'; though with France once again embroiled in the eternal quarrel between Frederick of Prussia and Maria Theresa of Austria – this time, thanks to the diplomacy of Maria Theresa's minister, Kaunitz, on the Austrian side – and with England, owing to her Hanoverian connections, moving towards an alliance with Prussia, a new war was clearly imminent, so that such a disguise would not be needed much longer. Indeed, in the Western Hemisphere, the English, in anticipation of the coming war, had already started attacking French ships and forts quite openly.

'To dispute the mastery of the Deccan with M. Bussy' was for Clive an attractive way of filling in the time until Pigot retired, relieving the tedium of being Deputy-Governor of Fort St David, which was now a backwater. It was arranged that he should take with him to India three companies of artillery, and three or four hundred of the King's troops, in a convoy of several ships. This force had to reach Bombay – from which the main attack was to be mounted – as quickly as possible, so on April 5, only eleven days after the signing of the agreement with the Company, Clive and Margaret boarded the *Stretham* at Deal. As they came aboard, they were saluted with nine guns: it was very different from Clive's previous departure from England.

For company on the voyage, Clive and Margaret had two cousins, who were going with them to India in search of a fortune and a husband respectively. One was 'Honest George' Clive, son of Clive's clergyman uncle Ben, a young stalwart with the round Clive face. The other was Jane or Jenny Kensall, the attractive but rather spoilt sixteen-year-old daughter of Margaret's uncle and aunt who had themselves recently retired from Bengal. Margaret was very fond of Jane, whose presence would to some extent have made up for the heartbreak of leaving behind her two infant sons: the one-year-old Ned and a second child, recently born and not very strong.

As they waited for a wind, Margaret must have wondered if it was worth it, though in the amusing daily letters which she wrote to Clive's parents she put up a brave face. Clive, whose health was still 'very indifferent', would also at times have had misgivings. His first journey to India had been to redeem the family fortunes, which he had succeeded in doing. The mortgage on Styche had been mostly paid off; allowing for the election expenses and his losses in remitting money from India, he would, at the very least, have been left with a capital sum of £20,000* and an unencumbered estate of £500 a year, which would have put him among the more prosperous of the smaller country gentry. In terms of present-day money, he would have been worth a quarter of a million, as well as owning an estate which brought him in about £6000 a year. He could have built a new house at Styche and settled down there in comfort.[18] But having once tasted success, he wanted more of it. Not for him the life of a country gentleman; he looked towards the greater world of politics and power. 'Want of ambition, etc., has never been laid to my charge,' he told Walsh, in reply to a homily on the importance of not misspending one's youth.[19]

Richard Clive and Mr Kelsall travelled down to Deal together in the hope of saying goodbye once again to their children. They arrived on April 23, just too late; the *Stretham* was already under way. Sadly the two fathers stood on the shore gazing at the ship as she vanished into the distance.[20]

* When Clive sailed for India this time, he left behind in England between £2000 and £4000, and sent at least £3000 to his agents at Madras. And it must be remembered that most of his fortune was still in India.

CHAPTER VII

Pirates and the Garden House

> I make no doubt but the newspapers will be swelled with a pompous account of the taking of the place (which proved a very easy conquest) and of the immense riches found within.
>
> CLIVE TO HIS FATHER AFTER THE GHERIA EXPEDITION

After a good voyage, which benefited Clive's health, the *Stretham* entered the splendid harbour of Bombay towards the end of October. To the east were the hazy peaks of the Indian mainland, and to the west the so-called island – in fact, a swampy peninsula – on which the English settlement was built. Dominating the waterfront of the island was the Castle, simply a fortress and not a walled town like Fort St George. Around and behind were the merchants' houses, less grand than those on the East Coast, with sloping tiled roofs and wooden verandahs of Moorish flavour. Bombay had no distinction between White Town and Black Town; the houses of the English were intermingled with those of the other communities, Indian, Portuguese, Armenian and Parsi.

Clive and Margaret would not have expected to be much impressed with the place, for Bombay still had the name of being 'the unfortunate island',[1] a backwater where nothing happened but disasters. It was regarded as less healthy than even Calcutta, owing to the climate, the swamps and the local practice of manuring the coconut trees with rotting fish. The English inhabitants were said to be parochial and inhospitable. Yet by 1755 the place was fast improving, so that Clive found it 'in a very flourishing condition'.[2]

Within a month of their arrival Clive and Margaret gave a ball, presumably to liven things up. But they and Jenny Kelsall were too bright for the stolid Bombayers. 'Nothing but running about the town from morning to night, laughing immoderately at just nothing, affecting to be very noisy and loud and making a great rout and bustle about nothing, witty chits flying about like wildfire' was how they appeared to Sarah Mathison, the wife of a local doctor.[3]

Sarah at first saw 'a vast share of good nature' in the 'very wild and merry' Margaret, to whom she was connected through Walsh.[4] Later, however, she wrote that 'Mrs Clive's and Jenny's behaviour has not been very genteel here, you must know they set up for great wits and reformers and accordingly have ridiculed and lampooned everybody upon the place.'[5] Sarah Mathison is unique among those who have left descriptions of Margaret in being unfavourable. She tells of Margaret's apparent callousness towards her maid, which is again surprising in that Margaret seems at all other times to have been particularly considerate to servants. The maid fell ill, and was attended by Doctor Mathison, who advised that she should be moved to a different room, as the one she was in had people going in and out all day. Margaret ignored this advice, and when pressed by Sarah replied that there was no other room available, even though Jenny Kelsall occupied not just one room, but two. When Sarah suggested that Jenny should give up one of her rooms at any rate until the maid got well, Margaret declared that Jenny couldn't possibly manage with only one room.

After this the Clives showed 'a great coolness' towards the Mathisons; no more friendly comings and goings as at first, just occasional formal visits from 'Madame Clive . . . in full dress and powdered out as if she had never seen me before.' Sarah was inclined to blame Jenny and Clive rather than Margaret herself. 'Madam Jane rules that family entirely and both the Colonel and Mrs Clive cannot do anything without first asking Miss Jenny. Don't you think their economy must cut a pretty figure to be governed and directed by a child, for I reckon Jenny very little better . . . This foolish little circumstance, trifling as it was, was conducted and carried on by the Colonel and Jenny for I found they were the managers of it, as if it was an affair of the greatest weight and importance, which makes him appear to me very weak and ridiculous, not in this affair alone but in many other respects.'

'The Madrassers don't like Bombay, we are all too reserved and grave for them,'[6] was how the aggressively unsmart and down-to-earth Sarah, whose chief interest was growing vegetables, summed it up. This would have been particularly true when the Madrassers happened to be the young hero of Arcot and two high-spirited girls aged sixteen and twenty. Yet while the thoughtless and upstage behaviour recounted by Sarah is wholly out of keeping with what we know of Margaret, and can only be attributed to her extreme youth at the time, the rather childish pettiness which she experienced in Clive was unfortunately very much a part of his character and became worse as he grew older, making him a host of enemies.

Jenny was soon provided with a husband–Captain Thomas Latham, commander of HMS *Tiger*, one of the ships of the naval squadron which arrived at Bombay in November, having spent some months on the East Coast, landing the first regiment of King's troops ever to go to India.[7] Clive took pride in his quick success with Jane, and suggested to his father that Sister Nanny and Cousin Judy should also come out, as there were 'stores of amorosos to be met with'.[8] But he had other things than matchmaking to occupy him. The Deccan expedition had now been shelved, owing to certain misgivings on the part of the Bombay Council. Instead, it was planned to make use of the troops and the naval squadron to attack Tulaji Angria, the pirate ruler of a territory along the coast whose fast-sailing *grabs* and forty-oared *gallivats* had long been a menace to shipping.

Clive offered his services to command the land forces in the proposed attack, and over Christmas busied himself with preparations. He found, on looking into the military affairs of Bombay, that there were several things of which he disapproved. Writing to a Director, he launched into a long criticism of the fortifications, and also of those of Madras; but pulled himself up by saying: 'Enough of what does not come within the compass of my knowledge and experience.'[9]

In the same letter, he expressed the hope of maintaining good relations with the Navy and the civil government.[10] But his touchiness was to cause ill-feeling between him and the Governor of Bombay over a court-martial, while the proposed division of prize-money brought him near to a dispute with the Navy. It was decided, before the expedition started, that the two senior officers of the squadron, Vice-Admiral Charles Watson and Rear-Admiral George Pocock, were each to receive a larger share than Clive, whose share would only be equivalent to that of a naval captain. Clive maintained that as Commander-in-Chief of the army he should at least get the same as Pocock. Watson settled matters by offering to make up the difference between Clive's amount and that of Pocock out of his own share. Such generosity was typical of him, for he was an English admiral in the best tradition, universally popular and loved by his men.

Angria's fastness of Gheria stood on a promontory inside a harbour. The promontory was guarded by a perpendicular rock, hence the popular belief that it was impregnable as Gibraltar. When, however, the English fleet arrived here on February 11, Angria panicked, left the fort in command of his brother and took refuge with the Marathas, who had approached from the landward and were supposed to be acting in concert with the English. Watson was visited by some of Angria's family, whom he ordered to be shown over his ship so that they could see the rows of gleaming guns. He gave them a thirty-two-pound ball as a souvenir, with the promise that if their master surrendered the fort peacefully, the English would give them protection.[11] By way of reply, the guns of the fort opened fire, so an engagement began. One of Angria's *grabs* was set alight by a shell, and the fire spread rapidly to all his flimsy craft, then to the magazine, the storehouses and to other buildings on shore, a holocaust which engulfed parts of the fort. The enemy guns were soon silenced, and Clive, with his army of eight hundred Europeans and as many Indians, was able to land. On the 13th, the fort surrendered, having been bombarded by the Navy. In it were found ten Englishmen and three Dutchmen off captured ships who had been kept as slaves.[12] Clive's chief concern during the action, in which the English casualties were no more than twenty killed and wounded, was to prevent his Maratha allies from entering the fort before anybody else and making off with the plunder. One of his officers threatened to cut off the Maratha general's head if he advanced a step further,[13] which had the desired effect, so that all the plunder in the fort, worth £140,000, fell to the English.

There was a touching scene when Watson, after the fighting was over, visited the womenfolk and children of the unfortunate Angria. Amid floods of tears Angria's mother lamented that 'the people had no king, she no son, her daughter no husband, the children no father',* to which Watson replied that 'from henceforward they must look upon him as their father and their friend'. Then Angria's youngest child, a boy of six, took Watson by the hand and said, between sobs: 'You shall be my father.' The Admiral was so moved that he, too, started to shed tears, and he had to turn away so that it would not be noticed.[14]

'I make no doubt but the newspapers will be swelled with a pompous account of the taking of the place (which proved a very easy conquest) and

* This was not strictly true, since Angria, though ruined, was still alive.

of the immense riches found within,' wrote Clive to his father. Though the reality was more modest, his share of the plunder, £5000, would at least 'balance the election'. A pleasant windfall, particularly so since he had recently lost between £2000 and £3000 in a shipwreck. He could have had an extra £1000 which Watson sent him to make his share equal to that of Pocock; but he would not accept it, saying that he had only asked for it to satisfy his officers.

Clive was now impatient to start work at Fort St David. He reckoned that if he were needed for the Deccan expedition, he could return quickly enough. In asking the Bombay Council for permission to leave, he patted himself on the back for his 'zeal and attachment to the Honourable Company's service' at a time when 'success could not be ensured or private advantages foreseen'—a dubious statement in view of the English superiority and the pre-arranged division of prize-money—and also for leaving the artillery in a much better state than he found it. But his tone became more modest when speaking of the Deccan expedition: 'I much suspect both want of abilities and constitution to command so great an undertaking.'[15]

Clive and Margaret, who was pregnant once again, sailed on April 27 in one of Watson's ships. They reached Fort St David on May 14, but he did not assume his Deputy-Government until he had been to Madras and taken his seat as Second in Council. It must have been as much of a homecoming as when they arrived in London. Particularly for Margaret, who was to be reunited with her brother Mun and her cousin Jack Walsh and who now had another cousin here, young Thomas Kelsall, Jane's brother. Clive was welcomed by friends such as Pigot and Lawrence, and also by Orme. And there was the *dubash* Venkatchelum and a host of servants and hangers-on who must have wept with joy at seeing Master and Madam back.

At the same time, there may have been undertones of jealousy. Aged little more than thirty, Clive had obtained promotion over the heads of his seniors. Henry Speke, captain of Watson's flagship, must have echoed a certain body of opinion when he wrote to Orme from Fort St David in June 1755, a year before Clive's return: 'I have a great deal about the Hero (who will lose his election) which I will show you when we meet to make you laugh. I think you need not entertain any fears of his rivalship—his reputation dwindles very fast.'[16] Speke, however, had not actually met 'the Hero' when he wrote those words, and his views would have been largely coloured by Orme himself, who wished to be Governor as much as Clive did, and was suspected by Clive's friends of trying to prejudice him by 'false reports'.[17]*

On June 22, 1756, Clive made his formal entry into Fort St David as Deputy-Governor, the guns booming a salute that was heard in Pondicherry. He now had the title of 'Worshipful', rode in a state palanquin and lived at the Garden House, with its portico, its grounds shaded by tulip trees, and its memories of his first military action nearly ten years previously. The house was put to rights by the Fort Engineer, and Margaret was able to add her own feminine touches to the lofty rooms with their furniture of teak and blackwood, their mirrors which at night reflected the wall-lights – candles flickering in the glass shades that were a necessary protection against sudden storms. Here Clive was to do the honours of the settlement, with eight chests of claret and two of hock sent out every year by his father.

At the age of twenty, Margaret became the first lady of the settlement. This might have turned the head of someone less genuine than she; but though she was henceforth to occupy a station far above that in which she had been brought up – rising from Fort St David to be the undoubted queen of Calcutta, and then, with scarcely a break, being metamorphosed into a very rich peeress in England – she never seems to have been in the least conceited. This is all the more to her credit since we know, from Sarah Mathison's criticisms, that she had it in her to be spoilt, and could also, if she wished, be sharp-tongued; it seems that as she rose in the world, her sense of responsibility increased and she managed to curb the less attractive side of her nature without losing any of her gaiety and high spirits.

Despite her exalted position, life at Fort St David was quiet compared with the balls and concerts of her Madras days. Yet she cannot have been lonely. Jenny Latham still spent a great deal of time with her, while the wife of the fort surgeon, Dr Hancock, was her old friend Philadelphia Austen who had come to India on the same ship as her in 1752.† More serious company – as well as spiritual comfort, which she needed when

* Clive's friends also blamed Orme for having put Saunders against him, for the ex-governor was reported as being not at all pleased at his promotion. In fact, Saunders's objection to Clive's appointment seems to have been merely on the grounds that he was not experienced enough in civil administration. (Home Miscellaneous Series, Vol. 806, memorandum by Saunders, October 5, 1755.)

† One wonders if she had any of the talent that was to appear in her niece, the yet unborn Jane.

she heard that her younger boy had died in far-off England—was provided by the genial, moon-faced Swedish missionary, the Reverend John Zachariah Kiernander.

Clive, more than Margaret, might have succumbed to idle boredom as he faced the prospect of anything up to five years in this backwater. Instead, he set to work with a vengeance, despite the sweltering heat of those days of June and July. During his first month at Fort St David, he looked into the details of his garrison and demanded more troops. He remedied a complaint that the *peons* who guarded the Bounds Hedge were levying an illicit toll on goods coming in, which made provisions in the settlement 'extravagantly dear'. He investigated a series of robberies, he took steps to improve the settlement's supplies of arak, he rationalized accounts. He even looked beyond Fort St David and considered plans for defending the nearby Danish settlement of Tranquebar against the French.[18]

CHAPTER VIII

The Black Hole

> That little company of Englishmen and one English woman . . . whose martyrdom on that night of doom, 20 June, 1756, had laid the foundation stone of British Dominion in Bengal.
>
> CURZON

I

On April 10, 1756, the Nawab of Bengal, Alivardi Khan, died. Though a usurper, he had managed to reign for fourteen years, in theory as one of the three great Mogul viceroys or *subadars*, in practice as an independent sovereign paying nominal homage to the Emperor. His kingdom, which included one of the most fertile regions in India, the vast plain of alluvial soil watered by the channels of the Lower Ganges—a country where everything was green, where crops grew in abundance—enjoyed a period of stable government under his rule. Trade and industry flourished.

Alivardi summed up his attitude to the Europeans—English, French, Dutch and Danish—who had settlements in his dominions by likening them to bees: you could enjoy their honey, but they would sting you to death if you disturbed their hive. In other words he left them alone as much as he could, while sharing in their wealth by means of periodic capital levies, as they would now be called, backed by a show of force. The Europeans naturally resented this; particularly the English, who traded under the protection of a *farman* or charter granted to them by the Emperor in 1717. For his part, the Nawab frequently complained that the English were abusing the privileges of their *farman*. The importance of their chief settlement, Calcutta, which since being founded from nothing in 1686 had grown into a city rivalling the Nawab's own capital of Murshidabad, a hundred miles to the north, encouraged the English to take more liberties with the Nawab and his government than the other Europeans did; and it caused the Nawab to view them with greater envy and mistrust.

Alivardi's grandson, Siraj-ud-daula, who succeeded him as Nawab, thus inherited an uneasy situation. But nobody would have imagined that this would lead, in a couple of months, to a full-scale war, in which the new Nawab would capture Calcutta. Siraj-ud-daula has been pictured as a monster of vice, cruelty and depravity. But though he may have suffered from the demoralizing effects of too much wealth and power at too early an age,* he was in fact no more cruel than most eighteenth-century Eastern despots – some of his Indian contemporaries criticized him for being over-merciful[1] – while his affection for his chief wife and his adherence to a promise made to his grandfather to give up drink, to which he had previously been addicted, do not suggest a particularly vicious character. His main fault was weakness, which caused him to be fickle and indecisive; he was also arrogant, of changeable temper, and lacking in courage.†

Weakness shows itself in his face, said to have been 'delicate' and 'famous for beauty'[2] – clean-shaven but for a small moustache and with large, rather frightened doe-eyes. Fear seems to have been his chief motive in attacking the English – the other possible motive, a desire for plunder, being disproved by the moderation with which he helped himself to the English property when it was in his power. His grandfather had felt a growing disquiet at what was happening in the Deccan and Carnatic, where the French and English had reduced the princes of the country to being their puppets. Siraj-ud-daula shared his grandfather's anxiety and was determined not to let the foreigners extend their military activities

* He was not, however, as is generally believed, barely out of his teens on becoming Nawab, but twenty-seven.

† The more spectacular allegations against him – that he amused himself by pulling the wings off birds, ordered boatloads of people to be upset so that he could watch them drown, and ripped open pregnant women to gratify his curiosity – can be dismissed as legend; there is nothing about them in the writings of his cousin, Ghulam Husain Khan, who was bitterly hostile to him; nor in those of William Watts and Luke Scrafton, the two Englishmen who knew him better than any of their compatriots and played a leading part in his overthrow. As to his supposed vices, these writers confine themselves to vague remarks about his love of low company, and his youthful over-indulgence in drink. There is a suggestion that drink caused permanent damage to his mental faculties, which seems unlikely if he was able to give it up at an early age.

into Bengal – which they seemed about to do, having for some months been improving the fortifications of their settlements. On becoming Nawab, he ordered them to demolish these new works. The French satisfied him by explaining that they were merely repairing the damage done by lightning; but he refused to believe the English when they assured him – without, as it happens, much truth – that the fortifications of Calcutta were against the French, rather than himself.[3] His mistrust of the English was exacerbated by reports that they had been intriguing with his aunt, Ghasiti Begum, and with his cousin, the Nawab of Purnea, both of whom he suspected of disputing his succession. These reports gained substance when the English gave sanctuary to Krishna Das, one of Ghasiti's clique who had embezzled the Nawab's revenues.

If the Nawab was ill-fitted for handling a crisis of this sort, so was the English governor, Roger Drake, a weak-minded and rather decadent young man with a reputation for vice that stemmed from his having married his deceased wife's sister. Like Siraj-ud-daula, he was unsure of his position, which had not yet been confirmed by London, and so was touchy and arrogant. He treated Siraj-ud-daula's envoy with contempt, which caused the Nawab to make his celebrated remark: 'What honour is left to us, when a few traders who have not yet learnt to wash their bottoms reply to the ruler's order by expelling his envoy?'[4]

Siraj-ud-daula occupied the English subordinate factory at Cossimbazar near Murshidabad and then marched on Calcutta. The English felt confident that they would be able to repel him. But their defences – despite the new works – were as inadequate as their garrison. After a few days it was resolved to abandon the town and the fort and take to the ships in the river. There was panic; the ships moved off carrying the women and children and some of the men – including Drake, who showed little courage on this occasion[5] – and leaving the rest of the garrison to the mercy of the Nawab.

Then followed that celebrated horror, the Black Hole,* which, like the character of Siraj-ud-daula, has been embellished with the years.† It is

* Its name alone is infinitely sinister, though in fact the room in Fort William where so many English died of heat and suffocation during the night of June 20, 1756, was known as such even before the event – 'black hole' being the recognized name for the detention cell in a military barracks until a century ago.

† Thus it was popularly believed that there were women and children shut up in the Black Hole, as well as men, whereas there is only contemporary evidence of there having been one woman – the brave Portuguese half-caste Mary Carey, who refused to be separated from her English husband.

founded almost solely on the writings of John Zephaniah Holwell, one of Drake's Council who was himself a survivor of the tragedy and who is known to have been a talented but not always truthful propagandist. Holwell's assertion that 146 people, of whom 123 died, were shut up in the Black Hole has been proved mathematically impossible by present-day Indian scholars, who put the total number of those incarcerated at between 39 and 69, with between 18 and 43 deaths.* Yet even for this lesser number it would have been horror enough to spend one of the hottest and most sultry nights of the Bengal June crowded together in a room fourteen feet by eighteen, unventilated but for two small barred windows giving on to a deep verandah.

More than anything else, the Black Hole has rendered Siraj-ud-daula hateful to posterity, though he was not directly responsible for it. In contemporary Madras, however, it does not seem to have caused any more of a sensation than the rest of the news from Bengal. When, on August 16, it was learnt that Calcutta had fallen, Clive was immediately summoned from Fort St David to attend the Council and the Select Committee.† After six weeks of wrangling, it was decided to go all out to recover Calcutta, even though it meant denuding Madras of troops. This policy – a brave and far-sighted one, in view of the imminence of war with France, when Madras would have been in danger from Pondicherry – was Pigot's; he was supported by Clive, who offered his services to command the expedition. Of the possible alternative candidates, Pigot himself stood down through lack of military experience, and Lawrence was too asthmatic for the damp heat of Bengal. But Colonel John Adlercron, commander of the King's Regiment – a pompous little parade officer of Huguenot descent – pressed his claim with such persistence that for a time it looked as if the command would go to him.‡ Then he overstepped himself, and refused to give the required assurances that he would return to Madras if needed and reserve a share of the plunder for the Company. So

* It seems that Holwell's figures were arrived at by deducting the number of persons assumed to have been killed in the fighting, or to have escaped in the ships or at other times, from the total number of Europeans in the garrison. But it is possible to account for more persons killed, or who escaped. As well as thus getting his figures wrong, Holwell probably embroidered as to the alleged cruelty of the guards. The Black Hole was not a deliberate outrage but a tragedy resulting from a mistake on the part of one of Siraj-ud-daula's officers, who seems to have been unaware of the smallness of the room.

† There had been a Select Committee or inner council at Fort St George since 1754.

‡ Adlercron had the power to withdraw the King's troops altogether from the expedition, if he was not given the command.

the command went to Clive, 'the capablest person in India for an undertaking of this nature'; or so he was described by Orme,[6] who had been largely instrumental in getting Pigot's policy adopted, and was now going all out to push Clive's military genius – perhaps in the secret hope that Clive would stay in Bengal and leave the way open for himself to become Governor of Madras.

Before Clive could sail, there was deadlock once again over the relationship between the expedition and the discredited Fort William Council, whose envoy, Charles Manningham, threw a heavy Bengal spanner into the Madras works. Eventually, it was settled that Clive, as commander of the expedition, should be responsible only to Madras and not to Bengal. It was quite unprecedented to put the military above the civil in this way. 'Had we not', wrote the Directors, on hearing of what had been arranged, 'the highest opinion of Colonel Clive's prudence and moderation, there would be no end to the disagreeable reflections we might make.'[7]

Clive arranged to take Mun, Walsh and Cousin George with him; Mun in command of a company and Walsh in the profitable capacity of Paymaster. Margaret, who was awaiting the birth of her child, stayed at Fort St David with Jenny Latham.

The expedition sailed on October 16. Five of His Majesty's ships and as many transports belonging to the Company carried some six hundred Europeans and rather more than nine hundred sepoys. In addition, there were three companies of King's troops serving as marines, the only contribution which the huffy Adlercron was prepared to make. This was, in the words of Macaulay, 'the army which sailed to punish a Prince who had more subjects than Louis XV or the Empress Maria Theresa' – though the expedition was not so much to punish Siraj-ud-daula as to force him to agree to a settlement favourable to the Company. The Madras gentlemen had decided that 'the sword should go hand in hand with the pen'[8] – so Clive was armed not just with muskets and field-pieces but also with a copy of the Company's *farman* and letters to Siraj-ud-daula from Pigot, Mohammed Ali and Salabat Jang. 'The great commander of the King of England's ships has not slept in peace since this news and is come down with many ships, and I have sent a great *Sardar* who will govern after me, by name Colonel Clive, with troops and land forces,' announced Pigot, with a suitably Oriental flourish. He then gave Siraj-ud-daula a chance of making amends. 'You are wise: consider whether it is better to engage in a war that will never end or to do what is just and right in the sight of God.'[9]

In short, the object of the expedition was to recover Calcutta and put the clock back to Alivardi's reign. For Clive, who was very much a child of the eighteenth century in the delicate balance of his motives between public interest and personal gain, there would have been another object, to make money and further his career. 'This expedition if attended with success may enable me to do great things,' he told his father.[10] Without exaggerating his sense of destiny, we can take it that he saw this as his big chance – far bigger than the Deccan expedition on which he had hitherto banked. His visit to Calcutta in the winter of 1749–50, though it must now have seemed an eternity ago in view of all that had happened since, had impressed the wealth of Bengal indelibly on his mind. He had been ready to leave his friends and throw over his position in the hope of sharing in this wealth by the laborious and uncertain means of trade; now, if he was lucky, an even larger share of it would fall to him as prize-money – the legitimate reward of the successful soldier or sailor in those days. He would have remembered how one of his business associates had prophesied, after Arcot, that he would make a quick fortune if there was a war in Bengal.[11] His anxiety lest the situation on the Coast should lead to his premature recall there is understandable.[12]

Clive's behaviour during the next few months, though as always not entirely consistent, would on the whole suggest that he went to Bengal determined to adhere to Pigot's firm but conciliatory policy. However, the possibility of taking a tougher line with the Nawab cannot have been entirely absent from his mind, as he sailed towards Bengal in that autumn of 1756. Orme, whose judgement he respected, had written to him four years earlier from Calcutta, where Alivardi was engaged in bullying the English settlement out of a large sum: 'Clive, it would be a good deed to swing the old dog: I don't speak at random when I say that the Company must think seriously of it, or it will not be worth their while to trade in Bengal.'[13] He must now have urged a still tougher policy towards Alivardi's grandson. Clive had no idea what such a policy would entail; just as he had no idea of the far-reaching consequences of a plan which at this moment was of much greater interest to him: to deprive the French of their chief Bengal settlement, Chandernagore. He regarded it as just another move against the French, a repetition of the wars of Lawrence and Dupleix, only waged in difficult and unfamiliar country. But though he went prepared for the 'woods and swampiness' of Bengal, and was uncertain enough of the outcome to commend his English agents for putting what they had left of his money into the Funds, rather than sending it to

India, as he had previously ordered,[14] he did not realize that he would have to pick his way through an even darker morass of intrigue and treachery. Fortunately, he had, in the words of Orme, 'the vigilance of a cat' as well as 'the intrepidity of a lion'. The cat image is significant, for there was a side to Clive's nature that was feline, as well as feminine. Orme spoke from a military point of view, but he touched precisely on the qualities which were to help Clive in the broader and more exacting world of politics and government that, unbeknown to him, lay ahead, making him 'a dangerous enemy, from the vivacity of his exploits and the perseverance with which he repeats them, thinking nothing done whilst anything remains to do'.[15]

2

The voyage to Bengal was anything but auspicious. Relentless gales blew the ships as far off course as Ceylon. Not until after nearly six weeks' sailing did Clive, who travelled in Watson's flagship, the *Kent*, notice the sea take on the distinctive colour of the Ganges mud; and while Thomas Latham's *Tiger* and the *Walpole* had also arrived, the rest of the fleet was yet to come.

They now had to wait for a high enough tide to take them up the Hughli, the westernmost of the two main branches of the Lower Ganges. By December 15, they had gone fifty miles up river to Fulta, a desolate waterside village backed by low-lying jungle and reeking, malarial swamp. Here they found the refugees from Calcutta and the other settlements, or rather those who had not yet succumbed to the unhealthiness of the place: haggard, threadbare and so overcrowded that some of them had, for the past five months, been obliged to sleep on the decks of the ships which had brought them down river, exposed to the Monsoon rains.

On the very day he arrived at Fulta, Clive wrote to Manik Chand, the Nawab's Governor of Calcutta, who was reported to be preparing to intercept the English force. Contemporary Indian chroniclers differ as to whether Manik Chand was arrogant or modest, a brave man or a coward.[16] His relations with the English seem no less equivocal.[17] Outwardly, he was one of the Nawab's Hindu favourites, yet he appears to

DUPLEIX

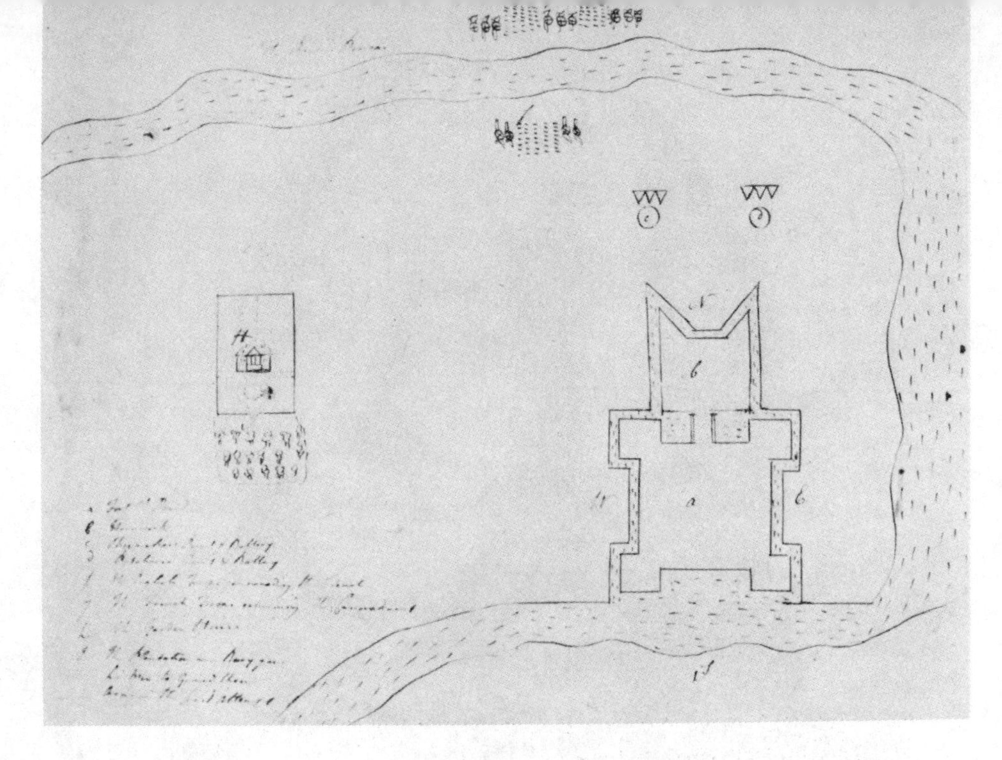

FORT ST DAVID, CUDDALORE

Sketch plan by Clive,
or made under his supervision

FORT ST DAVID, CUDDALORE
THE GOVERNOR'S GARDEN HOUSE

have had a private grievance against him. Whatever his true loyalties, he showed his humanity to the refugees at Fulta by supplying them with provisions. Clive thanked him for this,[18] to which he replied courteously, sending certain confidential information by word of mouth.[19] Presumably this concerned Siraj-ud-daula's terms for a settlement. During the past three months the Nawab had already made several peace overtures, but the gentlemen at Fulta had preferred to wait for the squadron and negotiate from a position of strength.

Before hearing from Manik Chand, Clive and Watson had both written stern letters to the Nawab. 'I have brought with me', wrote Clive, 'a larger military force than has ever appeared in Bengal.'[20] Manik Chand, who was to forward this letter to the Nawab, thought it contained 'many improper expressions' and sent Clive a more humbly worded draft.[21] Clive refused to use this, though he toned down his letter. He left in a piece of flattery which he had neatly combined with a boast: 'I know you are a great prince and a great warrior. I likewise for these ten years past have been constantly fighting in these parts and it has pleased God Almighty always to make me successful.'[22]

When Clive wrote this letter, Siraj-ud-daula was over a hundred miles away at Murshidabad, organizing a hunt and an elephant fight.[23] He did not have much of a chance to answer it, for on December 27, two days after it was written, the expedition set out. In fact, the correspondence with him and Manik Chand was merely to gain time, to prevent the garrison of Calcutta being reinforced while the English were delayed at Fulta,[24] waiting for a high enough tide to take the ships further up the river. One may accuse Clive and Watson of being two-faced, yet had they waited at Fulta for the Nawab to reply, it would have encouraged him to spin out negotiations while the English soldiers died like flies in that pestilential spot. Sickness made its appearance even in the few days they were there—Clive himself was laid low just before Christmas with a feverish cold.

Two more of Watson's ships, the *Salisbury* and *Bridgewater*, arrived before the expedition set out. But the *Cumberland* and *Marlborough*, which carried the better half of Clive's troops as well as most of his artillery, were obliged to return to Vizigapatam, north of Madras. Even with this reduced force, Clive was, by the standard of his previous campaigns, more than a match for Manik Chand, who had only two thousand men in all. Intelligence from Calcutta told of guns mounted on useless home-made carriages, of the forts downstream of the town being virtually undefended, of panic among the Nawab's troops at the news that the English were coming.[25]

Baj-Baj, half-way between Fulta and Calcutta, was little better than the other forts, but the English, who seem to have been misinformed in this respect, made their plans as though it were strongly garrisoned. The ships were to bombard it, and land the marine companies from Adlercron's regiment to take it by storm. The rest of the troops, under Clive, were to be stationed at a point on the Calcutta side of the fort, to cut off the garrison's retreat. To reach this point entailed an exhausting all-night march through swamp and jungle worse than Clive had ever expected, with numerous watercourses across which the artillery had somehow to be got. At any rate they did not suffer from heat, though for Clive the damp must have been even worse, making his cold bronchial.

Having set out at six in the evening, it was not until eight the following morning that the sight of the masts of Watson's ships appearing above the trees and undergrowth told them they had reached their destination. Clive disposed his troops ready to cut off the garrison from the fort. Then, quite suddenly, Manik Chand and his army appeared from out of the jungle and attacked. This, for Clive, was a complete surprise – he had obtained virtually no intelligence, having come through uninhabited country.

After a skirmish lasting an hour, Manik Chand and his troops retired. They had not expected to see Clive's field-pieces, imagining it would be impossible to bring them over the country which the English had just crossed. Manik Chand lost 200 killed, including his second-in-command – he himself was shot through the turban. The English also lost one of their best officers, together with nine other men killed and eight wounded.[26]

Clive felt this was more than they could afford to lose in so brief a skirmish.[27] The night march and Manik Chand's attack left him dispirited, and he began to doubt his chances of success in so difficult a country. He was later to complain that the march was against his wishes, that he had wanted all the troops to go in the ships but was overruled at a Council of War held on December 27.[28] Yet in writing to his second-in-command, Major James Killpatrick, on the 23rd, he himself advocated going by land.[29] One would suspect him of trying to blame the march on others, after it had proved a mistake.

In blaming the Council of War, Clive was, in effect, blaming the naval officers and the officers of the marine companies. Relations between him and the King's officers were bound to be difficult. The King's officers would have resented an amateur being senior to all of them except Watson. Clive, for his part, would have suspected the King's officers of insubordination, of trying to get more than their fair share of the kudos, of discriminating against the Company's troops.

It would not be true to say that Clive's experiences at this time gave him a lifelong prejudice against the King's officers, for he was later to include several of them among his closest friends. But it certainly gave him a prejudice against one particular officer – Captain Eyre Coote, a handsome, sharp-featured sprig of the Anglo-Irish aristocracy. Coote was a brave and conscientious soldier, but he was quarrelsome and hot-tempered and had the pride of his race. His natural ambition was doubtless intensified by the desire to live down the disgrace of having been court-martialled for alleged cowardice after the Battle of Falkirk.*

Coote was set on having the honour of storming Baj-Baj fort. The guns of the fort had been silenced by the squadron, and the marines, including his own company, landed. But before he could lead an assault, he was ordered to the assistance of Clive, who was then embroiled with Manik Chand. Later in the day, however, it seemed that Coote's chance had come, for his superior officer was taken ill, while Clive and Killpatrick, worn out by the efforts of the past twenty-four hours, were resting in one of the ships. But again he was thwarted. Clive sent him a message that the assault should be postponed till next morning[30] – he clearly wanted to lead it himself, or anyhow, to make sure that the Company's troops were in on it.

The matter was settled that night by a drunken sailor who took it into his head to storm the fort himself. He rushed alone into the breach, waving his cutlass, firing his pistol, and crying 'The place is mine!'[31] Fortunately for him the garrison, which was small enough at the best of times, had been slipping away under cover of darkness, so he only had a handful of enemy to contend with. His comrades, hearing his shouts, hurried to his support and in less than no time the fort had been taken,[32] though with the loss of a popular officer who was accidentally shot by one of his own men. Having restored order, Coote was able to assume command of the fort, but without the dubious honour of having taken it.

When the squadron moved on up river to Calcutta, Clive got his way, and he and his European troops travelled in the ships, the sepoys marching

* He was acquitted of cowardice, but convicted of having broken the 14th Article of War and sentenced to be cashiered. Though he managed to be pardoned, perhaps through the influence of the Duke of Cumberland, it would have left him under a cloud.

along the bank. The twenty-mile journey went without a hitch. At dawn on January 2, 1757, the squadron was in sight of the town. From this distance, and with the sun rising behind the buildings on the waterfront, it would have been hard to know that everything was not normal; except that the river lacked its usual forest of masts. Clive and his troops landed, and together with the sepoys advanced into the town from the southward; while the ships went on until abreast of Fort William. As they sheered round in the eddies of the tide, they came under warm fire. Then they anchored and returned the fire and Manik Chand and his garrison fled before Clive could catch up with them.

People on shore waved at the ships in greeting; somebody hoisted a Union Jack on a tree.[33] It must have been a great moment for Watson and his men, though they could see that the town was in a sad state. The fine classical factory building rising above the walls of the Fort, once the admiration of the East, was a burnt-out ruin. So were the mansions that graced the waterfront on either side.

Clive and his troops, approaching the Fort from the landward, would have seen even more damage. The church, several of the European houses and large areas of the bazaars were burnt or levelled. The trees of the park round the Great Tank had been cut down. Even part of the curtain wall of the Fort had been demolished, to make room for a mosque.

The Fort, for Clive, held another and more unwelcome surprise. It was already occupied by a detachment under Coote, who had orders from Watson not to relinquish his command. Coote took this to mean that he was not to let anybody in, not even the Company's troops; so when the advance guard of Clive's sepoys tried to enter, they were, as Clive said, 'ignominiously thrust out'[34] and their officer put under arrest. When he heard what had happened Clive was furious. He led his troops into the Fort and confronted Coote, threatening to put *him* under arrest. Coote agreed to hand over the Fort, but referred to Watson for further orders.

Messages then passed between Watson and Clive, each claiming to exercise the King's authority. Watson demanded that Clive should withdraw from the Fort, taking his forced entry as an insult to himself. Clive refused to move. 'If you still persist in continuing in the Fort,' wrote Watson, 'you will force me to take such measures as will be as disagreeable to me, as they possibly can be to you.'[35] This meant that the Admiral 'would fire him out',[36] as the captain of the flagship, Henry Speke, told Clive in an interview which ended with both of them losing their tempers, and Clive contradicting himself as he was liable to do when heated.[37]

In the end, through the good offices of Jenny's husband, Captain Thomas Latham, it was agreed that Clive should hand over the Fort to Watson himself when he came ashore, and that Watson would then hand it over to the Company.[38] Watson assured Clive that he had never intended to slight him, but Clive was convinced it was a 'dirty underhand contrivance' to forestall his own occupation of the Fort, and complained to Pigot of the 'mortifications . . . in point of prerogative' which he had suffered from the Navy.[39] His relations with Watson were soon to improve and he and Speke became good friends. But we can see in this incident a reason for his antipathy to Coote, who certainly behaved in a high-handed manner to the Company's troops.

CHAPTER IX

The Rose and the Lily

> Ranjit Rai . . . said to me in a mocking tone: 'You are a Frenchman, are you afraid of the English? If they attack you, defend yourselves! No one is ignorant of what your nation has done on the Coast. We are curious to see how you will get out of this business here!' I told him I did not expect to find such a warlike person in a Bengali merchant and that sometimes people had reason to repent of their curiosity.
>
> JEAN LAW

I

Drake and his Council were installed once again at Calcutta, little more than six months after having been thrown out. By late January, Calcutta life was sufficiently back to normal for one of the Madras officers to write of the grand houses and lavish hospitality.[1] Yet the houses lacked furniture, and in some cases, doors, which had been robbed for firewood. 'It is not possible to describe the distresses of the inhabitants of this once opulent and populous town,' Clive told his father. 'The private losses amount to upwards of two million sterling.'[2]

While acknowledging these losses, he had little sympathy for the gentlemen of the Bengal Select Committee and Council, whose one object, as he complained to Pigot, was the recovery of their own private wealth. *He* had come here to restore the prosperity of the Company. The Bengal gentlemen were proving even more troublesome than the King's officers. They objected to Clive's independent authority; they wrote asking him to relinquish it; they even wrote to the Madras gentlemen, questioning their right to give him such powers.[3] Clive told the Committee that he had no intention of giving up his powers, but that he would not use them unless obliged to do so.[4] Writing to Pigot by the same ship that carried the Committee's letter, he spoke more plainly: 'I would have you guard against everything these gentlemen can say; for believe me, they are bad subjects and rotten at heart and will stick at nothing to prejudice you ... the riches of Peru and Mexico should not induce me to dwell among them.'[5]

He suspected Holwell of putting the other Bengal gentlemen against him.[6] Certainly after the wild-eyed hero of the Black Hole had left for England at the end of January, things ran much more smoothly, and Clive found that he was able to work reasonably well with the Bengal Committee. He was even willing to tolerate Drake, so as to keep in with his uncle, a Director of the Company.[7]

January was a month of intrigues and preparations. The English had only recovered, as they said, 'the bare walls' of Calcutta.[8] If the Nawab himself had shown restraint, his troops and the populace at large had plundered as much as they could, for which the Company intended to present him with a large bill, as well as demanding that he should confirm their former privileges. To force the Nawab to meet these demands, the English had a good naval squadron and a very inadequate army; they also had the possible support of various local magnates. The Nawab confronted them with an army of at least twenty thousand, though it was by no means solidly loyal.

Whatever chances the English might have had against the Nawab alone, they could not run the risk of his being joined by 300 trained European troops from the French settlement of Chandernagore, where opinion was torn between mistrust of the national enemy—with whom France was now officially at war—and the fear of being at the Nawab's mercy if the English were brought low. As long as they were uncertain about the French, the English had to play for time. They also needed time for military preparations, and they were still waiting on the arrival of the *Cumberland* and *Marlborough* with the rest of their army.

Writing to Pigot on January 8, Clive was doubtful of success, even given time for these preparations.[9] A bout of depression and toothache, added to his troubles with the Bengal gentlemen and the King's officers, made him pessimistic: 'Between friends, I cannot help regretting that ever I undertook this expedition.'[10] At this juncture he longed to return to Madras, so wanted a quick settlement—another reason for insisting that only the Company's losses should be taken into account. Whereas the

Bengal gentlemen would have preferred a decisive victory with compensation for all, even if it meant a longer war. By flattering Watson and bestowing fifty bales of broadcloth on his gallant tars ('in the Company's present distressed circumstances', as Clive remarked bitterly),[11] they hoped to delay the departure of the squadron.

Since the beginning of the month, Clive had been busy putting Fort William to rights. The Fort, however, was only a last line of defence; he intended to await the Nawab outside the town. In choosing the site of his entrenchment, he again showed his talent for choosing ground—as well as having a narrow escape from a wild buffalo, which charged and killed one of the sepoys with him.[12] It was at Barnagul, north-east of the town, protected by the river, a salt lake and the Maratha Ditch. The Nawab's army, approaching Calcutta from the north, would have to pass close to here to get between the lake and the Ditch, and could thus easily be cut off.

The *Marlborough* arrived in the middle of the month, bringing most of the missing artillery; but the *Cumberland* and a reinforcement expected from Bombay still failed to turn up. Clive, therefore, raised a battalion of sepoys. The Bengalis were themselves not a warlike people, but the country abounded with soldiers of fortune from other parts of India.[13]

The Company and the King's forces had already formally declared war on the Nawab; and while Clive was engaged in his preparations two of Watson's ships sailed up the river and their big guns thundered at the Nawab's town of Hughli, just beyond the French settlement of Chandernagore and the Dutch settlement of Cinsura. Manik Chand and his troops, who had retired here from Calcutta, fled. Then parties of British scoured both banks of the river, plundering and burning everything in their path from the Nawab's granary to the house of the Armenian merchant, Khwaja Wajid, who was suspected of having encouraged the Nawab to attack Calcutta on account of a private grievance against the Company. This holocaust was intended to jog the Nawab into negotiating, and to destroy stocks of provisions which would have been of strategic value to him were he again to attack Calcutta.

As well as preparing for war, Clive wrote to some of the notables of the country—Manik Chand, Khwaja Wajid and the heads of the great banking house of Seth—asking them to bring pressure to bear on the Nawab.[14] The Seths were the most likely to be of help. This family of Marwari merchants, whose headquarters were at Murshidabad, had built up a banking empire with offices all over the north of India. Their wealth was legendary – they made about 40 lakhs a year in their capacity as bankers to the Bengal government alone – and as well as handling two-thirds of his revenues,[15] they exercised a special power over Siraj-ud-daula since their family had been instrumental in setting up Alivardi as Nawab. As bankers, it was in their interest that the English should prosper; there was also reason to believe that they were dissatisfied with Siraj-ud-daula's rule.*

The Seths agreed to use their influence, though they were angry about the burnings at Hughli.[16] Khwaja Wajid, himself the chief sufferer in that holocaust, was inclined to be philosophic about his losses and also offered to work for a settlement.[17] Clive, for his part, felt that the fires at Hughli had taught the suspect Armenian a lesson, so agreed to his acting as mediator. He gave him his terms, which were also to be communicated to the Seths. The fact that they included restitution to private individuals as well as to the Company could indicate that he was coming into line with the Bengal gentlemen – unless he just put in this extra demand to leave room for bargaining.

Siraj-ud-daula had been irritated by the letters which Clive sent him after his arrival in Bengal. The news of the burning of Hughli was the last straw, and he at once marched southward with his army. But after he had travelled part of the way, he began to talk of peace. His rage had subsided and he was having trouble with some of his officers, notably with the Paymaster, Mir Jafar, who was his great-uncle by marriage, being a brother-in-law of Alivardi. Mir Jafar could have been dangerous – eight years previously, the leaders of a revolt had offered to make him Nawab in Alivardi's stead.

As the Nawab approached the ashes of Hughli, the general alarm at what the English had done or were believed to have done would have had a sobering effect on him. His subjects had been particularly terrified at the firing of the heavy guns on the British men-of-war. It was imagined that if these ships could deal death and destruction as far inland as Hughli, they could go anywhere, even as far up river as Murshidabad.

Thus intimidated, the Nawab wrote to Watson on January 23, agreeing to allow the Company to trade as before, provided someone else replaced Drake as Governor.[18] To Clive, who was approached next day by his emissary, it seemed that he 'most earnestly' desired peace.[19] Clive's

* Seth was not a name but a title – the more senior of the two cousins who controlled the banking house at this time being known as Jagat Seth, or 'Merchant of the World'.

optimism had somewhat diminished by the 29th, and he was uncertain whether Siraj-ud-daula really intended to treat, 'or only to amuse us'.[20] Nevertheless, he and the Nawab started a friendly correspondence.

While he was writing these letters, the Nawab continued to move with his army towards Calcutta. He seems to have been playing a double game, and also acting on impulse. On the very day that he wrote to Clive, agreeing to make restitution, he offered attractive privileges to the French if they would help him against the English. It seems that as he approached Calcutta, his confidence returned. Thus, on February 1, he addressed Clive more sternly.[21] Had he always intended to deceive, he would not have risked arousing Clive's suspicions in this way: it is surely a sign of his instability.

Next day, however, it really seemed as if the Nawab was out to double-cross. He had asked Clive to send an envoy to meet him at Nawabganj, about six miles away; but on February 2, it was heard in the English camp that his army was approaching. During the two days that followed, Clive and his troops watched the never-ending stream of men, horses, elephants, camels and oxen passing close by them in the direction of Calcutta. This great host encamped to the east of the town, on both sides of the Maratha Ditch. Soon the Nawab's soldiers were firing the suburbs, and the women and sick of the settlement were being put aboard the ships – it was like the previous June all over again. Yet on the very day that his troops advanced to the outskirts of Calcutta, the Nawab was writing to assure Clive that they were only moving because of the inconvenience of their previous camp. He still expected Clive's emissaries and sent him flowers and vegetables.[22]

Whatever his motives, the Nawab committed a grave blunder in thus walking into the English net, and giving Clive a chance of attacking him while based on his fortified camp. He should have kept the English at a distance, and cut off their food supplies; in which case, according to Clive's own reckoning, the army and the squadron would have been obliged, after three weeks, to abandon Calcutta or starve.[23] But if the Nawab threw away his real chance, so did Clive. The enemy host passed slowly by his camp on the 3rd and 4th; he could have enfiladed it, and trapped it between the Ditch, the lake and the river. But apart from a feeble attempt at harrying, he did nothing. Did he get cold feet – reports put the enemy strength at 100,000, and they were known to have thirty pieces of cannon – or did he still believe that the Nawab wanted peace?

There were two good reasons for joining battle immediately – the fear of starvation, and of damage to the Company's trade, if the present situation were allowed to drag on; and the possibility that the French, who had refused to help the Nawab, might later change their mind. The fact that on February 2, the Committee added three further demands to those which had already been transmitted to Khwaja Wajid has been taken as a sign that the English were determined to fight, in which case Clive's gracious letter to the Nawab, written on the very day that his army went past, and ending 'I esteem your Excellency in the place of my father and mother and myself as your son, and I should think myself happy to lay down my life for the preservation of yourself',[24] was a supreme piece of hypocrisy.

Yet the addition of the extra demands, far from proving that the English never intended a settlement at this juncture, could show rather that they believed in the imminence of such a settlement; in that two of these demands were mere technical points, such as would only be raised if a treaty were in view.* And however unconvinced Clive may have been by the assurances of the Nawab himself, his hopes of a satisfactory settlement could have been raised by the agent of the Seths, who was in touch with him, while being in the enemy camp. His thinking could have been influenced by the ups and downs of various unrecorded transactions, such as eleventh-hour attempts to buy over the Nawab's officers. And in considering Clive's motives, one must always take into account his own unpredictable temperament, and bear in mind his admission, 'Irregular was in my very nature'.

Another explanation for Clive's failure to attack the Nawab's army as it passed his camp was that he was putting off fighting in the hope that the *Cumberland* or the Bombay reinforcements would arrive any day. Certainly this was his intention on January 28, when he told the Madras Committee that he hoped, as soon as the other forces arrived, 'to finish everything by a decisive stroke'.[25]

This 'decisive stroke' was forced on Clive sooner than he may have wished by the fleeing of his bazaar-people at the approach of the Nawab's troops. Starvation, from being three weeks off, was now imminent. He acted first by sending two emissaries – Walsh and Luke Scrafton – to the Nawab, as had already been planned. Scrafton was a shrewd and

* The extension of trading privileges to include free passage through the country for the Company's goods, and the counter-signing of the treaty by the Nawab's ministers. The third and major demand was that the Nawab should give up his jurisdiction over the inhabitants of Calcutta.

capable young Company servant, with a good knowledge of Indian customs.*

They found the Nawab in the country house of the great Sikh merchant, Omichand, which stood just on the Calcutta side of the Maratha Ditch. His headquarters was thus separated by the Ditch from the rest of his camp, but it was well defended by some of his best troops as well as by his cannon. Nothing was achieved with the Nawab that evening, and Walsh and Scrafton retired to their sleeping-tents ostensibly with a view to resuming talks next day. Instead, they slipped away under cover of darkness and returned to the English camp. They did so, according to Scrafton, because they expected treachery on the part of the Nawab. More likely, they reckoned that now was the moment for Clive to make a night attack, such as had been so effective at Arcot, or they may have heard that the Nawab was about to attack Calcutta next day, in which case it would have been imperative for Clive to strike his blow before the enemy host crossed the Ditch and poured into the streets of the town. They may have obtained this information from the agent of the Seths, to whom the Nawab had sent them with the promise that he would tell them 'something . . . very agreeable to the Colonel'.[26] Knowing the Seths' secret hostility to the Nawab, this 'something' may have been very different from what he meant it to be. It might have been a false account of his aggressive intentions, aimed at inducing the English to attack and destroy him.

It was ten or eleven at night when Walsh and Scrafton rejoined Clive, and as soon as he heard what they had to say, he decided on an immediate action. His plan was to lead his troops through the enemy camp, firing as they went, then to cross the Maratha Ditch by a causeway close to Omichand's country house so as to accomplish their main object, which was to attack the Nawab's headquarters and carry off his cannon.[27]

Before setting out, Clive asked Watson for five or six hundred sailors to pull his guns.[28] The sailors duly arrived, but not till 2 a.m. What should have been a night attack became an attack at dawn, for it was daybreak by the time Clive and his little army – 800 Europeans, 1300 sepoys plus the sailors – reached the enemy camp. They were greeted with a shower of

* He also had the reputation of being a cartographer, which gave rise to the belief that he and Walsh were sent to spy out the terrain of the Nawab's camp. In fact, when they started on their mission, the Nawab was thought to be still at Nawabganj, so they did not expect to enter the camp near Calcutta at all. Only when they were on their way to Nawabganj did they learn that he had moved on.

arrows and some fire-rockets, one of which blew up a whole platoon of grenadiers. Then a thick fog descended, and it became impossible to see further than a few yards.

Accounts differ as to whether this fog was a misfortune or a blessing. Since it was a regular phenomenon in the early morning at this time of the year,* Clive must have expected it; indeed, he may have counted on it as a substitute for darkness. In later years his enemies were to write sneeringly of him that he owed one of his victories to a fog, calling it a 'no-battle'.

Thus shrouded, Clive and his troops were able to march through the long, straggling camp causing havoc by firing on both sides. They could hear the shrieks and neighings, though they could see nothing. And then suddenly there was the thunder of hooves and out of the fog came three hundred charging horsemen, swords uplifted. The English had the presence of mind to stand fast and fire. The horsemen were only a few yards away and all but a handful of them crumpled up in their saddles and fell to the ground. They were the Nawab's Persian guards, who were stationed on this side of the Ditch.

The English now realized that the fog had played them false. They had strayed into the middle of the camp, instead of heading directly for the causeway leading to Omichand's country house. This gave the enemy time to recover from their initial confusion, so that when Clive's troops eventually did reach the causeway, it was so well defended as to be impossible to cross. The only hope was to make for a bridge about a mile further on, which meant struggling through paddy fields. As they floundered in the muddy plain, the sailors heaving and pushing at the field-pieces, the fog suddenly lifted; and under the bright morning sun they were a perfect target for the Nawab's cannon. And while his cannon thundered, parties of his horse came galloping up on all sides. Clive, however, rallied his men and they somehow managed to get over the bridge to safety, though two of their field-pieces had to be left behind in the mud. To attack the Nawab's headquarters was now quite out of the question; for had they attempted to return that way they would have been enfiladed from across the Ditch. There was nothing for it but to head for the town and Fort William.

Clive described this action as 'the warmest service I ever yet was engaged in'.[29] It left him and his men rather dispirited. Their losses were considerable, fifty-seven killed including Clive's aide-de-camp and his secretary; while the commander of his sepoys was among the wounded.

* Known as the *Cohassa*.

The sailors were at the point of mutiny at having been employed as coolies.

But if the English were dispirited, Siraj-ud-daula was scared. 1300 of his troops had been killed or wounded, including twenty-two of his best officers; and he had lost a great many of his beasts. The refractory elements in his army were now more than ever mutinous; and though there were those among his officers who urged him to continue the fight, he preferred to listen to the doves.

Clive and Watson followed up the attack with a virtual ultimatum. They told the Nawab that what they had done was merely a sample of what the English were capable of doing. Clive was sarcastic: 'I cautiously hurt none but those that opposed me.'[30]

On the day these letters were written, the agent of the Seths wrote to Clive telling him that the Nawab would agree to the English terms.[31] At the same time, the Nawab and his army decamped and retired to beyond the salt lake. Had they delayed a day longer, Clive would have erected a battery commanding the neck of land between the lake and the river, making it impossible for them to retreat.[32]

Watson thought the Nawab's overtures were merely to gain time for retreating and collecting reinforcements. He wanted Clive to make another attack, and advised him to consult his officers on the subject. He only intended him to consult them privately; but Clive, much to the Admiral's chagrin, held a full-blown Council of War at which he misrepresented Watson's arguments and consequently obtained the decision he wanted, namely that there should be no further military action.[33] Watson criticized Clive for his excessive prudence—hardly the schoolboy's image of the daredevil Hero of Arcot. But by refusing to fight any more at this juncture, Clive was putting aside the straightforward arguments of a soldier for the more subtle considerations of diplomacy. He felt that to attack the Nawab again would be to risk driving him into the arms of the French.[34]

So he submitted a treaty to the Nawab, which was broadly similar to the terms he had sent to Khwaja Wajid. There was no mention of private losses, but the Nawab verbally promised to pay three lakhs on this account—and, incidentally, to make good in full what Clive and Killpatrick had themselves lost. It looked as if negotiations would break down when he added evasive riders to some of the clauses; but he signed the treaty unconditionally after a stern warning from Clive. What really caused his change of heart was that he had just heard the disturbing news that

Ahmed Shah Abdali, the Afghan invader, was advancing towards Bengal.

Thus ended the second bout between the English and Siraj-ud-daula, who returned with his army to Murshidabad. Clive was well satisfied with the outcome. 'As this success has probably saved the Company, this is a proper time to push my interest,' he told his father. With this in mind, he wrote to several Directors, as well as to Fox, to Lord Hardwicke, to the Archbishop of Canterbury and to the Secretary of War, Lord Barrington, whom he had met during his Parliamentary attempt.[35] To his father and his noble friends, he gave the impression that the attack on the Nawab's camp was a victory; to the Directors, who would have had other accounts of it, he painted a less glowing picture. Instead, he appealed to their mercantile instincts, assuring them that 'as a civilian' he put the blessings of peace before military glory.[36] Already Clive showed his skill as a propagandist, and in gauging the likely reactions of others; though the latter ability was only sporadic, and he could at times be strangely insensitive to public opinion. To his father alone he revealed his latest ambition, which was to become 'Governor-General of India'.[37] Again, one can see the fine eighteenth-century balance between selfish motives and the public good – he wanted this hypothetical office for himself, yet also advocated its creation because he realized that the three Presidencies of Madras, Calcutta and Bombay could no longer afford to pursue independent and often conflicting policies as they had hitherto done. He had come here as a Madrasser; now, without losing sight of Madras, he was primarily concerned with the future of Bengal.

2

Three days after the February Treaty was signed, the Committee considered whether it might not be possible 'to force the Nawab into better terms'.[38] Certainly the three lakhs which he had promised for private losses fell far short of the estimated two million sterling. And as regards the Company, full compensation was limited to what the Nawab himself had taken; the much greater losses caused by the plundering of his troops were merely to be settled 'as his justice shall think reasonable'.[39] Clive and Killpatrick thought it unwise for the English to demand better terms in their present weak state, while sympathizing with the private sufferers, 'being considerable sufferers ourselves'. They did not mention the Nawab's promise to reimburse them.[40]

It was far from certain that the Nawab would keep the existing terms, as long as there was a chance of his joining with the French. There could be no true settlement until the French had either been driven out of Chandernagore, or else tied by an old-style neutrality agreement. Clive had thought about the capture of Chandernagore when he was still at Madras. Such a step, however, required the permission of the Nawab; otherwise, it would arouse his wrath as well as his deep-seated fears. Although some of his remarks at the time of the treaty could be taken as implying permission, his visit to Chandernagore on his way back to Murshidabad when he granted the French privileges similar to those he had just granted the English made it clear that he would not readily allow their destruction. His policy was to play off the two foreign nations against each other, so that neither should dominate.

The English, however, hoped that the Nawab could be prevailed upon to abandon the French, and they accordingly sent William Watts, one of the Bengal Committee, 'to urge the point' at the Nawab's Durbar or court.[41] As the archetype of that key figure of British India, the Resident, Watts was well chosen. The Nawab thought him 'a helpless, poor and innocent man'; but while being sincere, upright and apparently guileless, he was if anything over-suspicious, and well versed in the subtleties of the Oriental mind.

Watts was accompanied by another archetypal figure, the merchant, Omichand,[42] who was everyone's idea of the worst sort of Indian tycoon, immensely rich and infinitely slimy. This bearded Sikh from the Punjab had lived at Calcutta for forty years, becoming one of the largest—and worst—landlords in the town. He had saltpetre contracts with the English, and had long acted as agent for the Company's annual 'investment' or purchase of Indian goods for shipment to Europe. More recently, however, he had fallen from favour, so that, like his friend, Khwaja Wajid, he was suspected of having been an instigator of the Nawab's attack; on which grounds he had been imprisoned.[43]

The choice of so dubious a colleague for Watts is explained by the fact that the Nawab had asked Omichand to represent him in his dealings with the English.[44] And while he thus had the Nawab's ear, he would have been willing to play the English game, so as to get back into their good graces. Even before he and Watts reached their destination, he showed his worth by buying over the deputy-*faujdar* of Hughli. The name of this official

STRINGER LAWRENCE
by Sir Joshua Reynolds

ROBERT ORME
Bust by Joseph Nollekens

GEORGE PIGOT
by George Willison

THE ROCK OF TRICHINOPOLY
by Francis Swain Ward

FORT WILLIAM, CALCUTTA, 1754
by Jan Van Ryne

was to become as much a byword for Hindustani cunning as that of Omichand himself—for he was none other than the Brahmin Nundcomar,[45] who now started his long flirtation with the English that was to lead him eventually to an English gallows.

Nundcomar told Omichand that the Nawab had ordered him to give military assistance to the French, should they be attacked by the English. (As a sign of the Nawab's peaceful intentions, he also had orders to assist the English in the event of their suffering a French attack.) He was prepared to withhold such help from the French in return for a promise of 12,000 rupees. 'If you approve of giving this present,' Watts told Clive, 'all that you have to say to the bearer of this letter is *Golaub que Foul* or "a rose flower".'[46] 'The rose flower' was to become the word for English bribery.

Clive and Watson had anticipated the blooming of that not-so-sensitive plant by making their preparations for the attack on Chandernagore. In fact, Clive wanted to march and besiege the place and then, if the Nawab objected too strongly, to desist and 'make a merit of doing it'.[47] On February 18, he and his troops left the camp at Barnagul and crossed the river. But three days later the rosebuds were withered by a cold blast from the north. The Nawab wrote absolutely forbidding an attack on Chandernagore, and accusing the English of breaking the treaty by planning further hostilities against himself.[48]

There was nothing for it now but a neutrality agreement. The French deputies came to Calcutta and a treaty was drawn up. And then, when all seemed settled, Watson refused to sign the treaty until it had first been ratified by the supreme French government at Pondicherry.*[49]

Watson's refusal to sign brought a typical Clive outburst: 'All the world will certainly think that we are men of a trifling, insignificant disposition, or that we are men without principles.'[50] He threatened to return immediately to Madras, a threat which was none too serious.[51] The Committee

* Unlike the three English presidencies, which were independent of each other, the French possessions in India all came under the supreme government at Pondicherry. Watson argued that a provisional neutrality which might end after a few weeks if it was learnt that Pondicherry refused to confirm the treaty, would throw away the advantage to the French, giving them time to build up their forces. But the Admiral's slowness in raising his objection made it look as if he had in fact changed his mind when he heard of the arrival of the reinforcements from Bombay. He also at this time received the official Admiralty notice of the declaration of war against France, and he was carrying on a private correspondence with the Nawab which might, after all, have led to his granting permission for the attack on Chandernagore.

asked for an immediate attack on Chandernagore as being the only alternative; but Watson, with strange perverseness, objected to that too. Clive was growing tired of the Admiral's vagaries, but he warned them that a victory against the Nawab and the French together would be 'very precarious', and foretold a hundred years of British Indian history with the words, 'If you attack Chandernagore, you cannot stop there, you must go further.'[52] As the days went on, he became increasingly cautious, and insisted on having the Nawab's permission in writing, not just verbally.

Meanwhile, Watts, who was convinced of the Nawab's insincerity, was urging Clive to capture Chandernagore and face him with a *fait accompli*.[53] A tough line, he reckoned, was the only way of getting him to fulfil the articles of the treaty: 'His governing principle or reigning passion is fear.'[54] Certainly the Nawab delayed paying the first instalment of the money and handing over the factory at Cossimbazar until he had received an ultimatum from Watson[55] and was being threatened by an outside invader. But this was only a month after the treaty was signed—knowing the ways of Bengali officials, one doubts if it could have been any sooner.* Clive trusted the Nawab more than Watts did.[56]

In his efforts to clear the way for an attack on Chandernagore, Watts was faced with the necessity, as he put it, of 'opposing corruption to corruption, making friends of the Mammon of Unrighteousness'.[57] It was a duel with his French opposite number, Jean Law,† nephew of the Scottish financier, who was likewise obliged to resort to these methods, though every bit as much a gentleman as Watts himself. The rose grew more vigorously than the lily; Watts followed up his success with Nundcomar by buying over the chief of the Nawab's intelligence service. According to Law's own account, Watts had little need for such outlay, for most of the notables were already with him, seeing in an English victory a means of replacing the Nawab, whom they hated. This, he maintained, was particularly true of the Seths, though they concealed

* Certainly Watson showed himself ignorant of the methods of the East when he wrote of the Nawab's intentions: 'It is now three weeks since the peace commenced in which many articles were proposed by him. Are they yet complied with?' (S. C. Hill, *Bengal in 1756–7*, London 1905, Vol. II, p. 269). The hard-headed Yorkshireman at Cossimbazar, Francis Sykes, reckoned that everything would be fulfilled in time, 'if the Colonel writes frequently threatening letters' (Powis Collection, Box 22, Sykes to Walsh, March 9, 1757).

† Chief of the French factory at Cossimbazar; the much abler brother of Jacques Law, who commanded the French troops at Trichinopoly.

their true sympathies from Watts. Even Khwaja Wajid, who largely depended on French trade, thought it worth keeping in with the English and so he showed Watts the correspondence between the Nawab and the French, which he was handling.[58]

In believing all this, however, one must allow for Law's self-pity, the major fault of an otherwise brave and competent soldier and administrator. It must also be remembered that he was writing after the event, and trying to excuse his own failure. And being, even more than Watts—or for that matter, Clive—unsympathetic towards the Indian mind, which he believed to be chiefly motivated by 'fear and greed', it is possible that he saw politics in what was just an antipathy to him personally. If, as he makes out, he was for ever prophesying the destruction of the Nawab's regime—as though endowed with the second sight of his Highland ancestors*—he cannot have been very popular; the great men of Murshidabad would have preferred the apparently easy-going Watts to this Caledonian Cassandra in their midst.

Law's only hope was to appeal directly to the Nawab, and to work on his fear of the English. Watts countered by protesting that the English were peaceful. When the Nawab's suspicions were aroused by the news that Clive and his army had crossed the river, Omichand again turned up trumps. He told the Nawab that though he had lived in Calcutta for forty years, he had never once known the English to break their word. The Nawab was so impressed that he cancelled the order he had given for troops to be sent to assist the French.[59]

Omichand also took the opportunity to remind the Nawab of the consequences of an invasion by Bussy, who was reported to be about to enter Bengal from the south—he would end up as a French puppet, like Salabat Jang. At least one writer believes the Bussy scare to have been invented by Clive,[60] but there is no doubt that it originated with the French, who thought it would impress the Nawab, not realizing that it provided the English with a useful anti-French bogey.† Such was the Nawab's instability that towards the end of February he actually wrote to the bogeyman himself, asking for *his* help;[61] though in his calmer moments he would have liked nothing less than for his prayer to be heard.

Bussy was not the only bogey haunting the Nawab at this time.

* The Laws were in fact a Lowland family, but Jean Law's grandmother was a Campbell.

† Law seems genuinely to have thought that Bussy was coming (Hill, *op. cit.*, Vol. III, p. 187).

Abdali the Afghan, having overthrown the Mogul, was reported to be even closer to Bengal. The Nawab decided to march with his army to Patna, the capital of the province of Bihar, further up the Ganges, so as to oppose him; and played into the hands of the English by asking for their help[62] – for which he offered to pay them a lakh a month. He first wrote to Watson, who for some reason told neither Clive nor the Committee about it, but proceeded to negotiate with him single-handed.[63] Watson's refusal to sign the neutrality agreement may have been on account of this private diplomacy, which in the event came to nothing.

When Watson's 'shuffling' over the neutrality agreement had just about driven the Committee to the end of their tether,[64] Clive received a letter from the Nawab repeating his request for English military help against Abdali.[65] He reacted without hesitation, read the letter to the Committee and proposed that his troops should march northward on the excuse of going to help the Nawab, and in the hope that they would have permission to attack Chandernagore by the time they arrived there. In a committee of four, Clive and Killpatrick carried this opinion against the opposition of the peaceable Richard Becher, and the whifflings of Drake, which were voted 'no opinion at all'.[66] A somewhat dubious majority, as Clive's enemies were later to point out.

Clive and his troops moved northward on March 8, passing through flat fields of green and brown dotted with hardwoods, and by waterways coated with lotus so that the high-prowed boats on them appeared to be rising from a lawn. They marched leisurely, taking three days to cover the twenty-odd miles between Calcutta and Chandernagore. The French Council enquired anxiously as to their intentions, and Clive replied with this remarkable statement: 'I very sincerely declare to you that at this present time I have no intention to attack your settlement. If I should alter my mind, I shall not fail to advise you of it.'[67]

Cynical words, perhaps, yet literally speaking true. Clive did not intend to attack 'at this present time', but only later if circumstances were favourable, when he would – as he did – give the French adequate notice. He had already assured the Nawab, as 'a convincing proof of my sincerity', that on reaching Chandernagore he would 'wait without committing any hostilities' until he heard from him.[68] And indeed, he continued to insist to Watts that an attack on Chandernagore was unthinkable without the Nawab's consent.[69] But whilst waiting to hear from the Nawab, he took steps to embarrass the French by driving away their coolies and hangers-on.[70]

It would be easy to believe that Clive intended to attack Chandernagore, regardless of the Nawab, from the moment he left Calcutta; but this is to forget that there was another and perfectly genuine reason for his march, which was to join the Nawab against the Afghan invader. Clive took the Abdali menace seriously. 'If this plunderer get [*sic*] into the Province there will be an end to the Company's affairs for some time,' he told Pigot.[71] While to Orme he wrote, with a fine disregard for geography: 'I am going to Patna, or Delhi, or somewhere.'[72] Chandernagore was, with luck, to be captured on the way.[73]

By the time he reached Chandernagore, Clive was less insistent that the Nawab's consent was necessary. He had been in touch with Nundcomar, who still promised to stop his troops from helping the French. 'If the promise is fulfilled,' Clive told Watson, 'I shall look upon the Nawab's consent as obtained.'[74] He was inclined to be less cautious, having heard that part of the Nawab's army had already left for Patna, and also that the *Cumberland* had arrived. He had also managed to pick a quarrel with the French, whom he accused of giving his soldiers beer laced with arak so that they could be abducted while drunk.[75]

On March 12, the squadron was instructed to proceed up river, and a day or so later, Clive gave the French at Chandernagore the promised warning by summoning them to surrender.*[76] Having received no answer to his summons, Clive attacked Chandernagore from the west or landward side. This was his first action against the French since the Siege of Pondicherry, and the only time he ever commanded against a European enemy. He now had an army of 2500 including the Bombay reinforcements, and 200 sepoys who arrived from Madras after the action had started. The French had 237 regular soldiers, some of them sick, and 167 trained sepoys,

* By this time, Watson had received a letter from the Nawab which appeared to contain the long-awaited permission. The Nawab had dictated the letter after losing his temper with Law. His secretary, bribed by Watts, had then cooked it a little. This dubious document did not reach Watson until the night of the 12th, when he was already preparing to move. Watts's claim that it 'cut the Gordian knot' is therefore false, at any rate as regards the Admiral and the Committee. As for Clive, he heard about it from Watson in a letter written on the 13th, which may or may not have reached him by the time he commenced hostilities. But from the way in which the Admiral assumed that the attack on Chandernagore was about to be launched, and only mentioned the Nawab's letter as an afterthought, it seems that for Clive, too, the Gordian knot had already been cut. Watson's previous letter to Clive, written on March 11, implies that Clive's mind had even then been made up in favour of attacking without further delay (Powis Collection, Box X).

together with 400 motley troops including sailors, volunteers and English deserters. They also had 2000 troops on loan from the Nawab – under the control of Nundcomar.

Like Calcutta, Chandernagore had its fort by the river side, called Fort d'Orléans, built on more solid and Vaubanesque lines than Fort William. It was, however, in poor repair, and its walls were obstructed by the usual clutter of buildings. Pierre Renault, the Director, had been working hard to clear these away; but there were many houses still standing.

The French fought bravely among the burning houses, but by the 15th they were obliged to abandon the town and all the outworks to Clive's troops and retire into the fort. Thanks to the 'rose flower',[77] Nundcomar withdrew the 2000 loaned troops – on the pretext that the Nawab's victorious colours should not be involved in the French disgrace. It seems that the French officer in charge of these troops, by name of Ducré, had also to be bribed.[78] Clive had offered free pardon to English deserters and rewards to officers who came over – he is said to have announced this to the defenders by means of notes fixed to arrows[79] – and as a result the only artillery officer in the Fort, the one-armed Finn, Cossart de Terraneau, defected to him.[80]

Having captured the town and the outworks, Clive took things fairly easily until the arrival of the ships, which were delayed by fog, tides and lack of wind. He kept the French on the alert by cannonading, and set about constructing two batteries, to cover the river approach. This work had to be carried on under fire, and at one stage the enemy shot brought down a neighbouring verandah, which buried some of Clive's coolies under its rubble.

As he waited for the ships, Clive's main fear was that the Nawab should change his mind and send reinforcements to the French. The first few days seemed hopeful – the Nawab wrote to him swearing eternal friendship, though saying nothing of Chandernagore.[81] Then, on the 15th, it was heard in Murshidabad that Abdali's intentions were peaceful. The Nawab's tone changed; he told Clive he no longer needed his help, then ordered the English to make peace with the French, threatening to march against them if they did not.[82]

Clive hastened to smooth the Nawab down. 'I shall always be ready to hazard my life for your service,' he wrote, 'God only knows how great my desire is to have the pleasure of embracing you.'[83] Two days later, he pleaded like a naughty schoolboy. 'I beseech Your Excellency that my enemies may not . . . make you determine that for so small a place, already more than half conquered, and that must be mine in a day or two at farthest, my honour and reputation shall be called in question, I who till this day have by the blessing of God been victorious in every battle I have fought.'[84]

Meanwhile, Law was also pleading, and prevailed upon the Nawab to send off Manik Chand and another commander named Rai Durlabh with 5000 troops each to keep the peace; but soon afterwards, at the instigation of the Seths, they were ordered to withdraw.[85] As a last resort, the Nawab told Clive that Bussy was coming to the rescue of his compatriots; but Clive turned this round to imply that the Nawab was afraid of the bogey-man, and assured him that he had nothing to fear: 'I am no boaster, it is not my character, but I will venture to say that half the force I have is sufficient for any force he can bring against you.'[86] The Nawab could only return the compliment and assure Clive of *his* help against the imaginary invader.[87] By now, he had heard a premature report that Chandernagore had fallen, so he backed the winning side and wished Clive victory.[88]

The squadron had negotiated the tricky river passage by the 19th, and anchored downstream of the town. Now came the hardest navigational feat of all, for the French had blocked the final approach with sunken ships, booms and chains. However, the booms and chains were cut, and one of the *Kent*'s officers, observing the position of the sunken ships from their masts which appeared above the water at low tide, reckoned there was room for one ship at a time to pass between them.[89] So by a miracle of piloting, the *Kent* and the *Tiger* edged up alongside the Fort early on the morning of the 23rd, with the *Salisbury* some way behind them. The fire from Clive's batteries prevented the guns of the Fort from troubling the ships during the critical approach. When they were close enough, the *Kent* and the *Tiger* opened fire with all their guns, and at the same time Clive cannonaded from the landward side and his troops kept up a deadly musketry from the roofs of the houses.

The guns of the Fort did havoc to the ships, now that they were so close. Among the *Kent*'s officers, Watson himself and one other were alone in not being killed or wounded. Watson was lucky, for he was in the thick of the fight. At one moment he was told that the French were pointing a gun directly at him, to which he answered: 'Why then, they shall have a fair shot.'[90] And he stood still and smiled, while the ball passed close to him. But his smile turned to tears when he saw Captain Speke and his midshipman son Billy lying wounded together. Billy Speke submitted cheerfully to the horrors of amputation, his only concern being about his father; but in the end it was he who fell a victim to the inevitable blood-poisoning, whereas Captain Speke recovered.[91]

But though the ships took great punishment, their guns were too much for the Fort. After three hours, the walls were shattered and the batteries covered with dead. At a quarter past nine that morning, Renault surrendered. His losses and those of the English were about the same, 200 killed and wounded. On the English side, the casualties were almost entirely confined to the squadron. Clive had taken good care of his men, but it was bad for his reputation. To the light-hearted series of intrigues and walkover victories which were to make him master of Bengal by accident, the carnage on the decks of the *Kent* and the *Tiger* was the reverse of the medal. And it was, moreover, British blood, whereas in Clive's battles most of the killed and wounded were sepoys.

The spoils from Fort d'Orléans included full-length portraits of Louis XV and Queen Marie Leczinska, which were to adorn Government House, Calcutta, down to the present century.[92] It was fitting that the French King and Queen should thus become prisoners of the English, for the capture of Chandernagore broke French power in Bengal and was, as Clive put it, 'an unexpressable blow to the French company'.[93] Pondicherry and the French Islands lost most of their trade, as well as their food supplies.* From the point of view of private gain, however, the capture of Chandernagore was a disappointment; for the Fort yielded little in the way of plunder, the French being short of money and having sold off most of their merchandise. Knowing Clive's ambition, one wonders if he did not feel a certain sense of anticlimax at the prospect of returning to Madras. However, the outbreak of the Monsoon gave him an excuse to stay in Bengal for another four months.

* It was the French Islands, and notably Mauritius, which provisioned the French navy in Indian waters; so the loss of their food supply from Bengal was a serious strategic blow to the French.

CHAPTER X

The Conspiracy

> No oath which superstition can devise, no hostage however precious, inspires a hundredth part of the confidence which is produced by the 'yea, yea', and 'nay, nay', of a British envoy.
>
> MACAULAY

I

'I am persuaded you will be pleased at my success,' wrote Clive to the Nawab after the capture of Chandernagore.[1] His tongue must have been as much in his cheek as was the Nawab's when he replied that Clive's victory gave him 'inexpressible pleasure'.[2] And when, at the same time, the Nawab sent Clive a pair of leopards, trained to hunt deer,[3] one is tempted to suspect that he hoped they would turn on their recipient.

Now that the crisis was over, the Nawab himself planned to go hunting,[4] while Watts reported that the compensation money was coming in.[5] Relations between the English and Siraj-ud-daula could at last have set fair, if only both sides had not mistrusted each other. The English were certain that as soon as Clive's troops and Watson's ships had gone, the Nawab would not only repudiate the treaty but attack them once again. The Nawab, having been so foolish as to let the English get the upper hand, now made the mistake of not accepting the situation, and relying on their good faith.

Instead he showed signs of panic and even tried to dam the river to prevent Watson's ships from reaching Murshidabad. He hoped to restore the balance by calling in Bussy, writing to him of 'the perfidy of the English' at the same time as he was congratulating Clive.[6] The English, through Khwaja Wajid, learnt of this correspondence, and their suspicions were confirmed. It was now *their* turn to be scared of the bogeyman, who in fact was only 200 miles away in Orissa. The Bussy threat would continue so long as there was a centre of French intrigue close to the Nawab at Cossimbazar, where Law had collected a garrison of a hundred men who had either escaped from Chandernagore, or come from the other up-country French factory at Dacca. So it was necessary for the French to be driven out of Bengal 'root and branch',[7] and Clive started to work on the Nawab with this in view.

Hitherto, Clive's diplomacy had been makeshift, aimed at getting things settled one way or the other before he was recalled to the Coast. Now we see him with a fixed purpose, and thanks to the Monsoon, a clear four months in which to achieve it. From working in an uneasy partnership with Watson, to whom he was, after all, junior, he now acted alone, the Admiral having taken offence at the Nawab's slackness in answering his letters and retired from the contest.

Clive explained to Watts how he intended to handle the Nawab. 'The bent of our politics hitherto has been by haughty and by submissive letters such as the occasion required to persuade him to abandon the French to us. We must in pursuit of that system now endeavour to convince him that what we have done is best for both him and us.' To convince him that the English did not intend to extort provinces from him, as Bussy had from Salabat Jang, but that all they wanted was to continue as merchants while keeping a strong enough force to protect themselves, and him, from their enemies.[8]

At the same time, he regarded the Nawab as 'a weak and timorous prince, the spring of all his actions seems fear and whilst that is kept up by a respectable force he will always be very cautious how he undertakes anything against us'.[9] The Nawab had to be made to fear the English as well as to trust them. Clive knew just when to threaten and when to be tactful. Thus, when he moved his camp a mile to the north of Chandernagore, he did so not only to get out of reach of the arak, but also 'to strike some awe into the Nawab'.[10] However, he reassured him that he would be withdrawing the greater part of his troops to Calcutta as soon as there was accommodation ready for them.[11]

In pressing for his main object, he tried to show that this was for the Nawab's own good. 'There wants nothing to fix the peace of your kingdom, but that you would deliver up to us the French[12] . . . We shall then be without rivals, and our whole force ready to obey your commands.'[13] Clive's dream was to join the Nawab against Abdali, who still remained in the offing; this would convince him of the strength of the English, and of their sincerity at the same time. Such an expedition also opened up a prospect of private gain, for the Nawab would certainly have rewarded Clive richly for helping him to drive the invader away.

As he was liable to do when going all out to make a case, Clive sometimes used arguments which were not valid. He spoke of 'the treaty you have made with us that my enemies should be yours',[14] when no such treaty existed, but only a vague promise in a letter. He referred to how, when the English and the French had seized each other's subordinate factories in the south, the local potentates had not interfered; as though this were a convention, rather than just a sign of the breakdown of their authority.[15]

But while ceaselessly pressing his point about the French, and calling on the Nawab 'in the name of God and His Prophet' to fulfil the outstanding articles of the treaty,[16] Clive did his best to oblige him in other ways. He promised compensation for the debts which the French owed to many of his subjects. More significant, he offered to hand over Chandernagore to him once the fort was demolished, thus proving that the English had no territorial ambitions.

Suddenly, as though in a panic, the Nawab gave Law notice to quit. On April 13 the bewildered French Scot and his officers were summoned to the palace. They were kept waiting several hours while the Nawab disported himself in the harem, and were given what Law thought was 'a very bad dinner'. At length they were told to surrender to Watts. Law would not hear of this and, forcing his way into the Nawab's presence, managed to obtain permission to go to Patna with his troops.[17] So they set out on the first stage of a four-year odyssey among the courts of northern India. 'Remember my words, we shall never meet again' was Law's farewell to the Nawab.[18]

Clive showed no gratitude to the Nawab for dismissing Law's party, and demanded that they should be captured. The Nawab, who had recently suffered one of Clive's homilies on how the English always played the game, was able to reply that he, too, abided by Queensberry rules, and would not 'bind and deliver up the weak'.[19] From Law's own account, it seems that in letting the French go, rather than handing them over to the English, he was motivated purely by kindness. But the English suspected him of double-dealing and were confirmed in this belief a fortnight later when he actually did ask Law to return and help him against them. By this time, however, his attitude towards the English had changed.

2

It is hard to know whether or not the Nawab intended to fulfil his obligations under the treaty. He was certainly slow in 'parting with the ready money'[20]—he paid a lakh in April and asked for a year in which to pay the next four.[21] He was later to demand that the English should sign a paper stating that he had discharged his obligations to them in full, though he cannot have seriously imagined that they would agree to this. In other respects than money, he appeared to be doing his best. By the middle of April, much of what had been taken from the factories at Cossimbazar and Dacca had been restored[22]*—even the cannon, though he was himself short of guns.

Towards the middle of April, Luke Scrafton was sent to join Watts at the Durbar. If in Watts we can recognize the nineteenth- or early twentieth-century English sahib, Scrafton, though equally a public-school product, belongs to the tougher, more sophisticated world of the big deal and the takeover bid. Sallower even than most of his fellow-countrymen in the India of those days, he looked the cynic he was.

He set to work with gusto, and gave Clive a detailed account of his first audience with the Nawab, even to how he had taken the opportunity, while waiting to be received, of visiting a gentleman whose nose had been cut off by Nadir Shah, and who wore 'a clay substitute'. The Nawab recognized Scrafton from their previous meeting in Omichand's garden house, just before the attack on his camp, which might have been embarrassing. Instead, he 'fell a laughing and shaking his head' and exclaimed: 'Give him a horse and a dress, no, let it be an elephant.' Scrafton was duly arrayed in Indian costume, though he only got a horse.

* The fact that the Nawab restored the effects belonging to the factories at Cossimbazar and Dacca and not those of Fort William was taken by the cynical Scrafton as a sign that he intended to break faith—on the grounds that what was returned to the up-country factories remained in his power. The real reason why he was unable to restore the Fort William property was that it had been plundered by Manik Chand, who was slow in parting with it.

A few days later, Omichand fell ill. Scrafton went to visit him, and in the security of his bedroom the Sikh was really able to talk. The Nawab, he said, was certain that the English would never forgive him for the harm he had done them. Thus his friendship would never be sincere. If Abdali invaded the country, it would be different; but if that did not happen and if the Nawab in any way deviated from the treaty, there would be nothing for it but to set up another Nawab.[23] Thus was the Indian-born scheme that was to make the British the rulers of India first put across to a Briton – a Briton with a self-admitted taste for 'politics and power'.[24]

The conspiracy against Siraj-ud-daula had been building up for several months. Its chief instigators were the Seths, who provide an example of how Bengal, though ruled by the Muslim Nawab by right of Mogul conquest, was run by the indigenous Hindus. As bankers, they controlled most of the finances of the country, for there was no such thing as a national treasury. Alivardi, who largely owed his position as Nawab to their support, showed them great favour; but Siraj-ud-daula neglected them and insulted them in public, even threatening them with forcible circumcision.

The Seths might have taken these insults had there not also been economic considerations. Much of their wealth depended on the existence of the foreign trading settlements. In fact their rise, like that of the whole Bengal merchant class, had been tied up with the growing demand in Europe for muslins, calicos and other Indian products. So it was natural that when Siraj-ud-daula quarrelled with the Europeans the Seths should have become alarmed. The attack on Calcutta caused untold damage to trade – given the Nawab's unreliable temperament, there was no saying when it might not have happened again, even though his better self meant no harm to the English. Although the religious issue was not an immediate cause of trouble between Siraj-ud-daula and his Hindu subjects – indeed, his favourite, Mohan Lal, was a Hindu – it meant that the Hindus did not worry overmuch about European domination. To them, the Christians were no more alien than the Muslims. If anything, they would have welcomed the growth of European power as a check on Muslim despotism. However much a Nawab may have favoured Hindus like the Seths, however useful they may have been to him, there was always the fear that he would cast a covetous eye on their wealth.

Other notables joined the Seths in their conspiracy. They included Manik Chand and the minister and general Rai Durlabh, who resented being ordered about by Mohan Lal. Most significant of all was the support of Mir Jafar, the Paymaster of the army and the most powerful figure in the Muslim military aristocracy. The Nawab's mistrust had led him to plant cannon against Mir Jafar's palace, thus making an enemy of his chief supporter.

To obtain English help, the conspirators had to prevent the English and the Nawab from coming to a proper settlement. Law, who knew about the conspiracy before the English did, believed that the Seths encouraged the Nawab to be dilatory over the articles of the treaty.[25] They also made mischief between the Nawab and the English agents. It was the Seths and their fellow-conspirators who told Watts that the Nawab had threatened to impale him, or cut off his head.[26]* And, according to Scrafton, it was Manik Chand and others who, about April 20, incited the Nawab to one of his periodic anti-English outbursts, to coincide with their efforts to 'sell' the conspiracy to the English.[27] As usual, his mood quickly changed; but the news of his outburst reached Clive in a letter from Scrafton which also spoke of the tempting terms that could be obtained from a new Nawab in return for setting him up.[28]

Now followed the most critical week of all, when Clive and the Committee waited for more definite details about the conspiracy, and also for news of Abdali and a rebellious chief in the province of Bihar, with either or both of whom the Nawab might have become embroiled. Meanwhile, Clive made one last effort for a settlement. 'Trust me,' he begged the Nawab, 'and I will be faithful to you for ever.' He even agreed to supply him with some cannon he required.[29] That this was a genuine last attempt at diplomacy is proved by the accompanying show which would have been unnecessary and unwise had it been merely a blind. Clive sent for Nundcomar at midnight—his choice of hour denotes a keen sense of psychology—and when he refused to come, sent for him again, just before dawn. This time the reluctant Brahmin obeyed the summons, and went to the English camp, where he found Clive and his colleagues watching the army exercising on Chandernagore plain. After Nundcomar had been made to endure two and a half hours of this 'amusement', Clive took him aside and complained to him of the Nawab's bad behaviour.[30]

Nundcomar duly reported this demonstration to the Nawab, but added the false intelligence that Clive intended to march on Murshidabad the

* Most accounts give the impression that these threats were made to Watts's face, whereas they were only reported to him. Clive, with his customary exaggeration, told Pigot that the Nawab threatened to impale Watts 'twice a week' whereas according to the reports it happened on two occasions in all (Hill, *op. cit.*, Vol. II, p. 368).

very next day. So the report, far from having a sobering effect, put the Nawab 'all in a flame'.[31] His temper grew still worse when he heard from his spies that Clive was sending ammunition to the factory at Cossimbazar in a convoy of boats. The boats, when searched, were found to be empty; but the Nawab was now so angry with the English that he recalled Law,[32] and once again ordered Mir Jafar and his troops to march southward.[33]

All this, coupled with the news that Abdali was retiring and the Bihar trouble at an end, sealed the Nawab's fate.[34] An immediate decision was necessary, so that the military action could take place before the Rains. The plot became more definite, and the conspirators picked on Mir Jafar to succeed Siraj-ud-daula as Nawab. On May 1, a Committee consisting of Clive, Drake, Killpatrick and Becher decided unanimously to support the 'revolution'. They justified their decision with a string of alleged proofs that Siraj-ud-daula did not intend to keep the peace or comply with the treaty; and also with the more plausible argument that as a revolution was likely to take place whether the English gave their assistance or not, it was as well to take part in it and thus obtain advantageous terms from the new Nawab in return for giving him military support.

The terms which the Committee intended to impose on Mir Jafar were certainly advantageous; they included full compensation for all the previous year's losses, those incurred by private individuals as well as by the Company; together with a grant of more land around Calcutta and other concessions.[35] The Committee also agreed that Mir Jafar should give a private undertaking to make them a present of twelve lakhs, together with forty lakhs for the army and navy.[36] That the 'revolution' would thus be a means of enriching themselves cannot have failed to influence Clive and his colleagues in their decision to support it; however much they may have protested – and indeed, believed – that they did so purely through disinterested motives.

3

The terms were submitted to Watts, as proposals for a treaty with Mir Jafar. While this treaty was being negotiated, Clive had to distract the Nawab's attention from what was afoot by means of 'soothing' letters. 'I desire nothing so much as to live in peace and friendship with you[37] . . .

I almost despair of enjoying Your Excellency's friendship while you listen to the idle stories and falsities of men of mean extraction.'[38] Lest the Nawab should be suspicious at too great a change of tone, he took care to include the occasional reproach.

To the Victorian who liked to think of the British Empire as founded on valour and fair play, this was a distasteful chapter in the history of the Imperial race. 'Nothing can justify the dissimulation which Clive stooped to practise,' wrote Macaulay, just back from the established yet still heroic British India of the 1830s. But the standards of the Raj in its morning vigour cannot be applied to the representative of a small community of merchants in a strange country who unexpectedly finds himself playing a single-handed game against that country's prince, with no rules to guide him. A game is how we should regard it, as indeed Clive himself did; perhaps not cricket, but anyhow some elaborate Oriental form of poker.

If Clive deserves criticism at this juncture, it is for the way in which, having decided to overthrow the Nawab, he proceeded to blacken him: from being merely of 'a wavering pusillanimous disposition',[39] Siraj-ud-daula became 'a compound of everything that is bad' and 'a monster'.[40] But then Clive was a born propagandist. The modern general leaves the work of denigrating the enemy to the politician, who in turn leaves it largely to the Press. Clive had to be all three.

As well as beguiling the Nawab, and keeping his army ready to march at twelve hours' notice in support of Mir Jafar, Clive had to cope with the other members of the Committee, who objected to his single-handed role. But worse than these labours in the humid heat of Bengal was the agonizing day-to-day wait. 'I heartily wish matters were brought to a conclusion,' he wrote as early as May 10. 'Every day endangers a discovery.'[41] He had to wait another month, which for someone of Clive's nervous temperament must have been hardly bearable.

He waited in pleasant surroundings, having moved into the country house of the French director at Ghyretty south of Chandernagore. Standing in a large park by the side of the river, it was a palace rather than a house, with Ionic colonnades, curving Baroque steps and painted ceilings. In those anxious days and nights beneath goddesses made more than ever Rococo by the lizards that crawled across their damp-stained bosoms, and the bats fluttering beneath them like demoniac putti, Clive must have longed for the love and gaiety of Margaret, for he suddenly wrote and asked her to join him.

Having moved to Ghyretty, Clive kept part of his forces near him at

Chandernagore, and sent the rest back to Calcutta. They were ready to return by boat 'at a minute's warning';[42] the reason for sending them to Calcutta was to induce the Nawab to withdraw *his* forces to Murshidabad, so that Mir Jafar could confer with the other conspirators, and conclude the treaty with Watts. But the Nawab failed to respond. 'I know not how to refrain from showing my resentment at the Nawab's bad faith in not withdrawing his army,' wrote Clive, forgetting that he, too, was in bad faith.[43]

Then occurred one of those pieces of luck which always seemed to come to Clive when he needed them most. A messenger arrived, bringing what purported to be an offer from the Marathas to help the English and the other conspirators against the Nawab.[44] Clive suspected the messenger to be the Nawab's *agent provocateur*; on the other hand, he did not wish to offend the Marathas if the offer were genuine. So a tactful reply was written, to the effect that the English were on good terms with the Nawab and did not require help at present, which would not have done any harm had it fallen into the Nawab's hands.[45] Then Clive had the brilliant idea of letting the Nawab himself see a copy of the Marathas' offer, as a way of convincing him that the English were sincere.[46] Having been shown it by Scrafton, the Nawab 'broke forth into loud acclamations to the Colonel's praise',[47] and two days later, he ordered his troops to return.[48]

Meanwhile, the Committee's terms had been submitted to Mir Jafar by way of his trusted lieutenant Omar Beg, who was in favour with the English, having been kind to some of their womenfolk during the troubles of the previous year. Mir Jafar's reply was to send a blank sheet of paper with his seal on it.[49] Then came a blow. Omichand, up to now so helpful, showed the cloven hoof. He suddenly insisted that he himself should receive five per cent of Siraj-ud-daula's money, and a quarter of his jewels, and that there should be an article in the treaty obliging Mir Jafar to comply with this demand.[50] At the most conservative estimate of Siraj-ud-daula's wealth, this meant that Omichand would receive something like a million sterling.

Whether Omichand also threatened in so many words to betray the conspiracy to the Nawab if this exorbitant demand were not complied with, is not certain. We have Clive's statement that he did, and also that of Watts's colleague at Cossimbazar, Francis Sykes, who said that Omichand had threatened to 'have them all murdered that night'.[51] But these statements were made fifteen years later, after Watts himself was dead.

Writing to Clive at the time, Watts made no mention of any threat—though the threat could have been implied, even if Omichand said nothing.

When he heard about Omichand's blackmail, Clive proposed that two treaties should be drawn up, one real and one fictitious. The article in favour of Omichand would only be included in the fictitious treaty, which was the one that would be shown him. To look convincing, it would have to be signed by the English and Mir Jafar just the same as the real one; but Mir Jafar would be told which of the two was considered binding.[52]

The Committee adopted this plan, which later generations were to regard as the blackest deed of Clive's whole career. He himself defended the morality of it fifteen years later before the Select Committee of the House of Commons: 'He thought art and policy warrantable in defeating the purposes of such a villain, and . . . never made any secret of it. He thinks it warrantable in such a case, and would do it again a hundred times.'[53]

But morality was not the point—not, any rate, to the Victorians. 'Using no arguments but such as Machiavelli might have employed in his conferences with Borgia, we are convinced that Clive was altogether in the wrong,' thundered Macaulay. 'All that we could have gained by imitating the doublings, the evasions, the fictions, the perjuries which have been employed against us, is as nothing, when compared with what we have gained by being the one power in India on whose word reliance can be placed.'

Yet it was easy to be wise after the event. Clive was faced with a crisis calling for immediate action. To have agreed to include the article in favour of Omichand would have antagonized Mir Jafar. To have refused would have been to risk betrayal, and might have endangered the lives of Watts and his companions. There are those who maintain that Clive should have arranged for Omichand to be quietly done away with, as though murder were preferable to dishonouring the Englishman's word. But though Clive could be fierce, vindictive and at times unkind, he seems to have had a reluctance to take human life that was in advance of his time. In any case, to have had Omichand assassinated in Murshidabad would have been dangerous and difficult.

The opposite course would have been to let Omichand have his thirty lakhs—the sum he had agreed to settle for—by deducting it from the amount promised by Mir Jafar to the armed forces and the Committee.

Clive and his colleagues can be accused of preferring their presents to their good name. Yet there was an obvious way of getting out of the difficulty without sacrificing either. The real treaty could have included an article to satisfy Omichand, and Mir Jafar been told privately that he need not comply with it. Omichand's subsequent disappointment could then have been blamed on the new Nawab rather than on the English.*

That he chose the less subtle expedient of the two treaties would suggest that Clive was not merely concerned with getting out of the difficulty, but wished to have the satisfaction of doing Omichand down. Having been inclined to favour him unduly,[54] he would now have been particularly enraged by his ingratitude; and could have impulsively seized on a plan to disappoint him. It was a paradox of Clive's nature that while he was almost always merciful to a defeated army in war, he would punish and persecute those who opposed him in civil life far beyond what was necessary for their defeat; so that the punishment inevitably rebounded on himself.

The impression made by this affair on posterity was rendered worse by 'a strict principle of delicacy' on the part of Watson, which forbade his signing the fictitious treaty.[55] Omichand would have smelt a rat had Watson's signature been missing. 'But', in the words of Macaulay, 'Clive was not a man to do anything by halves. We almost blush to write it. He forged Admiral Watson's name.' More precisely, the forgery was done on Clive's behalf. According to Clive and his friends, it was actually authorized by Watson, whose scruples were confined to signing the document himself. But as Watson only survived the affair by a couple of months, his attitude towards the fictitious treaty is a matter of controversy. According to John Cooke, who was Secretary to the Bengal Select Committee at the time, 'he shrugged up his shoulders and said laughingly that he had not signed it but that he had left it to them to do as they pleased'.[56] Cooke made this statement fifteen years later to the Select Committee of the House of Commons, which also heard from one of Watson's officers, named Brereton, that the Admiral had never given his consent to the signing of his name. Brereton's evidence, however, was inconsistent, and he claimed that Watson objected not merely to the fictitious treaty, but to the whole conspiracy against Siraj-ud-daula.[57] Whereas we know that when Clive first discussed the plan with Watson,

* An anonymous and undated account of this affair in the Powis Collection (Box 73), probably written by Clive himself, states that even if the article in favour of Omichand had been included in the genuine treaty, it 'would never have been executed'.

at the beginning of May, the Admiral's misgivings did not concern its ethics, but its chances of success.

For this reason, and because it was purely a Company matter, he was at first reluctant to allow the King's forces to take part in it;[58] though he later relented and gave Clive his blessing.[59] He went further, and encouraged Clive to make an insincere promise to the Nawab.[60] In fact, at the end of May, he seems to have been in greater harmony with Clive than at any other time, although he knew about the fictitious treaty, having been present at the Committee meeting of the 17th.* It was easy to depict Watson after his death as the bluff, honest sailor who was disgusted with Clive's intrigues; but though he was a brave commander and an attractive personality, he seems to have been a much less straightforward character than this image would suggest.

The two treaties were drafted, the real one on white paper, the false on red. Clive reduced the sum stipulated for Omichand from thirty lakhs to twenty—a neat touch, to disarm his suspicions. 'Flatter Omichand greatly,' he told Watts. 'Tell him . . . that his name will be greater in England than ever it was in India.' Omichand was, in fact, up to more tricks. He divulged some secret information to the Nawab for which he was so handsomely rewarded that the paying out took till ten that night. The information, he assured Watts, was merely a concocted story, intended to throw the Nawab off the scent.[61] Watts, however, suspected that Omichand had told the Nawab about the conspiracy.[62] But if he did, the Nawab's vengeance on the English was slow in coming.

The Nawab must have known there was something afoot, if not through Omichand then certainly through spies or French agents; but he acted with his usual indecision. He suspected enough to ask his powerful neighbour, the Nawab of Oudh, for help. He also left half his troops in his fortified camp at Plassey, twenty miles south of Murshidabad, having assured Clive after the Maratha affair that he would withdraw them all.[63] Yet he dismissed the other half altogether, and further weakened his position by his slowness in paying the troops he kept.[64] And while leaving troops at Plassey he helped the conspirators by recalling Mir Jafar and Rai Durlabh to Murshidabad.

* It has generally been assumed that Watson did not attend this meeting, because his name does not appear in the Proceedings. But according to a letter which Clive wrote two days afterwards, both Watson and his second-in-command, Admiral Pocock, were present. Their names are omitted from the Proceedings because they were not members of the Committee (Hill, *op. cit.*, Vol. II, p. 388).

Whether or not Omichand had given anything away to the Nawab, Watts was determined to make him leave Murshidabad as quickly as possible. At length he was persuaded, and he and Scrafton travelled to Calcutta in palanquins. On the way, he gave his companion the slip and visited Rai Durlabh, who was still at Plassey. Watts suspected Omichand of encouraging Rai Durlabh to raise difficulties, which he proceeded to do after he had joined his fellow-conspirator Mir Jafar at Murshidabad. 'We had better depend on ourselves, and enter into no contract or have any connection with such a set of shuffling, lying, spiritless wretches', he wrote on June 3.[65] He had reason to be frantic. Mir Jafar had been in Murshidabad since May 30, yet he had still not managed to conclude the treaty with him.[66]

Meanwhile the Nawab's vengeance hung like the sword of Damocles over Watts's head, and Clive was showing signs of losing confidence in him. 'Why this delay?' he asked, impatiently. 'Surely you are deceived by those you employ, or you have been deceiving me.'[67] It was one of Clive's worst habits to jump to conclusions about people who were doing their best, though this time he had some reason, being frantic himself. 'The affair is now publicly talked of,' he told Watts, 'and if it does not take place within a short time after the receipt of this, I will set it aside, being determined not to undertake it in the Rains.'[68] There were all kinds of rumours: that the Nawab's best troops had been cut to pieces in Bihar, that Watts's head was being paraded through the streets of Murshidabad on a pole.

By June 5, Rai Durlabh had ceased making difficulties and Watts was at last able to have a secret meeting with Mir Jafar, being carried into his palace in a closed *dooley* such as was used by the women of the harem. Mir Jafar swore upon the Koran, and upon the head of Miran, his son, to keep the treaty. Watts and his two English colleagues now longed to make a bolt for it, but they had to stay until they heard from Clive that he had received the signed and sealed treaties, which were being carried to him by the trusted Omar Beg. While he waited, Watts endured agonies. Relations between the Nawab and Mir Jafar were fast deteriorating. Threatening messages passed from one to the other; Mir Jafar was dismissed from his office of Paymaster and banished from the Durbar.

By June 12, Watts could stand it no longer and he and his two companions, Matthew Collet and Francis Sykes, made their escape. They pretended to be going coursing, and told their servants that they would be back for supper. Once out in the country, they dismissed their grooms and hounds and galloped southward.

They timed their departure well, for Omar Beg had reached Calcutta on the 11th, and Clive's letter telling them to come was already on its way. On the 12th, Clive and the troops at Chandernagore were joined by Killpatrick and all the military from Calcutta, together with 150 sailors lent by Watson on the understanding that they would not, this time, be used as coolies. Next day, June 13, Clive's army marched.

CHAPTER XI

Plassey

Surely the most miserable skirmish ever to be called
a decisive battle.

PHILIP WOODRUFF

I

Clive had an army of 613 European infantry, and 171 artillery in charge of ten field-pieces; together with 91 topasses and 2100 sepoys. The Europeans travelled up the river in boats, the sepoys marched along the road on the west bank. Beyond stretched flat country broken by hard-woods, palms and stretches of jungle. On the 14th, when they were some twenty miles north of Hughli, they were joined by Watts and the other fugitives from Cossimbazar, who gave them encouraging news of the growth of Mir Jafar's party. On the 18th, Coote was sent ahead with a detachment to capture the fort of Katwa, which commanded both the road and the river, and contained a large supply of rice.

Coote quickly captured the fort, and the rest of the troops encamped on the plain around it on the 19th. Having had his first taste of campaigning in the full humid heat of the Bengal June, Clive now had his first experience of the Rains. No sooner had his army reached Katwa than the heavens opened, and there was a downpour of such violence that his troops had to leave their tents and shelter in the huts of Katwa village. Six years earlier, on the road to Arcot, a storm like this had brought Clive good fortune; but here in Bengal it meant that the country would soon be flooded, making military operations impossible. Murshidabad, and the Nawab's camp at Plassey, lay between two branches of the river, on the so-called Island of Cossimbazar. With the river only fordable in one place, it would have been easy enough to ferry the troops across to the island in the boats; but not nearly so easy to get them back again should by any chance the conspiracy have collapsed and the English suffered defeat.

With its success wholly dependent on the intentions of Mir Jafar and the other conspirators, Clive's march to Plassey seems more like the Jameson Raid than a rational military enterprise.[1] Not only did Clive stake everything on Mir Jafar's promises, but he also seems to have been far from clear as to what exactly *had* been promised. All Mir Jafar is recorded as having said he would do was to join the English in the event of an actual engagement between them and the Nawab's army, and perhaps seize the person of the Nawab.[2] But Clive, on his march north, seems to have been under the impression that Mir Jafar would join him with a large body of troops at Katwa, *before* there was any battle.[3] Unless such a promise was conveyed verbally by Omar Beg when he brought the signed treaties, it would seem like wishful thinking on Clive's part. Certainly the letters which Clive and Mir Jafar exchanged during the march northward—one of them sent in a slipper—suggest that the two men were not, so to speak, on the same wavelength.

If Clive took a risk in marching, he was encouraged to do so both by the Committee and by Watts, who reckoned it was now or never. The possible consequences of his defeat have been exaggerated. Clive might have lost his army and his reputation; certainly even a small setback would have destroyed the psychological advantage over the Nawab which he had built up during the past few months. But whether, as is frequently stated, such a defeat would have led to the loss of Calcutta a second time and perhaps even to the loss of Madras, which needed Clive's troops to protect it against the French, is doubtful. True, Calcutta was only garrisoned by a handful of invalids, artillerymen and sepoys; but it was also defended by the guns of the squadron. As for Madras, Clive's troops never went back there anyhow; and yet the settlement managed to hold out.

Clive's misgivings after he had marched were not simply on account of Mir Jafar's failure to do something which he does not seem to have promised. He heard reports that the conspiracy had been exposed and that the Nawab and Mir Jafar were reconciled.[4] The Nawab had in fact attempted to regain Mir Jafar's friendship, and the two had sworn amity on the Koran.[5] Mir Jafar admitted in the first of his letters to Clive that there had been a reconciliation; but added: 'what we have agreed on must be done'.[6] On the 20th, a messenger sent by Watts to Murshidabad returned having seen Mir Jafar and his son, Miran. He brought news that was scarcely encouraging. Mir Jafar would promise no more than that he would 'stand neuter'. Having sworn friendship to the Nawab on the Koran, he now felt he could not act against him.

Watts, who had never thought Mir Jafar would do much more than 'stand neuter', tried to convince Clive that his 'backwardness' was nothing to worry about.[7] Clive, once again more cautious than his colleagues, was not so sure. Supposing he crossed on to the Island of Cossimbazar only to find that Mir Jafar and the other conspirators had really made it up with the Nawab, he would have to face an army many times stronger than his own. This fact alone was nothing new to him; nor was he necessarily thinking in terms of facing an army of 70,000 as Scrafton and others talked about after the event[8] – reports reaching him at the time put the Nawab's available forces at as little as 8000, the rest of his troops being on strike for want of pay.[9] But the Nawab's army, whatever its strength, had the protection of the entrenched camp at Plassey. Clive would risk being cut off on the Island of Cossimbazar with the ground becoming hourly more impassable owing to the Rains.

In this critical situation, with so much depending on the doubtful word of Mir Jafar, Clive's resolution failed him. On the 17th and 19th, he wrote to the Committee, which consisted only of Drake, Manningham and Becher, asking their opinion as to what he should do next: 'I am really at a loss how to act at the present situation of our affairs.' He was, he said, unwilling to risk his force on the other side of the river unless Mir Jafar could be prevailed upon to join him; failing this, he proposed waiting at Katwa until after the Rains. There was enough food here, and his presence so close to Murshidabad would quite likely scare the Nawab into granting the English 'an honourable peace'.[10] It was typical of Clive's impulsiveness that having previously come to the conclusion that no such thing as an honourable peace was possible with Siraj-ud-daula, and that the only course was to dethrone him, he now should suddenly return to his way of thinking at the time of the February Treaty. It was also a sign of how far he was from being himself that he should have suggested calling in the Marathas as an alternative, knowing as he did the dire consequences of such a step.

The Committee advised him to give battle, provided there was a good chance of success;[11] their reply did not reach Clive until after he had acted and been victorious. Self-confident once again, he remarked sarcastically that it put him in mind of 'the famous answer of the Delphic oracle to Pyrrhus, "Aio te Æacide Romanos vincere posse".'[12] Very different from this non-committal advice were the rallying words of the naval captain, Henry Speke. Having once mocked 'the Hero', Speke now passionately believed in him: 'In you almost alone my hopes of success are centred . . . Every man here you deem your friend, or whose judgement you set any value upon, wish you may have marched . . . Aut Caesar, aut nullus is certainly the present motto for the English.'[13]

Speke's letter, like that of the Committee, did not arrive until too late, otherwise it might have prevented Clive from calling a Council of War on the 21st—something he lived to regret. Having informed his officers that Mir Jafar could not be depended on for anything more than 'standing neuter', and that Law's party was within three days' march of joining the Nawab, he asked their opinion whether in the circumstances they should engage in an immediate action, or entrench themselves where they were until the Monsoon was over.[14] Of the nine senior officers who voted, Clive, Killpatrick and five others were against an immediate action. Two were in favour, one of them being Coote, who gave his reasons for voting as he did. Of the junior officers who also voted, three were against immediate action and five in favour.[15] To Clive, the verdict of his officers might have been less decisive than the size of the majority would suggest. He seems to have deliberately presented the situation to them in the worst possible light, putting the enemy strength at 50,000, whereas when writing to the Committee on the same day he stated that the Nawab could not muster more than 8000 troops.[16] And it was seldom that a Council of War gave a decision in favour of battle, since the very calling of such a council made for pessimism.

After the Council of War had broken up, according to a tradition which originated with Orme and was made more romantic by Macaulay, Clive retired alone into a nearby grove, spent an hour there 'in deep meditation',[17] and 'came back determined to put everything to the hazard'.[18] But according to Clive himself it took 'twenty-four hours' mature consideration' for him to change his mind.[19] This was true in so far as it was at least another twenty-four hours before he finally made up his mind to march; though he postponed his decision not so much in order to have time for 'mature consideration', as in the hope of receiving 'some encouragement'[20] from Mir Jafar. This is what he told his colleagues in Calcutta when he wrote to them after the Council of War. And writing to Mir Jafar on the following day, the 22nd, he said, 'If you cannot go even this length to assist us I call God to witness the fault is not mine, and I must desire your consent for concluding a peace with the Nawab.'[21] Then, at three in the afternoon of that day, the long-awaited communication from Mir Jafar arrived. It was far more positive than his previous letters. He had marched from Murshidabad, and so had the Nawab. 'When you come near,' he told Clive, 'I shall then be able to join you.'[22] It was this letter which finally determined Clive to march, as he told Mir Jafar in a note sent three hours after receiving it.

On the other hand, we have Coote's statement that Clive told him on the 21st, an hour after the Council of War, that he intended to march next day. Clive, though he did not appear to remember much about this conversation, when it was recalled by Coote before the Select Committee of the House of Commons,[23] did not deny it. From the journals of Coote and another officer, we learn that the troops started crossing the river early in the morning of the 22nd, that is, before Clive received the letter from Mir Jafar;[24] although the accounts of Clive himself, Scrafton and others speak of the river having been crossed in the evening of that day.[25] Perhaps what Clive decided in the hour after the Council of War was to get his troops across the river as soon as possible so as to be able to march immediately on hearing favourably from Mir Jafar, and when he told Coote that he intended to march, he meant only this and not that he was going to engage the Nawab whatever happened. Or he may have decided at any rate to get part of the army across, which would explain why Coote speaks of crossing in the morning, whereas Clive himself and others did not go across until the evening.

Clive's remark to the Committee of the House of Commons that Coote was not of high enough rank to influence him,[26] and his statement elsewhere that he 'did not even then understand the subject upon which he delivered so peremptory an opinion',[27] seem like an attempt to play down Coote's part in his decision – as though Clive, jealous of Plassey as his own great victory, was endeavouring to conceal the fact that the battle might never have taken place but for Coote. It is possible to find the origin of Clive's hostility to Coote in his reluctance to share any of the glory of Plassey with his subordinate, though we know that Coote quarrelled with almost all his colleagues,* and that he and Clive had already quarrelled at the time of the recapture of Calcutta. Certainly, Clive's remark about

* Even the long-suffering Warren Hastings was to write of Coote: 'May success and honour attend him in every other part of the world, but God forbid that he should ever return to India again.'

Coote not being senior enough to influence him sounds like spite, for Coote came next in seniority to Killpatrick, having been given the local rank of Major by Clive himself a few days earlier.

There was, however, some truth in his assertion that Coote did not really understand the situation when he gave his reasons for attacking. Thus, he expressed the fear that if Law joined the Nawab, the French deserters would return to him; whereas there was never any question of their defecting to Sinfray, a former Councillor of Chandernagore, who commanded fifty Frenchmen in the Nawab's army. His foreboding that Clive's troops would 'be soon reduced to the greatest distress' if they entrenched themselves[28] at so great a distance from Calcutta failed to take into account the grain supplies at Katwa, as well as the excellent line of communication afforded by the river. He spoke of the evil consequences of a withdrawal to Calcutta, which was beside the point, as Clive intended to stay where he was. And he ignored the chief issue, which was how Mir Jafar and the other conspirators were likely to act.

Coote's reasons were those of a soldier, Clive was thinking as a politician. Plassey, described by a distinguished present-day Indian as not a battle but a transaction,[29] was far more significant as the climax of a brilliant political intrigue than as a piece of generalship. Had Clive regarded the event in its true light, he would have been justified in taking most of the credit. It would have been easy to believe him when he said that 'whatever he did upon that occasion he did without receiving advice from anyone'.[30] He could have argued that his mind was made up not by Coote or by the other officers but by the letter from Mir Jafar which arrived in the afternoon of the 22nd. But he had to invest Plassey with full military glory—doubtless his public expected it—which meant that the military genius of Coote called for its due.

2

Having crossed the river, Clive and his army marched for several hours in the dark, through pouring rain and over soggy ground. They reached Plassey about one in the morning, just in time to take possession of a village, a neighbouring mango grove and a hunting lodge by the river belonging to the Nawab, before the Nawab's troops, who were approaching from the north, could have done so. The grove, known by the picturesque name of Laksha Bagh or Orchard of a Hundred Thousand Trees, was enclosed by a ditch and high mud bank.* It formed a serviceable line of defence, some 300 yards long, protected on the left by the hunting lodge, a substantial building of brick, with cupolas and arcaded verandahs, surrounded by a high wall, which occupied most of the space between the corner of the grove and the river. The Nawab's front line, a mile to the north, was the entrenchment of the camp, where part of his troops had stayed ever since the capture of Chandernagore. This entrenchment ran inland from the river, then turned to rejoin it; and as the river here formed a loop, a long peninsula was thus completely enclosed.[31]

For what remained of the night, the English could hear the sound of drums, cymbals and clarions coming from the enemy camp. The soldiers slept through it, but few of the officers did; least of all Clive, though he lay out of the rain in the comparative comfort of the hunting lodge.

With the dawn of the next day, June 23, Clive was on the roof of the hunting lodge, surveying the broad green plain before him. Mist rose from the ground as the sun got up, and black Monsoon clouds rolled across the early morning sky. The Nawab's army had already started to emerge from the camp and was spreading out over the plain. With standards flying it made, in the words of Scrafton, who was present, 'a most pompous and formidable appearance'.[32] There were large numbers of elephants, covered in scarlet cloth and embroidery. The cavalrymen's swords glinted in the sun. The largest cannon were mounted on mobile wooden platforms, each pulled by forty or fifty white oxen and with a specially trained elephant shoving at the rear with his forehead.[33]

These immense Indian hosts were nothing new to Clive, but this one was disposed in a more regular and warlike manner than the armies he had so easily routed in the past. In numbers, it came up to his most pessimistic estimate of 50,000, and it was supported by at least forty cannon. And though the foot soldiers were untrained, the horsemen, mostly Pathans from the north-west, were far superior to the cavalry he had encountered in the Carnatic. As he watched the enemy advance, Clive said ruefully to his companion: 'We must make the best fight we can during the day and at night sling our muskets over our shoulders and march back to Calcutta.'[34] He was depressed at not having heard any more

* The name Plassey is also romantic, being derived from the palas tree or 'Flame of the Forest'. But if there were any of these trees here at the time of the battle, they would then not have been in flower.

from Mir Jafar; there was no sign now of his joining the English, nor could he necessarily be counted on to 'stand neuter'.

The Nawab's army divided in two, so that it seemed to the English that they were about to be surrounded. One part formed a broad arc stretching to the east of the mango grove. The rest moved forward to meet the English head-on, occupying as they did so two tanks or ponds with high banks which served as advanced positions for artillery. Other cannon were interspersed among the troops on either side.

Clive, however gloomy he may have felt, realized the need for a bold front, and so his troops advanced out of the grove to form a line facing the enemy. The Europeans were in the centre, flanked by artillery, the sepoys on either side. More artillery was placed in a brick kiln to the left. A fierce cannonade ensued, in which the English were able to make gaps in the enemy ranks. But they were too far away to disable the Nawab's guns, which quickly killed or wounded ten of Clive's Europeans and twenty of his sepoys. In view of the disparity of numbers, this was a far more serious loss than the havoc caused among the enemy by the English field-pieces. The fifty Frenchmen fighting for the Nawab under Sinfray did great punishment from one of the tanks. Their field-pieces, though smaller than the Nawab's massive ordinance, were European and therefore more sophisticated, with barrels raised and lowered by a screw mechanism.

After half an hour of this cannonade, Clive withdrew his troops into the shelter of the grove. Here, though the enemy fire shattered the branches of the trees, his men were protected; and they were able to return fire through holes in the bank, and from artillery placed in front of it. It seemed to Clive that the only hope was to hold out here for the rest of the day, and then rely on his old trick of a night attack on the enemy camp.

By noon the sky had darkened, and the noise of the cannonade was suddenly drowned by a crash of thunder. For half an hour the rain fell in torrents, soaking the ammunition of the enemy, so that their fire fell off. Thinking the English guns would likewise be silenced, a body of the Nawab's horse, led by Mir Madan, advanced; only to find that the English continued to fire, for they had covered their ammunition with tarpaulins. The enemy horse retired quickly, but not before the shell of a six-pounder had mortally wounded Mir Madan in the thigh.

It was a commonplace of eighteenth-century Indian warfare for the loss of the commander to mean the loss of the battle. As well as being the Nawab's best general, Mir Madan was one of three commanders, out of a total of eight, on whose loyalty he could rely. The other two were the favourite, Mohan Lal – unexpectedly soldierlike on this day – and his son-in-law, Bahadur Ali Khan, who perished about the same time as Mir Madan. It was the troops of these commanders alone, together with Sinfray's Frenchmen, who fought the English. The rest of the Nawab's army – reckoned at three-quarters of the whole – was disloyal and merely stood by and watched. That was why the troops forming the broad arc on the English right did nothing; for they were commanded by Mir Jafar, Rai Durlabh and other conspirators. But Clive still did not know this, and fired at them to keep them at a distance.

The Nawab, who sat awaiting the outcome of the battle, was greatly distressed when the dying Mir Madan was carried into his tent. He decided to send for Mir Jafar, in a last effort to regain his loyalty. When, after many messages, Mir Jafar agreed to come, the Nawab took off his turban and flung it at his feet, asking his forgiveness for all the wrongs he had done him and begging him to defend his life and his honour. Mir Jafar merely gave the Nawab the insidious advice that it was too late to make an attack that day, and that the troops should be recalled.[35] Rai Durlabh gave similar advice, and so the Nawab ordered Mohan Lal to retire. Mohan Lal at first refused to do so, saying that his troops were fighting well and that it would be a mistake to turn back; but when ordered again he submitted, and withdrew his troops into the camp.[36] After his meeting with the Nawab, Mir Jafar wrote to Clive urging him to attack, but the messenger to whom he gave the letter was afraid to proceed owing to the firing, and it did not reach Clive until five that afternoon, when the battle was already over.[37]

When Clive saw the Nawab's troops withdrawing, he retired into the hunting lodge to change his wet clothes, telling Killpatrick to let him know immediately* if the enemy made any further move. After he had been there a short while – according to Walsh, he did not even have time

* It was now that Clive was alleged to have gone to sleep, a story seized upon by his enemies, who made it sound as if he slept throughout most of the battle. As Orme points out, it would not necessarily have been to Clive's discredit if he had taken advantage of the lull in the fighting for a nap, particularly as he planned an action that night. But the story is denied on the important authority of Coote, who spoke about it some years later to the naval surgeon, Edward Ives (Edward Ives, *A Voyage from England to India in the Year 1754*, London 1773, p. 153). It appears to have originated from two newspaper letters written in 1763 by William Belchier, Clive's former banker and agent (Hill, *op. cit.*, Vol. III, pp. 403–4). Belchier had a personal grievance against Clive, who had ceased to employ him, having been warned of his dubious business methods by Sir Edward Clive and others. Their suspicions were justified, for he went bankrupt in 1760.

to get his clothes off[38] – he was told that some of his troops were moving forward. This was contrary to his orders, for he had intended his army to remain in the grove until after dark; it sounded like a piece of foolhardiness. He ran out, and found that Killpatrick had taken it on himself to occupy the tank from which Sinfray and his Frenchmen had just withdrawn. Clive was at first so angry with his second-in-command for acting without orders that he threatened to put him under arrest. But he realized that once there had been an advance there was no going back, so he called up Coote's division and ordered two companies of grenadiers to move to a bank close to the enemy and open fire with their small arms.

Clive aimed at drawing the enemy once again out of their camp, and in this he was successful. Part of the Nawab's troops poured forth, rallied by the French who now played their field-pieces from a redoubt at the angle of the entrenchment. Cavalry, brandishing their swords, made to charge the English. The enemy also kept up a smart musket fire from the redoubt and from a wooded mound. But Clive's field-pieces, which he quickly advanced, drove the cavalry back and prevented the Nawab's cannon from being brought out again by causing havoc among the oxen that pulled them.* This was the hottest phase of the whole battle, but it did not last long. Confusion broke out in the enemy ranks. Four of their senior officers had been killed. Elephants began to stampede.

Seeing the enemy were losing heart, Clive ordered up the rest of his troops for a general assault. He had ordered them up already, and then countermanded the order when the Nawab's troops to the right of the grove appeared to be moving closer, still uncertain that they were the troops of the conspirators. Now, at last, he was convinced they were friendly; so his main force was able to come up and the mound and redoubt were quickly stormed. The enemy fled, their confusion all the greater in that some of their ammunition blew up. The Nawab had already left the field;[39] he galloped back to Murshidabad on a fast camel. At five that afternoon the English were masters of the camp.

The battle of Plassey was over. It had been a comparatively bloodless battle; the Nawab, out of his great army, had lost only 500 men; the English had lost four Europeans and 14 sepoys killed; nine Europeans and 36 sepoys wounded. But the issue of the battle was decided not by the fighting, but by the treachery of Mir Jafar, Rai Durlabh and the other conspirators. It was unfortunate for Clive that this battle, which he

* Clive's enemies later made a joke of this, saying that he could not have done better had he been Master of the Butchers' Company.

SIRAJ-UD-DAULA, NAWAB OF BENGAL

from a contemporary portrait

VICE-ADMIRAL
CHARLES WATSON

Engraving by E. Fisher
after a painting by T. Hudson

SIR EYRE COOTE

regarded as the climax of his career, should have turned out to be such a walk-over. His enemies were able to say that he owed his fortune to a stroke of luck, or to the 'faint-heartedness' of 'the effeminate and luxurious Asiatics',[40] ignoring his long negotiations in the weeks before that fateful June 23, and his labours in the months that followed.

CHAPTER XII

The Nawab's Generosity

> Great princes dependent on his pleasure; an opulent city afraid of being given up to plunder; wealthy bankers bidding against each other for his smiles; vaults piled with gold and jewels thrown open to him alone.
>
> MACAULAY, *Essay on Clive*

I

'I congratulate you on the victory, which is yours, not mine,' wrote Clive to Mir Jafar on the morning after Plassey.[1] This remark, so patently insincere it might have been sarcastic, did not make the Nawab-designate, an elderly professional soldier with sleepy eyes and a grizzled beard, feel any less uneasy. When, on his arrival at the English camp, the guard turned out in his honour, he started back in fright.[2] He was only reassured when Clive embraced him and saluted him as *Subah* of the province.

Clive advised Mir Jafar to hasten immediately to Murshidabad. He and his troops followed more slowly, though Watts and Walsh were sent ahead to 'quiet the metropolis'[3] and get early information as to the state of the treasury. As the English troops marched northward, they were regaled with the sight of cannon, trains of oxen, broken carriages and wounded horses strewn over the plain. An elephant was found dead sixteen miles from the field of battle, with two six-pound shot lodged in its body. At Maidapur, near Cossimbazar, the army halted, and Clive waited for a favourable moment to enter the capital.

When Mir Jafar reached Murshidabad, he found the city in a state of confusion. Siraj-ud-daula was still in his palace of Mansurganj, across the river, having vainly tried to rally his troops by giving them money. Mir Jafar made no attempt to capture him on his arrival, but went to his own palace. That night, the unfortunate young Nawab slipped away from Mansurganj in disguise, and next morning he set off into the country, together with his favourite wife, Lutf-unnisa, his three-year-old daughter and a single faithful eunuch; heading in the direction of Patna, where the governor and the garrison were reported to be still loyal.

What with the inroads made by Siraj-ud-daula and also a certain amount of plundering, the treasury was found to contain only a fraction of what had been expected. And there was other disquieting news for Clive: rumours of a plot to assassinate him.[4] So he put off his entry into Murshidabad for two more days, until the 29th. 'It will be necessary for you to make some parade,' Walsh had told him, 'music, drums and colours I think should not be omitted. Two pieces of cannon would add to the pomp and I am persuaded give no kind of umbrage.'[5]

Once again, Clive entered an Indian city as its conqueror. The streets were crowded with people, watching awestruck as the great Sabit Jang went past with his escort of 200 Europeans and 300 sepoys. 'The city of Murshidabad is as extensive, populous and rich as the city of London,' Clive afterwards wrote, 'with this difference, that there are individuals in the first possessing infinitely greater property than any in the last city.'[6] He did not exaggerate the size of Murshidabad, for it stretched for five miles along the bank of the river and was two and a half miles deep. But from an account of the city written in 1759,[7] it consisted mostly of narrow, dirty streets and miserable huts, interspersed with the nondescript houses of the well-to-do, and with a number of mosques, temples and palaces by the river.[8]

Clive took up his quarters at Morad-bagh, a spacious house near the Nawab's palace, across the river from the city. It had a garden large enough to accommodate his escort. On his arrival here, as he told the Select Committee of the House of Commons, 'Jagat Seth and several of the great men, anxious for their fate, sent their submission, with offers of large presents . . . the Hindu millionaires, as well as other men of property, made me the greatest offers (which nevertheless are usual upon such occasions, and what they expected would have been required), and had I accepted these offers I might have been in possession of millions . . . but preferring the reputation of the English nation, the interest of the Nawab and the advantage of the Company to all pecuniary considerations, I refused all offers that were made me.'[9]

This was the boast that inspired Clive's most famous piece of oratory: 'When I recollect entering the Nawab's treasury at Murshidabad, with heaps of gold and silver to the right and left, and these crowned with jewels, by God, at this moment, do I stand astonished at my own moderation.'[10] From what we know of the prosaic realities of the financial transactions after Plassey – hagglings between the English, the Seths, Mir Jafar and Rai Durlabh – we can take this as little more than an example of Clive's gift for imagery. Some years before he spoke these words, he wrote in an offhand manner of the Nawab's treasury that he 'was never there but once out of curiosity'[11] – which sounds more like a visit to the strong-room of one's bank than to Aladdin's cave.

One can also be cynical about his boast that he refused all presents from the 'Hindu millionaires', knowing that he was offered, and accepted, a personal gift of sixteen lakhs or £180,000, from Mir Jafar, in addition to what he received as Commander-in-Chief and a member of the Committee. Having been made rich beyond all expectations by the monarch, he did not have to demean himself by accepting the money of mere subjects. And his remark about the Seths being 'anxious for their fate' is rather dubious, seeing they were his allies.

In the afternoon of the day of his arrival at Murshidabad, Clive went in state to pay his respects to Mir Jafar. He was accompanied by the son of the new Nawab, Miran, whom he knew to be one of those alleged to have plotted his murder. All the rajahs and great men of Durbar awaited him in the audience hall of the palace. Finding that Mir Jafar declined to seat himself on the *musnud* or carpet of state, Clive handed him to it, and saluted him as Nawab. He then made his submission to him by proffering the customary *nazar*, a token tribute of a few pieces of gold, and all the assembled magnates followed suit. It was, as Clive reported to the Committee, a ceremonial visit, at which no business was discussed. Perhaps this was just as well, for according to gossip Mir Jafar was in a stupor, having been roused too soon from his afternoon nap, before which, as was his habit, he had taken *bang*.[12]*

The really important business took place on the day after the new Nawab had been seated on the *musnud*. Mir Jafar paid a return visit to Clive, and the two of them went together to the palace of the Seths, where four thousand people were employed and where the family temple was adorned, somewhat incongruously, with Dutch tiles of Old and New

* A drug made from a plant like hemp or flax which also forms the basis of an intoxicating drink.

Testament scenes. Since the treasury did not contain nearly enough for him to fulfil his obligations under the treaty and also pay his troops and meet other expenses, Mir Jafar suggested that the Seths should mediate between him and the English. This suited Clive, although he suspected Rai Durlabh, who was now the Nawab's chief minister, of keeping large sums hidden away. The Seths settled that the Nawab should pay half of what he owed immediately, two-thirds in money and one-third in jewels, plate and goods; and the rest in instalments over the next three years. Clive regarded this as better than he had hoped for; but neither the Committee nor Watson was satisfied. In the end, it was decided that the Company should advance the other half of what the Nawab owed the soldiers and sailors.*

The Nawab's first payment made an impressive showing when it was loaded on to a fleet of native boats during the week following the conference. Each of seventy-five boats carried a lakh of rupees in a large chest; so that almost a million sterling was thus embarked. When the boats entered the Hughli, they were joined by an escort of naval craft, and they headed downstream to Calcutta, music playing, drums beating and colours flying, past the envious eyes of the Dutch at Cinsura and of the remaining French at Chandernagore.

* The conference at the Seths' palace was, according to Orme, followed by a dramatic scene when Omichand, who had accompanied Clive to Murshidabad, learnt that he would not be receiving the twenty lakhs. 'Scrafton said to him in the Hindostan language, "Omichand, the red paper is a trick; you are to have nothing." These words overpowered him like a blast of sulphur; he sunk back, fainting, and would have fallen to the ground had not one of his attendants caught him in his arms.' It is, however, doubtful if the scene recounted by Orme ever took place. Scrafton, writing three days after it was supposed to have happened, stated that Omichand still had not found out about the two treaties, although he knew by this time that he was not going to get his money (Powis Collection, Vol. 23, Scrafton to Drake, July 3, 1757). Clive's testimony before the Select Committee of the House of Commons would seem to confirm Orme's account–'when the real treaty came to be read, the indignation and resentment in that man's countenance bars all description'. But based as it is on Clive's uncertain memory, it is less valuable evidence than Scrafton's letter which was written at the time. One suspects Clive of having taken such pleasure in tricking Omichand that he wished to present the affair in as spectacular a light as possible. Orme goes on to say that the shock drove Omichand out of his mind–a statement which, while eliciting much posthumous sympathy for him among the British public, is not true. During the eighteen months or so that remained of his life, Omichand had various dealings with the Company, the records of which make no mention of his having been insane. Clive even wrote of him to the Directors as 'a person capable of rendering you great services', though this did not prevent the old Sikh merchant from attempting to sue Clive and the Committee in the English courts.

Great was the rejoicing when the boats reached Calcutta. 'We talk of great doings on this happy occasion and expect a world of guns to be fired and the ladies all to get footsore with dancing,' wrote Latham to Clive. 'I can assure you that a bumper goes to your health each day in every house from the Admiral's downwards.'[13] The inhabitants of the settlement, who had endured poverty for the past year, were in funds once again.

The twelve lakhs which Mir Jafar had originally undertaken to pay the Committee were now, through his 'bounty', almost doubled; so that ordinary Councillors were able to share in the money. The forty lakhs for the armed forces were upped to fifty. Each member of the Committee received about £27,000, each Councillor about £12,000, each subaltern in the army about £3000. Clive, as Commander-in-Chief, received two lakhs which, together with his share in the Committee money and the Nawab's special gift to him of sixteen lakhs, made him now worth about £234,000. The sixteen lakhs were part of a much larger present, the balance of which Clive distributed among some of his associates, including Watts, Walsh, Killpatrick and Scrafton. Watson was omitted, causing bad blood among the sailors.

This was only one of several 'great heats and dissentions'[14] resulting from the Nawab's golden shower. The army officers tried to prevent the naval detachment from sharing equally with themselves. Clive, who was determined to see justice done, had to rebuke them severely, and put some of them under arrest, before they climbed down.

While leaving him out of the Nawab's private gift, Clive took up Watson's case when he claimed a share in the twenty-three lakhs of the Committee and Council. The civilians had excluded him in a rather underhand way, on the grounds that he was not a member of the Committee, although he had been closely associated with all the Committee's proceedings ever since he came to Bengal. Clive proposed that each member of the Committee and Council should relinquish ten per cent of his share to Watson, but only four of them followed his example—the others pleading that they were too much in debt. Before anything could be settled, Watson was dead, a victim, like Killpatrick, of the terrible mortality among the British in Bengal during the months following Plassey; when the heat and humidity, the cholera and 'pucka fevers' of late summer and early autumn took an even greater toll than usual, and the Nawab's money, in the form of unlimited drink, had its own dire effect on the ordinary soldiers and sailors; so that of the Company's European troops who came here with Clive at the end of 1756, only a quarter were still alive a year later.*

Of the three million sterling paid out by the Nawab under the treaty, only the twenty-seven lakhs which the native inhabitants of Calcutta received as compensation for their losses – Clive and Watts suggested that the Indians' share should be increased out of the fifty lakhs allowed to the Europeans[15] – stayed in India. The rest would eventually have found its way to England;[16] a severe drain on the economy of Bengal, roughly equal to a whole year's revenues. Yet to criticize Clive and his colleagues for not possessing twentieth-century economic ethics is just as unfair as it was for Macaulay to apply nineteenth-century standards to the receiving of presents.[17] In the India of the 1750s, presents were the accepted custom. Dupleix and Bussy received them just as much as the English; Watson was no less anxious than Clive to participate in Mir Jafar's bounty, and saw nothing dishonourable or impolitic in so doing; though *he* was no mere Company servant but an Admiral of the Royal Navy. Clive did not hesitate to tell the Directors about the presents, and the Chairman congratulated him on his good fortune.

2

On July 2, while the English treasure fleet was being loaded, Siraj-uddaula returned to Murshidabad as a prisoner and in a wretched state. He had been recognized by a *fakir* or holy man near Rajmahal on the Ganges,

* Giving evidence in 1772, Captain Brereton described a touching deathbed scene when Watson was visited by an officer named Martin, who told him that his signature had been forged on the fictitious treaty, and also that the members of the Committee were dividing the money stipulated for Omichand among themselves, 'and excluding the Admiral'. To which Watson was purported to have said that 'as there was so much iniquity among mankind, he did not wish to stay any longer among them'. Brereton himself had to admit that Watson must have known about the forging of his signature before Martin's visit. As for the story about Omichand's money, it was clearly nonsense. And from Doctor Ives's day-to-day account of Watson's illness, it is clear that there was no deathbed scene. Watson had no idea he was going to die, and on August 12, the day Martin visited him, he was only a little indisposed. His condition only became grave a few hours before the end, by which time he was comatose and delirious. Martin had conveniently died by the time Brereton gave his evidence.

who had betrayed him to Mir Jafar's brother, Mir Daud, the local *faujdar*.[18] Within a few hours of his arrival at Murshidabad, he was stabbed to death. Next day his bleeding corpse was paraded through the streets of the city on an elephant. He was supposed to have been put to death by order of Miran, who was notorious for his cruelty; and there were those who believed the deed to have been done without Mir Jafar's approval or knowledge. But according to Scrafton, the son acted in collusion with the father, who was determined that Siraj-ud-daula should die immediately, lest Clive's 'clemency and moderation should plead for his preservation'.[19] If this is true, and if, as Orme states, Siraj-ud-daula's loyal officers advised him, after Plassey, to surrender to the English, it shows that Clive had the name for being merciful.

Nevertheless, it seems doubtful if Clive would have done much to save Siraj-ud-daula. After his capture, he confidently assured the Committee that Mir Jafar intended only 'to confine him and to allow him all the indulgence which a prison can admit of'.[20] With his experience of what happened to Chanda Sahib, he can hardly have believed that Mir Jafar would permit his defeated rival to stay alive. Like Lawrence on that previous occasion, he can be accused of washing his hands.

Mir Jafar feared Clive's displeasure enough to come and apologize to him the next morning, justifying the deed on the grounds that the captive Siraj-ud-daula was fermenting a mutiny among his troops. A flimsy enough excuse, yet Clive himself went further when he explained away Siraj-ud-daula's death to the Mogul by a complete falsehood—that he had been 'killed by his servants who followed him to demand their pay'.[21]

When Siraj-ud-daula was captured, Law and his band of Frenchmen were hurrying to his assistance. Clive considered it vital to the peace of Bengal that an end should be put to Law's peregrinations, so he sent a detachment under Coote in pursuit of him. He also wrote to warn Law that the whole country would be against him, and advised him to treat with the English.[22] The gentlemanly Law was touched by this apparent concern for himself and his men; but he refused to treat and continued his march up country. He had more than enough start over Coote, and had crossed into the territory of the Nawab of Oudh by the time the English reached Patna. So Clive agreed that the chase should be called off.

Coote's expedition was the longest and most arduous yet made by British soldiers in India; the first time the redcoats penetrated into the real Hindostan. He and his men covered four hundred miles in twenty-one days, suffering untold hardships. But Clive, in the comfort of Morad-bagh, failed to appreciate this feat of endurance. He accused Coote of being dilatory,[23] and was wholly unsympathetic to his request that his officers should be given extra *batta* or field allowance: 'I always thought their own reputation and the honour of their country would have been incitement sufficient with them to undergo hardships and fatigues, which could not much exceed those which the whole army suffered in their march from Calcutta to Cossimbazar. I am the more surprised at it, because their allowance is beyond everything heard of in any other service, without mentioning the good effects of the Nawab's generosity.'[24]

Clive may have felt that Coote and his officers could do something to earn their fortunes, though it was hard on them to have been singled out for this ordeal, while their fellows, who were to share just as liberally in the Nawab's gold, took it easy. But it was unreasonable to compare the march from Calcutta to Cossimbazar with Coote's march, which, if nothing else, was four times as long.

To make matters worse for Coote, Mir Daud's *diwan* complained to Clive that the soldiers of the detachment had plundered and insulted the women when they were in Rajmahal. Clive immediately wrote in the strongest terms to Coote, who denied these accusations and declared Mir Daud to have been a villain.[25] One suspects this was another instance of Clive's habit of jumping to conclusions, and that he was all the more ready to do so where Coote was concerned. It can be argued that Clive was continually finding fault with Coote because he disliked him – though he may genuinely have felt let down by Coote's failure to capture Law and held it against him subsequently. To get a false idea into his head and then base his later thinking on it was one of Clive's shortcomings. Yet Coote's letters should have convinced him that he was doing his very best. They are the letters of a brave and conscientious soldier – answering Clive's complaints with dignity and forbearance; never once saying anything to which a superior officer could take exception. 'I always was a sincerer friend of yours than you were made to believe,' he told Clive when he sailed for England a few months later,[26] which would suggest that Clive was influenced against Coote by others, possibly by the intolerant Walsh. That Coote's profession of friendship was genuine is proved by the way in which he subsequently helped to defend Clive against the attacks of his enemies, even though Clive never relented in his animosity towards him.[27]

3

Three days before the battle of Plassey was fought, Margaret and her infant daughter – named Jenny after Jane Latham – sailed from Madras in the *Marlborough* on their way to join Clive in Bengal. On the 24th the ship put in at Vizagapatam, the English settlement further up the coast, only to find the place invested by Bussy, and about to surrender to him. This did not, however, make much difference to the voyage. When Margaret asked Bussy if he would release some English sailors, he immediately agreed to do so, adding gallantly that his nation never refused 'the requests of the ladies'.[28]

By July 12, Margaret and her daughter were in Calcutta. Clive was then still at Murshidabad. There was talk of some of the wives going north to join their husbands, particularly two recent brides. 'I should not have been surprised if the two new married men had gone the length of Vizagapatam to meet their angels,' wrote Clive to Admiral Pocock. 'Let them think them so after a voyage to England together and I will confess I have been mistaken in my opinion of the sea. Partridges and pheasants are excellent dishes but the King of France's confessor was tired of them at last.'[29]

In the end, Margaret stayed in Calcutta. She managed to stand up to the climate. To keep her company, there were the Lathams. Jenny had followed her husband to Calcutta, where, as at Bombay, she managed to scandalize society. But a letter from Clive put matters right, whatever the trouble was; much to the gratitude of her husband.[30]

Margaret's letters to Clive at this time, and his to her, have disappeared. All we have are occasional messages and postscripts in letters written by Latham. When he began 'My dear Colonel', Margaret inserted the word 'charming' between the 'dear' and the 'Colonel'.[31] Under Latham's supervision, she busied herself in making 'a sort of uniform' – scarlet and gold lace – for Clive to wear at the Durbar.[32] She and Clive were reunited for a few weeks in August, when he visited Calcutta.

It was the desire of all who had benefited from the Nawab's generosity to leave India as soon as possible, particularly when they saw Watson and Killpatrick struck down before they even had time to count their money. Only Mrs Watts, with her Indian blood, wished to stay; but her husband hoped she would change her mind. Clive was as determined as anyone to go home, particularly after he had suffered a bout of illness in July. But as he told Pigot, strong as were his motives for going, 'a superior consideration' obliged him to postpone his departure for a few more months.[33]

The 'superior consideration' was to 'leave this country in peace':[34] to see Mir Jafar fully confirmed in his government, and the three provinces of Bengal, Bihar and Orissa 'firmly settled'.[35] This, Clive reckoned, would be achieved by January; and when writing to the Directors, as well as to Pigot, he took credit for his sense of duty in staying as long as that. Meanwhile, he asked his cousin, the Judge, to look out for an English landed estate that might suit him; since he regarded Styche as too small and too far from London.[36] As for the other requisite for becoming a person of consequence at home, a seat in Parliament, he had his hopes. But as he told his father, 'no more struggles against the Ministry; I choose to be with them'.[37] This time, he wrote fewer letters to the Great, as though he now felt his success would speak for itself—he warned a family friend that his father, if encouraged, might overdo the public relations: 'for although I intend getting into Parliament and have hopes of being taken some notice of by His Majesty, yet you know the merit of all actions are [*sic*] greatly lessened by being too much boasted of'.[38] That he intended to cut no small figure can be seen in his order for two hundred shirts—'the finest and best you get for love or money'.[39] But in the end, he did not go home for another two years.

CHAPTER XIII

Tricks, Chicanery and the Lord Knows What

I am possessed of volumes of materials for the continuance of your history, in which will appear fighting, tricks, chicanery, intrigues, politics and the Lord knows what.

CLIVE TO ORME

I

Clive stayed two years longer in Bengal to ensure 'the settlement of these provinces'[1] and the fulfilment of the treaty by Mir Jafar. Although he succeeded over the treaty, he was to leave the provinces more unsettled than ever, with the Nawab's government almost completely broken down and the English not yet providing a substitute. But if the English were still not ruling Bengal, they alone had authority. It was Clive who wrested this authority from the Nawab and put it, for better or for worse, into the hands of his own countrymen.

He did not consciously set out to do this. His original intention, as expressed by him with undoubted sincerity in his speech at Mir Jafar's installation, was that the English should not interfere in any way in the Nawab's government, but should 'attend solely to commerce' which was their 'proper sphere'.[2] The ascendancy which he built up grew out of the necessity of getting Mir Jafar to toe the line. Had the new Nawab been more amenable, the Company might have reverted to the position it had occupied in the days of Alivardi, only with more privileges. And even with Mir Jafar acting as he did, this might equally have happened had

Clive returned to England soon after Plassey, leaving the affairs of Bengal in the hands of someone less dynamic. Though the English, by deposing one Nawab and enthroning another, had shown the Indians where the power lay, the Nawab's government might have recovered its former prestige as these memories wore thin. Instead, the impression made by the events of 1757 was heightened during the years that followed, when Clive was virtual dictator of Bengal.

Apart from the essential prerequisite of being at the head of the only effective military force in the country, Clive was unusual among dictators. At the age of thirty-two, with only a few months' political experience, he became the most powerful man in a country approaching the size of France. He was a stranger in that country, he did not speak the language, he had no official position except by virtue of a small foreign community, whose power was in theory confined to the enclave around Calcutta.

Given these unlikely circumstances, Clive had plenty of the attributes of a dictator. He could be ruthless, while showing a reluctance to take human life. He had an 'explosive energy',[3] though he was often ill. He understood the principles of divide and rule and of the iron hand in the velvet glove. He had a poor view of human nature, or at any rate of the nature of that part of humanity under his sway. He was firm, and for all his impulsiveness, able to keep to a fixed line of policy. And he had something without which these endowments might have been of no avail: an almost magic ascendancy over the people.

As is always the case when power depends on a personality, the power declined when the personality was no longer there. Clive himself recognized this. 'These foolish people ground their opinion and confidence on one man's abilities alone,' he told Pigot at the beginning of 1758.[4] That he should have regarded the people as foolish in so doing shows that, unlike most professional dictators, he could still look at himself objectively.

Like all dictators, Clive knew the value of propaganda. The letters—more like manifestoes—which he had addressed to some of the chief potentates of India soon after Plassey not only covered up or justified Siraj-ud-daula's murder, but also exaggerated his own military strength: he had, he said, '25,000 matchless sepoys'.[5] To Salabat Jang, Nizam of the Deccan, he took the opportunity of pointing out that the English did not intend to wrest provinces from Mir Jafar, 'as I hear the French have done with Your Excellency'.[6] To his old friend Mohammed Ali, Nawab of the Carnatic, he spoke of having defeated an army of 100,000.[7]

Clive's purpose in writing to the Mogul was more than just to announce his great success. In order to invest his regime with the cloak of legitimacy, Mir Jafar had to be confirmed in his *subah*ship by the Emperor. It is significant that Clive should have written, rather than Mir Jafar himself; for by so doing, he appeared to come between the Nawab and the nominal source of his power. There were rumours that the Mogul disapproved of what the English had done in Bengal, but he was in no position to show his disapproval, having troubles of his own. And so, in return for a suitable payment, he sent Mir Jafar the necessary *sanad*; and for full measure, conferred on Clive the Imperial rank of a commander of 5000 horse and 6000 foot, together with the title of 'Flower of the Empire, Defender of the Country, the Brave, firm in War'.[8] This made him not just an *omrah*, or noble, but one of the great nobles or pillars of the state.

The initial honeymoon of Clive and the Nawab of his making did not last long. It is hard to know which side was more to blame. According to Scrafton, who for the first few months of the new regime was Resident at the Durbar, the Nawab grew haughty and unhelpful – he 'quite forgot the humble Mir Jafar'.[9] The English were certain that he would take the first opportunity to repudiate his debt, and suspected him of this whenever he was behindhand with an instalment. In fact, he was genuinely short of money, with the pay of his own troops in arrears.

It was only natural that Mir Jafar should come to resent the English yoke. Nothing could be done without what Scrafton called Clive's 'Great Seal'.[10] Clive started by asking to be consulted on the appointment of the Nawab's high officials and ended by ordering him and his son to get rid of their European hangers-on.[11] He was constantly urging him to dismiss half his troops and to become still more dependent on English arms.[12] To the indolent Mir Jafar, it must have seemed that the English were always nagging.

With the granting of additional privileges to the Company came the inevitable abuses. The English traded privately without paying dues, and encroached on to land to which they were not entitled. Even Scrafton, unbeknown to Clive, engaged in revenue farming under two fictitious Indian names, and lent money at exorbitant rates to *zemindars*.[13] For all Clive's preaching of 'equity and moderation',[14] Mir Jafar saw a constant erosion of the rights and privileges of his government, and came to look on the English as rivals rather than allies.

As well as mistrusting Mir Jafar, Clive and Scrafton were irritated by him. He certainly must have seemed more than ever obtuse as his faculties began to deteriorate through too much *bang*, coupled with the excesses of his new way of life. When first acquainted with Mir Jafar, Clive described him as 'a humane, generous and honest prince'.[15] Two years later he was referring to him as 'the old fool', and calling his son Miran a 'worthless young dog'.[16] The Nawab's attempts to preserve some independence and self-respect were to Clive a sign of Muslim ingratitude, of his 'wavering disposition' and 'the ear he gives to evil councillors'.[17]

Convinced as he was that his efforts were for the Nawab's own good, Clive could not see the other point of view. He was hampered in his relations with the people of Bengal, from the Nawab downwards, by his lack of sympathy with their mentality, and by the fact that he could not speak Persian – the official language of Mogul India – let alone Bengali. To a certain extent this was due to his narrow-mindedness and his almost total lack of interest in Indian customs and culture; but it can also be blamed on the circumstances of his career. It was only in the south that he was able to get to know the Indian people. There he had done business with both merchants and peasants and slept with the women; there, an atmosphere of trust and affection had grown up between him and his sepoys. In Bengal, he had not only spent much less time, but his important and arduous position meant that his dealings with the people – whom he found as different from those he knew in the south as someone familiar with the French would find the Hungarians – were limited to formal conversations and still more formal letters, which always had to be by way of an interpreter or a Persian translator. Clive's failure to learn Persian was again the result of circumstances. In the south, where it had been enough to speak the local *lingua franca* and a little Tamil, there had been no need to learn the language of the Nawabs and their courts. Now, when Persian would have been of use to him, he was far too busy to learn it.

Thus it is necessary to qualify the aphorism that Clive's understanding of the Indian character tended to be an understanding of the worst sides of that character[18] by confining it to his understanding of the people of Bengal. To ignorance was added a strong prejudice – particularly against the Bengal Muslims – for which the chief responsibility must rest with Scrafton. Unlike Clive, Scrafton had spent his whole Indian career in Bengal; he knew the language and had a genuine interest in Indian customs and history. His position at the Durbar gave him a chance of really penetrating the minds of the Nawab and the great men, whereas Clive's attention was half taken up by military affairs and he lived mostly in the purely British society of Calcutta and the camp. Yet Scrafton's view of Mir Jafar's court was even more cynical than Clive's. By the time Scrafton was replaced by Warren Hastings, Clive's opinion was irretrievably fixed. Scrafton's copious and almost daily letters – he himself admitted to verbal diarrhoea, or as he called it, 'a flux of pens'[19] – had done their work.

But though Clive became increasingly convinced of the need for the iron hand, he never removed the velvet glove. If, at Scrafton's prompting, he wrote the Nawab letters such as would 'enter his very soul',[20] they were designed to do so by way of his better nature. They were always the letters of a friend or partner: 'The fate of the English is twisted with yours like two threads.'[21] He called the Nawab his father,[22] and sent him valuable presents on behalf of the Company: a pair of lustres larger than anyone had seen; an enamelled blue and gold table, an onyx snuff-box set with diamonds, rubies and other precious stones; 'a clock or Chinese Temple in gilt metal with moving figures, an organ of six tunes and a Chinese striking the hour'.[23] 'The clock will be a fit present for the old Nawab,' observed Scrafton. 'He is a sour old chap and must be sweetened by applications of well-timed presents, though I believe nothing would be so acceptable as some fine liqueurs.'[24]

Clive's ascendancy was helped by the fact that the Nawab's ministers and officials were mostly Hindus, as they had been since the time of Alivardi. He thus started in a stronger position than that of Bussy in the Deccan, where the Nizam was backed by a powerful Muslim aristocracy. It was still more fortunate for Clive that within a few months of Mir Jafar's accession, some of his most powerful Hindu subjects were in trouble with him – notably Rai Durlabh, who, towards the end of 1757, was implicated in an alleged attempt to set up a new Nawab and owed his continuance as chief minister and probably his life as well to English intervention.[25] Clive's policy was to protect these magnates in return for their submission. Thus was he able to build up a party of influential men, whose prosperity and perhaps very existence depended on the protection of the English, to serve as a counterpoise to the Nawab.

In this way began the traditional alliance between the British and the Hindus. The Nawab reacted by trying to replace Hindu officials with Muslims, so as to strengthen his own position, causing further friction between himself and Clive. It also led to discord between Muslims and Hindus, something which had not existed under Alivardi or Siraj-ud-daula: an instance of the break-up of the body politic of Bengal after Plassey. And it may have been a factor in keeping the British and the

THE TAKING OF CHANDERNAGORE, MARCH 1757

by Dominic Serres

WILLIAM WATTS CONCLUDING THE TREATY OF 1757
WITH MIR JAFAR AND HIS SON MIRAN

attributed to John Zoffany

Indians so alien to each other. It would have been difficult for the British to become really friendly with their Hindu associates, who were barred by their religion from taking food with them; whereas the British and the Muslims could eat and drink together and shared a love of the chase.

2

Soon after his accession, Mir Jafar decided to march with his army to Patna. The purpose of the expedition was threefold: to discourage the Nawab of Oudh from any aggressive intentions by a show of strength, to scare the more rebellious Bihar rajas, and to settle with Ramnarayan, the Deputy-Nawab or Governor of Bihar, who had remained faithful to Siraj-ud-daula after his overthrow, and was suspected of intriguing with the Nawab of Oudh. The Deputy-Nawab had conveyed his submission to Mir Jafar, but was unwilling to go personally to Murshidabad, preferring to remain at Patna under the protection of his own troops. He was wise; Mir Jafar was planning to murder him and give the province of Bihar to his own son-in-law, Mir Kasim. The Nawab even asked Clive to promise English protection to Ramnarayan, so as to entice him into his clutches, but Clive replied rebukingly that 'it was not the custom of the English to be guilty of such transactions'.[26]

It was necessary for Clive's troops to accompany the Nawab on his expedition, for his own army was too ill-disciplined to make any sort of show against the fine troops of the Nawab of Oudh. Clive knew that if the English refused to help him in this way, they would lose their influence with him. On the other hand, he saw the possible danger of Calcutta being attacked by French warships while he and his troops were up country.[27] The French had increased their naval strength in Indian waters, and the British squadron was on the point of departure. Moreover, he was desperately short of men owing to sickness.

Before the march could begin, there was much haggling over the expenses, which the Nawab was bound by the treaty to pay. At the same time, Scrafton was engaged in more serious wranglings with the Nawab over the next instalment of his debt. 'He looked grim as a lion, told me he had no money and I must take jewels . . . we might pick and choose, but I think the old fellow is too fond of his fine diamonds (of which he exhibits new ones every day) to part with them.'

By November 7, Scrafton was on the point of throwing in his hand. 'If you don't set out,' he told Clive, 'with or without troops, permit me to go to Calcutta . . . I clearly comprehend the political disease of the Nawab's affairs, but it is you only that can apply the remedy.'[28]

In answer to Scrafton's call, Clive set out on November 9, with a force that included less than 500 Europeans. The Nawab was now at Rajmahal, where he had succeeded in assembling an army. Clive marched there to join him, but determined to go no further until money matters were settled. He reached Rajmahal on December 3, and soon afterwards was visited by the Nawab, who arrived in state, in a car pulled by two elephants. As a prelude to the hard bargaining that was to come, Clive showed the flag. His troops 'went through all their firings and evolutions' for the Nawab's benefit. 'The *Subah* seemed lost in amazement at the quickness and uniformity of their motions . . . he was altogether so well pleased with his entertainment that he ordered ten thousand rupees to be distributed among them, for which the soldiers returned him their thanks by three English huzzas.'[29]

Business was delayed until Rai Durlabh could be prevailed upon to come to Rajmahal. The minister had not seen the Nawab since the discovery of the alleged plot, and preferred to remain in the safety of Murshidabad, pleading a diplomatic illness. An 'elegant remonstrance' from Clive,[30] threatening to withdraw his protection, brought Rai Durlabh to the camp, and on December 30 a conference was held. To avoid the trouble of 'dunning the Nawab to no manner of purpose',[31] Clive proposed that his debt to the English should be discharged by a grant of *tuncas* or assignments of the revenues of certain districts. After Clive had spoken plainly to him, the Nawab 'felt his chains, and found that the more he struggled, the closer they sat' and so 'with a very ill grace' he agreed to grant *tuncas* on Burdwan, Nadia, Hughli and Ingelei.[32]

The *tuncas* covered only a part of the Nawab's debt, and their collection was to be one of the least reputable chapters both in Clive's career and in the history of British India. It is true that on occasion Clive reprimanded *zemindars** for extorting money from the peasants by force,[33] but his own treatment of the *zemindars* was no less harsh. The Raja of Burdwan lamented that he had to sell his furniture in order to be able to satisfy

* Tenants-in-chief in the Mogul land system, who paid rents to the state and in turn collected rents from the peasants.

Clive's demands; his country was in a bad way following a drought, and he was, moreover, upset by the death of his grandmother.[34] But Clive would take none of these excuses. He threatened to send a force to Burdwan; he confined the Raja's agent in the Black Hole;[35] he approved of the Raja's aunt being abducted by order of the Nawab.[36] The Raja, who seems to have had a most estimable affection for his female relatives, was much distressed. Clive did, however, insist that the lady should not be detained longer than necessary.[37]

The obtaining of the *tuncas* was not helped by the arrival of better news from Patna, which rendered the Nawab's expedition unnecessary. Nevertheless, the Nawab was determined to make a 'march of parade', even though it was going to cost him forty or fifty lakhs,[38] and so the combined expedition set out from Rajmahal during the first few days of January. Clive himself did much of his travelling by river, in a *budgerow*, a cross between a barge and a houseboat, with a long, many-windowed cabin. Depending on conditions it was sailed, rowed, or towed by another boat. Behind it followed 'cook-boats', and boats with servants and baggage.

Except in a storm, when the waves were big enough to swamp the boats, it was a pleasant mode of travel to glide slowly up the broad Ganges. Wood smoke curled into the sky from the villages and burning *ghats* on the distant, tree-lined banks; every now and then a cloud of brilliant green parakeets got up, or a flight of cranes passed overhead in dignified formation. The beat of tom-toms and the wail of Indian pipes drifted lazily across the water from native barges, with their turned-up prows and stubby sails. In the evening, when Clive's flotilla put into the shore for the night, both the sky and the river turned copper-coloured.

When the expedition was approaching Patna, Ramnarayan, who would not risk a visit to the Nawab's camp, came to the English camp with only a handful of followers, having heard from Clive that he could come with safety.[39] There followed some weeks of wranglings and intrigues. The Nawab tried every means, including bribery, to get Clive to agree to the destruction of Ramnarayan. At the same time, Ramnarayan and Rai Durlabh plotted the destruction of the Nawab, and tried to sow dissension between him and Clive. So charged was the atmosphere that a brawl between some of Clive's sepoys and a body of Ramnarayan's horse nearly developed into a general conflict.[40]

Meanwhile, Clive was laid low with gout, in great pain and unable to write.[41] By the end of February, he was better, and on the 23rd of that month the Nawab finally capitulated – there were fresh rumours that the

Nawab of Oudh was coming, and the Marathas were demanding arrears of their tribute. In full Durbar, Ramnarayan was confirmed in his office. Thus was Bihar secured to the English interest – a fact that became immediately apparent when the various local chieftains were summoned to pay homage to the Nawab; for some of them refused to come without first receiving assurances from Clive that they would be treated with justice.

When the threats from outside had once again receded, the Nawab delayed his departure from Patna, hoping that Clive would return to Calcutta and leave him with a free hand to attack Ramnarayan. But Clive was determined to stay by Ramnarayan until the Nawab and his troops had left, and it was not until two months later, when the Nawab had sent a large part of his army back to Murshidabad, that he considered it safe to go. He travelled in company with Rai Durlabh, and also took with him a new Hindu protégé, an able official named Shitab Rai, who was to be a staunch friend of the English. The Nawab consoled himself for his political defeat by making *his* return journey into a prolonged hunting trip, enlivened by the songs and dances of the best Patna actresses, whom he carried with him on his elephants.[42]

Owing to the misgovernment of Miran, Murshidabad was in confusion when Clive arrived back there. This, however, distracted attention from the Coast, where the French had built up their strength and now enjoyed military superiority. Clive was able to put it about that the English had won a great naval victory, news having reached Calcutta of an indecisive action against the French squadron fought by Watson's successor, Admiral Pocock.

The true state of affairs could not, however, be kept indefinitely from the Nawab. When he realized how strong the French were, he became more difficult, intriguing against Rai Durlabh so as to discredit him with the English. Suspecting he was about to be accused of mismanagement, Rai Durlabh asked leave to withdraw to Calcutta. Before he could go, he was nearly murdered by Miran's troops, but was rescued by Scrafton. If the English could not maintain Rai Durlabh in his post, they were at least able to protect his life, which was essential for their reputation and influence.[43] He went to live in Calcutta, and a detachment of Clive's sepoys later escorted his wife and daughter to join him there.

The situation on the Coast made it necessary to keep on the best of terms with the Nawab. Clive invited him to pay a visit to Calcutta, to put him in a good humour and – conceivably – to have him in his power should the news come that the French had attacked Madras.[44] The Nawab came and was well pleased with his entertainment, which happily coincided with the news of Pocock's second and more successful action against the French squadron. Business was totally neglected for balls, concerts and receptions. 'Thank God, His Excellency is at last gone,' wrote Scrafton, when it was over. 'He has led me a hell of a life here by the constant attendance I have been obliged to pay to him and his wenches, for he never went twenty yards from his house but they were with him.'[45]

By the time of the Nawab's visit to Calcutta, Clive had become Governor in name as well as in fact. On June 20, a letter from the Directors put an end to the anomaly of Drake being Governor; but proposed in his stead the even worse anomaly of the four senior members of Council holding the office of Governor in rotation, each for a month at a time. This was the work of Holwell, who, having failed to obtain the government for himself, had intrigued to get a scheme adopted where he would be Governor for one month in four.

The three other rotation Governors, Watts, Manningham and Becher (Holwell himself had not yet arrived), immediately offered to stand down in favour of Clive. At first, Clive felt that to accept would be to risk losing face with the Nawab if it subsequently turned out that the Directors did not want him as Governor.[46] He was hurt that they should not even have seen fit to include him in the rotation, though he must have known that when they wrote their letter they had not yet heard the news of Plassey. Four days later he changed his mind and accepted. He need have had no misgivings, for he had already been appointed to the post, the Chairman, John Payne, having yielded somewhat grudgingly to 'the public clamour' when the news of Plassey reached England.[47]

As Governor, Clive found himself more than ever isolated in that many of his colleagues, including Watts, left India at the end of 1758 or early in 1759. Scrafton stayed on a few more months, having returned to Calcutta from Murshidabad in August 1758. His place as Resident at the Durbar was taken by Warren Hastings, then aged twenty-five; an appointment for which Clive was responsible.

After Hastings had taken up his difficult post, Clive bombarded him with instructions. In money matters, he must be severe: 'It is the nature of these people to do nothing through inclination, a few sepoys or *chokeys* now and then will greatly expedite the payment.'[48] In matters of less importance, he was to avoid 'extremities', while showing 'as much spirit and resolution as will convince the Durbar that we always have it in our power to make ourselves respected'.[49] The military weakness of the

English made it necessary to give 'as little disgust as possible',[50] and to make full use of propaganda: 'Instil into the Nawab high notions of the great force which is coming out, huff away and assure him Pondicherry will soon be in our possession.'[51]

Above all, Clive warned Hastings not to trust the Muslims, who would 'never be influenced by kind treatment'.[52] He was able to give particular vent to his feelings on this subject in the autumn of 1758. A plot was hatched against the Nawab; his palace was surrounded by troops, clamouring for pay; there was to be an attempt on his life, but he was warned of it in time.

Soon afterwards, he showed Hastings a letter supposed to be from Rai Durlabh, implicating him in the plot.[53] Hastings thought it genuine, but Clive was convinced that it was a 'forgery from beginning to end', a scheme on the part of the Nawab and his henchmen to incriminate Rai Durlabh and seize his money. And he denounced the Muslims and their 'dark designs', having also heard a report that he himself was being accused of complicity on the plot, and that the Nawab was giving ear to these slanders.[54]

It is hard not to agree with Clive's verdict in this particular affair; for as he pointed out, Rai Durlabh, even if guilty, would never have put pen to paper; and he was right in maintaining that to withdraw protection from him on account of a dubious letter would 'entail disgrace and infamy upon the English nation'. The trouble blew over, but in the following April the Nawab made yet another attempt to discredit Rai Durlabh in the eyes of the English. In an effort to get to the bottom of the matter, Hastings pretended to share his suspicions; a deception of which Clive did not approve: 'I would leave all trickery to the Hindus and Muslims to whom it is natural, being well convinced that the reputation we have in this country is owing among other causes to the ingenuity and plain dealing for which we are distinguished.'[55] This is exactly the same argument as Macaulay was to use when condemning Clive's own deception of Omichand.

Scrafton wrote to Hastings as much as Clive did, and though he was by way of being Clive's friend, did not hesitate to criticize him to his younger colleague. Given the image of the tough-line Clive and the liberal Hastings, it is strange to find Scrafton lamenting to Hastings that Clive was being too lenient: 'The Colonel, now conscious of our weakness, will be daily giving ground to the Government and you know the consequence when once the rascals begin to encroach.'[56] But while wishing Clive to be tougher, he also mentioned the necessity of withholding some of his more impetuous letters to the Nawab.[57] 'The Colonel does not always think when he writes,' he told Hastings, giving us a clue to many of Clive's apparent inconsistencies.[58] Scrafton clearly found Clive difficult to work with. 'Whatever I ask of the Colonel is sure to meet with a blank refusal,' he complained, 'and I have done with asking favours.'[59]

Such friction as occurred between Clive and Hastings at this time was mainly due to the presence of Nundcomar, who in September 1758 was appointed to collect the revenues of the English *tuncas* in Burdwan, Nadia and Hughli.[60] Hastings, who loathed 'the Necromancer' from the first time he met him, complained of being subjected by him to 'daily indignities'.[61] But Clive was convinced of Nundcomar's 'known attachment to the English',[62] and seemed determined to shut his eyes to the fact that he almost certainly had a hand in the intrigues against Rai Durlabh and that it was his son-in-law who had made the monstrous accusation against himself. As Scrafton observed, 'It is something amazing to see how Nundcomar dupes the Colonel.'[63]

CHAPTER XIV

The Heaven-born General

> The hero Clive has taken Masulipatam and the Great Mogul's grandmother. I suppose she will be brought over and put in the Tower with the *Shah-goest*, the strange Indian beast that Mr Pitt gave to the King this winter.
>
> HORACE WALPOLE

I

While engaged in the tortuous politics of Bengal, Clive still concerned himself with military affairs. He saw the need for an up-to-date fort at Calcutta, to replace the old structure which had fallen so easily to Siraj-ud-daula's troops, and commenced the building of a vast, star-shaped citadel some distance to the south of the town.[1] Even to the Madras Committee he now made it plain that he regarded Bengal as of much greater consequence than any of the other settlements.[2] Pigot was resigned to getting no help from Bengal, though in April 1758 he had to face the arrival of a great French armament, commanded by Thomas Arthur, Comte de Lally;[3] he even agreed to part with one of his best officers, who was invited to Bengal at Clive's request to take the place of Killpatrick.

This officer was Lieutenant-Colonel Francis Forde, an Anglo-Irishman of sunny disposition and great ability, who had come out to India with the 39th Regiment. Clive first met him on the Coast in 1756, and immediately formed a high opinion of him. So keen was he to have him in Bengal that he added £2500 of his own money to a like sum granted by the Committee to make up the £5000 required by Forde as compensation for leaving his regiment.

Forde took up his quarters at Sydabad near Cossimbazar, and proceeded to carry out Clive's plan of incorporating the detachments from Madras and Bombay into the Bengal Battalion. On June 23, he and the army celebrated the first anniversary of Plassey, with wilder festivities than the parties and salutes which marked the day in Calcutta. Dancing-girls entertained the company until supper was announced, when each officer endeavoured to have the lady of his choice conveyed to his room for his subsequent delectation. There was much clamour as to who had picked whom: 'By God, this is mine, I know her by the ring in her nose,' shouted one officer, but when he went to call his servant to take her to his room, one of his comrades 'whips the ring out of her nose, and carries her off before his face'. Forde himself, as he told Clive, was no less unfortunate. While he was giving supper to Mrs Hastings—who must have been rather *de trop*—'the Adjutant had the assurance to carry off the lady he had fixed on to sing him to sleep after the fatigues of the day'.[4]

Clive and Forde also corresponded about more serious matters as together they watched developments on the Coast. 'I am not at all inclined to enter the lists with M. Lally,' wrote Clive on that first anniversary of Plassey. 'Experience, discipline and perhaps bravery likewise would be all against me.'[5] This was an open admission that he was not up to facing a crack European army.

Though Clive regarded Bengal as being of greater importance than the settlements on the Coast, he realized that if Madras fell to the French, Bengal itself might be in jeopardy. He had to do something. His eye was on the Northern Sarkars, the coastal strip of the Deccan between Orissa and the Carnatic, which had been wholly dominated by the French since the fall of Vizagapatam a year earlier. Recently, however, a powerful raja of that country, taking advantage of Bussy's departure to join Lally, had risen against the French, and had himself succeeded in capturing Vizagapatam. He now asked Clive for help, and proposed the reconquest of the four provinces which the French had obtained from Salabat Jang. Clive decided to give the raja as much help as he could; his aim being not so much to win territory as to prevent Lally's army from being reinforced with troops from the French army in the Deccan.

The expedition sailed at the end of September. It was commanded by Forde, who took with him 500 out of the 700 European troops in Bengal, together with 2000 sepoys. Clive's decision to send away two-thirds of his European troops caused great consternation among the inhabitants of Calcutta. But his gamble came off. On December 7, Forde put the French army to flight near Condore; and in the following April, he captured the important French coastal settlement of Masulipatam. This victory led to an alliance between the English and Salabat Jang, who like his subordinate, the raja, was tired of Bussy's domination.

More immediately important than the end of French supremacy in the Deccan was the fact that Forde's expedition, by depriving Lally of reinforcements, probably saved Madras. On December 14, Lally's troops entered the Black Town, and for the next two months Fort St George stood siege. A fierce and prolonged bombardment opened a breach, and reduced much of the settlement to ruins. But Pigot and Stringer Lawrence led a gallant defence, and though the English casualties amounted to 468 killed and wounded, the Fort held out until February 16, when the appearance of the ships bringing the long-awaited reinforcements from Bombay caused the French to retire. The defence of Madras by his old friends stirred Clive's emotions. 'I would gladly have given some of my riches to have shared some of your reputation,' he told his friend Henry Vansittart. 'I know it has been a conceived opinion among the old soldiers in England that our exploits in India have been much of the same nature as those of Hernando Cortes; but your foiling such a man as M. Lally, and two of the oldest regiments of France, will induce another way of thinking.'[6]*

2

'Every person is your friend,' wrote Mr Justice Clive to his cousin in the autumn of 1757, when the news of the recovery of Calcutta and the capture of Chandernagore reached England.[7] But he added that popularity was 'uncertain and fluctuating'—a truism that applied only too well to Clive, whose achievements were always to meet with a mixed reception.

* One at least of Clive's Madras friends did not share in this 'reputation', and that was Orme. When Lally's success at Fort St David put Madras itself in peril, he sold his effects, wound up his affairs and booked a passage home. He gave ill-health as the reason for his departure, which in the event was postponed until after the siege; but it led to his being charged with cowardice. He was also accused of trying to extort money from Mohammed Ali (Powis Collection, Box I) and so he resigned the service and returned to England as a relatively poor man.

The news sent Richard Clive hurrying up to Town to distribute the letters from his son among the 'Great Men'. Everyone he met said: 'Why is not the Colonel sent for home, then we may have success in England.'[8] But when he canvassed Clive's idea of being made Governor-General, the response was unfavourable,[9] and he found the Directors slow in proposing any concrete reward—on the contrary, Payne dissuaded the Duke of Newcastle from getting Clive an honour.[10]

To make up for this disappointment, Clive was praised both by the King and by the most popular English statesman of the day, William Pitt, then Foreign Secretary and Secretary for War, who had a personal interest in India, being the grandson of a Governor of Madras. The King was talking to the Commander-in-Chief, who asked if a certain young nobleman could go as a volunteer to the army of either the King of Prussia or the Duke of Brunswick. 'Pshaw!' replied the King. 'What can he learn there? If he want to learn the art of war, let him go to Clive!'[11]

Pitt's tribute came in his speech in Parliament on the Mutiny Bill. Having referred to the disgraces that had recently attended British arms, he said: 'We had lost our glory, honour and reputation everywhere but in India. There the country had a heaven-born general who had never learned the art of war, nor was his name enrolled among the great officers who had for many years received their country's pay. Yet he was not afraid to attack a numerous army with a handful of men, and overcame them.' 'Name him!' cried the House, and Pitt went on: 'Everyone knows that I mean Colonel Clive.'[12] He then proceeded to give Clive the highest possible character, saying that to read of his exploits gave him as much pleasure as reading Quintus Curtius, the historian of Alexander the Great.[13]

But even at this moment of triumph—witnessed from the gallery by Clive's Cousin Harry—a sneer was heard. Alderman William Beckford, the West Indian millionaire, spoke of Clive as having raised himself from 'a dirty writer' to a commander-in-chief. '*Dirty writer*,' exclaimed another member. 'The gentleman was a member of this House!' 'Yes!' retorted Beckford. 'For a day.'[14]

One is struck by how few people wrote to congratulate Clive, either in the autumn of 1757, or in the spring of 1758, when the news of Plassey reached England. In fact, Plassey seems to have made only a moderate impact on the British people. This was apparent to Scrafton from the letters he received at the end of 1758: 'Our successes here have not made the éclat that was expected,' he told Hastings, regretting that Clive himself had not followed the news back to England, as its publicist.[15] English military circles were sceptical as to whether the 'Heaven-born General'—a sobriquet that was to stick to Clive for the rest of his life, but used mainly in irony—knew anything about war, any more than did the King of Prussia.[16]

Such accounts as there are of Clive's fame being universal come from his family, who in the nature of things would have received many compliments about their distinguished relative. His father was in raptures. 'May Heaven', he exclaimed to his son, 'preserve you safe to Old England, where not only your friends and relations, but strangers who never saw you, will congratulate you for the glorious actions you have done your country. With what joy shall I embrace you! Oh, may I live to see that day! Your mother and sisters are sitting with me round the fire, drinking to your health and safe voyage.'[17] Nine months after the news of Plassey, he still could not read the letters of his wonderful son without bursting into tears.[18]

Clive's son Ned, now aged four, 'a fine, upright, lively child, not handsome but a very sharp little fellow', every day drank the health of Papa, Mamma and Mir Jafar.[19] It might have been of some consolation to the Nawab, among all his troubles, to know that he had made an honest English family really happy. Brother Dick and Sister Nanny, who had both been about to sail for India, in search of a fortune and a husband respectively, could now stay at home. As for Cousin Sally, Clive had promised to bring her back an Eastern prince. 'I have a taste to be a princess,' she told Margaret. 'Pray, is he a black in the Othello taste and I to be his Desdemona?'[20]

3

'Whilst you are employed in watching the motions of a vigilant and active enemy,' wrote Clive to Admiral Pocock, in 1759, 'we are employed in bullying and keeping under the black fellows.'[21] Chief among the 'black fellows' in question was no less a personage than the Shahzada or Crown Prince, son of the Mogul.[22] At this time, the Imperial family were little more than state prisoners in the hands of their Vizier, but the Shahzada had managed to escape and was, as Clive put it, 'fishing in troubled waters'.[23] Having gathered a following of soldiers of fortune, he planned to invade Bihar and Bengal, overthrow Mir Jafar and assume the government of the provinces himself. He had the approval of Shuja-ud-daula, the Nawab of Oudh, who gave him troops and a useful sum of money. By February 1759, he was approaching Bihar, his army having grown to 40,000.

The Shahzada chose an opportune moment. Mir Jafar's troops were still on the point of mutiny for want of their arrears; Clive was not much better off, with the greater part of his army away in the Sarkars. Nevertheless, he was determined to give Mir Jafar the utmost support. 'Rest assured', he told him, 'that the English are your staunch and firm friends, and that they never desert a cause in which they have once taken a part.'[24] Meanwhile, the Shahzada addressed 'the High and Mighty Protector of the Great, Colonel Sabit Jang Bahadur', in the hope of winning him over to his side. Clive sent an answer in which, as an Imperial Commander, he pleaded that he could do nothing without the Mogul's orders.[25] To the Nawab, he gave a highly coloured account of the Shahzada's overtures: 'They made me offers of provinces upon provinces, with whatever my heart could desire; but could he give, as well as offer me, the whole empire of Hindostan, it would have no weight with the English.'[26] The popular belief that Clive resisted the temptation of becoming an independent Indian potentate may stem from this remark.

Clive's letters alone could not drive the Shahzada away, so at the end of February he had to march, taking with him all his European troops – they amounted to no more than 450 – and leaving Calcutta to be guarded by volunteers and militia. Halting at Cossimbazar, he met the Nawab and lectured him on 'his treacherous behaviour and non-payment of the people in his service'.[27] The two of them rode on the same elephant together with Omar Beg; there was 'more dust kicked about them' than Major John Carnac – Clive's aide-de-camp and secretary, who was down below in his palanquin – could bear.*

Clive then headed for Patna as quickly as he could, by forced marches and by river. He was joined by Miran, with a considerable army, the

* Margaret did a childish sketch of Clive, the Nawab and Omar Beg on their elephant, with Carnac far below in his palanquin. Her note on the back reads: 'This proof of my folly should not have come with so serious a letter, but for the sake of comparing the Aide-de-Camp under his master to the Laurel of Parnassus, she could not forbear sending it. Let no one see it' (Sutton Court Collection, Box I).

Nawab himself preferring to stay behind. Carnac, for one, was less concerned about the Shahzada than about the dust, and his mind was also taken up with getting gloves and shoes to send to Margaret in Calcutta.[28] But close upon the news that the Shahzada and his army had crossed the Karamnassa* into Bihar, came an even more depressing report that Ramnarayan had visited the Shahzada's camp and made his submission. Clive immediately sent Ramnarayan a warning: 'What power has the Shahzada to resist the united forces of the Nawab and the English? Think then, what will be your fate.'[29]

Soon afterwards came better news: Ramnarayan had returned from the Shahzada's camp to Patna, and prepared to hold out against him. When the Shahzada's troops besieged the city, and tried to take it by storm, Ramnarayan drove them off. Clive sent forward a detachment to raise the siege, and when this was within ten miles of Patna, the Shahzada's army fled. 'If you do not come soon, you will lose the fine hunt I have prepared for you,' wrote Ramnarayan jubilantly to Clive,[30] whom he afterwards likened to Jesus Christ.[31] Clive had come quick enough by all accounts, his advance guard covering 400 miles in 23 days.

The Shahzada's army melted away as if by magic, and at the end of April the Shahzada was obliged to retire beyond the Karamnassa with a mere three hundred followers. He wrote Clive several plaintive letters, asking for his protection. Clive thought it imprudent to give him asylum within the Nawab's territories, but sent him 500 gold *mohurs* – £1000 – towards the expenses of his return journey.[32] Having thus dismissed the Shahzada, he felt equal to warning off his ally, the Nawab of Oudh – telling him that he would be happy to fight him after the Rains.[33]

It only remained to punish three rajas in the hill country of Boadgepore, who had declared for the Shahzada. Two of them came and made their submission immediately, a remarkable circumstance in that they had never before been known to venture out of their country – Clive ascribed it to their trusting the English.[34] They agreed to pay their arrears and were duly forgiven. The third raja, named Pulwansing, took to the hills. Clive thought it necessary to make a severe example of him. He led his army far into Pulwansing's country, destroying more than three hundred villages as he went – perhaps the only time in his career when he was cruel to the Indian populace. The going was difficult, owing to the hills, rocks and woods; the heat was greater than European troops had yet been called upon to endure;[35] but Clive reached Nookah, Pulwansing's capital, where

* The river forming the boundary between Bihar and Oudh.

he burnt the whole place, including the raja's house. Pulwansing, who had retreated even further into his hills, now wrote Clive a submissive letter, and as it was impossible to catch up with him, he was allowed to continue as the ruler of his ravaged country.

When Clive approached Murshidabad on his return from Patna at the end of June, the Nawab came to meet him, accompanied by one of the Seths, who handed him a document in a silken bag. Clive took it without opening it; he was later to assert that he had not known what it was.[36] When eventually it was translated, he found that he had been granted an annual income of 300,000 rupees—about £27,000. This was the famous *jagir*, which transformed Clive from a rich man to a man with one of the largest incomes in England. It was also to bring him infinite trouble; a case of Fate being over-kind.

Writing to Pocock soon after it was granted, Clive described the *jagir* as 'unasked, or indeed unthought of'.[37] This, like many of his assertions, was not strictly true, or at any rate it was a piece of hair-splitting. Clive's imperial rank as a commander of 5000 horse and 6000 foot carried with it, in theory, an annual salary of 300,000 rupees, which by custom was secured to him by means of a *jagir*, the grant of the revenues of a certain district. Knowing this, he asked the Seths, in January 1759, to use their good offices with the Nawab, that he might have a *jagir* equal to his rank.[38] The Seths at first seem to have ignored this request;[39] but a week or so later, when the Shahzada crisis was blowing up, and Hastings suspected them of intriguing with the invader, they wrote to say that they had raised the matter of the *jagir*, and that although the Nawab was not inclined to grant the revenues of a district in Bengal, he might have done something in Bihar.[40] As Bihar was then just about to be invaded, Clive took this answer to be 'an evasive one'.[41] He wrote no more about it, but in the following June, he received another letter from the Seths to say that the Nawab was now willing to grant him a *jagir* in Bengal.[42]

Clive seems to have convinced himself that the *jagir* was 'unasked and unexpected'. In a pamphlet he published a few years later, he made this assertion, and then told quite openly of how he had asked the Seths about the *jagir* in January 1759, as though unaware that the two statements were in any way contradictory. He was determined to answer the charge that he had bullied the Nawab into giving him the *jagir* by arguing that it was an unexpected reward for driving away the Shahzada, while making no attempt to conceal the fact that he had applied for it six months before. Although it was to all intents and purposes a reward for the Shahzada expedition, the *jagir* would have been easier to justify as the rightful salary of Clive's Imperial rank. He himself at first took his rank seriously, and planned to devote a large part of his *jagir* to maintaining a force of 500 European troops—he told Pocock of this intention in August 1759, but does not appear to have pursued it any further.[43]

Our judgement of Clive in this matter would depend on whether or not his Imperial rank was solicited by him. If it was, and he knew it would carry a *jagir*, he can be accused of greed—having, as he told his father, already been made rich beyond his 'most sanguine wishes'. But if the rank was 'unasked', he cannot be blamed for taking advantage of this extra windfall. In giving evidence before the Parliamentary Committee of 1772, he first of all admitted to having applied for the rank, then denied this a few days later, saying that on recollection he found he had been mistaken in his previous statement.[44] One feels that if he had been inclined to tell a lie, he would have done so in the first place; it was very much in character for him to speak without thinking and to be careless in remembering past events.

The Nawab found the money for Clive's *jagir* by assigning to him the quit-rent which he received from the Company for the district round Calcutta. It was just the right amount, and no immediate loss to his revenues, having been stopped, on account of what he owed under the treaty. The Company became, in effect, the tenant of one of its own servants—an anomalous situation bound to cause trouble.*

* Macaulay, so censorious about the present which Clive received after Plassey, regarded him as justified in accepting the *jagir* because it was 'no secret'. As a precedent for Clive's *jagir* there was the *jagir* granted to Dupleix. The popular soldier, Hector Munro, would have accepted a *jagir* of £12,500 a year in 1763, had not Clive's *jagir* been the subject of controversy at that time.

CHAPTER XV

The Happiest Woman Living

You are one of the happiest women living.

REBECCA TO MARGARET CLIVE, 1758

I

Margaret managed to keep her high spirits, despite the worry of Clive's expeditions up country, the loss of her daughter, Jenny, who died in the autumn of 1757, and the unhealthy and unpleasant climate of Bengal. Throughout these two-and-a-half years, she stayed in Calcutta, with visits to Clive's country house at Dum-Dum, a short distance to the north of the settlement. This house was originally a Dutch or Portuguese factory, a single-storey building of brick, massively buttressed, standing on an artificial mound. Clive added an upper storey to it with a pillared loggia in the centre, and he laid out a formal garden with walks and shrubberies.[1]

In Calcutta, there was no official Governor's house after the upheavals of 1756. Clive bought a house of his own at the south-east corner of the Park.[2] The colonnade of its upstairs verandah, crowned in summer with a row of the huge and rather grisly adjutant birds that fed on Calcutta's carrion, rose above its garden wall. Like most European houses in the India of those days, it was sparsely furnished: a few chairs, a few blackwood and marble-topped tables; large looking-glasses on the walls, and 'side lanthorns' to protect the candles from the wind; *almiras* or wardrobes and 'cots'. There was a certain amount of silver, and enough books for one room to be called the 'bookroom'.[3]

There was also Margaret's harpsichord and the many volumes of music which her mother-in-law sent her from England. While Margaret was making music, Clive, when he was at home, played cards with men friends such as Scrafton, smoking one of his hookahs, which were of blue and green lacquer, set with rubies and diamonds. He was never a gambler, but the stakes were high; his winnings amounted to 15,398 rupees in one month alone.[4] The house was always full of guests; even in his more modest days before Plassey, Clive reckoned that his year's supply of wine would cost him £500. Margaret never lacked the attentions of admiring males; but when the 'black grandees', as she called them, came to visit Clive, he observed the custom of the country and insisted on her concealing herself, 'not suffering me to appear till I was asked for, thereby to increase their respect'.[5]

After the Coast, with its intermingling of old-established Portuguese civilization and evangelical simplicity, Margaret found Calcutta society somewhat brash. Rather than sitting through the interminable dinner parties at which the throwing of bread pellets was a recognized diversion, she preferred the company of a few close friends. There was Philadelphia Hancock to replace Jane Latham, who had returned to Madras with the squadron. There were two clergymen: the Swedish missionary, Kiernander, now settled in Calcutta following the capture of Fort St David by the French, and 'Padre' Butler, recommended to Clive by the Reverend Dr Adams of Shrewsbury. There was her doctor, William Fullerton, and her 'gentleman usher', Major John Carnac, who lived *en famille* with the Clives when he was in Calcutta.

A former officer of the 39th, Carnac had accompanied Forde to Bengal as his secretary, and was then employed as secretary and aide-de-camp by Clive. Like Forde, he came from Ireland, but from the Huguenot middle class instead of the landed gentry; supporting an old mother and two deaf-and-dumb brothers in Dublin. Though nearly forty, he was noted for his fresh complexion. 'His blooming cheeks are dyed with colours all their own, Excelling far the pride of roses newly blown,' a Calcutta lady sang of him; while in Madras he was known as 'blind Cupid'.[6] He was inclined to fuss over himself in an unmanly way; yet at times he could be very much the military fire-eater.

It was to be expected that this bachelor, verging on middle age, should have become the devoted slave of Margaret, who was still in her early twenties. For her part, Margaret responded with mild flirtation. When Carnac was in Calcutta, the two of them chattered and laughed endlessly. Relationships of this sort were more understandable to the eighteenth century – or, for that matter, to the nineteenth, which saw the friendship between Disraeli and Lady Bradford—than to the present generation. It made no difference to Margaret's great love for Clive; nor did it lead to any jealousy between Clive and Carnac. On the contrary, they were to be lifelong friends; Margaret and Clive thought of Carnac as a possible husband for Cousin Sally. When Carnac was away with Clive on the Shahzada expedition, he and Margaret corresponded at great length. There was, however, a reason for this, in that she never ceased to want news of Clive, who was bad about writing to her. 'I frequently accuse him of writing less than any other husband, and so great is my imprudence that I mention these neglects before company.'[7] As Carnac observed to himself, she took no notice of a letter from him if it arrived at the same time as one from her lord and master.[8]

From these letters, we get a charming picture of Margaret's day-to-day life. We see her 'sitting at one of the small dinner tables, just in the wind of all the doors, with my drawer of letters at my elbow'.[9] On the table hops a tame mynah bird, 'learning of us women to talk nonsense'.[10] The mynah is not her only pet; she also has a 'young tiger, a bear, two porcupines, three of these new-fashioned birds and an owl as big almost as myself'.[11] From below come the voices of the servants, to whom she is 'Madam', or 'Bibi', rather than Memsahib, which has not yet come into use; though she herself sometimes refers to Clive as the Colonel Sahib. They include Chowry the butler, Black Robin, Maria the ayah, and Mercury, 'the boy the Frenchman gave me and whom I turned over to Doctor Butler to make a Christian and an Englishman of'. Suddenly, the voices rise to a commotion: 'So fruitless have been the honest Padre's admonitions that Mercury was very imprudently saying the Frenchmen were very good, and that all the English might go to a place whither Orpheus went to free his lady, as history says. This so enraged my loyal ayah, Maria, that she gave the boy that monstrous slap, "flap" as she calls it, or box on the ear, the drum of it must be cracked, since the boy cries so loud that we three are stunned, and he seems to not hear his own roaring.'[12]

It is just turned of eleven o'clock and the sun so fierce that our umbrellas and a gentle southerly wind which comes charging in at my windows are not sufficient to keep me from almost fainting . . . my genius is, I cannot say chilled or frozen, but quite (to use a country expression) expended,[13] and myself in danger of expiring. Thank you, good Chowry, you have quite restored me to health by your seasonable supply of toasted bread scrubbed with nutmeg,

> and the glass of Madeira wine. Having drunk half thereof, without any ceremony, as life and death were in the case, I tope off the remainder to the health of my friends in Camp . . . Mrs Hancock is squeezing mangoes down her throat to your health and safe return, and if she be not sincere, she wishes they may choke her. Amen, say I.[14]

Morning turns to afternoon, with her siesta. Then in the cool of the evening, she goes for a ride in the chaise with Philadelphia and Dr Fullerton. Then supper; 'made a meal of pancakes, and drank one glass of Madeira, of a bottle which was opened nobody knows how long ago'.[15] Then to bed, 'dreaming all our friends were returned'.[16]

This peaceful existence was frequently interrupted by 'squalls and hurricanes', 'north-westers' and 'south-easters',[17] and by 'swarms of flies, mosquitos, cockroaches and dumbledores [*sic*]'. 'We have all the plagues of Egypt together, for some of my visitors have boils.' Philadelphia was bitten by what Margaret called a 'cent pieds', managing to give the insect a Watteauesque elegance. She herself was the particular prey of the mosquitoes, despite the mosquito net on her bed. 'One would think we were young ladies just come out of Europe, they bite so, I thought I was too ancient to attract them.'[18] But apart from her bites, which she rubbed with lemons, she was remarkably well, particularly since she was pregnant again. By June, she was mocking Dr Fullerton for forbidding her from 'jumping and such things', and begging Carnac to 'take care of my husband and bring him back to his old woman, or little woman, or *large* woman'.[19] She eventually gave birth to another son, who was given the name of Robert.

For all her gaiety, her longing for Clive and her concern about him keep coming out. 'I thought I had in all my letters written with vast spirit and resolution, affecting more tranquillity than I really was blessed with. However, be assured I am now extremely easy, and shall wait with great composure for his return, against which I have a calf a-fattening. Don't make a pun, Carnac, and say that *I* am the calf.'[20] Carnac's letters, she told him, 'convey to me the highest consolation, that of hearing of the Colonel. The certainty of hearing often by your means keeps my mind in a state of tranquillity I never knew in that creature's absence. Why are the men of so much consequence to us?'[21] 'May the heroes return shortly to receive the wreath of laurel their ladies are preparing them! Alas! I think of mine too often for my repose, but on such an account who would not wish to be in my case? . . . Every one of my past melancholy ideas is far overbalanced by the most pleasing hope of seeing again the comfort[22] of my life.'[23]

On a more homely plane, she enquired after Clive's clothes: 'Has the Colonel a decent coat? I rigged him out well, but I suppose you are all by this time in rags and tatters.'[24] She also concerned herself in a light-hearted way with his spiritual welfare: 'Enjoin him to say Grace at dinner and supper every day constantly during his absence from her. She absolutely insists upon his doing it with an audible voice . . . Let who will object to it. An innovation in the camp! Bless us! What will the world come to? That such words should come from the Commander-in-Chief, who has been married these six years! This comes of playing cards on Sundays. Have not you heard of my turning Methodist?'[25]

While her letters to Carnac were a means of communicating with Clive, she did not forget Carnac himself. 'Your strange cat has forsaken the house and all the animals have lost their spirits since *our* clackings ceased.'[26] And she sent a 'salaam' to the other men with them, particularly to Henry Lushington and Clive's cousin, Thomas Amphlett. She made mosquito nets for the returning warriors[27] and had their 'cages'* rewired;[28] her great hope being that they would be back in time for the ball on June 23, the second anniversary of Plassey. She promised several dances to Carnac, but they would have to be minuets: 'It is not for people of my infirmities to venture themselves in a Bengal set of country dances, and you are not ignorant of how much we Indians fall short of a St. James's assembly in the gentleness and delicacy of our movements.'[29] But in the end her partners did not get back until after Plassey Day; it was poor consolation for her to be escorted to the ball by the attentive but stuffy Manningham.

2

Clive had barely returned to Calcutta in July 1759, when there was news of a large Dutch armament being on its way from Batavia. Despite the personal friendship between Clive and the Director of Cinsura, Adrian Bisdom, and the fact that a considerable amount of the English East India Company stock was Dutch-held, the Dutch had resented the growth of

* The cages of wire netting which protected them from insects when they slept out of doors during the hot weather.

English ascendancy in Bengal. Taking advantage of the growing friction between the Nawab and the English, the chief of the Dutch factory at Cossimbazar, Vernet, had carried on secret negotiations both with Mir Jafar and Miran for the introduction of a Dutch force into Bengal. The Nawab had expressed his hatred of the English yoke and welcomed an increase in Dutch strength as a counterpoise; it was Siraj-ud-daula's old policy, with the Dutch taking the place of the French.

To Clive, an increase in Dutch strength threatened the destruction of everything he had built up during the past three years. He was faced with a delicate situation. England and Holland were, as far as he knew, at peace, although the news from Europe told of worsening relations between the two countries. If the Dutch persisted in bringing their troops up the river and he used force against them, he would be guilty of starting hostilities against a friendly nation. But as he is reported to have said at the time: 'A public man may occasionally be called upon to act with a halter round his neck.'[30] So he determined to resist the Dutch, regardless of the consequences; though the risk was not as great as he afterwards made out, for it is unlikely that his action would not have been supported at home. Nor was he hazarding his private fortune as he claimed to have done when he told the Committee of the House of Commons that 'much the greatest part of his fortune was in the hands of the Dutch' at the time of his decision to resist them.[31] It is true that in August 1757, when faced with the problem of sending home his money, he had remitted £183,000 through the Dutch Company, which had, as it happened, been slow in honouring his bills. But even so, the money had been paid to his English agents by the early summer of 1759. At the time of the Dutch crisis, Clive would have been safe in assuming that the money was already in the hands of his agents—or would be before news of the affair reached Holland—considering how long it was since he had made the remittances.

Apart from the question of legality, Clive was faced with the immediate military problem of opposing a Dutch force reported to be twice the size of his own. The Madras gentlemen would not let Forde's troops return to Bengal from the Sarkars; Clive did, however, obtain the services of Forde himself, though in circumstances which caused him extreme disgust. A dispatch arrived from the Directors, disapproving of the conditions under which Forde had been appointed, and superseding him in favour of Coote.[32] On hearing this, Forde threw in his hand and set out for Europe by way of Bengal, where he broke his journey in order to command Clive's troops against the Dutch.

At first, Clive resorted to the time-honoured fiction, originated by Dupleix, of acting as an 'auxiliary' to the Nawab; requesting him to order the Dutch 'peremptorily' to send away their troops.[33] Despite his recent intrigues, the Nawab duly issued two *purwannas*, forbidding them from bringing any more troops into his dominions. The Dutch promised to obey the Nawab's orders, but Clive nevertheless garrisoned the fortifications downstream of Calcutta and gave orders for all boats coming up river to be searched.

Early in October, the Nawab paid another visit to Calcutta. Once again, he was lavishly entertained, at a cost of 79,542 rupees; his house was furnished with velvet and gold thread, lustres and looking-glasses; there was a theatrical performance and a ball; trumpets, horns and kettle-drums were sounded on every occasion. The presents given him by the Company included a number of waxworks: of a Turkish lady, of the Virgin Mary, of a boy and girl; as well as 'twelve standing Venuses to pull off behind' and 'six kissing figures'.[34] In the midst of all these festivities, news came of the arrival of the Dutch squadron at Fulta.

The Nawab agreed to summon the Cinsura council when he reached Hughli on his way back to Murshidabad, and to threaten to drive them out of Bengal altogether if their squadron did not go away. But according to Hastings, he received the Dutchmen 'very graciously', and gave them presents and promised them his protection.[35] He did not, however, commit himself openly against the English, and the Dutch made the mistake of waiting for him to do so, instead of forcing the river without delay, which would have convinced him of their strength, and perhaps induced him to join them. In fact, the Dutch had very little idea of what to do next. The Cinsura council was divided between the doves, led by Bisdom, and the hawks, led by Vernet.

Meanwhile Clive made ready to prevent the entry of the Dutch troops. It was vital to intercept them before they joined up with the Cinsura garrison. Three Company ships were ordered into the river; sepoys were stationed near Cinsura, to encourage the desertion of Dutch troops; there were even posters put up offering a gratuity of 100 rupees to anyone who entered the English service.[36] At length, the Dutch decided on action; Vernet and the war-party had a free hand owing to the illness of Bisdom, who was thought to be at death's door.[37] An 'immense remonstrance' was sent to the English on November 7, threatening reprisals if they continued the searching of boats. The English replied with some audacity that they had only done so by order of the Nawab; but that they were ready to interpose their 'friendly offices to mitigate his resentment'.[38] The Dutch reaction to the English reply was to seize some English small craft, and burn the houses of the Company's tenants near Fulta. This was just what Clive wanted: the Dutch had struck the first blow, and he was now able to retaliate without being guilty of starting hostilities.

On November 23, the Dutch troops, 700 Europeans and 800 Malays, landed down river. According to the well-known story, Clive was playing cards when he received a note from Forde informing him of this, and he scribbled to him in reply, 'Dear Forde, fight 'em immediately, I will send an order of Council tomorrow.'[39] Next day, at the same time as the English ships captured the Dutch squadron, Forde routed the garrison of Cinsura. He then turned his attention to the newly-arrived Dutch force. The resulting action, on the plains of Badara, was 'short, bloody and decisive'.[40] In less than half an hour, the entire Dutch force had either been killed, wounded or taken prisoner. The English casualties were no more than ten. In the face of this disaster, and threatened now by an army under Miran, who was prompted by the English success to rattle the sabre against his former friends, the Dutch capitulated. The English allowed them to remain in Cinsura, and in return, they agreed to limit their forces, and pay damages of ten lakhs. Clive was not present at Badara, which again suggests that he was determined to avoid risking his luck in another military action, least of all against a European enemy.

Among the measures which Clive felt obliged to take during the Dutch crisis was to seize the merchant Khwaja Wajid, who was suspected by Hastings of being 'the prime instigator of these troubles',[41] and bring him as a captive to Calcutta. Within a few days of being made a prisoner, he was dead, according to Clive of 'a fever and a flux'.[42] In later years, Clive's enemies were to accuse him of murder, but they chose the most unlikely victims. Nobody seems to have mentioned the case of Khwaja Wajid, where there are certainly grounds for suspicion. And if he died naturally, which he probably did, Clive would have to a certain degree been responsible for his death through having ordered his arrest.[43]

3

When the Dutch crisis blew up, Clive was already planning to go home.

His health was giving way, he had stayed on more than two years after Plassey; it was time to enjoy his riches in his native land. He wanted to be in time for any peace negotiations with France,[44] and, what was nearest to his heart, he hoped to get Coote's appointment reversed, so that Forde could become commander-in-chief of all the troops in India.[45] Such antipathy as Clive may already have had for Coote was fanned into a blind hatred by his appointment. 'I tremble when I think of the fatal consequences of such a mercenary man as Coote commanding here,' he told Vansittart, 'for God's sake, keep him on the Coast, there he can only get a little drubbing, but here he may ruin the Company's affairs for ever.'[46]

Anxious as Clive was for a share of the reinforcements from England, he willingly let the Madras gentlemen keep Coote's battalion so as to prevent Coote himself from coming to Bengal.[47] 'Take but the man and you shall have the 1000 men into the bargain,' he told Pigot.[48] It was some consolation to Clive that Coote did stay on the Coast, and that he was able to hand over the command of his troops in Bengal to Major John Caillaud. But far from taking 'a little drubbing' Coote won a decisive victory over the French at Wandewash in January 1760, opening the way for the capture of Pondicherry by the English a year later. The news of Wandewash reached Clive when his ship was leaving the river; it should have enabled him to see the last of Bengal with an easy heart, but one suspects he may have felt mortified.

There was dismay in Calcutta at the prospect of Clive's departure; eighty-seven people of the settlement signed a letter begging him to stay longer. 'It appeared', wrote a contemporary, 'as if the soul was departing from the government of Bengal.'[49] Clive travelled to Murshidabad to take leave of the Nawab, who at this moment was as anxious as anyone for him to stay, the Shahzada being about to invade Bihar once again, together with the Nawab of Oudh.

The return of the Shahzada was only one instance of the prevailing uncertainty. Clive had stayed two years longer in Bengal to ensure 'the settlement of these provinces', but to attempt such a settlement was like stopping up a sieve. By now, he had fewer illusions as to the permanency of his achievement;[50] it was a case of not so much a settlement as of a series of short-term expedients. This was all right so long as he was there, for he was a brilliant improviser; but it was only too easy for those who came after him to make a false move, with disastrous results. Clive had created a personal ascendancy over Bengal. 'Not a man in this part of the world dare send a bale of freight without my permission,'[51] was his proud boast.

The question was whether this ascendancy could be maintained by his successors. It had been as much as Clive could do to maintain it himself, leaving him no time for making any reforms in the body politic. Far from improving the Nawab's government, the English ascendancy caused it to become more corrupt, based as it was on the principle of divide and rule. While the Nawab's authority was undermined, his officials were shielded by the English, who were still unable to supervise them, so that it was all too easy for them to feather their nests.

Clive's settlement was not only shaky, but it left the Company with a deficit. The crore* of rupees paid by Mir Jafar as compensation, and the revenues of the lands near Calcutta which he ceded to the Company under the treaty, did not cover the cost of the new fort and of Forde's expedition, as well as the increased expenses of government. The Company also had to maintain an army to defend a country the size of France on a totally inadequate subsidy of a lakh a month which the Nawab only paid when he actually required its services.

However unsatisfactory may have been the situation in which Clive left Bengal, it was the work of a genius to have maintained his ascendancy for two and a half years, in the face of a recurring French threat and with inadequate military resources. The future existence of British India may have depended almost entirely on the subsequent work of consolidation; but it was Clive's empire on a shoestring which committed his countrymen to this work.

Clive wished for the task of those who came after him to be made easier by means of a garrison of 2000 European troops. This, he was sure, would prevent both the Nawab and Miran from giving trouble again. And if, by any chance, they persisted in being a nuisance, a force of this size would enable the Company itself to take over the sovereignty of Bengal. He was certain the Mogul would offer no opposition to so radical a step, but would see in it a way of getting his rightful share of the Bengal revenues which the Nawabs had long withheld. As for the people of Bengal, 'they would rejoice in so happy an exchange as that of a mild for a despotic government'. Clive wrote these words at the beginning of 1759. His thinking had come a long way since his assertion, only eighteen months before, that commerce was his countrymen's 'proper sphere' and 'whole aim in these parts'. Later that year, in the flush of his success against the Shahzada, he went further and dreamt of empire-building on a heroic scale. 'What an opening was here to release the Mogul and put him on the

* Ten million.

throne,'[52] he told Pocock, while to the Committee he wrote: 'A glorious opportunity now presents itself of making us considerable indeed in India and perhaps of giving a King to Hindostan.'[53] He soon had second thoughts about these wilder schemes, and for the rest of his life was consistent in opposing them; but he gave serious consideration to the possibility of taking over the sovereignty of Bengal as a means of finally securing the Company's position there.

He realized, however, that the Company was unlikely to provide sufficient troops for such an enterprise. The only hope was for the British Crown to be interested. And so, emboldened by Pitt's 'Heaven-born general' speech, Clive communicated these thoughts by letter to the Great Commoner himself; the one man in England to whom he considered it expedient, for the present, to impart them. He took care to hold out an attractive bait:

> I leave you to judge whether an income yearly of upwards of two millions sterling, with the possession of three provinces abounding in the most valuable productions of nature and of art, be an object deserving the public attention . . . an acquisition which, under the management of so able and disinterested a Minister, would prove a source of immense wealth to the kingdom, and might in time be appropriated in part as a fund towards diminishing the heavy load of debt under which we at present labour . . . this project may be brought about without draining the mother country, as has been too much the case with our possessions in America.[54]

To the twentieth-century mind, these are doctrines of colonialism and exploitation, while Clive's economic reasonings were proved to be at fault in his own lifetime. But when he wrote these words, they would have seemed good sense to a large proportion of his countrymen.

On February 21, 1760, Clive and Margaret sailed for England aboard the *Royal George*. Their party included George Clive and Carnac, and a number of Indian servants. The latter did not include Black Robin, who this time refused to come back to England – Margaret thought it odd in view of his being a Christian. They also took with them an assortment of wild beasts. As far as Clive knew, he was leaving India for good. Never more would he have to endure the pestilential climate of Bengal and its tortuous politics. His Indian career had been crowned with success beyond his wildest dreams; now, at thirty-four, he could look forward to a life of wealth and privilege in England.

Yet, as the *Royal George* passed from the river to the muddy waters of Ballasore Road, and then into the blue sea beyond, he felt a certain pang. 'It is not money which brings happiness,' his friend, John Call, observed of him at this time. 'I question if he is now so easy and happy as when he first left India.'[55] It was more than just his usual depression, for he had been in the throes of one such bout when he left India in 1753. That earlier departure had not been final; he knew he was coming back. Now that he was going for good, he found that the country he was leaving was taking a greater hold on him than he cared to admit. And then, he was not just bidding a final farewell to a country and its people; he was leaving a country where, for the past two years, he had been the uncrowned king. As is so often the case with those who become autocrats by accident, or even reluctantly, he had acquired a taste for power. He thrived on hard work; for a temperament needing challenge, as his did, to give of its best, the unending crisis of the past two years had afforded the perfect stimulus. And if being an autocrat gave full play to his strength, it was also a defence against his insecurity to occupy a position of undoubted supremacy, with not just the Company servants and the military, but also the Nawab and the magnates of Bengal hanging on his words and seeking his favours; and with his name revered by such distant potentates as the Nawab of Oudh and the Mogul. Great as might be the position which awaited him in England, he knew it would not be as great as this. Having once been a king, he could never again be entirely happy as a subject. If only he had gone home two years earlier, after Plassey, he would have been a young man who had brought off a tremendous *coup* and now had the world at his feet. Instead, at thirty-four, he was an unthroned monarch, facing a life which, after the life he was leaving behind, would always seem somewhat empty.

As for Margaret, she had a heartbreak of her own. Her baby son, Bob, was not well enough to travel, so had to be left behind in the care of Doctor Fullerton.

CHAPTER XVI

All over Estates and Diamonds

The solid pudding, th' adage says,
Is better far than empty praise,
When both concur, there's no great harm
To keep the heart and stomach warm,
And for your Lordship, there's this good in
Your case, that you've both praise and puddin'.

LINES ADDRESSED TO CLIVE ABOUT 1762

The voyage home was unusually quick. At St Helena, Carnac heard that he had been appointed Major of the Company's troops in Bengal, so left the *Royal George* and returned to India in the next outward-bound ship, taking some of Clive's Indian servants with him, including Chowry, the butler, and three 'black wenches', Lucy, Jezabel and another, about whose welfare Margaret was very much concerned.* He was very sad at being parted from Margaret, and wrote to her at length, saying how much he was looking forward to playing with little Bob, for whom he had bought 'a coral with bells'.[1] Bob was never to enjoy this pretty thing, for he was dead by the time Carnac reached Calcutta.

On July 9, 1760, the *Royal George* arrived at Spithead. Clive and Margaret travelled straight to London, and stayed with Clive's parents in Swithin's Lane. One can imagine the joyous reunion with all the family, in particular with Ned, now aged six. Five days after Clive set foot on English soil, he was received, together with his father, by the seventy-seven-year-old King at Kensington Palace. The Chairman of the East India Company and the principal Directors acknowledged his return by calling on him soon after his arrival, and in September the Company

* Carnac paid out £150 on Clive's account in order that they might have a proper cabin; nevertheless, one of them did not survive the voyage.

accorded him a unanimous vote of thanks. In the same month, he was given an honorary degree by the University of Oxford.*

But as William Smyth King had warned Clive, 'the brightest actions tarnish by time'.[2] Clive himself had foreseen that by staying on in India after Plassey, he would lose the advantage of arriving home when the news of his victory was fresh.[3] Even when this news first reached England, Horace Walpole had been blasé enough to write: 'I forgot in my last to say a word of our East India hero, Clive, and his victories, but we are growing accustomed to success again.'[4] Since then had come the *annus mirabilis*, 1759, the year of Minden, Quiberon Bay and Quebec. Having seen the body of Wolfe brought back to a hero's grave, the British public were less enthusiastic about Clive, when he returned home with his riches.

In fact, Clive caused a greater sensation as a Croesus than as the hero of Plassey. 'General Clive is arrived, all over estates and diamonds,' wrote Walpole. 'If a beggar asks charity, he says, "Friend, I have no small brilliants about me".'[5] Two years later, Walpole was still on the same tack: 'You would be frightened at the dearness of everything . . . I expect that a pint of milk will not be sold under a diamond, and then nobody can keep a cow but my Lord Clive.'[6] The *Annual Register* estimated Clive's fortune at £1,200,000, and alleged that Margaret had brought home a casket of jewels worth £200,000.[7] The name Clive became synonymous with wealth, like Vanderbilt or Rockefeller in a later age. People spoke of him as the richest subject in Europe.

This, of course, was a great exaggeration, even though Clive was a very rich man. In January 1759 he had estimated his total assets at £270,000, including money invested in ships and other trading ventures.[8] The *jagir* would make him richer by some £27,000 a year, but it was uncertain. Clive was definitely in the millionaire class by eighteenth-century

* He was presented by Dr Robert Vansittart, Fellow of All Souls, a brother of Henry Vansittart. Robert Vansittart was a member of Sir Francis Dashwood's 'Hell Fire Club' and it is possible that on this occasion he took Clive to dine with the club as his guest, which could be the origin of the legend that Clive himself was a member. If Clive did indeed dine with Dashwood's 'Brethren', it does not mean to say that he took part in an orgy; for as Mr George Martelli points out in his book, *Jemmy Twitcher* (London 1962), the popular conception of the club is based almost entirely on a contemporary work of fiction and other unreliable sources; it seems in fact to have been just another dining club. From Robert Vansittart's membership grew the oft-repeated belief that Henry Vansittart was a member, whereas it is established beyond doubt that he was away in India throughout the period of the club's heyday. (I am indebted to Dame Lucy Sutherland for this last information.)

standards, but he was far from being the richest subject in Europe. Many English noblemen at this time had incomes ranging from £10,000 a year to £30,000 a year.[9] Edward Wortley Montagu, husband of the famous Lady Mary, left something between £500,000 and £1,350,000 when he died in 1761, causing Horace Walpole to ask ironically: 'Did General Clive drop from Heaven only to get half as much as Wortley Montagu?'[10]

The stories of Clive's extravagance were as far from the truth as the accounts of his vast wealth. Clive was only extravagant inasmuch as he chose to live like a peer or magnate, which required a large country house and a town house, as well as the maintenance of a Parliamentary 'interest'. It was difficult to live in this way on much less than £10,000 a year.[11] With the buying or building of houses making inroads into his capital, with land bringing in less than five per cent on its purchase price, one can see that Cousin George was not far wrong when he stated that Clive's fortune, without the *jagir*, 'would not be sufficient for him'. His resources were further diminished by his generosity. Even before being granted the *jagir*, he had endowed his father with an annuity sufficient for him 'to retire from business' and keep a coach; he had given £2000 each to his five sisters and £25 a year to each of his aunts.[12] More recently, he had paid a debt of £9000 incurred by his father as collector of the Shropshire land tax;[13] and he settled £500 a year on Stringer Lawrence, which the old soldier accepted with reluctance.*

Clive also built his parents a comfortable new house at Styche. He never intended to live here himself, but hoped to acquire a country seat more in keeping with his aspirations; no easy matter at this time, when land was scarce and owners loath to sell. Towards the end of 1761, he bought, for £70,000, Lord Montfort's estate on the borders of Shropshire and Worcestershire: 7500 acres with no house. He considered building one there, to be named Plassey,[14] but delayed taking any final decision, preferring for the present to rent Condover, the seat of the Owen family, five miles south of Shrewsbury. A century later, Condover would have been everyone's dream of an English country house: Elizabethan, with gables and oriels, a great hall and a long gallery. But to Margaret, it was old-fashioned, and looked 'just like a church . . . windows from top to bottom but not a sash, all dismal casements'.[15] She tried counting the

* The popular notion of Lawrence's 'honourable poverty' was only relatively speaking true, for when he died he left something like £20,000. As a bachelor, who kept out of politics and smart society, he would have been very comfortable.

rooms – there were supposed to be a hundred – but gave up. Yet she liked the house and its gardens and park, looking towards distant blue hills.

A town house was easier to come by. Clive rented Lord Ancram's on the west side of Berkeley Square, for £600 a year, eventually buying it for £10,500.[16] He thus chose the most fashionable neighbourhood in London, but was content with what was a gentleman's town house writ large, rather than a palace; a fine enough house with its Palladian façade of stone, its grand staircase and its spacious rooms; but modest compared with the great mansions standing in their own grounds like Devonshire House.

Berkeley Square and Condover provided Clive and Margaret with the right background; yet it was still difficult for them to be accepted by the English aristocracy, which was probably more of a closed circle in the middle of the eighteenth century than at any other time, before or since.* Clive's enemies were later to imply that he had failed in Society on account of his awkward manner, his poor taste in clothes and his clumsiness on the dance-floor – he had, they said, to take dancing lessons.[17] More likely, he was regarded as a bore. It was later recalled how 'he would sit in company quite sluggish, while there was nothing to call forth his intellectual vigour; but the moment that any important subject was started, for instance, how this country is to be defended against a French invasion, he would rouse himself and show his extraordinary talents with the most powerful ability and animation'.[18] A world which accepted outsiders only if they had the wit of a Pope or a Sheridan would not have wanted to listen to Clive talking at length on how England was to be defended against a French invasion, even though he may have had all the attributes of a gentleman. Margaret's lively charm might well have made up for his seriousness, but, as Scrafton observed, few people bothered to find out what she was like.[19]

The Clives' circle was thus mainly limited to relatives and friends from India. There was Walsh and his sister, Eliza Fowke, there were Mr and Mrs Kelsall and Jenny Latham. Outside the family, there was Mrs Watts, who hated England, and eventually left her husband and her children and returned to India. Stringer Lawrence came to breakfast at Berkeley Square; John Dalton stayed at Condover, and so did Orme, despite what

* In the days of the Stuarts, and earlier, it was easy for outsiders to enter the aristocracy if they enjoyed Royal favour. With the coming of the Industrial Revolution, there grew up a moneyed class that rivalled the old aristocracy in wealth and was quickly assimilated by it. But in Clive's day, the successful businessman, with few exceptions, was not really rich enough to aspire to join the aristocracy.

MIR JAFAR, NAWAB OF BENGAL
by a Murshidabad artist

RAMNARAYAN
probably by a Murshidabad artist

SHUJA-UD-DAULA, NAWAB OF OUDH
Aquatint by P. Renault
after a painting by Tilly Kettle

THE MOGUL EMPEROR, SHAH ALAM II
probably by a Murshidabad artist

A EUROPEAN OFFICER TRAVELLING IN A PALANQUIN
Tanjore school

ELEPHANT ARMOUR BELIEVED TO BE A TROPHY OF THE BATTLE OF PLASSEY

Clive spoke of as his 'low cunning'.[20] Clive's wealth did not constitute a barrier between him and his poorer friends. He was not purse-proud; unlike so many of the newly-rich, he did not proceed to judge people by the extent of their riches. In the same way, Margaret never showed the slightest inclination to drop the friends and acquaintances of her humbler days. The only instance to the contrary of which we know was when, a few years later, she shut the door of Condover in the face of the Baron de Wüst, a French officer of Hussars who was frequently at the Garden House during her time at Fort St David, because he spied for the English, and for that reason incurred her contempt.[21]

One would imagine that Clive and Margaret were in some ways indifferent to Society, for they never seem to have given any balls, routs, or similar entertainments. Certainly Margaret disliked London, where she was, as she said, always 'in a flurry'.[22] She even avoided being there for the Coronation of the young King George III.[23] Clive, too, preferred the country, being fond of hunting. He spoke of the 'stagnated, smoky air' of London and went there not for pleasure, but to further his ambitions in the two worlds of politics and the East India Company.

These ambitions were thwarted by ill-health. The English climate did not agree with him. Soon after his arrival, he was struck down by a severe attack of what was described alternatively as gout or rheumatism. With it came a recurrence of the abdominal pain from which he had suffered on and off since 1752, accompanied by nervous prostration. He told Carnac in March 1761 that his sufferings during the past six months had been 'almost beyond what human nature could well bear', and that none of his friends thought he could have lived[24] – probably an exaggeration, for he was never one to make light of his illnesses.

Henceforth, he was obliged to spend long periods at Bath. He grew to like the place, and went there occasionally just for 'diversion'.* A lady

* While at Bath in 1761, Clive, Margaret and Ned sat to Gainsborough for a 'family piece'. The picture has mysteriously vanished, though a portrait of Clive now at the Royal Military Academy, Sandhurst, may be a surviving portion of it. It shows him in uniform, looking thinner and less self-assured than he does in the later and more famous portrait by Dance, though his face is a little flabby. His expression is sad. The fact that he is wearing the ribbon and star of the Bath, which was not actually conferred on him until 1764, does not necessarily mean that this portrait could not have been painted in 1761; for the order had been promised him at the time when the 'family piece' was painted. There exists a group by Reynolds, painted about 1763, of a gentleman and lady with a small child and an ayah, which was formerly believed to be of Clive and Margaret with one of their daughters, though there is now some doubt as to whether it is of them

who was at Bath at the same time found that he lived 'in little pomp, moderate in his table, and still more so in equipage and retinue'.[25]

Thanks to the efforts of his father, Clive had already made a start in English public life by the time he first fell ill. When in June 1759 one of the two Members of Parliament for Shrewsbury announced that he would not stand at the next general election, Richard Clive managed to get his son adopted to replace him – in the face of fierce opposition from the rich Earl of Bath, who had acquired the reversion to an estate in Shropshire and wanted the seat for his own son. Richard Clive carried the day with the help of the chief local magnate, the Earl of Powis, and was himself nominated to Powis's pocket borough of Montgomery. This was ostensibly a compliment to Richard Clive's famous son; but it may have been that Powis, who was chronically short of ready money, thought it wise to have the father of the Indian Croesus under his political wing.[26]

Clive was well enough to take an active part in the general election of March and April, 1761. He and his father were returned unopposed; he also managed to get Walsh, who had roots in that part of the country, adopted by the Corporation of Worcester. Walsh won his seat after a fight which cost him £5000. George Clive and Mun stood for Penryn in Cornwall – an election on which the four candidates spent £20,000 between them[27] – but were defeated.

Clive could thus command two votes in Parliament, his own and Walsh's, with his father's making to all intents and purposes a third.[28] There was the question of whom he would support. The obvious choice was Pitt, who had shown himself reasonably sympathetic to Clive's proposals for India, while foreseeing various difficulties. However, in October 1760, there had occurred the death of the King. His grandson and successor, the youthful George III, wanted to introduce his favourite, the Earl of Bute, into the Ministry, to which Pitt was opposed. The new King could hardly begin his reign by dismissing the man who had led Britain to victory, but he was able to undermine Pitt's position by separating the Duke of Newcastle from him.

Newcastle was willing to abandon the Great Commoner to keep in with the Crown, and worked to entice Pitt's followers over to himself.

---

at all. If this picture is indeed of the Clives - which, from the faces of the gentleman and lady, seems quite likely - it would suggest that Margaret imported an ayah for her children after she had returned to England; for it does not appear that she brought one back with her in 1760.

At first it seemed as though Clive would resist his overtures; then, however, he responded favourably.[29] Either he was disappointed at Pitt's reaction to his Indian proposals; or – which was more likely – he felt it best to support the Minister closest to the Crown, hoping as he did for a peerage.

Newcastle accordingly made a note that the first vacancy in the Order of the Bath was to go to Clive; and at the end of the year he procured for him an Irish barony. That Clive received his honours at his own solicitation in return for his political support, rather than as the spontaneous gift of a grateful monarch, shows the rather disappointing light in which his achievements were viewed.

So Clive became Baron Clive of Plassey,[30] and was henceforth addressed as My Lord even by his closest friends and relations – including Margaret and sometimes his father. As a peer and peeress, he and Margaret had direct access to the King and Queen: when Margaret gave birth to another daughter at the beginning of 1762, the Queen stood as godmother.

He did not, however, conceal his disappointment at his failure to obtain a British peerage, blaming it on his ill-health, which kept him away from the corridors of power, and also on the limitations of his fortune. He was certain that, had he been richer, he could have become 'an English earl with a Blue ribbon, instead of an Irish peer with the promise of a red one'.[31] Clive was under the impression that peerages could be bought – though declaring himself to be above that sort of thing[32] – and in this he showed his ignorance of his own contemporaries. Newcastle was no Lloyd George; money, in the middle of the eighteenth century, could buy the political power necessary for obtaining a peerage, but it could not buy the peerage itself.[33]

If ill-health robbed Clive of a British peerage, it also, according to himself, reduced his influence with the East India Company: 'It is natural to believe the interest of a dying man, (which was supposed to be my case), could not be very great.'[34] Unfortunate as his illness may have been, his relations with the Company suffered more on account of the bitter personal enmity that grew up between him and the Chairman, Laurence Sulivan.

At least one writer has tried to attribute Clive's dislike of Sulivan to the fact that he was an Irishman, supporting this theory by pointing out that Clive's other pet aversion, Coote, was also Irish.[35] But there were plenty of Irishmen with whom Clive was on excellent terms, ranging from Forde to his favourite servant, a Corkman named Ahern. And while Sulivan and

Coote both grew up in Ireland, they came from two separate and antagonistic worlds: Coote from the Anglo-Irish 'ascendancy', Sulivan from the dispossessed and impoverished Catholic and Celtic Irish. Nothing is known of Sulivan's origins except that he came from the County Cork sept of O'Sulivan More. Having been brought up as a Protestant—or changed his religion—he set out to make his fortune among the English,[36] going in a private capacity to Bombay, where he subsequently entered the Company's service. In 1752 he returned to England, becoming a Director three years later and Chairman in 1758.*

As autocrat of the Company during its most crucial period, Sulivan aroused great admiration as well as violent hostility. A not too friendly contemporary wrote of him as having 'great experience and some talents, great cunning, will go through thick and thin with his party while he remains attached to it, but not to be trusted for a moment when his own views lead him to be faithless'.[37] But in the words of the leading present-day authority on the history of the East India Company, he was 'one of the greatest of the Company's rulers, fertile in expedient, quick to recognize merit'.[38] Indeed, it was he, more than anyone else, who saw the merit in Warren Hastings. He was a highly competent businessman, though he was later to be unfortunate in his own affairs—for the reason that he valued his power in the Company above all else, regarding such power as an end in itself, unlike Clive, who simply saw it as a means of furthering his broader ambitions and his Indian policies.

There appears to be no portrait of Sulivan in existence; one imagines him as fussy and pedagogic, this impression being heightened by his spidery handwriting, the result of his poor eyesight. He tells us something of himself in a thirty-page letter of advice which he wrote to his son: we learn that, having been wild in his youth, he pulled himself together at the time of his marriage, since when he had led a life of industry and method, with meticulous attention to detail. 'I call upon my son if in the space of twenty-five years . . . he remembers me ten times in a tavern, eight times in a coffee-house, rarely ever from my family.' He was clearly devoted to his wife, consulting her in everything, regarding her judgement as superior to his own. He admits to being argumentative and hot-tempered.

* During the years when he dominated the Company, Sulivan did not continually occupy the Chair, nor was he even a Director for the whole time, on account of the rule that obliged Directors to retire in rotation. But whatever his technical position, he remained the autocrat of the Company, exercising his power through his friends, who formed the majority of the Directors.

He shows himself to have been a diligent observer of character, but mainly with an eye as to whose favour was worth cultivating and whose was not.[39]

In writing to his son, he evolved an elaborate code of pseudonyms, which clearly express his own opinion of the persons and things to which they refer. Clive's party he calls 'the Bees', which could equally describe himself and his methods. Much of the hostility between Clive and Sulivan could have arisen from the fact that they were too much alike. Both could at times be unscrupulous. Both were over-sensitive and hot-tempered. Both were inclined to be vindictive; but if Clive stalked his victims like a cat, Sulivan did mischief 'like a mole underground'.[40] They also had some virtues in common: tremendous industry, particularly when it concerned their own ambitions; the ability to grasp a situation and to improvise. Both were devoted family men.

But while they may have been remarkably similar in character, they were outwardly antithetic, so that not only could each have seen the qualities he despised in himself reflected in the other, but he saw them in a distasteful form. Sulivan, essentially a civilian and a man of peace, would have regarded Clive as a dangerous amateur soldier, and viewed his pretensions with a cynical Irish eye. Clive convinced himself that Sulivan was keeping out men of ability and working to bring the Company to ruin. In fact, the two of them were in agreement over most major issues; there was simply not room in the Company for two such dominant figures at the same time.

Clive had originally welcomed the advent of Sulivan, as a strong man with a first-hand knowledge of India; and had asked his father and his friends in England to support him when he was first running for the Chairmanship.[41] By the time he left India, however, he had twice given the new Chairman cause for offence. His suggestion to Pitt that the Government should take over the revenues of Bengal must certainly have reached Sulivan's ears – it was common enough currency to give rise to the story, repeated by Walpole, that Clive's father had told Pitt that, given the necessary resources, his son would send back enough treasure from India to pay the National Debt. For a servant of the Company to suggest to a Cabinet Minister that the State should take over a revenue that might have been the Company's was highly irregular – indeed, Clive himself would have thought so, had he not been carried away by the Great Commoner's praise of him.

The other matter which threatened to cause a rift between Clive and

Sulivan arose with Sulivan's attempt to inject new vigour into the Company's administration. In the General Letter of March 1759, he subjected the servants in Bengal to many sharp reproaches. As this happened to be the letter which announced the appointment of Coote and the supersession of Forde, Clive not unnaturally took umbrage, and he put his name to an insolent reply signed by all the Council.[42]

But although Sulivan dismissed four of the signatories, he avoided taking offence with Clive and the two were outwardly cordial at the time of Clive's arrival in England. Sulivan, in flowery terms, proposed the erection of Clive's statue at East India House. Clive visited Sulivan at his villa at Mile End, and Sulivan consulted him about various matters. But this cordiality was forced. 'We have all along behaved to one another like shy cocks,' wrote Clive,[43] who believed that Sulivan had not, in his heart, forgiven him for signing the offending letter.

Sulivan frequently assured Clive of his willingness to serve him. As late as 1762, Clive admitted that he had complied with most of his requests on behalf of his friends.[44] But Sulivan's promise that he would obtain a major's brevet for Carnac failed to materialize, much to Clive's disgust. Nor did he do anything about Forde, who was now back in England, and showed what he thought of Sulivan and the Directors by snubbing them within the very portals of East India House.[45]

Forde was only one of several malcontents who had returned from India, and who found support among those who were jealous of Sulivan's ascendancy. It was probably in order to prevent him from joining the malcontents that Sulivan hinted to Clive some time in 1761 that his right to his *jagir* might be challenged. He outwardly did so as a friend, warning him of the possible machinations of others, but it was clearly a piece of polite blackmail.[46] The *jagir* was Clive's Achilles heel. His right to it had not yet been formally confirmed by the Directors, even though when first told of it they had not objected. The contention of Clive and his friends that the quit-rent paid by the Company for the Calcutta lands was the Nawab's, to be disposed of as he saw fit, would have been justified if the Nawab had met all his obligations under the treaty. But as long as these obligations remained outstanding, the Company had a case for recouping itself out of the quit-rent, instead of paying it to Clive.

CHAPTER XVII

The Black Jagir

You I love my dearest life
More than Georgey loves his wife;
More than Ministers to rule,
More than North to play the fool,
More than Camden to grimace,
More than Barrington his place,
More than Clive his black *jagir*,
More than Bute the Royal ear;
More than Patriots their price,
More than Fox loves cards and dice.

ANONYMOUS SATIRE ON THE NOBILITY, 1773

I

The threat to stop his *jagir* 'bound Clive hand and foot'.[1] He had hoped that his Indian wealth would make him a great power in English politics; now he was obliged to use such political influence as he had to preserve his Indian wealth. Gone was that 'independence' which was to him 'the only desirable thing in this life'.[2] If only he could have done without his *jagir*, and been satisfied with the fortune he had already acquired, he might have been a far happier man; but his experience of what it cost to live as he wanted to live in England made him more than ever determined to hang on to it through thick and thin. He was ceaselessly lamenting to his friends in India what an 'extravagant' country England was, and advising them not to come home until they had acquired 'an independent fortune'. To Carnac he wrote: 'Of all places in the world, dread your native country the most if you are obliged to return to it in a state of dependence . . . he must be a philosopher indeed, and master of all the passions, who can live upon a little in England.'[3]

So the *jagir* came to dominate Clive's thinking. 'My future power, my grandeur, all depend upon the receipt of the *jagir* money,' he told his friend, Pybus. 'I should be a madman to set at defiance those who at present show no inclination to hurt me.'[4] Clive, who when his motives were in question would sometimes attempt to deceive even himself, was nothing if not frank in admitting to his friends that he was unable to stand by them for fear that his *jagir* might be taken away. 'I should not think it prudent to risk it by quarrelling with Mr Sulivan, although he should not pay that attention to my recommendations which I have a right to expect.'[5] But while telling his friends of his resolve to keep in with Sulivan, he did not hesitate to speak of him as 'a treacherous, deceitful fellow'[6] and 'this mushroom of a man'.[7]

The final split between Clive and Sulivan came as a result of the treaty which ended the Seven Years War.[8] Clive objected strongly to the preliminary treaty because it provided for the restoration to the French of all Indian possessions held by them in 1749, which meant that they would get back many of the acquisitions of Dupleix. 'The King of England has no right to give away the Nawab's dominions without his consent,' he declared,[9] hinting that the Duke of Bedford, who negotiated the preliminary treaty in Paris, had been bribed by Dupleix himself and by Bussy.[10] When the preliminary treaty was debated in Parliament, the Government, now led by the young King's Scottish favourite, the Earl of Bute, made a bid for Clive's support. Various baits were dangled before him, including, it seems, a British peerage and a £600-a-year sinecure for Cousin George.[11] But Clive rejected these advances and voted with the minority against the treaty.* If indeed he was given a firm offer of a British peerage, which he so much desired, it is to his credit that he stood firm; particularly as he must have known that to oppose the Government would put his *jagir* even more in jeopardy. He told his friends in India of how he had voted, with the exultation of a man who breathes the fresh mountain air after being a prisoner. 'I still continue to be one of those unfashionable kind of people who think very highly of independency, and to bless my stars, indulgent fortune has enabled me to act according to my conscience.'[12]

Sulivan, who was also a Member of Parliament, voted with the Government on the preliminary treaty, which gave rise to the belief that

* He was, of course, still in the House of Commons, being only an Irish peer.

he was ready to accept less advantageous terms than was Clive. In fact he deplored the preliminary treaty as much as Clive did, but preferred to conciliate the Government over it, believing that this would smooth the way for the definitive treaty to be amended as he and the Company wished.[13] This is actually what happened, and in the clause about the restorations, the date was put back so as to exclude the acquisitions of Dupleix.

Despite this reasonably satisfactory conclusion, the treaty negotiations left a legacy of ill-feeling. Sulivan had taken care to cultivate one of Bute's most influential supporters, the young Earl of Shelburne,[14] and so was consulted by the Government about the peace terms in preference to Clive, who since the departure of Pitt and Newcastle had lacked Ministerial friends. By letting Clive get out of touch with events, Sulivan antagonized him more than ever, which was particularly unfortunate seeing that the two of them were really in agreement.

Sulivan also succeeded in antagonizing Thomas Rous, who held the Chairmanship of the Company as his creature, while he himself stood down for a year as the rules required. Rous was a weak character but he had some influence; he and his friends now joined the Bengal malcontents. After hesitating a couple of months, Clive decided to throw in his lot with this now formidable opposition, and stake all on driving the Sulivan party from power.

The gloves were off, 'the great Civil War of the Company had broken out'.[15] If Clive succeeded, it would be the end of Sulivan's blackmail; if he failed, his *jagir* might be lost. It was one of those all-or-nothing gambles such as he had several times taken in his past career, like the night march to Utatur, the attack on Siraj-ud-daula's camp, or the dispatch of Forde's expedition. And, as on those past occasions, he realized that action was the only hope, for he had heard that Bute and the other Ministers were 'stirring up' the Directors to challenge his *jagir*,[16] in order to punish him for opposing them over the peace preliminaries.

2

The conflict between Clive and Sulivan was given an added dimension by events in Bengal. After a brief interregnum under Holwell, Clive's friend,

Henry Vansittart, became Governor. Vansittart's subsequent misfortunes have caused him to be depicted as well-meaning but weak, which is unfair; it would, as a modern writer points out, be more correct to regard him as a brilliant failure.[17] He was a visionary, always a dangerous thing in a man of power, who can push forward his schemes regardless of the warnings of his colleagues; and which was particularly dangerous in a situation calling for a hard-headed pragmatist of Clive's stamp. He was as handsome as he was brilliant, and only twenty-eight when he became Governor, which was young even by the standards of mid-eighteenth-century Calcutta. One suspects that behind his good-natured charm lay a certain arrogance, which amounted at times to instability. He also had the disregard for convention typical of his sort: he took his wife and Philadelphia Hancock with him when he went to confer with the Nawab, which shocked everybody, as Indian women did not show themselves in this way.[18]

On becoming Governor, Vansittart was faced with an acute financial crisis. The Company in Bengal had, since Plassey, reported itself to London as being so flush that London had ceased sending money out for the 'investment' or purchase of goods. But military expenses had quickly swallowed up all the surplus resulting from Mir Jafar's payments, so that there was now not enough either to meet the investment, or to pay the troops. To increase the Company's revenues in Bengal, Vansittart carried out a plan already envisaged by Holwell: he deposed Mir Jafar and set up his son-in-law, Mir Kasim, as Nawab, Miran having already come to a spectacular end by being struck by lightning. As the price of setting him up, the Company obtained substantial concessions of territory from the new Nawab, the revenues from which would meet its present deficit.

This, however, was not Vansittart's only reason for his *coup*. It was just as important to him that the young and vigorous Mir Kasim should take the place of the senile, hemp-sodden and intriguing Mir Jafar. For he rightly believed that Clive's system of a puppet Nawab and a precarious English dictatorship could not last for ever. Instead, he planned to establish a strong Nawab, hand back the real as well as the nominal power to him, and then pursue a policy of non-intervention.

Such a policy would have been applauded in the present century; but it proved a disaster in mid-eighteenth-century Bengal. For one thing, it was necessary, in order to strengthen the new Nawab's hand, that the English should cease guaranteeing the safety of the Hindu magnates whom Clive had used as a counterpoise to Mir Jafar. As a result, many of the Hindus who had worked with the English, including Ramnarayan and eventually the Seths, were deprived of their property and put to death. 'From that hour,' wrote a distinguished Bengal servant, Harry Verelst, 'we no longer had a friend in the country.'[19]

If Vansittart's policy foundered on the Scylla of Mir Kasim's vengeance, it also came to grief on the Charybdis of English greed. However much Clive may have tried to prevent abuses, it was natural that some of his countrymen should have taken advantage of their new position of superiority to get rich at the expense of the populace. The situation grew worse when his own colleagues, who had been well provided for under the 1757 treaty, were replaced by a new generation of Councillors with their fortunes to make. Europeans competed with the Indians in the internal trade of Bengal, particularly in the essential commodities of salt, betel-nut and tobacco. By freely misusing the Company's *dastak* or privilege, they evaded the duties which the Nawab's subjects were obliged to pay.* Under the crumbling regime of Mir Jafar, this could be done with impunity; but Mir Kasim was determined to put an end to such encroachments on his rights. Vansittart felt it his duty to co-operate with the Nawab in this, which brought him into violent conflict with his Council.

Clive who had, surprisingly, regarded Vansittart as the right man for Bengal, seeing in him a merit that shone 'with so peculiar and bright a lustre',[20] at first showed remarkable forbearance towards him, though he had undone so much of his work. 'I hope our friend Van will be forgiven this one false step,'[21] he told Carnac, and to Vansittart himself he merely pointed out that the deposing of Mir Jafar had made it clear to the world that *subahs* and nawabs were only there to do the work of the English, and that they derived their power not from the Mogul but from the Company.[22] His attitude to Vansittart was influenced by more than friendship. Vansittart occupied a key position with regard to the *jagir*. It was also Clive's intention to cause a rift between Vansittart and Sulivan. He managed to get hold of a copy of one of the letters which Sulivan was in the habit of writing to Vansittart's sworn enemy, Coote, and sent it to him as proof of Sulivan's treachery.[23]

* In theory, Englishmen were not supposed to engage in the internal trade of India. The private trade in which they engaged was between India and other places in the East, the trade between India and Europe being reserved to the Company.

3

The election of Directors in which Clive and his friends were to challenge the supremacy of Sulivan was due in April 1763. Although both sides endeavoured to create votes for themselves by 'splitting'* and stock purchases – in which Clive's party had the advantage of greater financial resources[24] – the majority remained in the hands of the uncommitted proprietors. The preliminary contest took place in March, when a General Court of Proprietors was summoned to exonerate Rous over the treaty. This was the first of those great debates in the General Court which were to attract as much public interest as the debates of the House of Commons. Clive spoke at length, accusing Sulivan of monopolizing all the power, and of preventing anyone becoming a Director who had 'experience, capacity, or general knowledge'.[25]

Sulivan, according to one of Clive's supporters, replied disjointedly, ignoring the points which he was called upon to answer. 'Mr Sulivan, sir,' exclaimed Clive's old friend, Mabbot, 'stand up and answer for yourself. I have been informed that you did propose to give up the whole Coast of Coromandel to the French.'[26] This 'staggered' Sulivan, and although he denied the charge, he had to admit that he had said in casual conversation that it would be better to give up the Coast of Coromandel than lose one inch of the Company's possessions in Bengal. 'You did say!' retorted Mabbot, 'and pray, Sir, if you give up the Coast of Coromandel, how are your ships to get to Bengal?' Sulivan was duly silenced, and when the question was put to the ballot, Rous was exonerated by 359 votes to 298.

At the election of Directors in April, which was the real contest, far greater numbers turned out to vote, and they were still largely influenced by Sulivan. Clive and his allies suffered a humiliating defeat. Less than a fortnight after the election, Sulivan punished Clive for daring to challenge his supremacy. A dispatch went out to Bengal ordering all payments of Clive's *jagir* to be stopped, on the grounds that it had not been confirmed by the Mogul. Clive retaliated by formally threatening Vansittart, as Governor, together with his Council, with legal proceedings if they obeyed these instructions – while writing privately to him as a friend, enlisting his help.[27] He endeavoured to obtain a proper confirmation from

* Everyone who held £500 worth of stock was qualified to vote, so that the larger proprietors were able to create votes by nominally selling their stock in £500 lots to their friends, who would sell it back to them after the election.

the Mogul, who was now none other than the former Shahzada, with whom Carnac was on friendly terms, having had him as his prisoner after defeating him in 1761. He also filed a Suit in Chancery against the Directors. But the outcome of any action at law seemed highly uncertain, and even if it were ultimately favourable, it would have meant that his money would be frozen for an indefinite number of years. Political influence was far more likely to be effective against the Directors than legal wranglings; but at this moment when Clive would most have needed Government support, he found himself in opposition. Such friends as he had among the Great were on the whole unhelpful.

Whilst working feverishly to save his *jagir*, Clive was at times inclined to be philosophical about it. One would take this as a passing mood, rather than insincerity. He spoke of going abroad so as to be able to live independently within his means,[28] just as on an earlier occasion he had vowed to have nothing more to do with the great men of England and to spend his life travelling.[29] The worries of that summer of 1763 did not prevent him and Margaret from celebrating Plassey Day with three days of festivities at Condover. The country people made merry all night outside the house, so that the host and hostess had to wrap their heads in pillows in order to get some sleep.[30] And despite his financial setback, Clive acquired the 6000-acre estate of the Walcot family in the south-west of Shropshire near the Welsh border, for which he had to pay the inflated price of £92,000. This was an estate which, given a few improvements, could be made into a country seat worthy of his rank. Walcot Hall, an old red-brick gabled house, was by no means grand; but it lent itself to being enlarged and modernized; and it was also superbly placed, on the side of a wooded spur facing across a valley of softly curving green slopes to purple hills beyond.

To Clive, however, the scenic beauties of his purchase were of less consequence than the fact that it included the chief Parliamentary 'interest' in the neighbouring town of Bishop's Castle. It was essential for him to obtain control of another seat in Parliament to give him more political bargaining power; and at the very moment when he took possession of Walcot at Michaelmas, 1763, one of the two Bishop's Castle seats was vacant, the member having died six days before. In order to be handy for the ensuing by-election, he, Margaret and the children moved to Walcot almost immediately, although Condover remained their headquarters in the country for the time being. Clive's candidate, Cousin George, was opposed by the other local 'interest', that of Walter Waring, who was standing himself. Waring was defeated, with fifty-three votes to George Clive's eighty. Though about to give birth, Margaret helped with the electioneering. 'The latter part of my time was taken up in company not of the politest,' she wrote to Carnac, 'for we were obliged to keep open house, and make dancings at home and in the town for our worthy friends, the burgesses'.[31]

When, towards the end of 1763, it became clear to Clive that his friends in the Opposition had no chance of an immediate return to power, he struck a bargain with the new Prime Minister, George Grenville. Grenville was to put pressure on the Directors to agree to a compromise in which they would pay Clive the *jagir* money for ten or twelve years.[32] In return, Clive would promise never to give them any opposition;[33] just as he promised Grenville his unswerving political support in return for taking up the cudgels on his behalf, and perhaps considering him for a British peerage.[34] Thus for a handsome endowment and a problematical coronet, Clive was willing to surrender his freedom of action, both in East Indian affairs and in Parliament. He began to support the Government in the middle of November, when he voted with them in their proceedings against John Wilkes. A month later, Walpole was telling a story of how Clive's father was at the Levee, and the King asked after his son, to which Richard Clive replied: 'Sire, he is coming to town, and then Your Majesty will have another vote.'[35]

Walsh begged Clive to keep his independence, and declared that he could not go with him into the Government camp; it would just be 'slavishly following the weaknesses of a master, not affording a sensible and manly support to a friend'.[36] Clive tried to justify himself by dismissing party politics as 'struggles of ambition only';[37] but he must have been mortified by his friend's plain speaking, particularly as he set as high a value on independence as Walsh did. And as Walsh had foretold, Clive's *volte-face* brought no immediate results, in that Grenville failed to influence the Directors, and did not press the point when the King showed himself dilatory over the matter of the British peerage.[38] Clive, however, felt that even if the Government did little to help him, they would at least refrain from injuring him, as they might have done had he been in opposition;[39] an argument which seems to have enabled Walsh to overcome his scruples.

4

Clive's growing concern about his *jagir* made him suspect Vansittart of teaming up with Sulivan against him.[40] It would have been hard for him not to be influenced by the letters of Carnac, who bore several bitter personal grudges against the unfortunate Vansittart. Relations between Clive and Vansittart deteriorated owing to a trifling affair at the end of 1763. The King had desired to see an elephant; so Clive had written to Vansittart asking for one to be bought on his account and sent to England. Vansittart dispatched two elephants, in separate ships, but he paid for them out of his own pocket and expected Clive to present them to the King in *his* name. This Clive refused to do, as he wanted the elephant to be a present from himself.[41] When the first elephant arrived, Clive was thwarted, for it was presented to the King by the captain of the ship in which it had travelled; it seems to have been ridden to the Palace surreptitiously, at two in the morning.[42] He told Vansittart that he would think no more of the matter, and remained outwardly on good terms with him; but to Walsh, he spoke of him as 'a very dirty fellow'.[43]

While Clive concerned himself with the affair of the elephant, poor Vansittart had more serious worries. The dispute over private trade, which had brought his Council into revolt, led to a rupture with Mir Kasim. After a senior Company servant, Peter Amyatt, had been killed in a skirmish with the Nawab's people on his way back from a mission to him, Mir Jafar was brought out from his retirement and reinstated. But though the English had thus deposed Mir Kasim, he still had his army and was allied to the Nawab of Oudh. Getting rid of him entailed a war, and he was able to take his revenge. Forty-nine Englishmen at Patna, including Clive's cousin, Thomas Amphlett, and the good-looking Henry Lushington, were cut to pieces by his orders, the work of butchery being supervised by a European adventurer named Walter Reinhardt, known from his dark countenance as 'Sombre' or 'Samru'.

By the beginning of 1764, it was known in England that Bengal was once again 'a scene of bloodshed and confusion',[44] although the news of the Patna massacre did not arrive until later in the year. There was panic, and the Company's stock fell by fourteen per cent. This was Clive's chance; he and his friends planned to put forward a proposal that he should return to Bengal with supreme military and civil power in order to save the situation there. He was to make his acceptance of the proposal conditional on the result of the election of Directors in April. If the election went in his favour, the matter of the *jagir* would then be settled.

This plan, which had the backing of Grenville's administration, was put into effect at a General Court of Proprietors on March 12. Various speakers stressed the need for a Governor with military as well as civil experience. Then, someone 'as by inspiration' suggested that Clive was the man. This proposal was carried with cheers, and Clive replied with a speech that had obviously been well prepared, stating that he would do his duty if called on, but would only consider accepting office if the Directors were as well disposed towards him as the General Court.[45] By this he meant that he would not accept office so long as Sulivan remained in control. There was another heated debate at East India House, accompanied by an even fiercer battle of pamphlets and newspaper articles, in which Clive's contribution, *A Letter to the Proprietors of the East India Stock*, ran into more than sixty pages. Meanwhile, both sides were busy splitting stock in preparation for the election of Directors on April 12.

The news that the English forces, under Carnac and Major Thomas Adams, had been successful against Mir Kasim, which reached England just before the election, made the stockholders less anxious for Clive's return to Bengal, so that the result of the election was a dead heat: six of Sulivan's party being elected and six of the opposition, together with twelve uncommitted candidates. Sulivan, however, with four of his followers, walked out 'in a pet'[46] when an attempt to get him elected as Chairman ended similarly in deadlock. This enabled the Clive party to put Rous into the Chair and to dominate the uncommitted Directors; commanding a majority that increased during the next few months. As though to celebrate Clive's victory, his statue by Peter Scheemakers—larger than life and in Roman dress—was set up in the Great Court Room of East India House in August, along with similar statues of Admiral Pocock and Stringer Lawrence. In a less heroic vein, Clive now took the opportunity of sifting through the East India House papers in the hope of finding something to discredit Sulivan; but these researches only served to convince him of his enemy's disinterestedness.[47]

It remained to settle the terms on which Clive would return to Bengal. After a bitter and stormy debate, the General Court allowed him his *jagir* for a further ten years by a majority of 583 votes to 396. At the same time, Clive submitted his plans for Bengal in a letter to the Directors. He intended to return to his old policy of giving protection to the magnates: lest the Nawab should have any cause for complaint, the Company ser-

MARGARET MASKELYNE, LADY CLIVE,
ABOUT 1760

CARICATURE BY MARGARET CLIVE
OF CLIVE WITH MIR JAFAR AND OMAR BEG

WARREN HASTINGS
by Tilly Kettle

HENRY VANSITTART
Engraving by S. W. Reynolds from a painting by Sir Joshua Reynolds

vants should be forbidden from trading in the three important commodities of salt, betel-nut and tobacco. He foresaw the possibility that he would be opposed by a majority of his Council, and asked for a 'dispensing power'. He insisted on having at least 3000 European troops constantly in Bengal, with absolute control over them, so that there should be no question of their being side-tracked to the other Presidencies as had happened in the past. Finally, he bound himself 'not to enrich himself one farthing by any pay or emoluments he might receive'.[48] He got his troops, and his supreme power, both civil and military. This, however, was given not to him alone but to a Select Committee of himself, Carnac and three others.

At the General Court of May 2, a resolution was passed prohibiting the taking of presents, without the consent of the Directors. That Clive, who had received larger presents than anybody, should be charged with enforcing this new rule, was certainly ironic; it might be imagined that the resolution was the work of Sulivan, as a scourge for his back. In fact, it was a non-party measure, a sign of the growing sense of responsibility among the ordinary stockholders.

Before Clive left for India, the King invested him with the Red Ribbon of the Bath. Newcastle's promise that he would have the next vacancy seems to have been forgotten; there was a vacancy in 1764, but this was destined for Colonel William Draper. It was, however, deemed important that Clive should arrive in India clothed with the Order,[49] or, as Walpole put it, 'My Lord Clive could not conquer the Indies a second time without becoming a Knight of the Bath.'[50] So the vacancy went to Clive, much to the annoyance of Draper, who said bitterly to his friend, the Duke of Bedford: 'Whenever I am employed again, I will be a most dirty dog, rob and pillage wherever I can, deserve to be hanged, and then carry every point for myself and my associates.'[51]

Four years after leaving Bengal as he thought for ever, Clive prepared to go there again. He had to turn his back on the pleasant life of a wealthy peer in England, on his political interest, on the improvements he was carrying out at Walcot and Berkeley Square, and face the hazards of a lengthy sea voyage and the prospect of exhausting work in a pestilential climate. He and Margaret had to be separated from their children, Becky, 'fat, rosy Charlotte', the baby Margaretta and the ten-year-old, monkey-faced Ned, who had just started at Eton.

Clive's return to Bengal is generally represented as a bitter pill which he had to swallow in order to save his *jagir*. He himself spoke of it as 'a very great sacrifice, a point of honour much against my own inclinations'.[52] Yet one wonders if he was not secretly pleased to be going back. 'We are not so happy in England as you imagine, and many of us envy your way of life in India,' he had told Carnac two years earlier.[53] Unbelievable as it may seem, the climate of Bengal suited him better than that of England. And from having had no more power than that afforded by a small political interest, he was once again going to be the autocrat of a country the size of France.

Margaret put on as brave a face as she could, and prepared to 'follow the fortune of my first and best friend, my husband . . . contributing towards making my Lord's stay in India less afflicting to him in such a separation from his children'.[54] At the last moment, however, it was decided that she was not well enough to travel, being pregnant again, and so she had to stay behind.

Clive sailed from Portsmouth in the Indiaman *Kent* at sunset on June 4. 'God only knows how much I have suffered in my separation from the best of women,' he had written to Margaret earlier that day.[55] With him went Mun, who was to be his aide-de-camp, Samuel Ingham, his doctor, and Henry Strachey, the clever and industrious young War Office clerk who, on Grenville's recommendation, had become his private secretary.[56] As well as this trio, and an assistant secretary, Clive took his steward, the Irishman Ahern, his valet, Philpot, a groom, a French chef and a band of four musicians. His luggage included twelve dozen chests of champagne.[57]

CHAPTER XVIII

The Augean Stable

Alas! How is the English name sunk!

CLIVE, 1765

The first stage of the *Kent*'s voyage, to Rio de Janeiro, was tediously slow, owing to contrary winds. Twice the ship lost a topmast, and Ahern fell down the hold and broke two ribs.[1] He recovered quickly, much to the relief of Clive and Strachey, for it was thanks to him alone that they were able to eat at all well; the young captain having failed to provide adequate stores. Even the skill of Ahern and the chef could not save them from an exclusive diet of pork and pease pudding during the last six weeks. To add to Clive's misery, there was Mrs William Sumner, the wife of his Second in Committee, who as he told Margaret, 'seemed possessed of every disagreeable quality which ever belonged to the female sex without being mistress of one virtue, (chastity excepted),[2] to throw into the opposite scale.'[3] Not only did she play the same 'two hum-drum tunes' over and over again on the harpsichord for four hours every day; but she also insisted that all the doors and windows should be kept open, so that everybody caught colds.

They reached Rio on October 7, and the Commander of an English warship[4] came aboard with a letter from Margaret. Clive answered it at greater length than it was customary for him to write to her. 'Nothing could afford me greater pleasure than to find you reconciled to my departure in a manner consistent with that good sense which I know you to be mistress of, and consistent with that superior duty which you owe to our children.' After telling her with some humour of the tribulations of the voyage, he went into the matter of Ned's education: 'I cannot say that I am at all uneasy that our son Ned does not make that progress in the

English language which he otherwise would if he had not so many irons in the fire. A master of the dead languages may become master of the living whenever he pleases. His want of ear and awkwardness in dancing I must own gives me pain.'[5]

Clive and his companions had to spend nearly two months at Rio, which was getting increasingly hot. The climate, however, suited him; it was like Bengal. He cast a professional eye over the fortifications and reported to Grenville that they were so ruinous he would be ashamed if he could not capture the place in twenty-four hours with a single battalion of infantry.[6] Before leaving, he was to rub this in to the Portuguese Viceroy himself. His musicians decamped; and, certain that His Excellency had enticed them away for the Rio opera, he wrote him a thundering letter, in which he ended by saying that he had received numerous applications from the local inhabitants to be taken to Bengal, but was 'too sincere a friend to the Portuguese nation to deprive her capital settlement of any of its defendants, especially in its present weak and almost defenceless condition'.[7]

About New Year's Day, 1765, they reached the Cape, where Clive gave a ball to celebrate the news of another military success against Mir Kasim and his ally Shuja-ud-daula, the Nawab of Oudh.[8] On April 10, the *Kent* dropped anchor in Madras Road, and Clive saw the familiar line of sand and palm trees and the white buildings of Fort St George. Here he learnt that Mir Jafar was dead. And either now or earlier, when the *Kent* met and spoke to a homeward-bound vessel, he heard news that was even more important. A decisive victory had been won over Mir Kasim, Shuja-ud-daula and the Mogul at Buxar in the previous October. The Mogul had put himself under English protection, Shuja had been driven into exile, and Mir Kasim had fled, stripped of his treasure and destined to end his days in poverty.

The English troops had followed up their success by marching onward in the direction of Delhi, getting as far as Allahabad. 'A march I highly disapprove of,' Clive told Rous. 'I mean absolutely to bound our possessions, assistance and conquests to Bengal.'[9] He still thought of himself as the representative of a trading company rather than an empire-builder, while accepting the fact that the Company no longer depended on commerce alone. Before leaving England, he had warned that if the Company failed to abide by the 'principles of moderation'[10] which he preached, it 'should by necessity be led from acquisition to acquisition', until the whole of India was 'up in arms' against it.[11]

In his letter to Rous, written from Madras, Clive went on to speak of the other side of his mission, the reform of the Company's administration in Bengal. 'See what an Augean Stable there is to be cleansed. The confusion we behold, what does it arise from? Rapacity and luxury, the unreasonable desire of many to acquire in an instant what only a few can, or ought to, possess . . . in short, the evils, civil and military, are enormous, but they *shall* be rooted out.' That he spoke with such certainty of these evils before he had even reached Bengal looked suspiciously as though he went there determined to find them.

On the morning of May 3, Clive stepped ashore at Calcutta, while the guns of his vast but still unfinished new fort thundered in salute. Drawn up on the waterfront to greet him were the Councillors – they must have looked absurdly young compared with the great men of England – headed by the outgoing Governor, John Spencer.* Clive took up residence in a house facing southward across the Esplanade, to which he later added two wings, making a handsome front.[12] Here he lived in greater state than he and Margaret had six years previously. To the retinue brought from England were added more than a hundred Indian servants, including his old friend, Black Robin. Wherever he went, he was attended by *chobdars*, or mace-bearers; he also had a European mounted bodyguard, resplendent in blue and gold, which had been instituted by Vansittart.

Barely pausing to read the letters of welcome – Rai Durlabh compared his coming to 'the sweet breeze of Spring'[13] – or to receive courtesy visits from his two old adversaries, Jean Law and Vernet, now Governor-General of the French possessions and Director of the Dutch settlement at Cinsura respectively, he set to work. The heat of Bengal gave steam to his restless energy. He had candles and writing materials put by his bedside so that he could continue drafting letters, minutes and memoranda if he woke in the night. While Strachey was trying to write his own letters, he would interrupt him over and over again with questions of business. On the day of his arrival, he took his seat in Council and made himself fully acquainted with what had happened during the past few months. That night, he wrote to Carnac, who was away with the army in Oudh, to say that he found the government 'in a more distracted state, if possible, than I had reason to expect'.[14]

Having spent the next day ploughing through papers, he was more than ever convinced as to the depravity of his Council. When he addressed

* The successor to Vansittart, who had sailed for England a few months earlier, taking his friend Warren Hastings with him.

them on the 5th, he emphasized that he and his four colleagues of the Select Committee would make full use of their special powers. Whereupon the handsome Ralph Leycester started to argue about the extent of those powers. Clive cut him short, saying that he would not allow the matter to be discussed. Then a young man with a prominent nose, a high-domed forehead and overhanging brow got to his feet. Clive knew him well. He was John Johnstone, who had commanded a battery of artillery at Plassey, and gone with Coote to Patna and with Forde to the Sarkars. Johnstone suggested that the Directors' orders with regard to the Committee should be read in the context of the other paragraphs of their letter. Clive took this as an attempt to invalidate these orders, and asked Johnstone if he dared to dispute the Committee's authority. Johnstone replied that he had no such intention. 'Upon which', wrote Clive to Carnac that night, 'there was an appearance of very long and pale countenances, and not one of the Council uttered another syllable.'[15]

From his enquiries and researches, Clive learnt that Spencer and the Council had hastened to appoint a successor to Mir Jafar. He was Najm-ud-daula, Mir Jafar's son by a dancing-girl. That he was quite unfit to govern was of no account, for Spencer and his colleagues had no intention that he should govern; they had learnt the lesson of Mir Kasim. Having installed the new Nawab, they bound him by a treaty depriving him of military strength and of the power to appoint his ministers. It was a settlement in the manner of Clive himself; that he criticized it as 'precipitate' would suggest that he resented not being its architect.

The army had already deprived him of the glory of restoring peace to Bengal. The laurels did not even go to his friend Carnac, but to Major Thomas Adams, since dead, and to Major Hector Munro, who had returned to Europe. It can thus be argued that he was determined to make the most of his role as a reformer, even to finding abuses that did not exist. However, he was still able to take the credit for carrying Spencer's settlement a crucial step further, and for concluding the peace treaty following Buxar. He might have remained content with these two achievements and avoided making a host of new enemies, had he not been genuinely convinced of the need for reform.

He found abuses in the very matter of the installation of Najm-ud-daula. A deputation, led by Johnstone and including Leycester, had gone to Murshidabad to execute the treaty with the new Nawab, and had received large sums of money as presents. Spencer and some of the other Councillors had also shared in the distribution. Their fault lay not so much in receiving presents, as in receiving them in defiance of the new regulation which obliged Company servants to sign covenants binding themselves not to receive presents except with the Directors' consent. This regulation reached Calcutta in January 1765; but Spencer and the Council did nothing about it, on the excuse that so important a matter should await Clive's arrival.

Clive had no doubt he would find still worse evils, evils 'shocking to human nature'.[16] At the Committee's first meeting, an inaugural letter from him was read, in which he declared: 'What do we hear of, what do we see, but anarchy, confusion, and, what is worse, an almost general *corruption*.'[17] Corruption, licentiousness, luxury, oppression. These words, particularly 'corruption', were to be Clive's constant refrain during the next eighteen months. But for a start, he and the Committee confined themselves to getting the covenants signed. Sign the Councillors did, though with bad grace.

Towards the end of May, the Nawab, a fat, sickly youth, came to visit Clive at Calcutta. He hoped to persuade Clive and the Committee to remove Mohammed Reza Khan, the chief minister imposed on him by the Spencer regime, and whom he accused of having distributed more than twenty lakhs out of his treasury among the Councillors. Mohammed Reza Khan had accompanied the Nawab to Calcutta. A naturally timid man, he was terrified on account of the Nawab's hostility to him. He knew, too, that Clive was prejudiced against him; although he was generally in favour with the English, having been helpful to them during his past career. When, after being kept some days in suspense, he was examined by the Committee, he testified that Johnstone and his colleagues had extorted the presents from him and the Nawab against their will.

Clive, without doubt, already believed this, and was looking for evidence to prove it. Relentlessly he pursued his enquiries. Moti Ram, the *faujdar* of Hughli, who had acted for Johnstone, was brought to Calcutta and kept in confinement with an armed guard while being examined. His servant was likewise seized. Such methods, while they may have been the custom of the country and necessary in order to prevent witnesses from making off, were a grave psychological error, enabling it to be said that Clive had obtained his evidence by intimidation.

The Committee reported Johnstone and his colleagues to the Directors. Before their letter was sent, Johnstone resigned in a fury, having, like the other accused, defended himself in a lengthy minute, in which he went so far as to make pointed references about Clive's *jagir*. It is difficult to know whether or not the charges against him were true. Certainly the Nawab can hardly have felt very generous towards the deputation, who were forcing him to sign an unfavourable treaty and putting him in the power of Mohammed Reza Khan; least of all towards Johnstone, who bullied him shamelessly.[18] And if Johnstone's hands were clean in this particular affair, they cannot have been so clean at other times. He was in partnership with William Bolts, one of the worst of all Company servants, in a trading concern which was accused of a great many oppressions and abuses. The firm was exonerated, yet when Johnstone sailed for home in October 1765, his fortune—which, if we accept his statement that he lost almost everything in 1763,[19] he would have made in only two years—was several times larger than the notorious present. Allowing for all this, it must be said that he was treated vindictively. 'I hope you will not forget Mr Johnstone's minute,' Clive told a colleague, 'and that you will make such discoveries as may enable you to give that gentleman such an answer as his impertinence and principles deserve.'[20]

In his blind determination to hurt Johnstone, Clive laid in a store of trouble for himself, as he so often did. For Johnstone had influential relatives; one of his brothers was married to the eventual heiress of Clive's old opponent in the Shrewsbury election, Lord Bath; another, George, was Governor of West Florida and shortly to enter Parliament. A tough, swashbuckling sailor, George Johnstone had organized a group which supported Clive in the India House election of 1764. He did so because brother John had been dismissed for rebelling against Vansittart, and he expected Clive, in return, to make his reinstatement a condition for going to India. John's disgust at Clive's failure to do this may have been the reason for an act on his part which Clive never forgave—he attempted to find a flaw in the title-deeds of the *jagir*.[21]

Clive's feud with Johnstone was an unhappy start to his second Government. One wonders if his treatment of him was wholly vindictive, and if he was not also making him a scapegoat for the genuine resentment he felt when he contrasted the rebelliousness of his present Council with the loyalty of his Council of six or seven years before. If he had come to Bengal happy at the prospect of being a king once again, he would have found that his crown had lost some of its lustre. This and perhaps his frustration at no longer having any crisis with the Indians and European rivals to act as a challenge—other than a minor rising in Bihar which was put down by one of his brigade commanders with no more help from Clive himself than the uncharacteristically barbaric advice to expose the heads of the chief rebels on poles[22] – seems to have embittered him. Up to his departure from Bengal in 1760, he was still in many ways the young hero of Arcot; now, at forty, he became middle-aged and increasingly cantankerous; more than ever liable to jump to wrong conclusions, often having to apologize to those he had treated unfairly through his 'warmth of temper'.[23] The man of action, the resourceful improviser, appeared to many to have turned into a purveyor of clichés, or rather of the single cliché concerning his determination to fight the corruption, licentiousness, luxury and oppression he found all around him. 'His zeal for the welfare of the Company transcends every other consideration,' one of his brigade commanders, Colonel Richard Smith, wrote of him in mocking imitation of his manner.[24] Yet the same none-too-friendly colleague was still able to see in him a 'penetration' which 'discovered events that must spring from certain remote causes, if remedies were not timely applied'.[25] And however fierce and unkind he may at times have been, he still kept his regard for human life. One of his first acts on his arrival was to order that in future the proceedings of all capital cases should be sent to him, for he refused to sign a death warrant unless he was fully acquainted with the circumstances and proofs on which a criminal was condemned.[26]

CHAPTER XIX

The Diwani

> The great act of the constitutional entrance of the Company into the body politic of India.
>
> BURKE

Although Buxar had disposed of Mir Kasim and ensured the peace of Bengal and Bihar, there was still the need for a settlement with Mir Kasim's two allies, the Mogul and the exiled Nawab of Oudh, Shuja-ud-daula. Clive decided to give Shuja back his kingdom, except for the districts of Allahabad and Korah which were to provide a sort of demesne for the Mogul; and on June 25, he set off up country to meet the two potentates, travelling by palanquin and budgerow. His retinue included Mun, Strachey and Ingham, as well as most of his servants: Ahern, Philpot and the chef; Munhir Khan, the butler and the under butlers; the bearers, *subahburdars* and *chobdars*; the fan men, the pastrycook, the hookah man, the betel-nut man, the shaving barber and the wig barber.[1] There was an army of keepers to look after Clive's elephant and horses, the hawks and the pack of hounds (imported from England) which he took for his amusement, the curious sorts of deer, and the gift tiger which were acquired on the way.[2] At night, or in the heat of the day while on land, this travelling circus transformed itself into an early example of that feature of the Raj, the Governor's Camp. There were in fact two sets of tents, one of which was sent ahead to the next stopping place, so as to be ready for the gentlemen when they arrived.

Clive's first business was with his own Nawab. He stayed outside Murshidabad, at a charming retreat called Motijhil, or the 'Pearl Lake', which had once belonged to Ghasiti Begum, a cool lakeside palace, with walled gardens full of flowering shrubs and birdsong. Mohammed Reza

Khan was confirmed as chief minister,[3] but Clive curbed him by appointing Rai Durlabh and the sons of the murdered Seths to act in conjunction with him.

During his talks with the Nawab, Clive put forward a plan that had been in his mind for some time. This was that the Company should receive the entire revenues of Bengal, Bihar and Orissa, and be responsible for paying the army and the expenses of the government. The Nawab would be given an annuity of fifty lakhs for his personal and family expenses.

In order that the plan should have a basis of legality, Clive intended to get the Mogul to appoint the Company as his *Diwan* for the three provinces. In the past, the Imperial *Diwan* had collected the revenues of a province, paying part of them to the Nawab, and part to the Mogul. With the break-up of the Empire, the Mogul had ceased to receive his customary share of the provincial revenues, and the office of *Diwan* had lapsed. Clive's plan put the Company over the Nawab in theory as well as in practice. And if the revenues left a surplus after the civil and military expenses, the Nawab's annuity and the annuity which Clive intended to allow the Mogul had all been paid, it would provide a magnificent addition to the Company's income.

The idea that the Company should assume the *Diwani* was nothing new. It had been offered to Clive in 1758 by the Vizier of the previous Emperor; and the present Mogul had offered it to Coote, Carnac and Munro, as well as to Vansittart, who thought it inadvisable. It was Clive, however, who put the idea into effect. The Nawab made no objection at all to the plan; in fact, he was overjoyed at the prospect of having fifty lakhs a year at his own disposal – in Clive's words, 'to squander away among whores, pagy fellows, etc'. 'Thank God!' he exclaimed, 'I shall have as many dancing wenches as I please.'[4]

Clive arrived in such good time at Patna, where he was to meet Shuja and the Mogul, that there was no sign of either of them; so he moved on, further into Hindostan than he had ever been, and on August 1 reached Benares. There is no record of what he thought of the fantastic waterfront of the Hindu holy city. To him, the main thing was that Carnac and Shuja were here.

Shuja-ud-daula, once the most powerful prince in Hindostan, was very different from the effete Nawabs of Bengal: an imposing figure with a Stalin-type moustache and features that suggest Tartar blood. His physical strength was legendary: the story was told of how he had lifted two British officers, one in each hand. Though now 'much fallen away', he was still able to perform his trick of cutting off a buffalo's head with a stroke of his sword.[5] Delighted at the prospect of getting his kingdom back, he made no objection to ceding Allahabad and Korah to the Mogul, or to paying the Company an indemnity of fifty lakhs.[6]

While his prime object in restoring Shuja was to limit the Company's responsibilities, Clive also hoped that he would thereby be attached to the English by 'gratitude'.[7] It was contrary to Clive's usual tenets to look for this sentiment in a Muslim potentate, and might have indicated a more mature attitude on his part had he not in the same breath asserted that the princes of Hindostan could not be attached to the Company 'by any other motive than fear'; so we must take it, instead, as denoting that Shuja made an exceptionally good impression on him. Gratitude apart, Shuja was to be tied to the English by self-interest: for they were alone among his neighbours in not threatening him. Oudh was to serve as a buffer between the territories controlled by the Company and the turbulent powers to the north-west.

The murky chapter of subsequent British relations with Oudh cannot be blamed on Clive, nor the fact that the buffer state proved ineffectual, though it survived until just before the Mutiny. If Clive made the mistake of thinking he had solved the frontier problem, it was a mistake which his successors were to repeat for nearly a century, until the British flag had reached the Khyber and the Arabian Sea; and they, unlike him, could have learnt from the past. Clive's settlement was the best that could be done at the time, and there is evidence that, when he was being honest with himself, he did not regard it as anything more than a short-term solution, hoping it might bring 'a peace for two or three years'.[8] In fact, it brought peace for eight years, until Warren Hastings allowed himself to be drawn by Shuja into the Rohilla War. Clive, whose shrewd if Machiavellian maxim was that the Company should 'take no open part with these Hindostan princes, but privately promote their quarrelling to all eternity',[9] might have preserved the peace still longer had he been in Hastings's place.

Instead of waiting at Benares for the advent of the Mogul, who was writing to him about 'the fragrance of odoriferous zephyrs',[10] Clive decided it would be quicker to go and see that prince at Allahabad. He arrived there on August 9, having travelled 600 miles in the steaming heat of the Rains since leaving Calcutta. Carnac could not remember him looking so well; however, the journey had proved fatal to several of his entourage, including Ahern, whose loss he felt deeply.[11] He met the Mogul, Shah Alam II, on the day of his arrival. This was the prince who, as Shahzada, had been his enemy: dark-skinned, with a 'grave deportment bordering upon sadness', the result of indolence and repeated disappointments.[12] At first he was inclined to be difficult; he even demanded that the English should put him back on the throne of Delhi, something which Clive had no intention of doing. But after two days he accepted Clive's offer. The revenues from Allahabad and Korah, and the annual tribute of 26 lakhs which the Company promised to pay him out of the Bengal revenues, made him better off than he had ever been.

In return, the Mogul granted the *Diwani* of Bengal, Bihar and Orissa to the Company. He did so on August 12, at a ceremony held in Clive's tent. For a throne, he was given a draped armchair, placed on Clive's dining-table which was covered with an embroidered cloth. The grant of the *Diwani* may have been the merest matter of form, issued under the seal of an Emperor who had ceased to rule; but if any one event can be signalized as the beginning of the British Raj, this is it. While thus engaged in making history, Clive did not forget to order hams, pickles and cheese to be bought for him off the ships from Europe; something poor Ahern should have done.[13]

Clive stayed about a week at Allahabad, 'tormented with bugs and flies'.[14] While he was here, he took the opportunity of getting the Imperial sanction for all the Company's territorial gains. In this orgy of *farmans*, Clive did not forget his old friend, Mohammed Ali, the Nawab of the Carnatic, who wanted some of his titles confirmed. This was only one of Mohammed Ali's many requests to Clive, which ranged from troops to perfume: 'Whenever I smelt that pleasant good smell I always remembered your intimacy in my heart.'[15]

The Mogul's confirmation still counted for something with the Indian princes, as well as with the other European nations settled in India. It was therefore useful for the English to have him in their power, a good reason for what some of Clive's critics regarded as his unnecessary generosity to an Emperor of straw. For the time being, the Mogul was protected by a brigade of English troops, who occupied the Allahabad Fort so that he had to retire to a neighbouring bungalow. Here he kept up 'a shabby sort of grandeur',[16] always hoping he could persuade the English to take him back to Delhi. Clive soon tired of his pesterings, and came to regard him as 'a most infamous villain'.[17]*

* Eventually, after Clive's departure, he regained the throne of Delhi with the help of the Marathas. Some years later he was cruelly blinded by a Rohilla chief, and he ended his days once again in the protection of the English.

Clive's return journey, mostly by river, took little more than a fortnight, for he was moving with the stream. As he relaxed in his budgerow off Benares, he began to write a long letter to Margaret, which is remarkable in containing no mention of the incomparable scene that must have been unfolding before his eyes as he wrote.

> I have received many letters from the dearest of wives and the best of parents who is seldom out of my thoughts one day together . . . it would amaze you to hear what diamonds, rubies and gold mohurs have been offered to Lady Clive because she has not signed covenants. However, I have refused anything . . .
>
> Action, as formerly, agrees better with me than indolence and laziness . . . I am as happy as a man at such a distance from his wife and family can well be. I have the testimony of a good conscience to support me in the most arduous task that ever was undertaken, no less than a total reformation in every branch of the civil and military departments, never was such a scene of anarchy and confusion, bribery, corruption and extortion seen or heard of . . .

He finished the letter when he was back in Calcutta, telling her that he was sending home 'a very small horse and a much smaller mare . . . we may have a Lilliputian breed, you being of that breed yourself'. From chaffing her affectionately, he ended on a peremptory note. 'In no circumstances whatever keep company with Mrs Hancock for it is beyond a doubt that she abandoned herself to Mr Hastings, indeed, I would rather you had no acquaintance with the ladies who have been in India, they stand in such little esteem in England that their company cannot be of credit to Lady Clive.'[18] These lines, though still legible, have been crossed out, almost certainly by Margaret, who wished to preserve Philadelphia's good name, while knowing already that her child was rumoured to be by Warren Hastings. The fact, however, that she also crossed out the sentiments that follow would suggest that she was ashamed of Clive's censorious outburst.

There was little time for writing to Margaret after his return to Calcutta. It was necessary to inform the Directors as soon as possible of his achievements. He composed a report running into six pages of folio, in which the *Diwani* had pride of place: 'an event which . . . must be productive of advantages hitherto unknown'. He reckoned there would be a clear gain to the Company of £1,650,900 during the coming year, which would finance the 'Investment' and the China trade, meet the demands of the other settlements and leave a balance.[19] Writing privately at the same time to the Deputy-Chairman, he claimed that when the revenues were properly organized, the Company would obtain an annual net income from Bengal of two million sterling, 'without oppressing or overloading the inhabitants'.[20] Writing to Orme, he grew ecstatic; he was clearly in the midst of one of his psychological periods of excitement, as well as genuinely delighted at his success. 'Fortune seems determined to accompany me to the last; every object, every sanguine wish is upon the point of being completely fulfilled, and I am arrived at the pinnacle of all I covet, by affirming the Company shall, in spite of all envy, malice, faction and resentment, acknowledge they are become the most opulent company in the world, by the battle of Plassey; and Sir Hannibal Hotpot shall acknowledge the same.'[21]

News of the defeat of Sir Hannibal Hotpot – alias Sulivan – in the 1765 election of Directors had already reached him: 'I feel no other satisfaction on that account than for the Company,' he told Margaret. He was confident that the *Diwani* would finish Sulivan for good; he even felt the compassion of the victor for the vanquished.

Clive also knew that the Company's stock would go up. Five months earlier, when he was at Madras, he had written instructing Walsh to buy East India stock for him without delay.[22] With typical carelessness, he sent this letter in the Company's cipher, so that its contents automatically became known to the Chairman and the Secretary. Thus it got about that for all his protestations that he would not make so much as a farthing from his Government, he had nevertheless contrived to benefit through the rise in the stock. He afterwards maintained that he had not yet decided to assume the *Diwani* when he wrote to Walsh; though there is evidence that he thought about it on the voyage from England. Walsh at the same time stated that he did not in any way regard Clive's letter as secret;* but advised many people to buy East India stock on the strength of it.[23] For various reasons, Clive's profit on the transaction amounted to no more than £1000, which was hardly worth the harm done to his reputation.

There were many criticisms of the *Diwani* in Clive's lifetime, and there have been many since. Clive's figures for the revenues were over-optimistic, being based on rents which were fixed in advance, rather than on what was actually collected.[24] No less unreliable was his estimate of civil and military expenses, which he confidently told the Directors would

* A somewhat dubious statement in view of the fact that Clive only used cipher when speaking about buying the stock, and wrote the rest of the letter *au clair*.

never be more than £600,000 a year in a time of peace. The expenses for 1766, when there was no war, turned out to be £980,000; within a few years they would exceed the revenues, bringing the Company close to ruin.

More serious from our own point of view – which was also the point of view of many of Clive's contemporaries – was the effect which the assumption of the *Diwani* had on Bengal. Apart from the basic economic evil of the draining away of wealth – something of which Clive himself was not wholly unaware[25] – the *Diwani* produced what was known as the Dual System, whereby the Company enjoyed the revenues and the power, while the Nawab's government was responsible for the administration. 'We may', Clive explained, 'be regarded as the spring which, concealed under the shadow of the Nawab's name, secretly gives motion to this vast machine of government.'[26] However powerful the spring may have been, the machine was wearing out; and with the Nawab no more than a shadow, there was nobody responsible for law and order and for the welfare of the people.

With the *Diwani*, Clive took over the old Mogul revenue system in which the *zemindars*, or tenants-in-chief, paid rents to the State and in turn collected rents from the peasants. If a *zemindar* produced the required sum no questions were asked about how much his peasants were squeezed. The advent of the Dual System made things worse, not only because there was now less supervision than ever, but because the English demanded too much. Clive preached against such rapacity, but his own inflated idea of the revenues made it inevitable. It was easy for him to impress the Directors and the English public with figures which did not have to be realized until after his return home; but it meant that his successor was expected to produce more than the country could stand. To compel the people to pay up, there was one of Clive's least fortunate innovations: an irregular force of sepoys known as the *pargana* battalions, which often behaved harshly.[27]

But when the faults of the Dual System have been considered, it is hard to know what could have been the alternative. Clive gave several reasons for not taking over the responsibilities of administration, of which the most conclusive was that the Company had not enough experienced English officials. It was the most the Company could do to administer the small territories ceded to it by Mir Jafar and Mir Kasim: the Calcutta lands, Burdwan, Midnapore and Chittagong. These lands were a good school, so that when, in the next decade, Warren Hastings finally did take over the administration of the whole of Bengal, he had a workable corps of administrators at his disposal. So as a transitional stage the Dual System was inevitable, and Clive cannot be blamed for introducing it. His fault lay in refusing to regard it as just a stepping-stone; he was to remain obstinately attached to it because it was his own creation.

It was unfortunate for Clive's reputation that the period of the Dual System saw the terrible famine of 1769–70, something beyond the control of man. But even before the famine, Bengal was 'verging towards its ruin'.[28] The country which, under Alivardi, was proverbial for its agriculture, its industry and its trade, had sunk, in the ten years following Plassey, to the point where people were deserting their homes and lands and becoming vagrants or *dacoits*. Whilst to a certain extent this economic decline was caused by the unsettled conditions which prevailed from the accession of Siraj-ud-daula to the overthrow of Mir Kasim, it was also due to the fact that the English, both the Company and individuals, took advantage of their new position of supremacy to monopolize the manufactures and trade of the country. The old-established Indian merchants were put out of business and replaced by the Indian agents of the English – the notorious *gumashtas*, who became a byword for oppression and greed. 'They swarm like so many bees', Clive wrote of them, 'and all have sepoys in their service . . . it is really very shocking to think of the distress of the poor inhabitants.'[29] But though he attempted to punish the *gumashtas*, it was little more than scratching the surface. The evils went too deep, Bengal was too large a country for someone of even Clive's energy.

And for all Clive's good intentions, he made things worse by his singular ineptitude in matters of economics.[30] There was the harm done by his inflated view of the revenues. He did further mischief by a disastrous if well-meant scheme of currency reform, which caused him to be unjustly accused of frauds on the coinage. Then there was the notorious Society of Trade. Clive was instructed by the Directors to 'regulate' the trade in salt, betel-nut and tobacco which had caused so many abuses in the past few years.[31] He and his colleagues accordingly drew up a plan restricting this trade to an exclusive concern in which a limited number of senior Company servants were entitled to shares, for which they had to subscribe the necessary capital. This, he hoped, would not only be a means of running the trade equitably, but would also serve to provide suitable rewards for the senior servants, something very necessary now that presents were forbidden and the maritime trade was in decline, while salaries remained purely nominal.

Always impetuous, Clive put the scheme into effect without waiting for it to be approved by the Directors. So when, as it turned out, the Directors disapproved of it, having already decided that the trade in salt, betel-nut and tobacco should be totally abolished, he had to delay winding it up in order not to cause hardship to the participants—thus giving rise to the charge that he had disobeyed his superiors. But this was only one of the welter of accusations and misrepresentations to which the Society of Trade gave rise, both in Clive's lifetime and afterwards. Clive was accused of getting rich by the very trade which he had been sent out to India to abolish. The Society was condemned as a monopoly of the most oppressive sort, and was even held responsible for the famine of 1769–70.

In their defence, Clive and his associates showed that the Society's prices for salt—the only commodity in which it effectively dealt—were fifteen per cent lower than what had been charged in previous years. They also pointed out that salt had always been a government monopoly.[32] Nevertheless, as a monopoly, the Society of Trade did cause hardship, and at a time when the economy of Bengal was already in a sorry plight. And apart from its direct effects, it gave what appeared to be a bad example, as though Clive and his senior colleagues had found a way of legalizing the illicit trade for their own benefit. This encouraged others to find ways of getting round the regulations. The example was all the worse in that Clive himself subscribed to the Society of Trade, as a means of rewarding Mun, Strachey and Ingham. In his desire to provide handsomely for his three companions, he went further, and took a share in a private salt-trading venture which by a piece of hair-splitting was deemed not to infringe the Company's orders. This yielded a mere £5000; like Clive's venture on the stock market, it was just not worth the opprobrium it caused. People went so far as to accuse Clive and his partners of privately monopolizing the salt trade of Bengal. He was accused of other monopolies: in cotton, a commodity in which he had no dealings at all; and in diamonds, which he simply purchased as a means of remitting home his *jagir*.

Clive's achievement as an administrator looks thin when considered in relation to Bengal as a whole, being limited to the founding of a postal system[33] and the institution of a land survey—which had the worthy object of enabling the rents to be more equably assessed. In the territories directly ruled by the Company, however, he initiated a series of effective reforms, ranging from a complete tidying-up of all the offices of government to the deportation of the 'poor whites' who had increased in number and were exploiting the humbler natives of Calcutta. These reforms were supervised by one of the Select Committee, Harry Verelst. Of recent Dutch extraction,[34] Verelst had both the appearance and character popularly associated with the nation of his forbears. His abilities were moderate, and he inclined towards indolence;[35] yet he was a man of generosity, integrity and 'great intrinsic worth',[36] qualities which Clive was said to have admired more than brilliance.

Clive's other lieutenant was the Yorkshireman, Francis Sykes, who had been one of Watts's assistants at Cossimbazar in the days of Siraj-ud-daula. His portrait shows a man of ability and drive who could be disagreeable when he wished; very different from the impassive features of Verelst. Moreover, he lacked Verelst's scruples. Yet Clive always regarded him as a man of integrity, and so did Warren Hastings. Though a member of the Select Committee, Sykes was appointed Resident at Murshidabad, where he was responsible for supervising the revenues, working with Mohammed Reza Khan and his associates.

If Clive did not trust any Indians in the way that he trusted Verelst and Sykes, there were nevertheless two in whom he placed a great deal of confidence. Both were Hindus, for whom he had kept his partiality, in preference to what he called 'these fat expensive Moormen'.[37] One was his protégé from the days of Ramnarayan, Shitab Rai, who was now in charge of the revenues of Bihar. The other was Nubkissen, who became Clive's *munshi* or Persian translator, as well as his *banyan*.[38] He accompanied Clive to Allahabad, interpreting for him in his negotiations with Najm-ud-daula, Shuja-ud-daula and the Mogul, drafting treaties and examining *farmans*. From being interpreter, he became Clive's unofficial intelligence officer and political agent, and was able to advise him on many subjects, since he spoke fluent English. Clive granted him land in the northern part of Calcutta, where he built the first of a remarkable complex of palaces still inhabited by his descendants. Here, unlike most Hindus, Nubkissen would entertain in European style, and Clive is said to have been his frequent guest.

CHAPTER XX

Angry Young Men

> A hot-headed and dangerous young man who will always be young.
>
> LAURENCE SULIVAN ON SIR ROBERT FLETCHER

I

The spirit of the victorious army of Buxar was none of the best. Before the battle, there was a mutiny of sepoys which Munro settled by blowing the ringleaders from guns. More recently, the officers had threatened a mass resignation because of the appointment of one Captain McPherson from Bombay.* Clive instituted a number of military reforms, aimed at improving discipline, reducing the Company's expense, and benefiting the troops. The custom whereby commanding officers took a commission from the bazaars which supplied the troops was abolished, a popular measure since it reduced the cost of living.[1] An attempt to prevent the Dutch at Patna from supplying the troops with arak must have been less popular; the bazaar-keepers were prohibited from selling the liquor under pain of having their ears cut off.† Clive even tried to have the worst of the regimental prostitutes banished for life to an island, in an attempt to control venereal disease.[2] But if he was severe in his fight against abuses and indiscipline, he was not without compassion. He asked the Governor of Bombay to find a job for an officer who had been cashiered for a false

* They had the support of Carnac himself, who told Clive on his arrival that it would be a popular gesture if he set McPherson's appointment aside. Clive, to his credit, would do no such thing.

† There does not seem to be any record of this punishment having been inflicted.

muster.[3] He ordered the sentence of 1000 lashes on a deserter to be reduced.[4]

At the same time as Clive reformed the army, he reorganized it, dividing it into three brigades, of which the First and Third were both stationed in Bihar, at Monghyr and Patna respectively; and the Second at Allahabad. Each brigade was commanded by a colonel, who held a position of great responsibility. Sir Robert Barker, of the Third Brigade, was reliable if colourless. Dick Smith, of the Second, was a brave and conscientious soldier, though vain, touchy and rather precious.* But Sir Robert Fletcher, the commander of the First Brigade, was a disgrace to his rank. In his portrait, he seems not so much a man as a schoolboy of arrogant good looks; and indeed, when put in charge of his brigade, he was no more than twenty-eight. One cannot, however, blame his treachery, his belligerence, his capacity for intrigue, his greed for both money and promotion, on his youth, for these faults increased as he grew older. So unpopular was he with the officers of his brigade that there was even an attempt to reprove him from the pulpit with the text: 'Can the Ethiopian change his skin, or the leopard his spots?'[5]†

2

Johnstone and Leycester were not alone among the Councillors in questioning the absolute powers which Clive and the Select Committee had assumed; and indeed, these powers were in theory supposed to lapse after peace had been established. When Clive was away on his journey

* His origins were obscure, which gave rise to many stories, as did his alleged lack of education; though his letters seem far from uneducated, in a high-flown style full of classical allusions: campaigning in the depths of Hindostan, he read Voltaire. He travelled out in the *Kent* with Clive, who found him very irritating.

† Fletcher's background was Scotch-Irish; he went out to Madras as a writer, transferred to the army and was soon dismissed for insolence. Coote had him reinstated and he served with gallantry in the Manila expedition of 1762, for which he was knighted. He was appointed to command a brigade in Bengal through the influence of Sulivan, but Clive took pains to assure him that this would not be held against him (Clive MS. 218. Clive to Fletcher, May 19, 1765) and seems to have been as good as his word. Sulivan was later to regret having favoured Fletcher.

to Allahabad, there was an attempt at opposition, led by Leycester, George Gray and others. Clive, when he heard about it, described the Councillors as 'children and fools, as well as knaves',[6] and was determined to punish them. It seems more than just a coincidence that having heard of the Councillors' misbehaviour, he was given evidence that Gray's *gumashtas* were oppressing the peasants.[7]

By the middle of October, Sykes had collected 150 witnesses against the same Councillor,[8] whose employee, Ramnath Das, had been seized and imprisoned. Clive even accused Gray of taking money from the whores of Calcutta, to which he replied that he had merely accepted the customary present offered to him in his capacity as Collector by the 'poor women', intending to use it for starting a hospital for their 'loathsome distempers' – like Mr Gladstone at a later date, he found his good intentions misconstrued.

Gray and Leycester complained about the arbitrary imprisonment of Ramnath, which led to a violent argument in the Council as to whether Clive's government was military or civil. Carnac lost his temper with Leycester and told him that in certain circumstances 'he himself would go at the head of six sepoys and seize him by the collar'. Clive remarked good-humouredly that it would be as well for Carnac 'to have a man with a guglet of water ready to pour upon his head whenever he should begin to grow warm in debate', but Leycester took the General's fulminations to heart and told his friends that a military dictatorship was about to be set up. Clive punished him for this by taking advantage of an accidental majority in the Council to have him suspended.

Clive's treatment of Leycester was certainly unjust. Leycester was not allowed to vote in the case, whereas Clive and Carnac both did, though they were the accusers. And while it may have been true, as Clive asserted, that Ramnath's imprisonment was due to his own 'heinous crimes and misdemeanours' rather than on account of his connection with Gray, he was confined for so long without a trial that it looked suspicious.[9]

Soon after Leycester's suspension, Gray resigned. A humorous Rabelaisian Scot who had been a schoolfellow of Boswell, he consoled himself while waiting for his ship by trying unsuccessfully to cut out Sykes with his fiancée, and by circulating rude verses about Clive and the Committee.[10] Writing in a more serious vein, he described Clive's language as 'calculated for the meridian of Billingsgate or Grub Street', and painted a dramatic picture of witnesses being paraded through the town under a military guard and 'carried before the frowning President'.*

After the resignation of two more Councillors, Clive and the Committee were supreme. 'Clive is really our king, his word is the law', wrote Richard Barwell, a shrewd young Company servant up country. He compared the Committee to characters of mythology. Clive was Cerberus, guarding the path to Elysium, 'constantly barking at everybody and very loth to permit any to pass him'. Sumner was Sisyphus, Verelst Tantalus; Sykes was 'a greedy Midas with asses' ears'; Carnac was 'the ever-famed Thersites, that warrior of warriors, distinguished equally by brazen lungs or nose of brass'.[11]

Barwell had a private grudge against Clive, who had caught him out bullying the Nawab's officials with Company sepoys for his own purposes.[12] But others joined in the chorus of protest. Major James Rennell, the surveyor, compared Clive to Henry VIII;[13] while Henry Vansittart's younger brother, George, spoke of his being 'guilty of so many acts of violence and oppression that his name must ever be abhorred in Bengal'.[14] Dick Smith recalled how when Clive, Carnac and himself were discussing Carnac's behaviour during Henry Vansittart's administration, Clive had told Carnac: 'General, had I been in Vansittart's place, I would have soon gained the majority, for I would have sent you in arrest and then voted you away to the army.' 'This', observed Smith, 'was *à la mode de Clive*, fruitful in resources.'[15]

For the rest of his time in Bengal, Clive continued his enquiries, which, if they were sometimes motivated by his own vendettas, nevertheless served to expose several Company servants whose conduct was genuinely scandalous.

There was, for example, William Billiers, the Chief at Patna, who extorted money from the entire local population. Clive began to investigate the matter within a month of his arrival in Bengal, but before he had proceeded very far Billiers committed suicide, stabbing himself thirteen times. It was generally believed that Clive's reputation for severity made him kill himself, though he also seems to have been mentally unstable.

* The alternative title of the Governor.

3

To celebrate the peace treaty with Shuja, Clive held what he called a 'fandango', lasting four days. There were wild beast fights on the Maidan near the new Fort, watched by the whole town: buffaloes versus tigers, an elephant versus a rhinoceros, as well as elephants and camels fighting among themselves. The greatest excitement was caused by an elephant which ran amok, killing seven of the spectators and lifting the roof of a nearby house. That Clive was not unaffected by this tragedy can be seen from a remark of his after a similarly fatal spectacle held in his honour by the Nawab a few months later.[16] It was not, however, allowed to spoil the rest of the entertainment, which included a dinner for three hundred people, a ball, a supper, fireworks and—perhaps a slight anti-climax—a performance of *Romeo and Juliet* by the young gentlemen of the settlement.[17]

Clive certainly believed in the psychological value of a *tamasha*. He was also of what modern Indian writers tend to regard as the mistaken school of thought which believed that Indians were impressed by the trappings of power.[18] He knew how to arrange a Durbar; he set such store by salutes that the army grumbled about waste of powder; he even spoke of an Indian Order being started, though he was joking when he suggested that it should be called the Order of Plassey.[19] And while impressing the Indians with his power, he impressed the Europeans of Calcutta with his lavish entertainments, though this may have caused an even greater multitude of fingers to be pointed at his wealth.

People were also impressed by Clive's day-to-day living: the quantity of plate, the splendid equipages, the palanquin adorned with tigers' heads in silver. The account in Carraccioli's generally unreliable book seems to ring true: 'His table was served with delicacy and profusion, and all his most exquisite wines of Europe were at the discretion of his guests.' From his housekeeping books, and what we know of his tastes, it may be added that for all the creations of the French chef, the homely curries were by no means absent. As a touch of informality, one of the gentlemen would always make the salad.

Carraccioli goes on to give a picture of Clive as his guests saw him.

> If he was in good humour, he would encourage a free circulation of the bottle, and by intervals stimulate mirth and jollity; but he soon relapsed

in his natural pensive mood, and was after silent for a considerable time. His conversation was not lively, but rational and solid. As he seldom drank freely enough to be seen without disguise, he was impenetrable excepted to a few confidants to whom he entrusted the execution of his schemes and designs. It was not often that his guests were allowed a great latitude of freedom, as he was always stately and commonly reserved.[20]

One would doubt if Clive was quite so reserved – Leycester complained that he discussed state secrets in front of the ladies – but otherwise this picture seems genuine, except for an allegation that he was in the habit of retiring, after supper, 'with some favourite woman'. The tales of Clive's amours during his second Government as told by Carraccioli – like the other scurrilous printed libels on him which appeared towards the end of his life and shortly after his death – are too obviously mere hack material to be taken seriously. There is the inevitable coy reference to a 'little seraglio'.[21] There are the proverbial etchings: a captain's widow storms out of Clive's house because he invites her to see 'a great curiosity' in his bedroom.[22] To another object of his desires, he is made to give the wholly unlikely Oriental pseudonym of Mirza;* and when the lady (as most of the reputable ones do) repels his clumsy advances, she takes the opportunity of lecturing him on 'the horrors of famine' – which betrays the fact that the story was invented after 1770.[23] It is significant that Clive's enemies, whose letters to each other are full of derogatory references to him, appear to have made no mention of his indulgence in any amours. One feels certain that if they had heard of any, they would have retailed them with relish.

As a contrast to the lurid goings-on recounted by Carraccioli, there are Strachey's descriptions of quiet bachelor week-ends at Dum-Dum, himself, Clive, Mun and Ingham living together in perfect harmony, Mun spending most of his time potting at the crows and jackals.[24] One can imagine Clive thumbing his way through the vast supply of reading matter which he had sent from England: a whole year of *Gazetteers*, *Ledgers*, *Advertisers* and *Gentleman's Magazines*, together with pamphlets like *A Vindication of the Ministry* or *The Grievances of the American Colonies Candidly Examined*. Such was his affection for the place, with its memories of week-ends with Margaret six years before, that he and his three companions took to living here most of the time, riding into Calcutta each morning and returning in the evening by chaise.[25]

* Anyone with knowledge of the East would know that this is not a woman's name at all, but the title of a Muslim nobleman, a lesser equivalent of *Mir*.

Much of Clive's leisure must have been taken up with acquiring curious and beautiful presents to send to Margaret; pictures and swords, a hoopoe, a 'gold bird', a pair of antelopes, and 'a deer no bigger than a cat'.[26] He also bought her shawls, muslins, dimities and diapers, and sent cloth to his friend John Call in Madras to be made into shifts for her. As a pattern, he told Call, 'you must get a shift from the smallest lady in the place'.[27] Clive's feelings for Margaret come out in a letter which he wrote at this time to Ned, at Eton. 'Attend diligently to your studies and to the advice of your Tutor but above all follow the instructions of your mother, let her excellent example be your guide and you will render yourself truly worthy of that great fortune which Providence seems to have designed for you.' Earlier in the letter, which begins: 'My dear and only son,' and ends 'your father and your friend', he compliments Ned on his style and grammar: 'You have laid the foundation of that knowledge which alone can make you the gentleman, and distinguish you from the herd of your fellow-creatures.'[28]

One of the five surviving letters from Margaret to Clive would have reached him at the end of 1765. 'I will write a few lines to my beloved Sabit Jang . . . language is ever too weak to express the feelings of a tender heart.' She had hoped to send him a miniature of herself but had failed to get a good enough likeness.[29] The letter is neither as long nor as gossipy as those which she continued to write to Carnac, who vied with Strachey in keeping her informed about Clive's health.

Margaret was now living mainly at Westcomb, a pretty villa near Blackheath belonging to the Duke of Bolton, which she rented so as to be handy for getting the Indian news as soon as it arrived. When the *Admiral Stevens* brought accounts of the *Diwani* and the treaty with Shuja she was so overjoyed it almost made her ill. But her joy was closely followed by sorrow: her youngest child, Elizabeth, born after Clive's departure and described as a beauty, died of convulsions resulting from smallpox. This was the fourth time she had lost a child.

At Westcomb, Margaret had the company of Jenny Latham, now widowed; while her brother, Nevil Maskelyne, the recently appointed Astronomer Royal, lived not far away at Greenwich. She had her music, and for further diversion studied Italian. This quiet life was interrupted by visits to Berkeley Square, for meetings of Clive's attorneys, of whom she was one, and to keep in touch with Company affairs. When the 1765 election of Directors was coming off, she wrote to people like her Bath acquaintance, Mrs Ducarel, asking for their votes.

Such efforts were superfluous, for Sulivan and his party were crushingly defeated. Clive's star rose high at East India House—higher than ever, now that Scrafton was a Director—as well as in the country as a whole. There was applause from all sides for the man who had obtained unheard-of revenues for the Company. One can even detect a note of genuine admiration in the mocking voice of Walpole: 'Lord Clive has just sent us the whole kingdom of Bengal, which the Great Mogul has yielded to this little Great Mogul without a blow . . . and when all expenses are paid, there will be remitted to England yearly a million and a half—we may buy another war in Germany, and subsidize two or three Electors.'[30] With remarkable foresight, 'Athenian' Stuart had recently designed a medal of Clive, flanked by a globe to symbolize territorial gains and a cornucopia representing money.

The news that his wonderful son was doing more great things in India acted as a tonic to old Richard Clive, who was now rather frail,[31] and given to complaining of how Clive's other attorneys were skimping the new stables at Styche. Clive had preferred to concentrate on Walcot, though even there his building schemes were modest. Under the supervision of Sir William Chambers, the old house was given a modern dress, the gables, oriels and porch being replaced by a parapet, sash windows and a pillared portico; while the ceilings of the main rooms were decorated with trophies of bows and arrows and musical instruments—signifying, perhaps, the two main interests of Clive and Margaret.

Chambers also supervised the work that was going on at Berkeley Square. Writing to Margaret from the Ganges, Clive had desired that the main rooms of his town house should be 'furnished in the richest and most elegant manner'. Accordingly, the two first-floor drawing-rooms were given ceilings of gilded foliage and their walls covered in scarlet damask. At the same time, the house was provided with every modern comfort, including 'veined marble water stools'.[32]

4

To fill the vacancies in the Council caused by the departure of Johnstone, Leycester and the others, Clive decided to import four 'untainted' Madras servants.[33] The Bengal servants, furious at being thus passed over, formed an association in which everybody was obliged to join under pain of ostracism. One of the leaders was the Secretary, a young man of twenty-three named William Majendie; he encouraged his fellows to hold what would now be called a 'sit-in' in the Council Room and the public offices so that everything was held up at the busiest time of the year when the ships were being dispatched.

At first, Clive was not greatly perturbed by the behaviour of the young men, which he merely regarded as 'puerile'.[34] But when they decided to refuse all invitations from himself and the Committee, and to send the Madrassers to Coventry, it seemed all too like the revolt against Vansittart. But as he wrote to Walsh, 'I am and can be as determined as any man so long as something within tells me I am *right*.'[35]

He made an example of Majendie and had him dismissed, hoping this would bring the other young men to their senses. He also deprived George Vansittart of his post as Translator, because he had lent his house for a meeting of the association. Clive was hurt by George's behaviour, having, as he said, been like a father to him: but doubtless for Henry's sake, he intended, after a while, to 'forget and forgive'.[36]*

At the end of March, the young men were still unrepentant enough to hold a party to celebrate Clive's departure up country and to ask to borrow his private band for the occasion. But by July, they had climbed down. 'The spirited Bengallers appeared in a body one morning at the table of their lord and master,' wrote Barwell. 'All means, all methods, were adopted to break the association: severity, kindness, violence, and these, I am sorry to say it, have at last worked the effect.'[37] But while there do not seem to be any recorded instances of Clive's severity in this affair, there are indications that he used kindness. The four Madrassers were invited to Verelst's house and given a little surprise; four fine horses, all caparisoned, were brought to the door and they were told to take their pick, with Clive's compliments.[38]

5

Clive's departure up country, which caused the young men to celebrate,

* He did so before leaving Bengal, recommending George Vansittart for the important and lucrative post of Resident at Midnapore.

was in order to attend the *Punyah*, the annual meeting of *zemindars* and collectors at which the next year's *bandobast* or rent roll was fixed. On March 26, he started up river with a large party; his two budgerows, one for dining and one for sleeping, were accompanied by more than twenty others, some of twenty-two oars, and some of ten or twelve; together with a dozen 'tow boats' and four or five 'cook-boats'.[39] On April 1, they reached Plassey, where they were greeted by the Nawab. If Clive went inside the historic hunting-lodge, it is to be hoped that he did not notice the elaborate graffito which one of Carraccioli's informants purported to have seen there: 'In this sublime design the Heaven-Born General was represented fast asleep on his back, in his palanquin, with his mouth wide open, and Fortune in that posture in which the nicest and most exalted ladies must on some occasion condescend to place themselves, was beneficently dropping into the mouth of her distinguished favourite, from that part to which Fame applies her posterior trumpet, riches, titles, ribbons, and honours.'[40]

Two days later, Clive was at Motijhil, able to relax amid the cooing of doves and the splashing of water. The *Punyah* was held here on April 29, the first since the English assumed the *Diwani*. Clive took care to observe the traditional customs. As the Mogul's representative, he sat on a throne beside the Nawab. All the great officers of state and *zemindars* were assembled in their gorgeous clothes. It was a memorable *tamasha*, costing over two lakhs, which would have seemed justified by the revenues it promised. But in the midst of this pageantry, the tiger-fights and the dancing-girls, there came a bombshell: a letter from Sir Robert Fletcher informing Clive that all the officers below the rank of major in his own and the other two brigades had pledged themselves to resign their commissions unless an extraordinary allowance known as 'double *batta*', which had been abolished at the beginning of the year, were restored.*

This news threatened a crisis of the first magnitude. If the troops were suddenly abandoned by most of their officers, they would almost certainly mutiny. To make matters worse, an army of 50,000 Marathas had approached within a hundred miles of Allahabad; Smith's brigade was watching them. The officers were clearly in earnest; they had signed a

* *Batta* was an allowance given to officers in the field. The double *batta* had started as a piece of generosity on Mir Jafar's part, but came to be regarded by the English officers in Bengal as their right. Clive had instructions from the Directors to abolish it, which he did at the beginning of 1766. This, up to now, had appeared to cause no worse reaction than a protest.

penalty bond, agreeing to forfeit £500 each if they returned to duty before the double *batta* was restored, and they had raised a fund of 140,000 rupees to help their more needy comrades.

Clive did not hesitate. The officers could resign and be damned; he would 'fall a sacrifice to their fury rather than give up the point'.[41] Those last days of April and the first days of May seemed to reflect his thunderous mood: the atmosphere was sultry and oppressive, the trees around the Pearl Lake took on an unearthly shade of green against a darkening sky; and every now and then lightning flashed and thunder rent the air.[42] Yet Clive's mood was not all defiance; one of his staff noted how worried and distracted he had seemed during the evening of May 2.[43] That day, he had been feverishly writing letters: asking for officers from elsewhere in India, and ordering his Brigade Commanders to accept the officers' resignations, to arrest the ringleaders pending a court martial, and to do their best to secure the loyalty of the sepoy *subadars*.

He was certainly right in acting as he did. Had he given way to the officers' threats, the army would for ever more have been able to dictate to the civil government. Yet it was felt by some that he should have temporized with the officers and not risked a mutiny of 24,000 well-trained and well-armed sepoys; while there were many who sympathized with the officers' claim that the cost of living was fifty to a hundred per cent higher up country than it was in Calcutta, though as Clive pointed out, the Bengal officers were in general far better off than those elsewhere.*

The First Brigade at Monghyr was Clive's chief concern, for he believed the conspiracy to have started there and he did not entirely trust Fletcher. He felt that his presence would keep the troops from mutinying, and set out for Monghyr as quickly as he could. His first stop was at a garden house a short distance from Murshidabad, where the Nawab insisted on coming to say goodbye, though he was suffering from a fever which affected his nose. Four days later, he was dead. There is no reason to suppose that his death was not due to natural causes: apart from his fever, he was grossly overweight and riddled with venereal disease. Neverthe-

* To help the hard cases, Clive had recently started a fund, into which he put five lakhs, described by him as a legacy from Mir Jafar. Many were sceptical about this legacy, suspecting him of having cadged the money from the subsequent Nawab. It is certainly strange that he never mentioned it until he announced his military fund in April 1766, while claiming to have known about it since May 1765. Yet from Carnac's letters, written earlier that year, it seems that Mir Jafar expressed a particular veneration for Clive, and so might well have left him a legacy on his deathbed.

less, Clive's enemies were to hint that he had poisoned him, though for what motive it is hard to say; unless it was to save the Company thirteen lakhs a year. For when the dead Nawab's brother, Saif-ud-daula, was installed in his place, his allowance was reduced by this amount.

To reach Monghyr by May 14, the day before the officers were due to leave, meant a hurried journey in almost insupportable heat. There were relays of bearers along the route, yet some of them dropped dead. Clive was feeling far from well, but he did not allow himself more than three hours' sleep in twenty-four. On the 13th, they came to a river where the bridge had been washed away and which was too swollen to be crossed until that night, even on elephants. This made it impossible to reach Monghyr until the 15th.

Meanwhile, the officers had already left, having decided to go a day sooner than they had originally planned. Their departure caused some of the European troops to mutiny, but they were quietened, partly by having the saluting battery pointed at them by a body of sepoys, partly by a hand-out of cash with the band playing 'The British Grenadiers' to keep up morale.[44] The sepoys remained faithful, and one of their *subadars* was actually put in charge of a battalion of Europeans.[45]

Clive had been told of a plot to assassinate him as he arrived at Monghyr fort, but made light of it. His mood of anger and worry had by now given way to his old exhilaration in the face of danger. He entered the frowning, castellated gateway accompanied by a major and nobody else. A battalion of European troops was drawn up under arms on the square; he approached them 'with a steady pace and composed countenance' and ordered them to ground their arms. On being instantly obeyed, he said: 'Now I am satisfied you are British soldiers and not, as I was erroneously informed, assassins!'[46] Next day, he addressed all the Europeans, telling them of the iniquity of the officers' behaviour. He also, through an interpreter, spoke to the sepoys, commending their steadfastness which he rewarded with two months' double pay.[47]*

As for the mutinous officers, who were encamped outside the town, Clive ordered them to leave for Calcutta, prior to being shipped back to Europe. 'Many of them', he wrote, 'went away with tears in their eyes.'[48] There were certainly many who regretted having gone to such lengths, particularly as they now faced the loss of their livelihood. The news that the officers at Monghyr had failed made Smith's officers submit, and he

* Clive's critics later pointed out that this generosity cost the Company as much as giving the officers their extra *batta* for two years.

reinstated all but the ringleaders; while in Barker's brigade, where there was much less mutinous spirit, the officers had already repented and been forgiven. Within a week of Clive's arrival at Monghyr, the crisis was over.

Clive made the most of the 'Batta Mutiny', both in order to gain the maximum credit for its suppression, and as yet another instance of the depravity of Bengal. It might, he maintained, have led to a 'civil war' between the loyal troops and bands of freebooting officers; it had 'cast a stain upon the Company's service, which all the water of the Ganges can never wash away'.[49] Clive's enemies were able to compare this furore with his comparative silence over the McPherson affair in which his friend Carnac was implicated.

Most of the disgraced officers lost no time in writing to Clive, begging to be taken back. He was ready to forgive all but the ringleaders and the more senior Captains who should have known better, and those who were 'low and illiterate'.[50] On being reinstated, the officers did not lose their rank, but were made to sign contracts. The ringleaders were tried by court martial for stirring up mutiny; but they mostly suffered nothing worse than being ordered immediately back to Europe, the Court being uncertain as to the extent of its jurisdiction. Captain Stainforth, who was charged with no less a crime than threatening to assassinate Clive, received only a cashiering; Clive himself having put in a plea for mercy, on the grounds that he 'bore a very good character, was recommended strongly to me by some of our friends, and is nephew to the Bishop of London'.[51] Inevitably, however, the broken officers took home many stories of Clive's harshness and ruthlessness. In particular, there were Captain Parker, who complained of having been imprisoned for more than a month in 'a dismal hole' at Patna while awaiting trial – though this seems to have been without Clive's knowledge – and Captain Duffield and Lieutenant Robertson, who suffered the discomforts of house arrest in the heat of Calcutta, having attempted to evade deportation to England.[52]

Far more important to Clive than the punishment of these irresponsible youths was the bringing to light of the real instigator of the mutiny, who turned out to be none other than Sir Robert Fletcher himself. Before they left Monghyr on May 14, some of the officers told Clive's advance party that it was he who had first persuaded them to resign their commissions.[53] Certainly Fletcher's behaviour was most suspicious. He admitted to Clive at the end of April that he had known since January of the officers' conspiracy, but had failed to report it to him. Then in June he tried to deny that he had had any knowledge of the conspiracy until April.

EAST INDIA HOUSE, LEADENHALL STREET
by Thomas Malton

STATUE OF CLIVE
by Peter Sheemakers

GHYRETTY HOUSE
by Samuel Davis

CLIVE'S GOVERNMENT HOUSE AT CALCUTTA
DURING HIS SECOND PERIOD AS GOVERNOR (1765–67)
From T. and W. Daniell, Oriental Scenery

He was arrested in July and tried by a general court martial at Patna, presided over by Dick Smith. Faced with the evidence of a great many officers, he contradicted himself, and in his defence repeated what he had told Clive some time before, namely that he had encouraged the officers in their conspiracy so as to gain their confidence and thus more easily frustrate their schemes.[54] This defence, if true, would have shown him as little better than an *agent provocateur*. In fact, it seems beyond doubt that he incited the officers to revolt so as to win popularity with them, and also perhaps to distract attention from the many abuses of which he was guilty, such as taking a commission on the illicit sale of arak to the troops. When he saw that Clive was determined not to give way to the officers, he abandoned them. The Court found him guilty of mutiny, and sentenced him to be cashiered.[55] Apart from the slur on his reputation, this was not a very severe punishment; his fortune was already considerable, and he had for some months talked of resigning.

CHAPTER XXI

The Last of Bengal

Joy to you, my friend, on the event of this day, this important day, which assures us of the departure of his Lordship.

RICHARD BARWELL, 1767

From Monghyr, Clive went on to Patna, where he had a meeting with Shuja, who gave him a magnificent pearl necklace for Margaret. He accepted it, contrary to his rule; no doubt he could not resist seeing it on her slender neck. Having taken his leave of the now ailing Nawab of Oudh, he set off back down the broad river.

On his arrival in Calcutta, he found a dispatch from the Directors ordering him to make 'the strictest enquiry'[1] as to what presents were received by Company servants from Mir Kasim. As it happened, he had already made enquiries regarding Vansittart, who, it transpired, had accepted a present from Mir Kasim of five lakhs. He did not, however, intend to make this information public unless Vansittart openly went over to the Sulivan camp; he still hoped to keep the influential former Governor on his side. For this reason, he did not welcome the Directors' instructions.

Nevertheless, they provided an opportunity of getting rid of Sumner, who had been the nigger in the Committee woodpile ever since he had shown weakness towards the recalcitrant Councillors in the previous year. Clive also despised him for being, as he thought, 'entirely governed' by his 'odious' wife. He knew that Sumner had himself received two and a half lakhs from Mir Kasim, and therefore told him that the Directors clearly had him in mind when they ordered an enquiry.[2] Sumner took the hint, invented a diplomatic illness and resigned. With Sumner out of the way, the next Governor would be the solid and reliable Verelst, who, according to Dick Smith, regarded Clive as 'the greatest man that ever existed'.[3] Clive generously told Verelst to 'let . . . if possible, all the odium fall upon me, who am going home, that your Government may be easier'.[4]

Having settled who would be the next Governor, Clive now introduced a measure for raising the dignity of his office. The Governor would henceforth bind himself by a public oath not to engage in trade, and in return would receive a commission of $1\frac{1}{8}$ per cent on the revenues. Clive took the oath against trading on October 1, in the presence of the Mayor and Aldermen, the Council and most of the inhabitants, some of whom regarded the ceremony with scepticism, and grumbled that it held up the proceedings of the Mayor's Court.

This was the last public act of Clive's Indian career. In November, ill-health, which had stayed away for a remarkably long time, returned with a vengeance. It was the usual combination of malaria, excruciating abdominal pain and nervous collapse. For a month he could do no work, nor see anyone but his closest associates. At times he thought he was dying, and he afterwards maintained that he could not have survived but for opium, of which he took as much as fifteen grains in twenty-four hours. He was reduced to hysterics worse than Carnac had ever seen, but Ingham never thought he was in danger, and considered the nervous attack to be no more serious than that which he had suffered a few years previously in England.[5]

By the middle of December, the pain had gone, and the hysterics given way to languor and depression. Strachey tried to get him to write a couple of lines to Margaret, but he was still not up to it; not until New Year's Day did he write to her. Gradually he recovered his interest in business, and his conversation improved. To raise his spirits, there was a letter from the Directors, expressing their warmest approval of his work.[6]

At the same time, however, there was less cheering news from Walsh and Scrafton.[7] Vansittart had openly joined Sulivan; Walsh had therefore seen fit to inform the Chairman about his present of five lakhs from Mir Kasim. The Directors were talking of prosecuting him, and also Johnstone, which had the inevitable effect of driving the two former enemies together, in the opposition camp. This, to Clive, was particularly unwelcome news. He still had no wish for his friend Vansittart to be exposed, although he continued his search for ammunition to be used against him if necessary.

Before Clive left, George Vansittart said that if an account were made of what he had done to root out licentiousness and what he had done to encourage it, the balance would be against him.[8] A harsh verdict, but not one to be ignored, even though its author was prejudiced. On the credit side, there were his reforms within the ceded territories, and his attempt to provide Company servants with legitimate rewards. The latter, however, did no more than establish a principle, which was not properly acted upon until twenty-five years later.

On the debit side, there was the bad example he gave by his private salt venture, and by urging the Directors to allow Carnac to keep a present of two lakhs from the Mogul, while failing to do anything about a similar present which had been promised to Munro. Not only did this show favouritism, but it looked like a deliberate attempt to play down Munro's victory of Buxar lest it should outshine Plassey. Then there was the casuistry of his claim not to have benefited by his Government. To support this claim, he prepared a detailed account of receipts and expenses.[9] The receipts totalled about £80,000 against which he set expenses of over £85,000, showing that he ended up £5,816 out of pocket. But he counted among his expenses the £13,049, £15,942 and £9161 which he gave as 'emoluments' to Mun, Strachey and Ingham, respectively. Endowing his brother-in-law and friends with these magnificent 'emoluments' was one way of benefiting himself.

One cannot pass a fair judgement on the efficacy of Clive's reforms because of the abandonment of his scheme for providing suitable rewards for Company servants, which meant that they had to continue making money as best they could. It was after Clive's time that Bengal produced the really rich 'Nabobs'. Barwell was eventually worth about half a million and Sykes was not far behind him. Even the admirable Warren Hastings sent home over £200,000, though it melted away through bad management. These great fortunes, however, were not so much a sign of Clive's failure as of changed conditions. The assumption of the *Diwani* opened up ways of making money which had been unknown to the likes of Johnstone. And it is perhaps significant that the two most notorious of all the Nabobs, Thomas Rumbold[10] and Paul Benfield, obtained their ill-gotten fortunes not in Bengal but in Madras.

On February 1, 1767, Clive sailed for home in the *Britannia*. Seven years earlier, he had thought he was seeing the last of Bengal; but now it really was the last. George Vansittart believed that even the four Madras gentlemen were pleased to see him go, and that the anniversary of his departure would long be celebrated.[11] But if the day of the *Britannia*'s sailing was a red-letter day for many, it was for Nubkissen 'the most melancholy I have ever known'. As consolation, he now had the title of Maharaja, granted to him by the Mogul at Clive's behest. But he also wanted a picture of Clive and Margaret: 'They are already drawn in my heart, but I would have them ever before my eyes.'[12]

This time, Black Robin agreed to come back to England. Clive also took a slave boy, a number of dogs and birds, and a monkey complete with clothes. The rest of his menagerie went by a later ship. His luggage included diamonds and other stones insured for £8000, some of them for Margaret, others representing part of his *jagir*. Then there were what he described as some 'curiosities' for the King from the Mogul – a gold and enamelled casket studded with diamonds, a jewelled dagger, a gold and enamelled sword. There were, in addition, a pair of diamond drops, worth at least a lakh, a present for the Queen from Mohammed Ali, who had also wanted Clive to take a present for the King. Clive had returned the latter, with the crushing message that His Majesty would never condescend to accept a present from 'so petty a prince'.[13] He had also returned a diamond which Mohammed Ali wanted him to take to Margaret; the rule about presents presumably applied to diamonds, but not to Shuja's pearls.

After an uneventful voyage, the *Britannia* dropped anchor at Portsmouth on July 14. It was the sort of English July which is more like April; Clive must have shivered as he stood on the deck of the ship. He wrote a line to Margaret, saying that he would be dining with her next day at Berkeley Square, and sent Strachey and Ingham ahead of him to tell her the good news. When they arrived in London, Strachey presented Ingham with a beautiful new chariot which he had ordered to be built specially as a surprise for him, in return for 'keeping my crazy body in tolerable repair'.[14]

CHAPTER XXII

The Return of the Proconsul

> My languid spirits once again revive
> And pay their tributory praise to Clive!
> That, to succeeding ages, all may know
> A perfect man resided once below...
> The richest subject e'er Britannia knew
> European Princes cannot cope with you.
>
> LADY DOROTHEA DUBOIS, 1767

Walsh told Clive that he should henceforth be independent, and stand on his popularity with the Sovereign and the public.[1] His popularity with the Sovereign augured well; he received the Royal summons within a couple of days of his arrival, when the presents from the Mogul were still in the hands of the customs, who had held up his luggage. A fifty-pound tip to the right official secured their timely release,[2] and Clive was able to enter the audience chamber with a page at his side weighed down by the Mogul's gems and jewelled weapons, not to mention his own more modest offering of drawings and maps.

The King and Queen were most gracious. 'I have the King's command to lay before him my ideas of the Company's affairs,' wrote Clive afterwards, 'with a promise of his countenance and protection in everything I might attempt for the good of the nation and the Company.'[3] It seemed that the elusive British peerage was once again in sight.[4] Mohammed Ali's diamond drops were a tremendous success with the Queen; their fame spread as far as Florence, where the Grand Duchess of Tuscany was reported to be very envious.[5] The Mogul's presents caused an equal sensation, though Clive had valued them at less than £2000. 'Lord Clive is arrived, has brought a million for himself, two diamond drops worth twelve thousand pounds for the Queen, a scimitar, dagger and other matters covered with brilliants for the King, worth twenty-four thousand more,' wrote Walpole. 'These *baubles* are presents from the deposed and imprisoned Mogul, whose poverty can still afford to give such bribes.'[6] There were naturally those who believed that the bribes were really from Clive himself. John Johnstone spoke of his 'leaving the diamonds in pledge for the Royal favour'.[7]

As for the public, Clive's return brought him many letters of congratulation from strangers as well as from people he knew. Begging letters came from all over Europe, some of them in verse. His fame was acknowledged by Arthur Young, who published an open letter to him, suggesting that he should devote part of his fortune to starting an experimental farm.[8] He was invited to become President of the Lying-in Hospital, he was elected to the Royal Society, and the burgesses of Shrewsbury celebrated his return with a feast, to which he contributed a turtle bought when the *Britannia* called at Ascension Island.

The public which Clive particularly wanted to impress was centred on Westminster and Leadenhall Street. Having found, on his arrival, that Mohammed Ali had persisted in sending Margaret the diamond he had refused before leaving India, he was able to make a pretty gesture by surrendering it to the Directors, who promptly returned it to him, expressing their appreciation of his 'delicacy and disinterestedness'.[9] Their tongues, however, must have been in their cheeks, for at a General Court in the previous March, Walsh had proposed that Clive's *jagir* should be extended for a further ten years in recognition of his services. It is surprising that Walsh, whose sense of the fitness of things was greater than Clive's, should have been guilty of such a grave tactical error; but the move seems to have originated with him and Scrafton. Clive, it is true, was himself considering the possibility of getting his *jagir* extended, but there is no sign of his having communicated his thoughts to his friends in England.

Walsh's proposal made it seem as though Clive had carried on his unpopular policy not out of duty, but in order to obtain this extra prize. It was adopted by a thin majority of 29, while raising a general cry that he had been rewarded enough. There were wild reports of his profits from the salt trade; according to one printed lampoon, in which he is called 'Lord Vulture', Walsh 'Skeleton Scarecrow' and Scrafton 'Jaundice Braywell', they amounted to £50,000 a year and his total income was £96,000.[10] Walsh had to 'turn publisher in the papers' to refute the worst of these libels.[11] It was hardly the right atmosphere for the return of the proconsul.

Even before the end of 1766, Clive's popularity at East India House had declined.[12] Johnstone and the other ex-Councillors had set to work; Vansittart had 'sounded the war whoop',[13] and together they had rallied behind Sulivan. This growing opposition was just as much against the Directors, with whom Clive should have made common ground. Instead, his friends joined with the Sulivan party in demanding that the Company's dividend should be raised, to which the Directors were prudently opposed, though they bowed to the popular clamour.

Before Clive reached England, the Directors were again obliged to surrender: they raised the dividend still further and they agreed to drop the prosecutions against Johnstone and the other returned servants. At the same time, they gave way to the Government. When in July 1766 Pitt—now Chatham—had become Prime Minister, he had planned a Parliamentary enquiry into the Company's affairs. Historians were to take this as a sign of his imperial vision, but in fact he merely wished to challenge the Company's right to the revenues of Bengal, so as to appropriate them for the Treasury. Eventually it was agreed to postpone any decision as to the Company's future status for two years, during which time the Company was to make an annual payment to the Treasury of £400,000.

Clive regarded this agreement as too precipitate, and felt that in return for its money the Company should have obtained some definite measure of security for its territories abroad.[14] On the whole, he believed that the nation would benefit more from the revenues of Bengal if they remained in the Company's hands, rather than being used to strengthen the Government.[15] Walsh, however, seems to have assured Chatham that Clive would support the Government in its claim for a share in the Company's revenues, and Chatham in return gave him to understand that he would be sympathetic to any proposal for extending the *jagir*. But the prospects of such an alliance faded in the spring of 1767 when Chatham was stricken by a mysterious nervous illness rather similar to Clive's. For the next few years he lived as a recluse, and the leadership passed into the hands of the young and pleasure-loving Duke of Grafton, who was as ineffective in controlling his heterogeneous Government as he was in dealing with the growing discontent at home and the worsening situation in the American colonies.

Rather than ally himself with Grafton's Goverment—which included Sulivan's patron, Shelburne—Clive resumed his connection with

Grenville, hoping that he would soon be back in power. He benefited from Grenville's advice not to interfere in the day-to-day controversies of the East India Company; at the same time, however, he was encouraged by that pedagogic statesman to think of himself as the Company's overlord, who had a right to be consulted in everything.[16]

As on his previous return to England, Clive's plans were thwarted by illness. It was the same old thing, nausea, agonizing pain, insomnia and constipation, with the inevitable nervous collapse. People likened his case to Chatham's: 'his whole system of nerves destroyed, sometimes dying, sometimes tolerable well, sometimes crying'.[17] But whereas Chatham was sixty, Clive was no more than forty-two. At this age, it was cruel for a man of Clive's boundless energy to be incapacitated for months on end. With ill-health came hypochrondria: a pricking sensation about the stomach now assumed as much importance in his mind as a rebellion had formerly.

After a few weeks at Bath, during which time he saw the now-penitent Majendie, and agreed to use his influence to get him reinstated, he was well enough to go to Shropshire, and to eat oysters which had been sent all the way from Colchester. He was reunited with his parents, and had his first sight of the newly remodelled Walcot, though his interest in the place had waned as he was sure it would be too damp for him. Towards the end of September, he and Margaret, accompanied by Jane Latham, Strachey and Ingham, set out for London. When they reached Birmingham, Clive suffered a severe relapse and sent for his Will. Most ironically, the townspeople rang the church bells, to welcome their distinguished visitor, not knowing that he lay prone, apparently at death's door. In London, people heard that he had died. But once again the crisis passed. 'Proclaim it to all our family and friends,' wrote Margaret, who had been nursing him day and night. 'If all the bells in England are set a-ringing, I'll pay the ringers what they please.' She felt, she said, like a condemned criminal restored to life.[18]

For some days they stayed at the house of a local doctor, and Clive gradually mended, though he suffered a slight setback through drinking a glass too much of the wine which Pigot—now an Irish peer and living grandly in Staffordshire—sent him. Margaret gives a very Oriental picture of him, reclining on his bedroom carpet draped in satin and surrounded by books, reading an historical romance, *The Countess of Salisbury*, 'at a great rate'. Then she speaks of him 'sitting up very hearty and talking about the things of the world, forming schemes of future good behaviour as to eating and drinking and keeping quiet and in great spirits'. There followed a period of indecision as to when he would resume his journey, and to where. One moment he was for continuing to London, the next he had decided to return to Walcot. False starts and repeated changes of plan were to become part of the normal life of his family and entourage—as though being away from India made him restless.

Eventually, he settled for Walcot, and then went back to Bath. His prolonged absence from London led to a 'cool situation' between him and the Directors.[19] He regarded them as 'timid and irresolute',[20] he felt they were jealous of his influence.[21] That he was to some extent justified in the latter opinion is confirmed by no less shrewd an observer than Sulivan;[22] but if the Directors deliberately played down Clive's achievements, as he accused them of doing, they did so in order to quieten the dividend clamour, rather than out of jealousy.

Then there was the question of the *jagir*: the Directors had thrown 'a great deal of cold water' on Walsh's proposal.[23] This proposal had to be ratified by a General Court at the end of September. Clive, when he returned to England, could have asked for it to be withdrawn, and redeemed the unhappy situation which Walsh had created. But he missed this opportunity, and the extension of his *jagir* was duly confirmed. The Directors had given it their 'unanimous though languid' support;[24] but he showed them no gratitude; and he annoyed the ordinary stockholders, who had voted for his reward, by off-loading nearly £100,000 worth of his stock immediately after the matter was settled, as though he had no faith in his own rosy picture of the Company's affairs.

One of Clive's grievances against the Directors was that they consulted him in 'a mean, sneaking manner', rather than openly. This was hardly fair, in that they seem to have shown great deference to his views; they even asked him to nominate army officers. They postponed their decision on various matters so as to have a chance of discussing them with him; but he could not, or would not, come to London. Scrafton begged him to give the Directors his wholehearted support, in return for the support which they gave him when he was in India; warning him that a lack of solidarity in the present regime could only bring back Sulivan.[25] Clive replied to this sensible advice with the arrogance of which he was sometimes capable: 'Know, Scrafton, I have a judgement of my own, which has seldom failed me in cases of much greater consequence than what you recommend. As to the support which you say was given to my Government by the Directors, they could not have done otherwise.'[26] One has to remember that when he wrote these words, he was suffering from a painful bilious colic. Clive's opinion of the Directors was bound to get back to them; they heard rumours that he aspired to weed out four of their number–including the Chairman, the long-suffering Rous, and his old Madras chief, Thomas Saunders–and to become a Director himself.[27] He denied these reports with characteristic hauteur: 'The being a Director may be an object to the Directors, but not to Lord Clive.'[28]

The situation between Clive and the Directors was further complicated by Vansittart, who was now in financial difficulties.[29] To recoup himself, he wished to go back to Bengal as Governor; and he hoped that Clive would secure his reappointment in return for his having supported the extension of the *jagir*. His brother-in-law, the former Governor of Madras, Robert Palk, whose clerical past–he originally entered the Company service as a chaplain–and friendship with both Clive and Sulivan fitted him for the role of peacemaker,[30] sounded Clive on his behalf. Clive, while strongly opposing his reappointment to Bengal, was ready to help him become Governor of Madras. In November, there was a meeting between the two former friends; Clive, at the time, was only half recovered from a nervous breakdown, while Vansittart was in a distracted state of mind owing to his money worries. There followed a hideous misunderstanding: Vansittart went away convinced that Clive had agreed to recommend him for Bengal, and put this about, to the astonishment of the Directors.[31] Clive maintained that he had agreed to no such thing, and called Vansittart 'the greatest hypocrite, the greatest Jesuit and the meanest, dirtiest rascal that ever existed'.[32] The final break came a couple of months later, when Vansittart, through the indiscretion of Rous, learnt of Clive's dossier of evidence against him. This time it was Vansittart who would not forgive. Meanwhile, the Directors were clamouring to be shown the dossier, but Clive would not release it, for it incriminated others as well as Vansittart. Thus did relations between him and the Directors deteriorate still further.

At the beginning of 1768, Clive was advised by his doctors to go abroad. He accordingly set out for France, crossing to Calais on January 22. His party consisted of himself and Margaret, Mun, Strachey and Ingham, Jane Latham and two other ladies, a gentleman-factotum named Crespin,[33] and seven servants. Black Robin was not among them, having, at his own wish, returned to Bengal; and there is no more mention of the slave boy.

It was thought by many that Clive would not see England again. Lord Carlisle, who was at Turin and heard a false report that he was bringing him his insignia of the Bath, grumbled that he would 'die by the way and my riband travel back to England with a hearse and undertakers'.[34] Carraccioli, on the other hand, makes Clive's journey into a series of amorous adventures such as would have taxed the most robust of constitutions; and which is more of an expression of the popular English beliefs regarding the French nation and the Church of Rome than a libel on Clive personally. Superimposed on this chronicle of promiscuous wives and complaisant husbands, of unchaste nuns and abbés who act as procurers and writers of *billets-doux*, which might have been lifted from some picaresque novel of the period, are remarks as to how the French looked critically on Clive's awkward manner and poor taste in clothes, and how some of them stuck pasquinades about his monopolies on the door of his *hôtel*.

If the reality was free from such discreditable episodes, it also lacked the audience with Louis XV and the meeting with Bussy which Carraccioli gives as the highlights of Clive's tour. The party headed slowly in the direction of Paris, visiting many churches and looking at works of art. One suspects that Clive went sightseeing largely to please Margaret. They visited a convent, which was very different from the seminaries of vice depicted by Carraccioli: 'two agreeable, cheerful English nuns' sold them some needlework. ('Poor women!' was Jane Latham's comment on them.[35]) By the end of the month they were in Paris, where they stayed a fortnight. Clive's health had by now improved beyond all expectations,[36] and he was able to stand up to an intensive programme of sightseeing, opera, and French and Italian comedy. He also bought pier glasses for Berkeley Square, and spent more than £60 on dresses for his sister, Anne Sempill,* to take to India with her.

The next stop after Paris was Fontainebleau, where they found the palace too 'gothic' and irregular for their taste. At Dijon, they attended a masquerade; at Nîmes, the ladies first brought out their parasols. On March 29, they reached Montpellier, where they rented a 'sweet villa' called L'Enclos de Despioch, with gardens looking towards the town and the aqueduct, and a drawing-room 'most lovely to behold, furnished with chintz and adorned with Indian pictures in gilt frames'.[37]

The leading families of the place, including the Intendant and his wife,

* She had married her cousin, Colonel George Sempill, a few months earlier.

received them with hospitality. There was also a large English community here. Clive attended the weekly *pique-niques** of the English gentlemen, for which Margaret provided curries that were a great success. While tolerating them in Indian guise, Clive and Margaret had the traditional English horror of grease, garlic and 'strong things'. 'My whole nature shudders at the appearance of a ragout,' wrote Margaret, who described Clive's sufferings after he had inadvertently eaten 'oyster highly scallop'd and well garlic'd'.[38]

Apart from social life, Clive passed his time riding, fishing and playing cards and chess – his men were of Indian ivory, the kings seated in howdahs on the backs of elephants, the bishops on camels and holding parasols. But always his mind kept returning to politics and Indian affairs; he hung on the English mail, and fretted for Walsh and 'Daddy' King. He also missed Strachey, who had gone home to fight an election at Pontefract, on the strength of Walsh's newly-acquired interest there. Strachey was defeated, but Walsh intended to petition because of a riot at the poll. 'Walsh may be a Don Quixote if he pleases,' wrote Clive in philosophic mood, 'but by God, I should not follow his example. In ten or twelve years we shall most of us in all probability be disposed of by the worms, after that it matters not whether dog worry hog or hog bite dog, whether old England become a province of America or America be given up to the savages.'[39]

Nevertheless, when Strachey told him that Lord Rockingham, whose vast estates were not far from Pontefract, wanted to buy his prize Arab stallion, he wrote: 'If the horse can be made the means of securing a certain seat in Parliament, or ensuring a certain person's future interest at Pontefract, let him go.' But he added: 'Does His Lordship think Lord Clive capable of selling anything, or does His Lordship suppose I will make him a present of the horse?'[40]

Margaret also kept up a correspondence with Strachey, the same sparkling and slightly quizzical letters that she had formerly written to Carnac, every now and then breaking into French, and referring to herself as his 'mamma'. 'What, you think to be written to again and again?' she asked him mockingly.[41] She hoped he would join them at Nice, but in the end they went no further than Pézenas, a few miles south of Montpellier, where they took a ramshackle château within sight of the sea; returning for visits to L'Enclos. The constant moving backwards and

* Gatherings at which each person present contributed some of the food. The word did not denote a meal eaten out of doors until the following century.

forwards between the two houses suited Clive. 'He is never long well without travelling,' observed Margaret,[42] and soon they were off on a longer journey, up into the mountains to Lodève. The local bishop put his fishing at Clive's disposal, and in return Clive made him a present of an English horse, which so pleased him that he lent them his palace. Here they stayed in great comfort, 'visited by a multitude of priests who seemed cheerful good-natured people'. Margaret and Jane were shown all over a convent; Clive was invited to accompany them – 'a very particular compliment to His Lordship' – but he declined.[43]

They stopped in Paris on the return journey for another fortnight of sightseeing, tailors and dressmakers. It was now June, and in the evenings they walked among a gay throng in the boulevards or the Tuileries Gardens, or watched the fireworks at St Cloud. More fashionable entertainments, however, had ceased owing to the death of the Queen; so that when they visited Versailles, it was only as tourists.

More exciting to Clive than a glimpse of Louis XV getting into his carriage was the belated appearance of Walsh and 'Daddy' King, who accompanied the party to Brussels, Aix-la-Chapelle and then Spa. Here Clive and Margaret seem to have entertained more lavishly than they ever did in England, numbering among their guests Prince and Princess Ferdinand of Prussia, the brother and sister-in-law of Frederick the Great, who showed them 'many marks of distinction'.[44] When not entertaining Royalty or drinking the waters, Clive read Orme's *History* and Dow's *History of Hindostan*.

Clive returned to England at the beginning of September; he hoped he would be strong enough to attend Parliament during the forthcoming session. He had put on weight, he could now 'trot on horseback for fifteen or twenty miles'. He had given up opium. Yet he knew that he would never again be really well, as he told Strachey in a sad letter written while he was still at Pézenas.

> I suffer in the manner I did on board the *Britannia*, both from the bile and my former nervous complaint, but not more; which convinces me the roots of both disorders still remain, and I much fear I must be unhappy as long as I live, though I am certain there is nothing mortal in either of them and in all probability I shall drag on a miserable life for fifteen or twenty years longer as I have already done ever since the year 1752.[45]

Yet when he wrote these words, Clive had a special reason to be gloomy. Sir Robert Fletcher, who was working tooth and nail to vindicate himself, had obtained a written opinion in his favour from Stringer Lawrence and Caillaud, as the two most senior retired officers of the Company. Clive was deeply mortified that his old friend and commander should have put his name to such a document, though of the two, Caillaud was more to blame, for Lawrence was elderly and out of touch.

Thus armed, and with another testimonial from General James Murray, the first British Governor of Canada (who was, incidentally, an uncle of the Johnstones), Fletcher put the question of his reinstatement before the General Court in April. Walsh, by dint of hard work, managed to secure his defeat by a narrow majority of thirty. But there was still a chance that 'the dead dog', as Strachey called him, would come to life again, particularly as he had now managed to get into Parliament. His choice of borough, Cricklade, in Wiltshire, was more than a little galling to Clive, for Margaret's ancestors had represented the place in the previous century, and Mun, having bought an estate in the neighbourhood, hoped to do so himself; but was thwarted by an uncharacteristic piece of stinginess on Clive's part.[46]

Clive's behaviour over Cricklade was typical of the rather half-hearted way in which he regarded the 1768 general election. Having fought for his *jagir* in order to become a great power in English politics, he now seemed reluctant to exploit it to the full. Perhaps it was his illness, or perhaps he did not wish to make any more enemies.

In the election of 1761, he and his friends had been obliged to go hunting for boroughs. Now, boroughs fell into his lap; he was invited to nominate candidates all over the country. This was a sign of his popularity with the general public rather than of the attraction of his wealth, for at the time of the previous election, he was reputed to be just as rich. But either he refused these offers, or else they came to nothing.

Most of Clive's efforts and resources at this time were concentrated on obtaining complete control of Bishop's Castle, which he did by buying Waring's estate for rather more than £30,000 in December 1767. He also had to face a threat to his own seat at Shrewsbury when the Johnstones' brother, William, decided to stand there in the Pulteney interest, which he had inherited by marriage. But the interloper was repelled.

As a result of the 1768 election, Clive's party increased by three. There was his younger brother, William, to whom he gave the second seat at Bishop's Castle, as well as an estate in the neighbourhood; there was Carnac, elected for Leomister in Hereford; and Strachey, who had won the appeal at Pontefract. Brother William had to give up his seat a few months later, as Clive wanted it for Grenville's friend, Alexander Wedderburn. An able but slippery Scottish 'lawyer on the make', Wedderburn had come south ten years previously, and had pursued a relentless upward course that was to lead eventually to the Woolsack and an Earldom.* He had a name for being unctuous to those he wished to please, and bitingly sarcastic to his opponents in court; his many enemies delighted in telling of how he took lessons in speaking English without his native accent, and how as a child he was knocked over by a turkey-cock.[47]

In 1769 came the storm over the repeated expulsions from the House of Commons of John Wilkes, who was making a comeback following his previous expulsion for libel five years earlier. Grenville, who had opposed Wilkes in 1764, now supported him as he was himself in opposition; and Clive did likewise, though he had recently been the victim of an attack in Wilkes's newspaper, the *North Briton*.[48] Wedderburn, who sat in the interest of another climbing Scot, the millionaire contractor, Sir Lawrence Dundas, was prevented from voting for Wilkes because Dundas wished to keep in favour with the Government. So to please Grenville, Clive offered Wedderburn the Bishop's Castle seat, enabling him to sacrifice the patronage of Dundas and come over to the Opposition. Clive was present at a dinner held at the Thatched House Tavern in Pall Mall, in honour of Wedderburn's 'martyrdom', and he gained some credit with the radicals of the City of London, not least with Wilkes himself.

Wedderburn had Clive's permission to vote whichever way he pleased, but he did not forget the ties of gratitude, and was to serve his new patron extremely well. Outside Parliament, he acted as Clive's legal adviser, and at times roused him from the slough of illness by his Caledonian vigour and agile mind. Yet it was unfortunate for Clive's reputation that the chief political ally of his later years should have been someone so generally disliked.

Clive had originally regarded his Indian achievements as a means of enabling him to play a part in English politics. Then, when his *jagir* was threatened, he had to use English politics to secure his Indian wealth. Now that he had secured his *jagir*, he was free once more to concentrate on the English political scene. But India now had a grip on him. He thought about it, he talked about it, he corresponded at length with numerous friends and acquaintances who were still there. It dominated his life far

* He was eventually created Earl of Rosslyn, but is better known by his previous title of Lord Loughborough.

CLIVE RECEIVING THE DIWANI OF BENGAL FROM SHAH ALAM

by Benjamin West

HENRY STRACHEY
by James Northcote

HARRY VERELST

more than it had done five years earlier; it was almost an obsession. Henceforth, except when he was defending himself against the attacks of his enemies, his efforts as a politician were almost entirely devoted to what he thought to be the Company's good, and the good of its territories. Even if he thought wrong, one has to admit that his motives were those of the elder statesman rather than the political opportunist.

His chief object in Parliament at the beginning of 1769 was to support the Company in the debates on its future status, which was due to be settled this year following the expiry of the 1767 agreement.[49] The Government's proposals were little more than a renewal of this agreement for another five years, with the addition of a few minor concessions. Although a majority of the General Court – including Clive himself – regarded these proposals as unsatisfactory, they were accepted by the Company. Clive watched with sorrow as the Directors became increasingly disunited. While still dining with them 'on a turtle' in the City, and asking them back to dinner at Berkeley Square, he despised the 'low intriguing Cardinals', as Walsh called them,[50] more than ever. How could they be expected to control a land the size of France? In a pessimistic mood, he was inclined to doubt whether any of his countrymen were equal to the task of running an empire. 'Our wide and extended possessions are become too great for the Mother Country or for our abilities to manage,' he wrote at this time. 'America is making great strides towards independancy, so is Ireland. The East Indies also I think cannot remain long to us, if our present constitution be not altered.'[51]

Clive would have been the last to admit it, but there was one man in England capable of directing the Company in the crucial years that lay ahead, and that was Sulivan. To a greater extent than Clive, he had the necessary vision; or rather, his vision was constant and clear, whereas Clive's came in flashes, interspersed with periods of blindness. Sulivan's views on the Company's agreement with the Government were identical to Clive's, just as their views on the 1762 peace treaty had been the same. It was a tragedy that these two men, who stood high above the rest of the Company's rulers and advisers, could not have been friends.

CHAPTER XXIII

In the Wood

They are in a wood, and want a skilful guide to lead them out of it.

ROBERT PALK

Still fresh in Memory's eye, the scene I view,
The shrivell'd limbs, sunk eyes and lifeless hue;
Still hear the mother's shrieks and infant's moans,
Cries of despair and agonizing groans.
In wild confusion, dead and dying lie:
Hark to the jackal's yell, and vulture's cry.

LINES WRITTEN ON THE BENGAL FAMINE OF 1769–70
BY LORD TEIGNMOUTH, FIFTY YEARS AFTER HE HAD WITNESSED IT

Having borrowed £100,000 with which to buy stock for 'splitting', Sulivan and Vansittart were both elected as Directors in 1769. The previous Directors, however, remained in the majority, and the new Chairman was one of their number, the dapper little banker baronet Sir George Colebrooke. Far from healing the dissensions within the Company, the return of Sulivan seems to have increased the spirit of faction. There were now three warring parties, one led by Sulivan, one by Colebrooke, and one associated with Clive, who at the same time kept out of the wranglings of the General Court, in accordance with the role of 'public man' envisaged for him by Grenville. He even remained silent when, as a result of the shift in the balance of power, Fletcher was reinstated and appointed to Madras as a Colonel.[1]

By way of consolation, Clive saw two of the lesser ringleaders of the mutiny, Parker and Vertue, take a sound beating in the Court of King's Bench, where they had brought actions against him for assault, injury and wrongful imprisonment. His reaction was characteristic: 'I rejoice on the

Company's account that a verdict was given in my favour.'[2] La Compagnie, c'est moi.

India House affairs, Shropshire politics, a trip to Spa and the birth of another son enabled Clive to keep his enemy, boredom, at bay during the summer of 1769. In June he provided himself with another interest by acquiring Claremont, near Esher in Surrey, which he intended to make his principal seat. He bought it from the Duchess of Newcastle, widow of his one-time political patron, beating her down from £40,000 to £25,000,[3] which shows that he could bargain, though he used to grumble that when people saw him coming they put their prices up.[4]

For his money, Clive became the owner of a wide-spreading house by Vanbrugh, and a park that had been transformed by William Kent into an idyllic landscape of lakes, wooded hills and gently rolling sward; adorned with temples, lodges, and a castellated belvedere. He decided almost immediately to pull down the old house and build a new one. His enemies were to twit him for not finding the ducal mansion grand enough; he has been depicted as a Ludwig II, building palaces to give a semblance of reality to his delusions of power. In fact, he condemned the old Claremont because of its damp, low-lying site, and he replaced it with a house which, if not actually smaller, was certainly less imposing.

He chose as architect the landscape gardener, Lancelot 'Capability' Brown, who worked in partnership with his future son-in-law, Henry Holland. Their design represented a new concept of domestic architecture in its simplicity and neo-Classical ornament,[5] a move away from the far-flung pavilions and colonnades of Palladianism, which would have been more likely to appeal to Clive had he been at all ostentatious. A compact block of two storeys on an unusually high basement,[6] it was adorned with a Corinthian portico and contained a few fine rooms round a central staircase. It was not to be a palace, but a gentleman's house of great elegance and comfort; the country equivalent of Berkeley Square. In so far as Claremont expresses Clive's taste, it 'appears to reflect a sane and practical idealism'.[7]

Within a few months the old house had gone, and the white brick walls of its successor had risen to plinth height. The home farm had been done up as a temporary residence for the family, and the park fence raised to keep in Clive's spotted and hog deer, and his various sorts of antelopes, which were moved here as soon as possible, together with the Cape geese, the Guinea hens, the large cyrus birds, and the other 'foreign creatures', with strict instructions that they should be kept warm. The raising of the fence did not prevent a nylghau from jumping out and getting as far as Cobham before it was caught; while a female of the same species suffered a worse fate, being killed, as Clive put it, 'by the amorous violence of Dr Hunter'.[8]* This, and other losses, were soon made good, for Clive had ordered antelopes to be sent to him by every ship.

Unfortunately for Clive and the Company, the ships from India did not just bring cyruses and 'curcurras'. There were also letters in which the news was usually bad. Dick Smith, who had succeeded Carnac, was quarrelling with the rest of the Committee. Verelst was showing signs of weakness and irresolution. Nubkissen faced a death sentence on charges of robbery, rape and abducting women in Clive's name.[9] It was hard on the unfortunate Maharaja that while he stood thus accused, George Johnstone was telling people in London that he was known among his fellow-Hindus as 'The Catamite',[10] which could have carried a particularly nasty allegation against Clive. However, the charges against Nubkissen turned out to be fabricated, and he regained his respectability, giving daily alms to propitiate his gods on Clive's behalf, making a new road in Clive's memory.[11]

In May 1769, the news was far more serious. The French appeared to be turning their attention to India once again, as Clive had prophesied they would a few months earlier. Worse, Hyder Ali, a common soldier who had usurped the government of Mysore, was ravaging the Carnatic right up to Madras. Clive had some time ago urged that Hyder's power should be reduced, but the war now being waged against him was proving a failure. This was the first time in eighteen years that the English had not been victorious against the Indians, and the psychological effect was devastating. East India stock fell from 273 to 239, and there looked like being a panic. Many were ruined, in particular Sulivan and Vansittart, who still had stock on their hands which they had bought with borrowed money for use in the election.

To counter the growing Government influence over the disunited Directors, Lord Rockingham, on behalf of the Opposition, had worked to bring about an alliance between Clive, Sulivan and Colebrooke. He now redoubled his efforts. Soon, Colebrooke was on such familiar terms with Clive that when Margaret fell ill following the birth of her son, he wrote: 'If I am informed right, that Lady Clive's illness is owing to the

* He referred, no doubt, to an animal from the private zoo of the great surgeon, Dr John Hunter. The naturalist, Joseph Banks, also proposed breeding from Clive's nylghaus.

effects of your vigour since her lying-in, I am physician enough to say she must be debarred the use of something else, for the present, besides that of pen and ink.'[12] However little use Clive may have had for Colebrooke and his boardroom chaff, he was willing to respond to his advances, and he also agreed, albeit half-heartedly, to negotiations being opened with Sulivan. For his part, Sulivan saw in a *rapprochement* his only chance of continuing as a Director, now that his financial losses made it impossible for him to fight another election.

Clive took advantage of the crisis to press once more for the appointment of a Governor-General.[13] Sulivan also favoured such an appointment, but was determined to get Vansittart back to India so that he could recoup their joint losses. It was obvious that Clive and his followers would never tolerate Vansittart in the supreme position; so the autocrat gave place to 'The Three Kings of the East',[14] three Supervisors with overriding powers. One was to be Vansittart, and one Scrafton, representing Clive's interest. The third Supervisor was intended to hold the balance between the other two; but Clive and his party were able to tip the scales in their favour by securing the appointment of Forde.

There was general satisfaction when, towards the end of September, the Supervisors sailed aboard the *Aurora* frigate. It really seemed as though there might be a *rapprochement* between Clive and Sulivan. Clive was not last in wishing the 'Three Kings' success; and as a sign of the prevailing goodwill, he collaborated with his other pet aversion, Coote, in a plan for altering the Company's military forces.[15] But all hopes as to what the Supervisors would achieve came to nothing; for the *Aurora*, after leaving the Cape on December 27, was never heard of again.

Clive's reactions to the loss of the *Aurora* are not recorded. He must surely have had some moments of anguish. The ghost of poor Vansittart may have risen from those far-away depths and reproached him for his muck-raking activities. Yet it could be that his heart was hardened, and he felt grateful to the ocean for having relieved him of an enemy. But it had also robbed him of his friends Scrafton and Forde.

Clive was to need such friends in the years that lay ahead. Perhaps the first sign of his declining popularity came with the fall of the stock, which continued even after it was known that the war with Hyder Ali was over. In certain quarters Clive was blamed for deliberately bringing this about, by spreading gloom.[16] He was certainly regarded as a barometer by a great number of stockholders; yet it seems unlikely that he could have been so irresponsible as to cause a general collapse in order to ruin Sulivan, which would have been his only possible motive for doing so. Sulivan himself found this hard to believe.[17]

Where Clive was to blame was in his excessively optimistic reports, which had certainly caused the ruin of many by over-inflating the stock. He had been rash enough, after his return to England, to give the stockholders an exaggerated estimate of the Company's revenues during the next two years. Poor Verelst, when he heard of this, was greatly distressed, knowing that he would be blamed for his inevitable failure to achieve Clive's target. 'To be sure, this is one of the Noble Lord's strokes!' exclaimed Dick Smith. 'Why, such an estimate given in by him must have raised the stocks very considerably, and when they were at the highest, he sells out. Bravo! Bravissimo!'[18] It may have been a ruined stockholder who inspired, or even wrote, a couple of letters threatening his life which Clive received in the spring of 1770, and which purported to be from an Indian victim of his 'plundering'.[19]

The loss of Scrafton and Forde severed two more links with Clive's great days in India. Now, the only person left from those days among his intimates was Carnac, apart from Walsh and other members of his family circle. His flickering friendship with Orme died altogether after his final return to England: we find him speaking of 'my friend Orme, that was'.[20] Orme felt neglected by Clive, and wrote censoriously to his crony, Dick Smith:

> Old Lawrence has a reputation in England which may well be envied (with all its fortune) by the name of Clive. It is these cursed presents which stop my History. Why should I be doomed to commemorate the ignominy of my countrymen, and without giving the money story that has accompanied every event since the first of April, 1757, I shall not relate all the springs of action, that is, I shall be a Jesuitical historian . . . I foresee that the Parliament will in less than two years ring with declamations against the plunderers of the East. How fair, how great it will be not to see your name in the list.[21]

Orme's prophecy came true, if not quite as soon as he envisaged; but Smith, who returned home with a quarter of a million, was just as much a 'plunderer of the East' as Clive or anybody else.

On another occasion, when complaining of how Clive dropped his old friends, Orme remarked that he rode post through life and changed his horses at every stage.[22] Knowing Clive's lifelong attachment to such cronies as Walsh, 'Daddy' King and Carnac, this allegation seems hardly fair; though there is something uncanny in the way that all relations seem to have ceased between him and John Dalton. One doubts, however, if he dropped Dalton, for that was not his way; more likely the friendship ended in a quarrel, as did his friendship with Vansittart.[23]

For his part, Clive often complained that his old friends neglected him. This was probably for the reason that they found him a difficult companion, inclined to lay down the law, not liking to be contradicted, a little touchy. Like so many self-centred people of a certain age, he tended to get on better with those who showed deference to his years and position, than with his contemporaries and equals. He was not, however, a prey to sycophants, except in one notable instance; rather, he collected disciples; men of worth, like Strachey, who had a genuine appreciation of his own good qualities and were prepared, through gratitude or interest, to tolerate his failings. Strachey came to be Clive's best friend as well as his man of business and his Parliamentary private secretary.

In May 1770, Strachey also became a cousin, for he married Jane Latham.[24] After their marriage, the Stracheys continued to spend a good deal of time with the Clives, so that Margaret was not deprived of Jane's company. And she now had a new companion, Maria Ducarel, the daughter of her Bath acquaintance. Clive, who regarded Mrs Ducarel as an 'old jade',[25] tolerated Maria though she got on his nerves. She seems to have admired him from afar, but her admiration may have stemmed from the hope that he would give her clergyman suitor a living.

Margaret now divided her time between her music, her languages, and her telescope, orrery and growing collection of terrestrial and celestial globes, for she had inherited her family's interest in astronomy. When in London, she surrounded herself with a little circle of highbrows, including a blind poet named Brodick, whose sight she tried to restore by paying for him to have an operation. Though she saw a little more of smart society than before, it was only sporadic: occasional balls and masquerades, sudden descents on Claremont by the Great, who were curious to see what Clive was doing there. The Shropshire house-parties were still made up of relatives and Indian connections, with 'Daddy' King as part of the furniture.

Life at Walcot was interrupted in September 1770 when Clive suffered a particularly bad nervous attack. From what Margaret wrote, it seems that he was upset by something to do with Fletcher, who had not yet left for India.[26] The pattern of his illness was, as always, up and down, with a continual urge to be on the move. He suddenly cheered up, bundled Margaret into the coach, and they set off for Shrewsbury. After an hour's travelling, he 'relapsed into dejection',[27] and he arrived at Shrewsbury 'full of horrors'. A little wine and roast partridge and a doze in a chair made him well enough to go to Underdale, one of his lesser estates, where he had a small house. Here he grew worse. At times, he was convinced he was dying, and at other times he wished for death. When he tried to walk, he fell. 'I wonder if I exist myself!' wrote Margaret, distractedly.[28] Her only consolation was that having been through it all so many times before, she could hardly believe that he was now really in danger. She had ceased to take his death-wish seriously.[29]

With the help of musk and ether, bark, and cold baths ('For God's sake be cautious in the use of this powerful remedy!' counselled Lord Powis),[30] he recovered sufficiently to be able to pay a visit to his Montfort estate, even riding part of the way; but on the way back, he again became depressed. There followed a crisis which scared even Margaret. 'I was so near falling, too, that I went to lie down, with no comfortable prospect of rising any more to joy.' But after an hour and a half, he sent for her, and she found 'his reason, head and stomach . . . all at ease'.[31]

By now Clive had reached the stage of imagining himself to be ill. When Strachey suggested a ride on a fine morning, he said it was 'absolutely impossible, that he would never ride more, nay, that he would never eat again'. Strachey pressed him to take exercise and he grew angry. But a few minutes later he came downstairs, ordered the horses, and trotted away at Strachey's side.[32] Though at times he was sunk in despondency, at other times he was so impatient to get well that Walsh had to warn him against 'chemical and dangerous experiments'.[33] Walsh, who was of scientific bent,[34] was the only person to whom Clive would listen in matters concerning his health.[35]

At the beginning of November, Clive was well enough to go to Bath. While he was here, he heard that Grenville had died. This, though not unexpected, was a great blow, depriving him of a political leader. Commiserating with each other, Clive and Wedderburn agreed to remain in opposition.[36] A few weeks later, Wedderburn went over to the Government, like most of Grenville's former supporters, and became Solicitor-General. It was a shock for Clive to see his Scottish friend sitting on the Treasury Bench, next to the new Prime Minister, Lord North, particularly as he intended to attack the Government for failing to send a fleet to India during the current crisis with France.[37] However, he forgave him, while continuing for his own part to react coldly to Lord North's overtures.

Within a year of becoming Prime Minister, Lord North brought about the long-hoped-for coalition between the supporters of Clive, Colebrooke and Sulivan. Financially ruined, abandoned by Shelburne and deserted by the Johnstone group, who roved the battlefields of East India House like a band of freebooters, Sulivan had suffered defeat in the 1770 election of Directors. In this 'low and humbled' state he was befriended by Lord North, who persuaded the Directors, as an act of kindness, to include him among their candidates for the 1771 election. He was duly elected, though without any of his friends, and in theory the *rapprochement* between him and Clive had at last come about. In fact, however, it was a defeat for Clive, who, as the Directors came to be increasingly dominated by Sulivan's personality, found himself edged out into the cold.

Sulivan's return followed the news of the Bengal famine of 1769–70, a fearful visitation which wiped out millions, and threatened the Company's main source of wealth. Gone were the golden hopes of the *Diwani*: Barwell was able to speak of 'the *ignis fatuus* with which Lord Clive dazzled mankind'.[38] To deal with this disastrous situation, a new Governor of Bengal was appointed, with increased powers. The man chosen was Warren Hastings. His friendship with Vansittart made him very much Sulivan's man, but his appointment seems to have been settled before Sulivan was re-elected as a Director in April 1771. It was a non-party measure in which Clive claimed to have had a hand.[39] Whether or not that claim was justified, Clive was certainly responsible for getting Hastings sent back to India in 1769. But only to Madras, and because Hastings was a friend of Sykes; for he had then regarded him as 'so great a dupe to Vansittart's politics' as to be unfit for Bengal 'in any station'.[40]

Three months after Hastings's appointment, Clive wrote him a long letter of advice. He urged economy in all spheres, and recommended his own policy of facing troubles as they arose, by means of improvisation: 'This you must do with cheerfulness and confidence, never entertaining a thought of miscarrying till the misfortune actually happens; and even then you are not to despair, but be constantly contriving and carrying into execution schemes for retrieving affairs, always flattering yourself with an opinion that time and perseverence will get the better of everything.' He ended by saying that Hastings had the abilities and opportunity to become 'one of the most distinguished characters of this country', a surprising flash of foresight in view of his rather moderate view of his great successor.[41]

Clive invited Hastings to correspond with him on Indian affairs. But any hopes he may have had of thus influencing the destinies of India were ended when it became clear that Hastings was working hand-in-glove with Sulivan. Hastings was all too ready to obey the Directors when, on Sulivan's initiative, they ordered him to remove Mohammed Reza Khan and take over the management of the revenues himself.

This order, which was dispatched on August 28, 1771, put an end to the Dual System and meant that Clive was henceforth wholly out of sympathy with the Company's policy, both at home and abroad. It was unfortunate that he should have remained obstinately wedded to his system, the shortcomings of which had stood out all too plainly even before the famine, rather than accepting that it had served its purpose and been replaced by something more permanent. Clive, more than anyone, should have known how quickly policies in India were rendered obsolete by changing circumstances. He had seen how, in nine years, the peaceful co-existence of the English and the French Companies had given place to the hegemony of Dupleix and then to English domination. He had seen how, in another nine years, the Calcutta of Governor Drake had turned into the Bengal of the *Diwani*; and during that period his own thinking had evolved accordingly. Now, six years after he had established the Dual System, he seems to have imagined that circumstances were the same as in 1765. It was as though his mind, once so fertile in expedient, so quick to grasp the realities of a situation, had become ossified. While to Hastings he counselled the pragmatism which was so much a part of his own nature, he adhered to the one system of government with the tenacity of the most rigid of doctrinaires. This can only be explained by his almost pathological need to justify himself; he had to believe in the efficacy of the Dual System just as he had to believe in the military glory of Plassey.

Clive also, and with more reason, deplored Hastings's intention to deprive the Mogul of his tribute. This seemed to him short-sighted, in that the shadow Emperor afforded the Company a useful protection against the 'high hand' of the British Crown. It was all right, as Clive saw it, to take advantage of the Mogul's death or defection to cease paying the tribute; but to do so without any such excuse would destroy the pretence that the Company's revenues were granted by him, rather than obtained by conquest. Once the latter was admitted to be the case, the Crown could claim the Company's gains for itself.[42] Clive was torn between loyalty to the Company and a growing conviction that the Company was incapable of ruling its vast territories. 'It is beyond my power to do the Company any further service,' he had written in February 1770 to Margaret's cousin,

Thomas Kelsall, who was still in Bengal. 'The best and soundest advice I can give you is to return to England rather with a moderate competency, while you have youth and constitution to enjoy it, than by staying longer, lose that youth and sacrifice that constitution which no riches can possibly compensate for.'[43] Did he wish that he himself had been satisfied with his 'moderate competency' in 1755, rather than going back to India? But having lost his youth and constitution, though he was only forty-five, he had to make the most of his riches.

In 1770, when he had enjoyed his *jagir* for more than ten years, Clive reckoned that he was worth £555,685.[44] Most of this was invested in land; he had, since his last return from India, bought estates in Monmouthshire, Radnorshire and Devon, as well as increasing his Shropshire acres. The Devon estate, Okehampton, gave him an extra seat in Parliament. As a great landowner, Clive did not ignore the precepts of Arthur Young, but carried out many agricultural improvments, as well as awarding silver cups to his tenants for their turnips and their cattle.[45]

In June 1771, Clive acquired Lord Powis's Oakly estate in Shropshire, which not only brought him an interest in the neighbouring borough of Ludlow, but unlike most of his other land purchases was also a place to live. The house there was not impressive – a jumble of half-timber and brick – but its setting was superb, for it stood by the River Teme in a glorious old park that had once belonged to Ludlow Castle. Having previously thought Shropshire too damp for him, Clive now found that Oakly suited him as well as anywhere, and he began to regret having embarked on his 'grand designs' at Claremont. But he kept on with them all the same, and at Oakly confined himself to rebuilding the more awkward parts of the house.

With the purchase of Oakly, Clive now had five houses, not counting the partly-built Claremont or its farm, the dwellings on his minor estates, or his little house at Shrewsbury. For as well as Walcot, Styche and Berkeley Square, he had bought the lease of Chatham's house at Bath. Styche was now more or less unoccupied, his father having died in May 1771. When Clive heard that the old man was ill, he ordered him to be sent 'a hogshead of the best port wine which can be had for money',[46] but it was to no avail. His mother did not long survive his father.

Until the beginning of 1771, Clive seems to have been reluctant to spend money on works of art. Then, in the early months of that year, he started buying pictures as determinedly as he had bought land. Though he had his likes and dislikes, he did not trust his own judgement, but followed the advice of the young American historical painter, Benjamin West, and a Scottish connoisseur named William Patoun, who helped him to build up a collection that was typical of the period, except that it included nothing by the Caracci, and only one very cheap and doubtful Guido. The highest price he paid at this time was £546 for a Madonna by Carlo Dolci.

In April, Sir James Wright, a groom of the King's Bedchamber, offered Clive what he pretended was his own private collection. According to Strachey, Wright was 'an arrant (or errant) picture dealer, a haggler and by no means to be treated with as a gentleman';[47] and indeed, he started by asking the fantastic price of £6250 for the eight 'most capital pieces', one of which was condemned by West as a copy, while another – a Guido *St Francis* – did not appeal to Clive on account of its subject.[48] After much hard bargaining on the part of Strachey, Clive obtained six of the original eight, and one other, for £2000. When Walpole sneered at 'those learned patrons of taste, the Czarina, Lord Clive or some Nabob' who would give fifty thousand for what was worth eleven,[49] he was near the truth as regards three of these pictures, which together fetched less than £100 when sold at Christie's after Clive's death. But the purchase from Wright also included an authentic and very important Veronese, the large and beautiful *Visitation*.[50] This was easily the best picture in Clive's collection until he acquired, early in 1773, one of the most beautiful of Claudes, *Cephalus and Procris*, as well as a magnificent Poussin, the joyous and delightful *Finding of Moses*. The former cost £507 3*s*., which was not excessive considering that Claude was then the highest-priced painter on the English market; while at £327 12*s*. the Poussin was also reasonable by the standards of the time.

The pictures were hung at Berkeley Square, though most of them were destined for Claremont. For Claremont, too, Clive planned to commission a set of Gobelins tapestries, and he accordingly visited the factory when he was in Paris in October 1771 on his way back from Spa. He also visited the studio of Claude Joseph Vernet, where he was so 'enchanted' by a pair of sea pieces painted for the Elector Palatine that he wanted a similar pair for himself; but he was put off when the artist quoted 12,000 livres as his lowest price.[51] Two years later, however, he was able to acquire a pair of Vernet's sea pieces for £455; they had been painted for the King of Poland, the unfortunate Stanislaus Poniatowski, but not yet paid for.

On his journey to Spa in 1771, Clive was accompanied by Margaret and Maria Ducarel. He was rather bored with having to go round the sights of Paris once again for Maria's benefit. At Spa, however, he found plenty to entertain him: a fine new playhouse, a charming old Electress who was an Emperor's daughter, parties and whist. 'I am ashamed of all this tittle tattle and scandal,' he told Strachey at the end of a gossipy letter, 'but it is a sign I am free from bile and that the waters agree with me.'[52] He was enjoying the calm before the storm.

CHAPTER XXIV

A Bad Liver and a Worse Heart

> If any of our readers will take the trouble to search in the dusty recesses of circulating libraries for some novel published sixty years ago, the chance is that the villain or sub-villain of the story will prove to be a savage old Nabob, with an immense fortune, a tawny complexion, a bad liver, and a worse heart.
>
> MACAULAY

Just as a wind, a cloudburst and a tide, all happening at the same moment, can cause a flood that inundates a city, so did three circumstances combine during 1772 and 1773 to produce the torrent of vilification which broke upon Clive and threatened to bring him down. Public opinion turned against the Nabobs, of whom he was the outstanding example. His enemies made a concerted attack on him. And the worsening state of the Company required a scapegoat.

It was natural that the rich Nabobs, who by the beginning of the 1770s were coming home in appreciable numbers, should have aroused hostility. People feared their growing influence in Parliament. The scandal of Dick Smith bidding against his fellow-Nabob Thomas Rumbold for the borough of New Shoreham gave their political methods a bad name. Then there were the stories of their ostentation and vulgarity, which were largely a figment of popular prejudice; for on the whole, the men who had made fortunes in India were well-bred and of good education. The Nabob image was largely based on Dick Smith and Sykes, who were of more humble birth than most of their colleagues. While Sykes built his great Palladian house at Basildon, a few miles from Smith's no less splendid mansion, rumours went around that he had started life as a 'menial servant' in Yorkshire.*

When accounts reached England of the horrors of the Bengal famine, humanitarianism joined with snobbery and envy in condemning these men who had grown rich by reducing whole provinces to starvation. The fact that Clive was the richest and best known of all the Nabobs meant that he came in for the greatest share of the odium, even though he had left India three years before the famine which, as Rumbold rightly pointed out, 'no human foresight' could have prevented.[1] Clive's alleged salt monopolies fitted in well with the popular belief that the famine had been caused or aggravated by the monopolizing of rice by Company servants. 'The groans of India have mounted to heaven, where the *heaven-born* General Lord Clive will certainly be disavowed,' exclaimed Walpole. 'What think you of the famine in Bengal, in which three millions perished, being caused by a monopoly of the provisions, by the servants of the East India Company?'[2]

For the rest of his life, Dr Johnson would speak of the crimes by which Clive had acquired his fortune, telling of how Capability Brown was shown a chest by Clive's bedroom door which had once contained Indian gold, and had expressed surprise that he could sleep with it so near.[3] Macaulay may have been exaggerating when he wrote of how the Surrey yokels thought that Clive's great wall at Claremont was not so much to keep in the antelopes as to keep out the Devil; but he had himself heard old men, who knew nothing of Clive, yet 'still retained the prejudices conceived in their youth, talk of him as an incarnate fiend'.

While public opinion was thus conditioned to listen to attacks on Clive, the disreputable former Company servant William Bolts appeared on the scene, to prosecute Verelst for alleged ill-treatment of himself and his Armenian agents, whom he brought with him as witnesses.† He was naturally drawn to the Johnstones, having once been in partnership with John, and they saw in him a means of getting their revenge on Clive. The Johnstones were also encouraged in their aggressive designs by John Petrie, one of the officers cashiered in 1766, who had collected information in

* In fact, he was of good yeoman stock, and married, as his second wife, the daughter of a Yorkshire peer.

† A Dutch adventurer who entered the company service by a back door, Bolts engaged in numerous underhand dealings, and was eventually expelled from Bengal for intriguing against Verelst's government.

India concerning Clive's alleged monopolies and currency frauds, which he now proceeded to lay before the Directors.*

Even without the stimulus afforded by Bolts and Petrie, the Johnstones would probably have taken advantage of the prevailing climate of opinion to launch an attack. George Johnstone published an anonymous pamphlet against Clive in 1771, and towards the end of that year, he and Ralph Leycester worked 'to club intelligence', which was fed to the Directors to substantiate Petrie's charges.[4] It also served as grist to the mill of Bolts, who burst into print early in 1772 with an inaccurate and intemperate book entitled *Considerations on Indian Affairs*, which was widely read and even translated into French. Bolts repeated the charges about monopolies and frauds on the coinage, and hinted that Clive had murdered Najm-ud-daula, emphasizing his insinuations by an artful use of large and small type.

Even Leycester thought that Bolts went too far,[5] and it soon got about that he was a 'bad character'.[6] But Bolts's book was followed by a more reputable work, Alexander Dow's 'prefix' to the third volume of his *History of Hindostan*. Dow was an officer of literary bent who had been involved in the 1766 mutiny and was hostile to Clive; his charges, though similar to those of Bolts, were presented in a more reasonable way.†

Both works were 'swallowed greedily by the public'[7] together with the more scurrilous attacks on Clive which appeared at the same time, and of which 'Gun's' letter in the *Public Advertiser* is a fair sample: 'If the opium has not blunted every nerve, if you have one latent spark of feeling left in your whole frame, I will search out the place where it inhabits and plant a dagger there . . . I will not represent Your Lordship as the Conqueror of India but as a buyer and seller of salt . . . surrounded by the parade of government, and the ensigns of dignity and command, Your Lordship was making a riot in the streets of Calcutta, at the door of a common prostitute.'[8] It was fortunate for Clive that he had long grown 'callous' to such 'encomiums' – as he remarked to Palk some years before – having already been subjected to them in plenty.[9]

The third force by which Clive was threatened, the desire on the part

* Petrie was an old associate of John Johnstone. Having been allowed by Clive and Verelst to stay on in India after he was cashiered, so that he could wind up his affairs and those of Johnstone, he had taken the opportunity to engage in gun-running.

† Warren Hastings dismissed both works as 'medlies replete (though not in an equal degree) with abominable untruths, base apprehensions and absurdities' (B.M. 29127, Hastings to Palk, November 11, 1772).

of the Directors to make him a scapegoat for the Company's ills, was less evident at the beginning of 1772 than it was a year later. Clive's previous biographers have suggested that Sulivan was the master-mind of the Johnstones' campaign,[10] which is unlikely since he never forgave them for deserting him in 1770.[11] It seems, however, that the Directors deliberately made use of Petrie's charges to embarrass Clive, for they sent them to him with no indication as to their authorship, or what they thought of them; although they knew that many of them could be confuted by reference to the public records.[12]

In an attempt to forestall the public clamour for Parliamentary intervention in the Indian crisis, the Directors drew up a Bill 'for the better regulation of the affairs of the East India Company'. Sulivan, as a Member of Parliament, introduced this Bill on March 30. The House was crowded for the debate and so was the gallery, where the exotic figures of Bolts's three Armenians attracted attention. Less conspicuous was the emaciated form of Chatham, looking down on the scene of his former triumphs. After Sulivan and a few other speakers, Clive rose. For two hours he held the attention of the House. Up to now, he had been heard but seldom; but this speech, the first of many, established him as one of the great orators of his time. 'Had not his voice suffered from the loss of a tooth,' wrote a newspaper, 'he would be one of the foremost speakers in the House. In fluency he has scarce an equal; in a speech of three hours hesitating less than any person could imagine. His delivery is bold, spirited, but yet gracious.'[13]

Today, his speech was supposed to be against Sulivan's Bill, but in the words of a fellow Member, 'It was almost all digression, and meant to vindicate himself from all sorts of aspersions and to carry the war into the enemy's quarters.'[14] He began by saying how, when he arrived in Bengal in 1765, there were three paths open to him. He could have taken the path 'strewed with abundance of fair advantages', and countenanced the abuses which he found there. Then there was the path of 'folly and cowardice': he could have left as soon as he found his powers disputed. But he chose a third, and 'intricate' path: 'I was determined to do my duty to the public although I should incur the odium of the whole settlement . . . It was that conduct which has occasioned the public papers to teem with scurrility and abuse against me, ever since my return to England. It was that conduct which occasioned these charges. But it was that conduct which enables me now, when the day of judgement is come, to look to my judges in the face.'

He proceeded to answer Petrie's charges in detail. 'How a monopoly of salt, betel-nut and tobacco in the years 1765 and 1766 could occasion a want of rain and scarcity of rice in the year 1770 is past my comprehension . . . as to cotton, I know no more about it than the Pope of Rome.' He then paid tribute to Mun, Strachey and Ingham, saying of Grenville, who had recommended Strachey: 'Many and great are the obligations I have been under to him, but the greatest of all the obligations was his having recommended to me this gentleman.'

After protesting that he had spoken too long, at which the House cried 'Go on, go on!', Clive launched into his celebrated account of the temptations which faced a young man on first arriving in Calcutta. 'He observes that other writers arrived only a year before him live in splendid apartments, or have houses of their own, ride upon fine prancing Arabian horses, and in palanquins and chaises; that they keep seraglios, make entertainments, and treat with champagne and claret.' When the young man tells his *banyan* what he has observed, the *banyan* assures him that he, too, can live in this way. 'The *banyan* is the fair lady to the Company servant: he lays his bags of silver before him today, gold tomorrow, jewels the next day.' The Company servant falls into the clutches of the *banyan* who commits acts of violence in his name. 'Hence, Sir, arises the clamour against the English gentlemen in India.' But these gentlemen, when they retired to England, showed themselves to be perfectly honourable members of society. 'If in short, there has not yet been one character found amongst them sufficiently flagitious for Mr Foote to exhibit on the theatre in the Haymarket, may we not conclude that if they have erred, it has been because they were men placed in situations subject to little or no control?'

This light relief was followed by raps over the knuckles all round. He denounced the Government, the Directors, the General Court; he even blamed the troubles in Bengal on the weakness of poor Verelst, who was sitting above him in the gallery. He ended on a rhetorical note: 'I have now opened my budget, it is not a ministerial budget, it is an East India budget, which contains many precious stones, diamonds, rubies of the first water and magnitude; and there only wants a skilful jeweller, an able artist, to polish them and ascertain their real value.'[15]

Chatham afterwards spoke of Clive's speech as 'one of the most finished pieces of eloquence he had ever heard in the House of Commons.'[16] The *General Evening Post* was less complimentary. 'Poor dear innocent lamb!' it mocked. 'Was it maliciously accused?'[17] Clive's defence of himself did not in any way silence the attacks on him in the Press. Thus, a few days later, 'Junius Asiaticus' in the *Advertiser* called him 'an obscure urchin, picked up, fostered and very unmeritedly raised to the highest pinnacle of affluence and pageantry by that deluded Company'.[18] Another writer in the same paper told a story of how one of the Indians who was being interrogated by Clive's government had dogs tied to him by their tails, so that they tore him to death.[19] It must be remembered, however, that these letters were not so much a reflection of public opinion, as a campaign on the part of Clive's enemies; for in the eighteenth century it was regarded as somewhat disreputable to write to the papers. The scarcity of letters in his defence was merely a sign that he had hired no 'scribblers'. To the scribbler Cawthorne, whom he had once employed in the past, and who now importunely flattered him, in the hope of being employed again, he gave short shrift.[20]

Clive spoke too soon when he said that the dramatist Samuel Foote had not yet seen fit to satirize the Nabobs. Three days later, Boswell and George Gray dined with Foote and discussed his speech.[21] The result was a new comedy, *The Nabob*, which enjoyed a good run both in London and Dublin. Its chief character was 'Sir Matthew Mite from the Indies', a vulgarian who 'profusely scattered the spoils of ruined provinces' and spoke a jargon compounded of such words as 'lakhs', 'jagirs' and 'ships' husbands'. He was variously said to be based on Clive, Dick Smith and Sykes; he bore no resemblance to any of them, but helped, more than ever, to give the British public their idea of a Nabob.

The debates on Sulivan's Bill continued in the middle of April. In one of them, Clive's remarks as to how Eastern potentates had 'forced their favours upon him' occasioned the one-eyed Colonel Isaac Barré, Shelburne's Irish henchman, to observe that this was like the lady of Toulouse, who after having been raped by 'a dozen blooming grenadiers', said: 'Thank God, I have now had my bellyful and nobody can reproach me with sin.'[22] After the second reading, a private Member on the Government side, Major-General John Burgoyne, proposed that before the Bill was voted on, a Parliamentary Committee should be set up to enquire into the state of affairs in India. Burgoyne's motion was carried amid cheers.

The Select Committee of 1772 has been represented as an inquisition set up by Clive's enemies in order to destroy him. This is not fair. Although its thirty-one members included George Johnstone and his brother William Pulteney, as well as Barré, who looked after the interests of

Sulivan, they also included Clive himself and Strachey. The majority were reasonably open-minded, or, like Lord George Germain, definitely biased in Clive's favour. The Chairman was Burgoyne, a handsome and rather flashy soldier, whose past career had featured a runaway marriage with an Earl's daughter and a narrow escape from imprisonment for causing violence at an election.* He fancied himself as an orator, a wit and a playwright, but was of only moderate intelligence. It is hard to know how much he genuinely stood for responsible and humanitarian opinion in and out of Parliament, and to what extent he was merely acting as the tool of Clive's enemies.

The Committee set to work at once, and continued its sessions during the summer months, after Parliament had risen, and on into the following winter. A large number of witnesses were examined, including Walsh, Carnac, Sykes, Coote, Pocock, Munro, Sumner and Verelst, as well as Bolts and his Armenians. It was like an Old Bengal Reunion, with even such figures from the past as Manningham and Becher.

To turn the Committee into a weapon against Clive, George Johnstone had successfully put forward a proposal that its investigations should go right back to 1757. So everything that happened in Bengal during the past fifteen years was closely investigated: the conspiracy against Siraj-ud-daula, the Battle of Plassey, the treaty with Mir Jafar, the troubles with Mir Kasim, the *Diwani*, the Society of Trade. Johnstone produced witnesses hostile to Clive, like Bolts, and he subjected Clive's friends to long cross-examinations, in the hope that they would reveal facts to his discredit. Clive, who himself gave evidence to the Committee, mostly during its early sessions in May, was similarly interrogated. It cannot have been pleasant for him, but one suspects he made it out to be more of a martyrdom than it actually was when he complained of being examined like a sheep-stealer.

On the whole, he faced his ordeal coolly. He did not contradict himself, though occasionally his recollection was at fault, and his bitterness towards the memory of Vansittart led him to make a wild allegation which Walsh, who was giving evidence at the same time, had to deny.[23] He made no serious attempt to hide discreditable facts, though he appeared to one of his colleagues as being somewhat guarded, and he also rather foolishly refused to disclose the amount of Mir Jafar's private gift to him, until pressed to do so by the friendly Lord George Germain. Where, at times, he did dis-

* Later, he was to gain notoriety as a commander in the American War.

tort the truth, was in the matter of his own motives. He argued unconvincingly that he had not made up his mind in advance that the Bengal stable was Augean. He repeated his highly dubious assertion that when he attacked the Dutch in 1759, he believed that most of his fortune was in their hands. And he exaggerated the temptations to which he was exposed when he entered Murshidabad as the victor of Plassey, the vaults heaped high with gold and jewels, ending by striking his brow, and making his most famous remark, 'By God, at this moment, do I stand astonished at my own moderation!'[24]

On balance, Clive should have been grateful to the Select Committee. If it dragged a number of skeletons out of his cupboard, it also laid many ghosts. The less reputable incidents of his career were now recorded in full detail: his deception of Omichand, his stock-jobbing activities, his ungenerous treatment of Munro.[25] On the other hand, the Committee dispelled the ugly rumours that had surrounded the death of Najm-ud-daula; it presented the Society of Trade in a far more respectable light than that in which it had hitherto been seen; and if the existence of Clive's private salt-trading venture was now proved to have been a fact, it was shown to have been nothing like a monopoly. And if the world now had it in black-and-white that Clive received large sums from Mir Jafar, they were not nearly so large as people had imagined.

After the attacks of his enemies and the ordeal of the Select Committee, two events that summer and autumn must have served to restore Clive's ego. The first was his formal installation as a Knight of the Bath in June; not of any real significance, in that it followed automatically on his appointment to the Order eight years previously. But any thoughts he may have had about being regarded as a sheep-stealer must have been temporarily dispelled as he proceeded into the Prince's Chamber at Westminster, resplendent in plumed cap and scarlet mantle.

The second event was of greater consequence. In September, Lord Powis died. He had held the office of Lord-Lieutenant of Shropshire, to which Clive now aspired. At first it seemed hard to know how he would go about obtaining it. Having received no support from North against his enemies, he felt reluctant to ask a favour of him. On the other hand, to have gone direct to the King would have been to snub the Prime Minister, which he knew was unwise in view of the likelihood of an attack on him in Parliament.[26] The ever-helpful Wedderburn solved the problem by putting in a word, and North was only too willing to take the initiative in obtaining the Lieutenancy for Clive. He had been looking for a way of winning him over to the Government which did not entail supporting him in the Indian controversies.[27]

Whilst he could still remain neutral in the controversies that raged around the name of Clive, Lord North could no longer shut his eyes to the question of India. Up to now, the Directors had managed to keep the Proprietors in ignorance of the critical state of the Company's finances, even to paying dividends which they knew were quite unjustified. But in September 1772, they were obliged to reveal the true state of affairs and stop the dividend altogether. The Company's stock fell from 219 to 160.

The Directors were brought to this pass by an international financial crisis which threatened to become a second South Sea Bubble. It started in June with the failure of the Scottish banker, Alexander Fordyce, whose collapse brought down many other bankers. Colebrooke, Chairman of the East India Company once again, was among those hit. He managed, however, to postpone his crash for a few months, and in the meantime put up a show of affluence by rebuilding the church near his country house in Surrey, 'an expiatory step for the hecatombs of human offerings sacrificed by his friends in India to the God of Avarice', as a newspaper described it.[28] The Company suffered from the general panic caused by the crisis and the resulting shortage of credit. The knowledge of its Chairman's own financial difficulties did not help to restore confidence.

In order to carry on, the Company had to ask the Government for a loan of one and a half million pounds. The granting of such a loan made it inevitable that the Government should intervene in the affairs of the Company. Lord North's first move was to set up another Parliamentary Committee, the Committee of Secrecy, which, unlike the Select Committee, really did get down to investigating the current problems and abuses. It was, however, primarily intended to defeat the Directors in their eleventh-hour attempt to ward off Government intervention, which they hoped to do by sending a fresh batch of Supervisors to India. Accordingly, the Committee recommended that a Bill should be introduced to restrain the Company from sending out the Supervisors. When, on December 18, the Bill was debated, Clive supported it—a sign of how far he had gone over to the Government. He took care, however, not to appear as though he had deserted the Company in its hour of crisis.[29]

The debate was interrupted by the appearance of the Company's lawyers,[30] who came to argue that the Bill was unconstitutional. They also enlarged on the 'rogueries' of the Company servants in Bengal, no doubt to show that the Company was able to diagnose its own ills without the help of a Parliamentary physician.[31] To Clive and other 'East Indian' Members, these revelations were ominous: a sign that the Directors, in their desperation, were looking for scapegoats among their servants, past and present. Sykes, who was also in the House, seems to have lost his head. An irregular tax, known as the *mathaut*, from which he had personally benefited, was being discussed, and the old and decrepit chief clerk of the Company was called as a witness. Sykes was foolish enough to ask him what the *mathaut* was used for, and the old man, either deliberately, or because he did not know to whom he was speaking, replied: 'Mr Sykes received annually 24,000 rupees for his table, 18,000 rupees for his dress, and for his *munshi*, 18,000 more.'[32] Poor Sykes went red in the face and the whole House turned and looked at him. *Mathaut* became another dirty word to be thrown at the Nabobs, not excluding Clive, although he maintained that he had never heard of this tax until the summer of 1772.

The Bill was carried by a large majority and Lord North was able to proceed with the plan for 'regulating' the Company which was slowly forming in his head. The result was the Regulating Act, which became law in the following June, and subjected the Company to partial Government control as well as reforming its constitution both at home and abroad. As might be expected of Lord North's brain-child, it was meant to be a compromise; but, while it was regarded by the Company as a gross violation of its rights, the Government control which it provided was far from satisfactory.

In November 1772, Clive gave Lord North a memorandum on India, based on his own ideas and worked up by Strachey. He told Strachey his reason for doing so: 'I will not patiently stand by and see a great Empire acquired by great abilities, perseverance and resolution, lost by ignorance and indolence.'[33] His description of the Company's sphere of influence as 'a great Empire' shows how far his thinking had progressed since the days when he had merely aimed at securing English trade.

At least one of Clive's biographers suggests that the Regulating Act was a watered-down version of this memorandum,[34] which Clive appears to have discussed with the Prime Minister at Downing Street on the day after the debate about the Supervisors. Dame Lucy Sutherland, however, shows it to have been of more hybrid ancestry, deriving just as much from Sulivan's abortive Bill.[35] The Act certainly embodied a number of Clive's ideas, but they were not his ideas exclusively. It made the Governor of Bengal into a Governor-General, it followed Clive's precepts in allowing him a liberal salary – £25,000 a year – and also investing the supreme authority in a Council of five. Whatever may be said about Clive being an autocrat, he was sufficiently a child of eighteenth-century England to take it for granted that there should be a check on a Governor's powers.[36] The smooth working of his own Committee of five convinced him that no Council should be larger; a fallacy, in that whereas a Governor can generally find a majority of men of good will in a larger body, with a Council of five it is easy for three to team up against him and make his life a hell on earth, as the notorious 'Triumvirate' did to Warren Hastings.

CHAPTER XXV

Refund, Refund!

May such rapacious rogues as Sykes
Be doomed to die like dogs in dykes!
And as the proofs are fixed on Clive
May he in ignominy live!
While every night around his bed,
The shadowy shapes vindictive tread,
Of Siraj-ud and Omichund,
Crying aloud: 'Refund, Refund!'

VERSE PRINTED IN 'PUBLIC LEDGER', 1773

During the months when the Regulating Act was taking shape, the storm which had broken over Clive's head a year before doubled in violence. With creditors howling for their money and Proprietors howling for their blood, with Lord North slowly hammering out the chains that were to bind them, the Directors now made a frenzied attempt to justify themselves by throwing the blame on their servants. Sulivan was heard to declare, when speaking of Clive, that he would '*mark* the *man*' and 'show that all the distresses of the Company arose from *him*'.[1]

Not content with mud-throwing, the Directors proceeded to claim against Clive and some of his former colleagues in respect of transactions which had taken place during his second Government. Some of these transactions – such as Clive's exchange of his salt profits for a commission on the revenues which continued for seven months after he had left Bengal – were controversial, to say the least; but they had been entered in the Company's records and approved, at any rate tacitly, by the Directors five years before. Clive replied to these claims with sarcasm so biting that Wedderburn advised him to tone it down.[2] In any case, he could not afford to waste his energies against the Directors, who, to use a popular expression of the time, were already 'in the suds'. He now had to face the final onslaught, led by his enemies in Parliament and backed by an increasingly hostile public opinion. Their losses in East India stock caused the good people of England to be even more resentful of the Nabobs than they had been when they heard of the Bengal famine; it seemed to the anxious Palk that they were yearning for examples to be made, as at the time of the South Sea Bubble.[3]

During the first half of 1773, the Press campaign against Clive reached a crescendo. The accusations of Bolts and Dow were repeated over and over again; the evidence from the Select Committee reports was presented to appear as incriminating as possible. Then there were the more frivolous attacks. *Lloyd's Evening Post* announced the runners in 'The Great Mathaut Sweepstakes for ten thousand lakhs of rupees', which included 'Mr Omrah's bay horse Jagir, got by Nabob out of Rapino's dam, full sister to Satan'.[4]*

One might easily imagine that in the face of all these attacks, Clive led the life of a pariah. It is therefore a surprise to find that on March 30, when the campaign against him was nearing its climax, he and Margaret were at a party at Carlisle House, where the fellow-guests included the Dukes and Duchesses of Gloucester, Northumberland, Portland, Grafton, Ancaster and Gordon.[5] And among the attacks, there were voices raised in Clive's defence; he also received a number of letters from well-wishers.

In April, Clive had the satisfaction of seeing Sulivan and his followers driven from power. By now, however, the battlefield was no longer East India House but the House of Commons. The conflict opened on May 3, when there was a debate on North's Regulating Bill. Clive spoke for two and a half hours, mostly in defence of himself; though it seemed to Walpole, who was present, that he was being bold and frank, rather than apologetic.[6] Early on he referred to his much-criticized stock transaction: 'The transaction was neither illegal, nor dishonourable, yet I say, Sir, I should not have given my enemies even this slender twig to hold by.'

* The newspapers, however, cast few if any aspersions on Clive's sex-life, with the exception of the *Town and Country Magazine* which featured him (Volume V) as 'Baron Jagir' alongside his alleged mistress, 'Miss Fanny Ch—n', in its notorious series of *Tête-à-Tête* portraits. According to the accompanying article, Clive had, when in India, tasted 'the sweets of Asiatic beauty', but was put off when a dusky nymph tried to poison him. Apart from this revelation, it reads soberly, and one might have been tempted to believe it, if one did not know that the *Tête-à-Tête* articles were written by none other than Carraccioli (see *Notes and Queries*, 10th Series, Vol. IV, pp. 241–2) and that in the eighteenth century nobody bothered to treat material of this sort as libellous.

And with equal frankness he remarked how when he arrived in Bengal in 1765, 'there was not a living European that was not trading in salt',[7] so that there seemed nothing wrong in engaging in his private venture.

As he warmed to his subject, 'he often attempted wit and satire and sometimes succeeded'.[8] The House was 'entertained and astonished', particularly the ladies in the gallery, though for much of his speech he was suffering from hoarseness. 'It was not', wrote Walpole, 'a piece of regular and set oratory, but the artful effusions of a man, master of his cause, of himself, and of the passions of others, which he raised, interested, or amused, as he found necessary . . . his allusions and applications were happy, and when he was vulgar he was rarely trivial . . . while the Ministers and the Parliament sunk before him, he shone eminently as a real great man, who had done great things, and who had the merit of not having committed more (perhaps not worse) villainies.'[9]

It was now that Clive made his celebrated remark about having been examined like a sheep-stealer. 'I am sure, Sir, if I had any sore places about me, they would have been found. They have probed to the bottom; no lenient plaster has been applied to my sore, they have been all of a blistering kind, composed of Spanish flies and many other provocatives. At the India House, Sir, the public records have been searched from top to bottom as charges against me.' From this, he inevitably turned on Sulivan, 'so assiduous in my affairs that really, Sir, it appears he has entirely neglected his own'. Sulivan, who was present, must have writhed. But Clive was becoming increasingly good-humoured and suggested that as the Jacobite heads on Temple Bar had fallen down, they should be replaced by his own head in the middle with Sulivan's on one side and Colebrooke's on the other. At this, the House burst into applause and laughed for nearly ten minutes.[10]

Thus encouraged, he painted a picture of the Directors enjoying an expense-account meal, 'devouring the turtle and all kinds of viands out of season and in season, and swilling themselves with whole hogsheads of claret, champagne and burgundy'.[11] From this, he went on to criticize North's Bill, though again in a light-hearted way. The result of it, he said, would be 'some noble Duke, or other high in blood, high in female connections, appointed Viceroy or Governor-General' while 'some of those first-rate geniuses who spend their thousands at Almack's and Arthur's'—a hit at Charles James Fox, who had been on the Select Committee*—

* Clive wrote of Fox: 'A pistol will be his end' (Sutton Court Collection, Vol. V, Clive to Strachey, April 3, 1774).

would become Councillors. 'Instead of returning home Nabobs, as we have done, they will all return home Great Moguls.'[12] Fortunately for British India, none of these prophecies came true, and England was never to know a race of Super-Nabobs.[13]

Though most of Clive's fellow-Members enjoyed his speech, it did not, according to Walpole, convince them. Nor was it favourably reported in the Press. The *Public Advertiser* spoke of his 'low buffoonery' and printed an ominous warning from 'Aristides': 'Perhaps a certain Assembly may pluck up a resolution which may rescue them from that *contempt* with which you seem to treat them. Then, my Lord, beware of PAINS AND PENALTIES!'[14]

Clive's enemies had, in fact, been planning Parliamentary action against him for some time; his speech served only to provoke them. Later on May 3, Burgoyne, who now seems to have been definitely in the Johnstones' camp,[15] 'gave notice in a pompous style' that he would move the House to take the Select Committee reports into consideration along with North's Bill.[16] Meanwhile, a group within the Government, hostile to Clive, was pressing North to take action. This group consisted mainly of followers of the late Duke of Bedford, the nobleman whom Clive had offended by hinting that he had been in the pay of the French when he negotiated the peace treaty of 1762. They were led by the Attorney-General, the tough and pushing Edward Thurlow, who had borne a personal animosity towards Clive ever since the days when he had acted for the Company in the *jagir* dispute. North was loath to attack Clive himself and drive him into the arms of the Opposition; on the other hand, he was prepared to adopt what his biographer has called a 'Pilatesque' attitude[17] and sit quiet while Thurlow, 'a proper blood-hound to pursue such a tiger',[18] and the rest of his pack were turned loose. So the resulting proceedings cut across the ordinary alignment of Government and Opposition. Clive's chief accuser was the Attorney-General, and his chief defender was the Solicitor-General, Wedderburn: 'no honester than the accuser or the criminal', as Walpole remarked cynically.[19]

The other powerful group within the Government, the so-called 'King's Friends', appeared, for most of the conflict, to be uncertain which way they would go, though at least one of their number, Charles Jenkinson – who had, incidentally, married Watts's daughter – was favourable towards Clive. There were many who, like Walpole, believed in the mythical influence of the diamonds which Clive had brought from India for the Queen; so much so that when, at one stage in the proceedings, this Court party appeared to be veering towards Clive's enemies, a newspaper reported that 'a flaw has been discovered in the diamond given by Lord C——e to a great lady'.[20] In fact, the King himself at this juncture seems to have echoed the prevailing opinion against what he called 'the fleecers of the East Indies',[21] while Burke, who supported Clive not through any particular brief for him, but because he regarded the attack on him as a threat to public liberty, spoke of the Court party as being among Clive's enemies.[22]

Burke's own party, that which followed Rockingham, was divided. The other chief opposition party, made up of old followers of Chatham now grouped behind Sulivan's friend, Shelburne, was in the forefront of the attack, led in the Commons by Barré with his single staring eye and mordant wit. Among the Members who were uncommitted by either personal motives or party loyalties, one might say that all shades of what would now be called left-wing opinion united against Clive: thus his antagonists included Charles James Fox, the liberal aristocrat, Sir William Meredith, the dedicated humanitarian, and Jeremiah Dyson, representing the latent forces of Nonconformism.

However much Clive's enemies in the Government worked behind the scenes, they left it to Burgoyne to open the attack, which he did on May 10. 'We have had in India revolution upon revolution, extortion upon extortion,' he declared to a crowded, frenzied and sweltering House. 'In the whole history of mankind, I defy mankind to produce such a continued system of oppression.' He spread himself over the Omichand affair, and according to a newspaper, when he mentioned the forgery of Admiral Watson's name, 'the House could scarce restrain their indignation'.[23]

His speech ended with three resolutions: that all territorial acquisitions made by subjects belonged to the Crown, that it was illegal for private persons to appropriate the revenues of such possessions, and that there had been appropriation of such revenues.[24] The last two resolutions were aimed at Clive and his colleagues, and could, if passed, have led to a Bill for the confiscation of the money they had received from Mir Jafar, a Bill of 'Pains and Penalties' as the newspaper had forecast, or an impeachment such as Warren Hastings was later to suffer.

'With all the arts of his profession, and all the resources of oratory'[25] Wedderburn opposed the resolutions, dwelling on their 'vague and dangerous impropriety', as well as alluding to Burgoyne's unsavoury methods of electioneering.[26] Clive only spoke for about five minutes, 'with arrogant haughtiness that did not conceal strong dismay'.[27] He had, in fact, been warned beforehand by Wedderburn not to be in too much of a hurry with his final defence.[28] Lord North made two bumbling speeches in which he managed to contradict himself, and slept during the most interesting parts of the debate. Barré repeated the old invidious comparison between Clive and Wolfe, who, he said, had won an empire for Britain yet had not been enriched; he was also about to tell one of his dirty stories, but desisted on account of there being ladies in the gallery.[29]

Wedderburn's speech had swayed the House in Clive's favour, and it seemed that Burgoyne's resolutions would be heavily defeated. Then Thurlow rose, 'and in a moment revived and heightened the odium against Lord Clive'.[30] By now, it was past ten; the younger Members came trooping back from dinner, flushed with wine, and found the debate had become boring – according to the catty Walpole, they also feared the heat of the Chamber 'would melt their rouge and shrivel their nosegays'.[31] So they voted for Burgoyne's resolutions and passed them, merely so as to put an end to the night's proceedings.

'You can hardly conceive what satisfaction almost every person one meets with expresses today at the event of yesterday,' wrote Lloyd Kenyon, an up-and-coming legal friend of Thurlow's, on the 11th. 'I am told that Lord Clive's friends look wonderfully crestfallen.'[32] The King was less confident that 'national justice' would prevail against the 'fleecers'.[33] Burgoyne's resolutions were too general to be of much effect. But he and his backers intended to follow them up with something more explicit. 'On Friday next, the public censure of the Commons of Great Britain will be followed, it is expected, by a vote for RESTITUTION,' announced the *Morning Advertiser* portentously.[34] Edward Gibbon was less certain of the outcome. 'The hounds go out again next Friday. They are in high spirits but the more sagacious ones have no idea they shall kill.'[35]

The next act in the drama was in fact postponed to the following Wednesday, May 19. Burgoyne opened with another attack on Clive, which a Member described as 'very heavy, unedifying and unsatisfactory'.[36] He waxed eloquent on the *jagir*, erroneously stating it to have been granted after Plassey, yet failed to take it into account when considering Clive's actual gains, which he put at £234,000 – a figure representing only his share in the treaty money and Mir Jafar's private gift. Before sitting down, he stated his intention of proposing a resolution that Clive 'had illegally acquired the sum of £234,000 to the dishonour and detriment of the State'.[37] This, for Clive, was highly ominous. The resolution, if passed, would almost inevitably have led to proceedings for the confiscation of his fortune. Although Burgoyne did not include the *jagir* in his figure, it would not have been in any way safe, for it was acquired, like the other money, when he was at the head of British troops.

The ensuing debate was described as 'irregular and episodical';[38] Lord North found it 'neither amusing nor instructive'.[39] Everyone agreed that the only speech worth listening to was Clive's. He spoke for an hour and twenty minutes, 'in a very decent manly manner',[40] as a Member remarked; though he was afterwards said to have trembled as he spoke. There were no more witty remarks or raps over the knuckles; he was fighting with his back to the wall, appealing to the better nature of the House to save his reputation and his money. 'After the long and painful services which I have rendered the State, . . . I did not conceive it possible that a motion could ever be brought into this House to deprive me of my honour and reputation. I am sure the House will not accuse me of vanity, . . . they will not accuse me of presumption for stating to the House what those services are . . .'

He proceeded to give an account of his career, making the most of the early period which had not been publicized by the Select Committee. Then, he said, forgetting his takings as Commissary, he had 'reaped barren laurels', which might have given him 'some pretensions to have reaped laurels more fruitful'. He told of Arcot, of Arni, of Kaveripak, of Trichinopoly, paying tribute to Stringer Lawrence, which gave the impression that he was not being too boastful. In the same way, when he had passed on to the events in Bengal, he paid tribute to the memory of Admiral Watson.* Regarding the Omichand episode, he declared: 'Where the lives of so many people were concerned, and when the existence of the Company depended upon it, I would not have scrupled to have put Mr Watson's name to that treaty even without his consent. I said so in the Committee, I say so here.'

His speech ended on a pathetic, pleading note.

> I cannot look upon myself in a much better light than a bankrupt, I can look upon myself as having nothing left but a family estate of about £500 a year, which has belonged to us for many generations. I am not ashamed to live

* But with typical carelessness, he told the irrelevant story of the bribing of the French officer Ducré before the capture of Chandernagore, which created a bad impression in some quarters. It was even said to have got back to Ducré himself, causing him much anguish.

> upon that family estate, perhaps I may enjoy more health, more satisfaction, more content ... Do I stand condemned by an *ex post facto* resolution for receiving presents sixteen years ago? ... I can never bring myself to believe that this House will ever adopt such a horrid idea, such a shocking, dreadful, detestable idea as to punish a man for what he could not know he could be guilty of. I have done. I have read an author who says that it requires much more resolution to support prosperity than adversity. Sir, my acquaintance is not a very extensive one, but I believe that those that do know me know that I have supported prosperity in moderation. I am not afraid to meet adversity, *frangas non flectes* I may be broken but I will never stoop to ill-fortune. I may be distressed, I may be ruined, but as long as I have a conscience to defend me, I will always be happy ... I have only one thing more, that is a humble request to the House, I make it not for myself, but for them, the request is this, when they come to decide upon my honour, they will not forget their own.[41]

The House, always impressionable, was very much moved. But his enemies had not finished. Burgoyne proposed to read the evidence of the Select Committee reports. Sir Richard Sutton, who had been on the Committee, argued strenuously that this evidence could not be used against Clive, as it included a number of confessions which he had made voluntarily.

There followed an interminable discussion on procedure,[42] during which, as it was afterwards remarked, many of the Members showed signs of embarrassment. From having regarded the attack on Clive as representing the righteous indignation of the British people, they now saw it as somewhat disreputable. If the newspapers are anything to go by, this change of attitude was shared by the public at large: Clive's enemies were called 'Bourbonite hirelings',[43] and the inevitable comparison was made between his case and the victimization of Admiral Byng seventeen years before.[44] At the Thatched House Tavern on the night of the 19th, 'a gentleman of rank' bet fifty pounds to a thousand that Clive would not have to part with any of his fortune.[45]

Nevertheless, Parliament could be fickle. When, on the 21st, the fate of 'this every way great criminal',[46] as Walpole called him, came to be decided, there were many who were uncertain of the outcome. Amongst their number was the hard-headed Sykes, who admitted to having suffered more mental anguish that night than when he was a prisoner of Siraj-ud-daula.[47]

Clive's speech that night was short. There was, however, according to

JOHN JOHNSTONE

After a painting by Raeburn

SIR ROBERT FLETCHER

Engraving by W. Dickinson from a portrait by Sir Joshua Reynolds

WALCOT, THE ENTRANCE FRONT

CLAREMONT, THE ENTRANCE FRONT

Caillaud, who was present in the gallery, 'an energy and propriety in his manner and expression' that affected the House.[48] Having made his celebrated plea, 'leave me my honour, take away my fortune',[49] he bowed and walked out, with tears in his eyes, followed by loud and repeated cries of 'Hear, hear!' Entering his carriage, he drove back home, not knowing whether he had 'a sixpence to call his own in the morning', as Sykes put it.[50]

At Berkeley Square, many of his friends were waiting to hear what had happened. He greeted them calmly, played a few hands of whist, had supper, and then at midnight went to bed, asking to be woken if the news was good, but if not, to be allowed to sleep on.[51] Margaret and the rest of the company sat up in the big drawing-room, waiting to hear the outcome of the debate. One can imagine her putting on a brave face and trying to keep her guests amused, and then, as one in the morning became two, and two became three, her spirits drooping, like the candles which flickered and died against the scarlet damask walls. There is no indication as to who were the other people in the room; but we can be pretty certain that Jane Strachey was one of them, for Strachey was at the fateful debate. During the past eighteen years, Margaret and Jane had often sat together, waiting.

Three became four and four became five; the dawn rose from behind the houses on the far side of the Square. The birds in the trees outside the windows started their morning chorus. And then, another sound was heard: distant horses' hooves and the rumbling of a carriage over the cobbles. The sound grew nearer, louder; everybody made a dash for the windows. They saw the carriage stop, and out of it got Strachey; he looked up and smiled. All was well.[52]

Earlier that night, when Clive walked out of the House with tears in his eyes, several Members burst into tears, too. Some of them only just stopped themselves from breaking the rules and clapping. As soon as Clive had gone, Burgoyne proposed his resolution. He had toned it down. It no longer accused Clive of obtaining his £234,000 illegally; but it still said that in doing so, he had 'abused the powers with which he was entrusted, to the evil example of the servants of the public'. He was seconded by Meredith, who leant over backwards to praise Clive's earlier achievements. And then Hans Stanley, a junior member of the Government, and Rose Fuller, a distinguished Parliamentarian described as 'an old, honest, independent veteran of integrity',[53] proposed that Burgoyne's resolution should be cut in half, so as to separate the bare statement that

Clive had received the £234,000 from the passage about his having abused his powers and given a bad example.

There followed a long and heated debate on this amendment. Fox called Clive 'the origin of all plunders, the source of all robbery'.[54] Barré remarked in rather poor taste that Clive's lakhs could hardly have been 'given him for his beauty'.[55] Lord North, in the words of Burke, 'blew hot and cold, and veered round the whole thirty-two points of the compass of uncertainty and indecision'.[56] Burke himself, and other members of the Rockingham group, now rallied to Clive's defence, the most significant voice among them being that of Admiral Sir Charles Saunders, who, 'with rough naval indignation', declared that Clive was being treated like Sir Walter Ralegh.[57] The Admiral spoke as a 'Rockingham', but he also spoke for the ordinary, decent men in the House, the country squires, the soldiers and sailors. These men regarded Clive as the hero of Arcot and were determined to stand by him, however little brief they may have had for the other Nabobs. They also stood for the proverbial English fair play, which now came to Clive's rescue, just as the English sympathy for the under-dog, another facet of the same national virtue, had brought the liberals on to the side of his enemies.

When the 'King's Friends' from the Government followed the 'Rockinghams' into the Clive camp, the issue was a foregone conclusion. Stanley's amendment was carried by 155 votes to 95, Lord North voting with the minority. The first, and harmless, part of Burgoyne's resolution was then passed; the severed tail containing the sting was rejected without a division. Wedderburn then took the initiative and moved 'that Robert, Lord Clive, did, at the same time, render great and meritorious services to this country', which was carried almost unanimously. 'Lord Clive has thus come out of the fiery trial much brighter than he went into it,' wrote Burke on the day after the debate. 'His gains are now recorded, and not only not condemned, but actually approved by Parliament. His reputation, too, for ability, stands higher than ever.'[58]

There were many who wondered how Clive had managed to achieve this, for him, happy result. 'Some lakhs of rupees have been employed in obtaining this victory,' muttered Lloyd Kenyon, who hinted that they went into the pockets of the 'Rockinghams'.[59] A newspaper put it out that Clive's vindication cost him a quarter of his fortune, adding that he had 'settled £3000 a year for life on a well-known Weatherbeaten councillor'.[60] Not only are such aspersions proved groundless by Clive's account books; but it would have been unthinkable to buy over English public men in the 1770s by means of direct cash bribes, however possible it may have been to sway them by 'interest'. As for the suggestion that Clive paid for Wedderburn's services, this would have been quite unnecessary since Wedderburn was already indebted to him for his seat in Parliament.*

The diamond myth was also revived to explain the final attitude of the 'King's Friends', who in fact seem to have voted as they did through the example of two of their number, Clive's old acquaintance Lord Barrington, the Secretary at War, and Jenkinson,[61] whose father-in-law had benefited from the gold of Murshidabad to a greater extent than anybody, barring Clive himself. Whatever their reason, the 'King's Friends' went against the King, who expressed his feelings in a letter to Lord North: 'I own I am amazed that private interest could make so many forget what they owe to their country, and come to a resolution that seems to approve of Lord Clive's rapine. No one thinks his services greater than I do, but that can never be a reason to commend him in what certainly opened the door to the fortunes we see daily made in that country.'[62]

Without resorting to bribery, Clive and Wedderburn certainly canvassed all the support they could get. The amendment proposed by Stanley and Fuller may have appeared spontaneous, but in fact it had been planned several days beforehand. Stanley had been approached as an acquaintance of Clive's and the brother-in-law of one of Strachey's best friends.[63]

As well as affording time for such negotiations, the eleven days' delay between the opening of Burgoyne's attack and his final resolution enabled both Parliament and the public to have second thoughts. There was the fear of 'retrospects and laws *ex post facto*';[64] the whole business smacked of envy and was suspected by some of being an attempt by the Government to grab the Nabobs' money.[65] Then it must have occurred to the more thinking humanitarians, as it did to one gentleman who was present during the debates, that none of the accusers of Clive and his fellow-Nabobs appeared to have 'the smallest idea of restoring to the injured natives of India the territories and revenues said to have been so unjustly acquired'.[66] Finally, and most important, it seemed, even to many of Clive's accusers, that there was not enough evidence on which to convict him.[67] As a modern biographer points out,[68] there was no real case against Clive, such as was brought against Hastings fifteen years later, causing him to be impeached.

* A confusion of the word 'seat', in the Parliamentary sense, with 'country seat', may have given rise to the legend that Clive rewarded Wedderburn with an estate.

Clive was also more fortunate than Hastings in that the attack on him did not become a straight issue between Government and Opposition. Members were able to think for themselves, rather than follow the party line; and they thought sensibly. 'I felt a pleasure in the good humour of John Bull,' wrote one of Clive's opponents after the debate. 'He will speak and write daggers, and hang and cut off heads without mercy in the newspapers; but when a culprit has submitted and John has him absolutely in his power, he will not hurt a hair of his head.'[69]

CHAPTER XXVI

See Naples and Die

The ghost of Clive haunts me.

LAURENCE SULIVAN, 1775

Because Clive died by his own hand within two years of being attacked in Parliament, it has been generally assumed that he never recovered from the ordeal, and that for the last few months of his life he was sunk in melancholy.[1] This is a myth, originally put about by his enemies, to imply that he suffered remorse for his alleged misdeeds, and then used by the historians of a later age to show that his persecutors drove him to suicide. It was easy to believe that the depression, from which he had suffered at intervals since his youth, should now have overwhelmed him; although this depression was pathological, and seems to have occurred more as a reaction to success than as a result of adversity.

He is only once recorded as having suffered from depression during his last months. These months may well have been happier than any other time since his return from India. He was coming to terms with ill-health: 'I am so well acquainted with my own constitution at present that I think I may venture to say that with care and attention I may make the rest of my days tolerably easy,' he wrote in April 1774.[2]

He saw his enemies confounded. Sulivan was well and truly in the wilderness. For John Johnstone, the failure of his and his brothers' great plan of revenge was followed, later in the year, by near ruin, caused by the bankruptcy of Bolts.[3] On a lower plane, the egregious Fletcher, who returned towards the end of 1773, having quarrelled with his colleagues in Madras, only succeeded in making a fool of himself when he attempted to discredit Clive as a means of getting rid of the mutiny slur, for which he was still 'universally despised'.[4]

One feels that historians have exaggerated the extent to which Clive suffered from 'the popular obloquy that had descended upon him, which no resolution of the House of Commons could remove'.* To prove that this 'obloquy' was by no means universal, he was invited, soon after his exoneration, to stand as a Parliamentary candidate for Liverpool, in opposition to Sir William Meredith, whose attack on him had been unpopular with the electors.[5]† And having always been rather remote from Society, he would have been unlikely to notice much change in people's attitudes to him, if indeed there was any change. Long years as a controversial figure had thickened his skin; it must be remembered, too, that such derogatory remarks as we know to have been made about him by the Great are mostly in letters which he would never have seen. Thus the King may have written privately to Lord North about Clive's 'rapine'; but to Clive himself he continued to be nothing but gracious.[6]

Clive had recovered enough of his self-esteem to go to Portsmouth in June, along with many other 'persons of distinction', for the great naval review in honour of the King.[7] Within a week of the fateful May 21, he was back in Parliament, speaking in the debates on the Regulating Bill. Whatever his influence on the framing of the Bill may have been, he certainly influenced its working after it became law; though unfortunately in a negative way. The Act appointed Hastings as the first Governor-General, with a Supreme Council consisting of Barwell, General Sir John Clavering, Colonel George Monson and Philip Francis. The last three were the notorious 'Triumvirate' sent out from England, who teamed up against Hastings and formed a hostile majority in the Council, virtually 'making the working of the Act impossible'.[8] Clavering was on friendly terms with Clive, but it was chiefly through the youngest Councillor, Philip Francis, that the Triumvirate came to adopt Clive's policies, in opposition to Hastings. Soon after his appointment, in July 1773, Francis was invited to spend a fortnight between Walcot and Oakly, presumably at the suggestion of Strachey, who had known him since the days when they had worked together at the War Office. He immediately became the rising star in the Clive firmament.[9]

Clive was doubtless impressed by Francis's 'bright metallic intelligence',[10] and saw in him a likely agent for influencing the government of India according to his views. Francis saw in Clive a powerful backer, and would have admired his personality and been eager to pick his brains. So

* A. Mervyn Davies, *Clive of Plassey* (London 1939), p. 489.

† He wisely declined.

he went all out to please, played quadrille for more than he could afford and lost cheerfully.

Additional cement for the friendship was provided by Margaret, who was delighted to find that Francis shared her love of cats.[11] Francis entertained her with his waspish wit; he doubtless took care to conceal his disbelief in Christianity, while joking with her about Clive's poor attendance at evening prayers. Allowing for the sycophancy of his bread-and-butter letter, one can take it that when he left he was just a little infatuated with her, and genuinely dazzled by his excursion into High Life. His house at Margate seemed very small after Walcot and Oakly; he missed the luxurious beds and upper-class talk; no other lord or lady treated him on such equal terms.[12]

Margaret pressed Francis to come again and bring his wife. She took to Betsy Francis as quickly as she had taken to Francis himself; she even enthused about their maidservant.[13] Much of Francis's remaining time in England was spent at one or other of the Clive houses. 'I wish Lord Clive would communicate a portion of his fortitude to his humble servant,'[14] he wrote as he sailed for India with his two colleagues in the following April; but fortitude apart, Clive had impressed enough of himself on Francis, at any rate as far as his ideas and prejudices were concerned. And he had armed him with sheaves of memoranda on his system of government, just as Margaret had given him a bottle of her best attar of roses (a present from the Mogul), to carry in his pocket.

That Clive indoctrinated Francis with his views and encouraged him to revive his policies, is certain. In so doing, he would obviously have criticized the policies of Hastings; but whether he actually ran down Hastings's character to Francis is a matter of conjecture. According to Francis, he did;[15] but then Francis would have been liable to put constructions on whatever Clive said, particularly if it suited his ambition. Outwardly, at any rate, Clive and Hastings were still on friendly terms.

In June 1773, when his mind was on the Regulating Act and the recent drama in Parliament, Clive was also thinking about the final education of the nineteen-year-old Ned. It was planned that he should spend two years studying in Geneva, with a tutor named Fraser. Clive wrote a lengthy 'Direction' which shows him once again to have been, in some respects, a Victorian before his time.

In order to lead a happy life, Mr. Clive must take care of his health and he must acquire those qualifications that render a man a useful and valuable member of Society in Great Britain and in his particular station ... The manner of preserving and cultivating a healthy constitution, Mr. Pope has expressed with great truth and precision: '*Health consists in temperance alone*.'

It is morally impossible to make any man without experience ... feel the close connection that there is between these qualifications and the happiness of his life, because before Man can discern their full value and influence he must not only be possessed of them, but he must also have acted in these nice, difficult and great situations, that demand the exertion of such qualifications; ... In order to supply this defect of experience, let Mr. Clive substitute and rely upon my experience; and I, his father, his most cordial and affectionate friend, whose happiness is linked with his, do most peremptorily recommend to him the acquisition of those great and valuable qualities which constitute the character of a good man and a useful citizen, because I know from experience their real importance to Mr. Clive's happiness ...

I know it frequently happens that gentlemen abroad, in the situation of Mr. Fraser and Mr. Clive, form separate societies. This, I must absolutely prohibit, for it is often, if not always, attended with the worse consequences to the unexperienced party; and there can be no justifiable reason for it, as no company can be fit for Mr. Fraser that is improper for Mr. Clive, nor ought Mr. Clive to frequent any company that is not fit for and approved of by Mr. Fraser ...

As to expense, Mr. Clive must be sensible that the more he spends at present, the less he will have to expect in time to come ...[16]

If Clive showed some vanity in suggesting that he possessed the 'great and valuable qualities' which he recommended to his son, he also seems to have been certain that he had achieved happiness. We know how he could delude himself, yet we know, too, how convinced he was that he had always acted right. There would have been happiness enough in this conviction.*

* Just before Ned set out for Geneva, Clive received a letter from a Mr Stuart asking if he could recommend some books on India for the aged Voltaire, who was then writing on Indian affairs (Powis Collection, Box 67, Andrew Stuart to Clive, July 9, 1773). This is the origin of the legend that Voltaire attempted to get in touch with Clive, whereas his request only reached Clive at third-hand. Stuart seems to have been a friend of Wedderburn, who told Ned to 'load his trunk' with books for 'the old gentleman', and suggested that Clive should address a few lines to Voltaire at the same time. But he feared that Margaret would 'scruple at a correspondence with so free a writer' (*ibid.*, Wedderburn to Clive, July 9, 1773), which may explain why Clive does not appear to have acted on Wedderburn's suggestion.

Of the rest of Clive's children, the three girls were on the threshold of their teens; Charlotte, the Queen's god-daughter, promised to be a beauty, though she was delicate. When in the country, the girls were drilled three times daily by a sergeant—'part of a lady's education which you have not yet heard of', as their older cousin, Jane Latham, remarked after describing this 'military exercise'.[17] Clive's younger son, Bob, now aged four, was soon to acquire little Phil Francis as a playmate. In the following year, Bob and Phil were put at a boarding school in Cavendish Street, run by a Frenchman named Monsieur Ribouville.

Perhaps it was on account of the children that Margaret did not accompany Clive when he left for Italy at the end of 1773; for though she did not much appreciate Italian art, she loved the sound of the Italian language. As a parting gift, he gave her a new dress, 'all over diamonds and white satin', which she was to wear at Court for the Royal Birthday.[18] Clive's companions for the trip were Thomas Kelsall, now back from India, and another 'East Indian', the portly Anselm Beaumont. He also took Patoun with him, for his main object in going to Italy, apart from the need to escape the English winter, was to increase his art collection.

He started as soon as he reached Paris by buying pictures and fine furniture; and he engaged a sculptor to work for him at Claremont.[19] Shortly before the New Year, the party reached Milan. Here they found the Duke of Cumberland, brother of George III, and his Duchess, but Clive did not think it necessary to call on them, as he expected to see them in Rome. On January 2 they arrived in Florence, where they met Zoffany, who was painting a picture of the Tribuna. Clive wanted to have a similar picture, but, as the artist remarked ironically, 'poor man, he could not go to the expense'.[20]

Soon after his arrival in Rome, Clive was received in a very friendly manner by the Pope.[21]* The city was full of English nobility, most of whom, including Clive himself, hurried off to Naples in the middle of January to see an eruption of Vesuvius which did not materialize.[22] Clive intended to spend the rest of the winter here, but the climate did not suit him and he returned abruptly to Rome after little more than a month. It appears that he suffered one of his fits of depression, for Sir William

* Clement XIV, better known by his surname of Ganganelli, a friar of humble birth elected through the influence of the French and Spanish Courts, on the understanding that he would suppress the Jesuits, which he had done in 1773, gaining the applause of English Protestants. Like Clive, he was destined to die before the end of the year, and in circumstances which gave rise to many dark rumours.

Hamilton, who entertained him, remarked: 'I am much doubtful whether it is in the power of any air to cure His Lordship's disorder, which seems to be mostly of his spirits.'[23]

Father John Thorpe, a cultivated English priest living in Rome, observed how the artists and dealers of that city were all set for Clive's return, 'preparing to lessen his millions'.[24] It was rumoured that he would give up to £2000 for a really good picture;[25] in particular, he was looking for 'a capital Guido'.[26] But in the end, the largest sum he paid out was £500 to the banker and dealer, Thomas Jenkins, for an authentic Tintoretto *Assumption* and a so-called Sassoferato, which Thorpe doubted was worth as much as £50.[27]

The living artists of Rome were even more disappointed than the dealers. Clive declared that 'he would only purchase the works of the Old Masters, and leave his son to encourage the moderns'.[28] His patronage went no further than paying £35 to the Reverend William Peters* to copy for him a Barocci Madonna at one of the Papal palaces.

While in Italy, Clive kept in close touch with affairs at home by corresponding with Strachey. That session, the main business of Parliament was America. Strachey told Clive that Lord North, in accordance with his self-appointed role as protector of the East India Company, was taking a dim view of the Company's tea being thrown into Boston harbour.[29] Now would have been the time when, according to a legend which seems based on no earlier foundation than an article of 1784,[30] Clive was offered the supreme command of the British forces in America, but refused on account of his health. Had this offer been made, and had he enjoyed better health, one feels he would still not have accepted it, being too much aware of his limitations as a general. And more than most of his countrymen, he realized the strength of the American colonists. His memorandum on Indian affairs of November 1772 contains an irrelevant yet none the less remarkable prophecy: 'That the Americans will be sooner or later master of all the Spanish possessions and make Cape Horn the boundary of their empire, is beyond a doubt.'[31]

As may be imagined, Strachey's letters are more about the politics of the Company than those of the nation. For the present, Clive and his friends held the balance in the General Court, thanks to the menace of George Johnstone and his new ally, the erratic Duke of Richmond. The Government could not carry any measure against the Directors without Clive's support, while the Directors preferred the tender mercies of Clive

* Chaplain to the newly-founded Royal Academy.

and Lord North to those of Johnstone and the Duke.[32] Lord North offered Clive 'carte blanche' in the choice of a list of candidates to run against the outgoing Directors in the April election.[33] The outgoing Directors were victorious; but Clive took the disappointment philosophically; at least Johnstone and Sulivan had been kept out.[34]

Strachey also kept Clive informed on the progress of Claremont, which was now nearing completion. West was conferring with Brown about the decoration of the Eating Room, which was to feature his paintings of the chief events of Clive's Indian career. Had it been carried out, this would have been one of the richest and most remarkable English interiors of its period: the vast canvases of battles, treaties and the gorgeous East flanked by delicate gilded plaster work.* Clive wanted nothing but the best. But although it was fitted with every modern luxury, including water-closets and an immense sunken bath of grey marble, complete with pipes and taps, the house cost no more than about £30,000 in all – very different from the £100,000 it was popularly believed to have cost.

While Strachey kept an eye on the architectural details of the new house, Margaret was busy with the furnishings. In four of the five surviving letters from her to Clive, each written, to save postage, at the foot of a final page of Strachey's, she told him of the chintzes which she was having made up.[35] And speaking of when Claremont would be habitable – Clive wanted to move in as soon as he returned from Italy, Strachey doubted if it would be ready till the autumn – she said: 'You know how pleased I should be to enter a charming new house with a charming old husband.'[36]

Clive left Rome towards the end of March and travelled by way of Bologna and Venice to Geneva, where he stayed with Ned. He arrived back in England on May 16; his family found him 'in such high health and spirits' that they 'looked forward to an age of comfort and delight'.[37] We do not know if he carried out his plan of moving into Claremont, or if he never stayed so much as a night in his new house; knowing builders, one fears the latter. Certainly he would not have been able to spend much time there, for at the beginning of June, he and Margaret, with Maria Ducarel, went for a fortnight to Tunbridge Wells.

* Unfortunately, West only painted one of the series, that depicting the grant of the *Diwani*. He allowed himself a certain amount of artist's licence, setting the scene not in Clive's tent, but in a hall of many pillars; and putting Thomas Kelsall and Anselm Beaumont in the group of Englishmen behind Clive, though they were certainly not with him at Allahabad in 1765.

He had little need for the Tunbridge waters, his health being still excellent. 'My Lord looks very well and seems in better spirits than I ever saw him,' wrote Betsy Francis, who had not accompanied her husband to India, and was at Tunbridge recovering from a bad stomach occasioned by his departure. She found everybody 'very happy and cheerful' at the Clives' house on Mount Ephraim, except when at dinner Margaret proposed the health of the absent Francis and burst into tears. On Sunday, Margaret and Maria went to church, but Clive was conspicuous by his absence.[38]

At the end of June came the migration to Shropshire, where Clive spent a happy summer, mostly at Oakly, with a constant houseful of guests. There was to be a general election in the autumn, which kept him busy. His fellow-member for Shrewsbury had decreed to stand for the county instead of the town, thus giving a better chance to the interloping Pulteney, who had taken advantage of Clive's absence abroad to launch a campaign. This was the Johnstones' last shot at Clive in his lifetime, and it turned out to be more noise than metal: Pulteney had taken his wife's family name, but was unable or unwilling to spend much of her money. In the end, Clive and Charlton Leighton, a neighbouring squire, were elected with a good majority, though not without some rigging of the electoral roll.[39]

The general election increased Clive's party to seven,[40] though it cost £11,000 to retain one of the two Worcester seats for Walsh, and to win the other one for Thomas Bates Rous, son of the former Company Chairman. We do not know whether Clive would have followed Strachey's advice and taken advantage of his greater voting strength to press for 'the only object you have in life', a British peerage;[41] for he did not live long enough to do anything in this respect. The troubles of 1772 and 1773 had brought him into the Government fold and he had remained there, despite attempts by the 'Rockinghams' to win him over; but he was reluctant to ask favours of North,[42] who in return for being supported gave nothing more tangible than protestations of his friendship. He did, however, ask a favour on behalf of Strachey, who wished for a place in the Government.[43]

The summer passed. A friend of Strachey's came to stay a fortnight in August, and he and Clive pored over maps of India together. He thought Clive had 'a very sound and clear head with an intrepid resolution'.[44] Towards the end of the month, Clive and Margaret went to Shrewsbury races, an event they did not much enjoy but attended out of duty.

Summer turned into a wet autumn. Clive stood too long by the river at Oakly supervising an improvement and caught a bad cold. On November 5, he left for Bath, full of catarrh, and when he arrived there he was too ill even to drink the waters. After a fortnight he was worse, but insisted on going to London: according to some sources, he went at the request of Verelst, who was in the process of being sued by Bolts's Armenians. The journey to London was a nightmare; he was unable to eat or even to swallow. By the time they reached Berkeley Square on the night of November 20, he was once again tormented by his old abdominal complaint. He kept pointing to his belly and groaning, as he suffered acute spasms of pain. The next day was as bad; he tried to make up his mind whether to return immediately to Bath or to stay in London; he took every medicine he could think of, including larger doses of opium than his physician, Dr John Fothergill,[45] considered safe.

On November 22, he appears to have been better; he decided to return to Bath, and ordered his carriage for the afternoon.[46] In the late morning, he joined Margaret, Strachey and Jane for a game of whist. He had taken a purge, and at about noon was obliged to retire to the water-closet.[47] There, it would seem that his pain returned with all its violence; and in a paroxysm of agony, he thrust his penknife into his throat.

Clive's family tried to conceal the fact of his suicide, with the result that his death has remained something of a mystery down to the present day. The newspapers put out contrary reports: some said he had died of an apoplectic fit,[48] others that he had taken an overdose of opium against his doctor's orders.[49] That he died of an overdose was the general belief in the first few days following his death.[50] But even then, there were rumours of suicide. By the middle of December it was generally believed that he had cut his throat.[51] Had this belief been false, Clive's family would surely have contradicted it. Instead, when Strachey wrote to Francis on January 3, telling him of Clive's death, he was suspiciously silent as to the circumstances. At the same time, Sykes, who would have been as close to the circle of Clive's intimates as any outsider, and who would have wished to present Clive in the best possible light, told Hastings that he had without doubt cut his throat.[52] Then there is the account in Malcolm's biography, written with the help and approval of Ned, which implies suicide while not stating as much in so many words.[53]

Most conclusive of all is the eye-witness account given by Jane Strachey to her son some time before her own death in 1824. Her memory may have played her false as regards the details, but she certainly would not have distorted the central fact to Clive's detriment. According to this account, when Clive failed to return, having been out of the room for some time, Strachey said to Margaret: 'You had better go and see where my Lord is.' Margaret 'went to look for him, and at last, opening a door, found Lord Clive with his throat cut. She fainted, and servants came. Patty Ducarel got some of the blood on her hands, and licked it off.'[54]

There remains the question of how Margaret reacted to Clive's suicide. She was deeply religious; she would have been taught that suicide meant certain damnation. Having loved Clive as much as she had, the knowledge of how he died could have made the rest of her life unbearable; whereas we know she enjoyed a good measure of happiness in the years to come. Walpole's friend, Lady Mary Coke, heard a report that when Margaret came out of her faint, she thought that Clive's suicide was merely a bad dream, a delusion which her family encouraged, telling her afterwards that he had died naturally.[55] But she was far too intelligent to be deluded in this way, and in any case she was present at the meeting of Clive's executors on November 23,[56] which settled the details of his funeral, an event conducted with haste and secrecy such as would hardly have been called for in normal circumstances.* And even if this did not strike her as suspicious, she would surely have wondered why there was no tablet or monument over his resting-place in Moreton Say Church.

That she knew, and was reconciled to, the truth seems clear from a letter she wrote to her brother, the Astronomer Royal, six months after the tragedy: 'My health and spirits are much better, and now that I feel less anguish, I feel renewed my former sensation of love, of gratitude, of the softest affection for my own dear Lord, whose qualities had almost ceased to present themselves to my mind for the few days that it was so distracted in London.'[57] A year after his suicide she was able to speak of Clive as 'one of the most virtuous of men';[58] her religion, far from telling her that he was damned, made her thank God for her 'years of felicity' with him and to offer up her 'large draught of sorrow . . . towards the attainment of the favour of Heaven'; a Heaven in which her 'own dear Lord' must surely have had a place.[59]

'My good cousin supports herself with as much strength of mind as can be expected,' Jane Strachey wrote of Margaret, a year after Clive's death, 'but she will never again be what you and I have known her.'[60] Nevertheless, from her letters, it seems that Margaret recovered most of

* Yet it cannot have been quite such a hole-in-the-corner affair as was popularly imagined, for it cost £1066, not including £340 for servants' mourning.

her old spirits. She still had more than half her life ahead of her: she was only thirty-nine when Clive died, and she lived to be eighty-two, speaking of 'Buonaparte' in the way she had once spoken of Dupleix. She spent most of her time at Oakly, which always seems to have been full of guests; she remained the centre of a lively circle of family and friends right up to the time of her death, so that far from complaining of the solitude of old age, she welcomed the rare occasions when she could be alone with her cats and her telescopes. She also kept in touch with Clive's old acquaintances, and did her best to further the interest of their children and grandchildren when they went out to India; though she wondered what influence she really had, being only, as she rather touchingly called herself, 'a *cidevant* princess'.[61] Her links with India were renewed in 1798 when Ned became Governor of Madras; she was able, through him, to relive her own happy Madras days, envying him the blue skies of Coromandel as she sat shivering in the gloom of an English winter.

While Ned was in Madras, his brother-in-law, the second and last Earl of Powis of that creation, died unmarried.* The vast estates of this branch of the Herbert family, including the glorious rose-red Powis Castle, went to Ned's elder son;[62] on the strength of which Ned was himself made Earl of Powis in 1804.[63] For full measure, the descendants of his younger son, to whom Oakly passed, eventually became Earls of Plymouth. Thus in his posterity, Clive achieved an eminence far beyond that for which he had striven in his lifetime, just as having struggled to be accepted as the leading national authority on Indian affairs, he now has his place among the immortals as Clive of India.† It would be hard to find another historical figure whose ambitions were quite so abundantly realized after death as Clive's were.

Clive's ambitions for India were less clear-cut than those for his family and himself. As a Company man, who declared categorically against 'carrying our arms beyond Bengal',[64] he might not wholly have welcomed the prospect of a British India stretching from Cape Comorin to the Khyber, from Burma to the Arabian Sea, and of the granddaughter of George III reigning in place of the Mogul, which was the state of affairs little more than a century after he obtained the *Diwani*. Yet before he died he had grown convinced that the gentlemen of Leadenhall Street

* Ned had married Lady Henrietta Herbert, daughter of Clive's old friend, patron and debtor, Lord Powis, in 1784.

† As another sign of his immortality, there are still parents in the English-speaking world who christen their sons 'Clive'.

could never be equal to ruling an empire such as he had won; and having repeatedly expressed the fear that his empire would be lost through ineptitude, he would surely have rejoiced in the knowledge that the men who came after him would, on the contrary, enlarge it many times over.

But for the labours of these men, of Warren Hastings, Wellesley and Dalhousie, of Elphinstone, the Metcalfes and the Lawrences, Clive's empire would not have endured. Whether that empire would have existed at all had it not been for Clive is another question. There were plenty of soldiers like Coote or Munro who were just as good at winning battles as he was, possibly better. And there was a much greater statesman and administrator in Hastings. But to conjure up an empire in eighteenth-century India, where autocrats meant more than committees, it required that the mystique of the victorious general and the ability to rule should be combined in one man, as they were in Clive. In addition, it required a much rarer quality, which Clive also had, in common with many of the great men of history, notably Churchill: that almost superhuman power and energy to get things done, and to inspire others to give of their best. Clive might well have been the only Englishman in the India of his time who had this power to the extent necessary for bringing an empire into being, and tiding it over the first few perilous years.

Along with Clive's gift of inspiring others went a fantastic capacity for hard work; something he had in common with most of his successors in British India and particularly with Curzon. This was not the only similarity between Clive and Curzon; there were others less fortunate. Both of them suffered constant pain and both lacked magnanimity. One can to a certain extent blame Clive's pettiness on his friends, Walsh, Scrafton and especially Carnac, who even more than the first two could be quarrelsome and vindictive. But if Carnac was little more than a courtier, Walsh and Scrafton served Clive well in other respects. Clive was generally fortunate in his followers and friends, unlike Hastings. He was particularly fortunate in having Strachey by his side, to make good his defects as an administrator; though at the same time Strachey did a disservice to his memory – as well as to British India – by bringing Francis on to the scene.

The fact that Clive – or rather his ghost – was, so to speak, on the wrong side in the controversy that raged around the name of Warren Hastings has weighed heavily against him in the court of history. Clive suffers by comparison with his great successor more than ever now that empire-builders are judged solely from the point of view of the subject peoples; for one can find a sympathy for Indian aspirations in Hastings that was

DRAWING ROOM OF CLIVE'S HOUSE, BERKELEY SQUARE

CAPABILITY BROWN'S DESIGN FOR THE EATING ROOM AT CLAREMONT, SHOWING BENJAMIN WEST'S PAINTING OF CLIVE RECEIVING THE DIWANI, IN POSITION

'THE DIRECTORS IN THE SUDS'
Sir George Colebrooke in the centre, Clive standing on the right.
A satirical print from the Town and Country Magazine, *1773*

THE GHOST OF OMICHAND

A satirical print from the Westminster Magazine, *1773*

lacking in Clive. At the same time, it should be easier to form a fair opinion of Clive—without suppressing the less palatable facts—now that the standards of the Victorian Raj are no longer unquestioningly accepted. And we can also see the hypocrisy of Clive's enemies, whose crocodile tears for the suffering peasants of Bengal blinded them to poverty and misery much nearer home.

Notes and Source References

CHAPTER I

1. *Shropshire Parish Records*, Vol. VIII, quoted in A. Mervyn Davies, *Clive of Plassey* (London 1939), p. 19; *Burke's Peerage*.
2. Thomas Auden, *Memorials of Old Shropshire* (1906), p. 220, quoted in A. Mervyn Davies, *op. cit.*, p. 28.
3. Sir George Forrest, *Life of Lord Clive* (London 1918), Vol. I, p. 2.
4. By Stukely, in 1724.
5. Powis Collection, Box VII, Bayley to King, December 30, 1728.
6. *Ibid.*, January 26, 1728/9.
7. *Ibid.*, January 11, 1728/9.
8. *Ibid.*, June 9, 1732.
9. Sir John Malcolm, *Life of Robert, Lord Clive* (London 1836), Vol. I, p. 38.
10. According to the article on Clive in the second edition of *Biographia Britannica*, an eighteenth-century equivalent of the *Dictionary of National Biography*, Dr Eaton remarked that he was braver and more intelligent than the other boys, adding: 'If that lad should live to be a man, and an opportunity be given for the exertion of his talents, few names will be greater than his.' But as the article was published in 1784, ten years after Clive's death, this prophecy may have been invented in the light of his fame.
11. We first hear of the tower story in the *Biographia Britannica* article. The other stories are even less reliable, since they were told by the townspeople to Sir John Malcolm, Clive's first serious biographer, a century after the time they were supposed to have happened. In most respects, however, Malcolm is a reliable authority, for his book, published in 1836, is based on Clive's own Papers and on information supplied by his son (who was then still alive, though in his eighties) and other members of the family. Macaulay's essay on Clive is a review of it.
12. A. Mervyn Davies, *op. cit.*, p. 22.
13. This is the picture given us in the *Biographia Britannica* article: 'From a dislike to restraint, and an abhorrence of all compulsion, Clive's academical attainments seldom received, or deserved, from his masters, any particular applause; but they all agreed in giving him the character of the most unlucky boy they ever had.'

14. Lady Mary Coke, *Journal* (Edinburgh 1896), Vol. IV, p. 432; Walpole, ed. Steuart, *Last Journals* (London 1910), Vol. I, p. 232.
15. *Biographia Britannica.*
16. Charles Carraccioli, *Life of Robert, Lord Clive* (London *c.* 1777), Vol. I, pp. 11–12.
17. Powis Collection, Box IV, Clive to Vansittart, February 3, 1762.
18. Charles Carraccioli, *op. cit.*, Vol. I, pp. 11–12.
19. 'We may take it . . . that of a hundred men arriving in Madras in any one year, half would probably be dead in five years' time – but that some twenty would still be living many years afterwards' (Henry Dodwell, *Nabobs of Madras* [London 1926], p. 111). The survival rate among Clive's particular associates seems to have been considerably higher than this. Mortality was, of course, very much less among the 'officer class' than it was among the ordinary soldiers and sailors. Not only were the living conditions of the men infinitely worse than those of their superiors, but they were more intemperate. They also suffered through their ignorance of tropical hygiene, whereas the more educated Europeans in eighteenth-century India usually devoted a great deal of thought and care to matters of health.
20. There is a theory that the American insurgents captured some of these ensigns from tea ships at the time of the Boston Tea Party and used them as their own flags and that the Stars and Stripes was thus adapted from them; the stars taking the place of the Union Jack in the corner of the original ensign.
21. Powis Collection, Box VII, Clive to his father, September 10, 15, 1744.
22. *Ibid.*
23. *Ibid.*
24. *Ibid.*
25. India Office Marine Records, log of *Winchester*.
26. *Ibid.*
27. Although the verandah, that most characteristic feature of the Anglo-Indian house, was then not as common as it became later in the century.
28. Francis Collection, Box 58, Betsy Francis to Francis, June 17, 1774.
29. Orme MSS, Vol. 37, Smith to Orme, January 7, 1767.
30. Powis Collection, Box VII, Clive to his cousin, February 16, 1744/5.
31. *Ibid.*, Clive to his father, September 10, 1744.
32. Sir John Malcolm, *op. cit.*, Vol. I, p. 45.
33. One can detect in this the seeds of the superiority which the Indian Civil Servant, the direct descendant of the Company Servant, was to feel over the businessman or 'box wallah'; though of course in the 1740s the Company Servants and free merchants were all equally in trade.

34. Fowke Collection, Vol. 21, Margaret Clive to Mrs Casamajor, December 7, 1775.
35. Powis Collection, Box VII, Clive to his father, September 10, 1744.
36. Basically arak and water, but with five ingredients in all, hence its name, from *panch*, the Indian for five.
37. Powis Collection, Box VII, Clive to his father, September 10, 1744.
38. *Ibid.*, January 31, 1745/6 (? 44/5), quoted in Sir George Forrest, *op. cit.*, Vol. I, p. 23. (January 21, 1745 in Powis Catalogue—the letter itself is missing.)
39. *Ibid.*
40. *Ibid.*
41. According to the story, which is told in the *Biographia Britannica* article, he duly apologized and was invited by the Secretary to dinner, to which he ungraciously replied: 'No, sir, the Governor did not command me to *dine* with you.'
42. The story is mentioned by no earlier writer than Malcolm, whose authority for it is merely that it was 'long current'.
43. Clive to his father, quoted in Sir George Forrest, *op. cit.*, Vol. I, p. 23.
44. Powis Collection, Box VII, Clive to Daniel Bayley, December 12, 1744.
45. The inhabitants of Madras did, however, suffer from one particular inconvenience in Clive's time: the *dhobis* lived out in the country and only delivered the laundry once a month. But while showing themselves to be both modern and Western in this respect, they adhered to the traditional practice of beating the clothes against a stone, so that, as Clive lamented to his father, 'in eight or ten times washing they are all in rags'.
46. In Madras in the mid-eighteenth century, as indeed today, the European was addressed by servants and others as Master or Madam. Sahib and Memsahib belong further north, and to a later period.
47. Ormathwaite Collection, Vol. II, Eliza Walsh, later Fowke, February 1, 1750.
48. The Indians themselves sometimes did so. Thus Nubkissen, Clive's 'political banyan' of later years, was to write to him: 'Both black and white rejoiced with me and praised God for the many blessings Your Lordship brought upon us.' Powis Collection, Box 52, Nubkissen to Clive, March 25, 1768.
49. A century later they would have been despised as Eurasians. Even in Clive's day Horace Walpole spoke sneeringly of the daughter of one of these Madras families as that 'most deplorable sooty gentlewoman'.
50. Sir John Malcolm, *op. cit.*, Vol. I, p. 38.
51. Powis Collection, Box 21, Father Severini to Clive, March 5, 1754.
52. It may have been originally built up by a seventeenth-century Governor, the scholarly Elihu Yale, benefactor of the University of his native Massachusetts which bears his name.

53. Home Miscellaneous Series, Vol. 260, pp. 1–54.
54. Much of this comes from the diary of Ananda Ranga Pillai, Dupleix's Indian factor, who had Oriental ideas about a woman's place and consequently hated Madame.
55. Ananda Ranga Pillai, *Diary* (English translation, Madras 1904–22), Vol. II, pp. 39–45.
56. *Ibid.*, Vol. II, p. 319.
57. Yvonne Robert Gaebelé, *Créole et Grande Dame* (Pondicherry 1956), p. 135.
58. B.M. 44061, Clive to Orme, July 9, 1762.
59. Arnold-Forster MSS, Lady Clive to Mrs and Miss Maskelyne, June 1812.

CHAPTER II

1. The house still stands, and looks much as it does in a sketch made by Clive himself, or under his close supervision. Orme MSS, Vol. 333, p. 29.
2. He was officially only a Deputy-Governor, in that Fort St David was subordinate to the Presidency at Madras, but he was now acting instead of Morse.
3. This again first appears in the *Biographia Britannica* article.
4. *Biographia Britannica.*
5. Dispatch from Fort St David, quoted in Sir George Forrest, *op. cit.*, Vol. I, p. 61.
6. Lawrence was born at Hereford.
7. Yvonne Robert Gaebelé, *op. cit.*, pp. 135–6.
8. Powis Collection, Box 20, Clive to Richard Court, January 24, 1747/8.
9. B.M. 44061, Clive to Orme, 1762.
10. *Ibid.*
11. Gaebelé, *op. cit.*, pp. 183–9.
12. B.M. 44061, Clive to Orme, 1762.
13. Madras Public Proceedings, Gingens to Council, February 26, 1753. This incident is recounted in some detail in *Biographia Britannica.* Clive is said to have called Allen out; Allen then struck Clive from behind on the ear. This would have been punishable by cashiering, but Clive was content merely to lay his cane gently on Allen's head and declare that 'he was too contemptible a coward even for a beating'. Next day, according to the story, Allen resigned his commission.
14. Gaebelé, *op. cit.*, pp. 197–8.
15. Ormathwaite Collection, Vol. II, letter from Eliza Walsh, 1749.
16. Orme India MSS, Vol. II, pp. 490–1, Dalton to Clive, July 26, 1752.

17. Ormathwaite Collection, Vol. II, letter from Eliza Walsh, 1749.
18. *Ibid.*
19. Orme MSS, Vol. 288, Dalton to Clive, October 21, 1752. A recent work (*The Rape of India* by Allen Edwardes, New York 1966) portrays Clive as an insatiable amorist. But the author himself describes his chief source of material as 'often fragmented and of doubtful authorship and/or authenticity'. This is borne out by the fact that his account of Clive's earlier life is based on a document described as the Journal of Dr John Rae, who is referred to by the author as 'Civil Surgeon at Fort St George' during the period when Clive was there as a young man; whereas the records of the East India Company make it clear that there was no surgeon called Rae either at Madras or elsewhere in India during the eighteenth century; nor does anybody of that name appear in the lists of European residents at Madras and the neighbouring settlement of Fort St David, between 1741 and 1758.
20. Dodwell, *op. cit.*, p. 41.
21. *Ibid.*, pp. 19–20.
22. Fort St David Consultations, March 3, 1748/9.
23. *Ibid.*
24. *Ibid.*, statement of Captain James Cope.
25. Madras Records, Dispatches to England, General Letter, November 2, 1749.
26. Fort St David Consultations, Clive's statement, March 3, 1748/9.
27. *Ibid.*, Dalton's statement.
28. *Ibid.*, Fordyce's complaint.
29. Madras Records, Dispatches to England, General Letter, November 2, 1749.
30. Thomas Babington, Lord Macaulay, Essay on Clive.
31. *Cambridge History of India*, Vol. V, p. 117.
32. Chanda Sahib was a Muslim; his name, which sounds Hindu, was in fact a pseudonym. His son, Raza Sahib, was generally referred to by the English of the time as 'Raja Sahib', which makes things even more confusing, Raja being a title never held by Muslims.
33. Prosper Cultru, *Dupleix, ses plans politiques, sa disgrace* (Paris 1901), p. xi.
34. Robert, Lord Clive, *Letter to the Proprietors of the East India Stock* (London 1764), p. 4.
35. Orme India MSS, Vol. I, pp. 219–25, Clive's account of the two attacks on Devikottai.
36. *Ibid.*, some details from Robert Orme, *History of the Military Transactions of the British Nation in Indostan* (London 1763–78), Vol. I, p. 115.
37. This is from the contemporary printed version of Lawrence's narrative, in R. O. Cambridge, *Account of the War in India* (Dublin 1761), p. 14. In the three manuscript versions the name Pondicherry appears instead of Devikottai. But as the narrative was 'ghosted' for Lawrence, these are not

necessarily more reliable than the printed version. The fact that Lawrence was a prisoner during the Siege of Pondicherry suggests that Devikottai is correct.

38. Clive, quoted in Sir George Forrest, *op. cit.*, Vol. I, p. 109.
39. In his first draft, he made a rude remark about Boscawen, then crossed it out. Powis Collection, Box I.
40. Madras Public Proceedings, February 7, 1753; Powis Collection, Box XVII; Orme MSS, Vol. 287.
41. There is a story of how, when he was more senior, he asked a young man in the Company service what profession his father was. The young man replied that he was a saddler, whereupon Orme asked: 'Why did he not breed you up a saddler?' The young man asked Orme what profession *his* father was, to which Orme replied: 'My father, Sir, was a gentleman', to which the young man retorted: 'Pray sir, be so good as to inform me why he did not breed you up as a gentleman.' Love, *Vestiges of Old Madras* (London 1913), Vol. II, p. 423.
42. Madras Records, Letters to Fort St George, Lawrence, Starke and Powney to Prince, August 8, 1750.
43. Powis Collection, Box VII, Clive to Brown, December 13, 1750.
44. Ormathwaite Collection, Vol. II, Eliza Fowke to her aunts, February 5, 1750/1.
45. *Ibid.*, Eliza Fowke to her aunt Fanny, August 1, 1751.

CHAPTER III

1. Ananda Ranga Pillai, *op. cit.*, Vol. VI, pp. 184–6 and 212–13.
2. Philip Woodruff, *The Men who Ruled India* (London, edition of 1963), Vol. I, p. 82.
3. Ormathwaite Collection, Vol. II, Elizabeth Fowke to her aunts, September 13, 1750.
4. *Ibid.*, October 10, 1750.
5. The removal of Floyer was the work of the Reverend Mr Fordyce, who, when he returned to England, revenged himself on the Governor and Council by telling the Directors of their addiction to gaming. This charge turned out to be true, and after some enquiries Floyer and all his Council were dismissed.
6. Orme to Payne, March 11, 1758, quoted in Love, *op. cit.*, Vol. II, p. 489.
7. John Dalton's Journal.

8. Madras Records, Country Correspondence, Mohammed Ali to Saunders, received June 30, 1751.
9. Orme states that he had 300 sepoys: Stringer Lawrence's narrative puts the number at 500, Forrest at 600.
10. Orme MSS, Vol. 14, pp. 157–66, 'The Sergeant's Diary'.
11. Home Miscellaneous Series, Vol. 211. Considerations on the former and present state of the East India Company by Clive, November 24, 1772.
12. Powis Collection, Box 20, Prince to Clive, August 29, 1751.
13. *Ibid.*, September 10, 1751; Saunders to Clive, September 17, 1751.
14. Orme, *History*, Vol. I, p. 183.
15. Ananda Ranga Pillai, *op. cit.*, Vol. VIII, p. 60.
16. Orme, *History*, Vol. I, p. 184.
17. Orme MSS, Vol. 287, Saunders to Clive, September 3 and 6, 1751.
18. *Ibid.*, September 6, 1751.
19. *Ibid.*, September 3, 1751.
20. *Ibid.*, Prince to Clive, September 5, 1751.
21. Powis Collection, Box 20, Prince to Clive, September 8, 1751.
22. Orme MSS, Vol. 287, Pigot to Clive, September 6, 1751.
23. The fort at Arcot was meant as an inner citadel, the city having originally been surrounded by an outer wall five miles in circuit. According to Orme, this wall no longer existed in 1751, which is surely an exaggeration; two hundred years ago there must have been more left than there is today, when only the massive Delhi Gate remains standing.
24. Orme MSS, Vol. 287, Prince to Clive, September 5, 1751.
25. Orme, *History*, Vol. I, p. 185; Orme MSS, Vol. 14, pp. 157–66, 'The Sergeant's Diary'.
26. John Dalton's Journal.
27. Orme MSS, Vol. 14, pp. 157–66, 'The Sergeant's Diary'.
28. Virginia Thompson, *Dupleix* (New York 1933), pp. 296–8.
29. Ananda Ranga Pillai, *op. cit.*, Vol. VIII, p. 65.
30. Virginia Thompson, *op. cit.*, pp. 296–8.
31. Ananda Ranga Pillai, *op. cit.*, Vol. VIII, p. 65.
32. Powis Collection, Vol. 20, Prince to Clive, September 29, 1751.
33. Orme, *History*, Vol. I, p. 189.
34. Fort St David Consultations, October 21, 1751.
35. Orme MSS, Vol. 14, pp. 153–6, 'The Sergeant's Diary'.
36. Orme, *History*, Vol. I, p. 189.
37. *Ibid.*; Powis Collection, Box 20, Prince to Clive, October 29, November 1, 1751.
38. Fort St David Consultations, October 21, 1751.
39. Virginia Thompson, *op. cit.*, p. 299.
40. Orme, *History*, Vol. I, p. 190.

41. Orme MSS, Vol. 14, pp. 157–66, 'The Sergeant's Diary'.
42. The Rajah was a minor.
43. Orme, *History*, Vol. I, p. 192.
44. Powis Collection, Box 20, Prince to Clive, November 4, 1751.
45. John Dalton's Journal.
46. Fort St David Consultations, November 18, 1751.
47. Orme, *History*, Vol. I, p. 194.
48. *Ibid.*
49. Virginia Thompson, *op. cit.*, pp. 300–1.
50. Orme, *History*, Vol. I, p. 194.
51. Virginia Thompson, *op. cit.*, pp. 300–1.
52. Orme MSS, Vol. 14, pp. 157–66, 'The Sergeant's Diary'.
53. Orme, *History*, Vol. I, p. 195.
54. Philip Woodruff, *op. cit.*, Vol. I, p. 88.
55. It was hard to estimate the enemy losses. Orme puts their killed and wounded at 400, the sergeant at 200.
56. Orme, *History*, Vol. I, pp. 195–6; Orme MSS, Vol. 14, pp. 157–66, 'The Sergeant's Diary'.
57. Orme MSS, Vol. 288, Mohammed Ali to Clive, undated.
58. Orme MSS, Vol. 287, Saunders to Clive, December 8, 1751. When the news of the siege reached England in the following spring, Clive's father is said to have remarked of him: 'After all the booby has sense.' But as there appear to be no surviving letters between Clive and his family from 1746 to the end of 1752, his father's attitude to him at this time is a matter of speculation.

CHAPTER IV

1. Orme MSS, Vol. 14, pp. 157–66, 'The Sergeant's Diary'.
2. Powis Collection, Box 20, Prince to Clive, December 3, 1751.
3. Orme, *History*, Vol. I, pp. 197–9; Orme MSS, Vol. 14, pp. 157–66, 'The Sergeant's Diary'.
4. Orme, *History*, Vol. I, p. 199; Orme India MSS, Vol. II, p. 297, Clive's account of Arni.
5. Powis Collection, Box 20, Prince to Clive, November 19, December 3, 1751.
6. Fort St David Consultations, December 9, 1751.
7. Madras Records, French Correspondence 1752, Depositions of Robert

Revell, William Leemin and James Crighton, July 19, 1752, December 11, 1751.

8. Fort St David Consultations, December 14, 1751.
9. Orme MSS, Vol. 14, Wilson to Orme, December 16, 1751.
10. *Ibid.*
11. Orme, *History*, Vol. I, p. 200.
12. Madras Records, French Correspondence, Deposition of Robert Revell, July 19, 1752. Orme implies that the letter did reach Clive, and says nothing of Moden Sahib's intervention.
13. Powis Collection, Box 20, Prince to Clive, December 15, 1751.
14. *Ibid.*, December 14, 1751.
15. John Dalton's Journal.
16. *Ibid.*
17. Powis Collection, Box 20, Prince to Clive, February 20, 1752.
18. Fort St David Consultations, February 24, 1752. Orme, writing long afterwards, put the strength of the enemy at much more: 400 Europeans, 2000 sepoys and 2500 horse. One suspects this to be the usual European exaggeration of Indian numbers, if not part of Orme's build-up of Clive, for which Clive himself may or may not have been responsible. Orme, *History*, Vol. I, p. 209.
19. Fort St David Consultations, February 24, 1752.
20. One can comfortably visit most of his battlefields in a day's excursion from Madras.
21. Fort St David Consultations, March 2, 1752.
22. Orme India MSS, Vol. II, pp. 299–300.
23. The impression conveyed by Orme and by Malcolm and other writers is that the idea of the surprise attack was originally Clive's, and that he sent Shawlum to reconnoitre for this purpose. But Clive's own account of the battle makes it clear that the idea originated with Shawlum, who was sent out to find an escape route. Dalton, though a friend of Clive's, goes so far as to say that Shawlum told another officer of his discovery, and that this officer – presumably Keene – immediately set off with a detachment on his own initiative. This would suggest that Clive had no hand at all in the affair. But it seems unlikely that Keene would have undertaken an enterprise of this sort, involving so many troops, without orders from Clive.
24. Orme India MSS, Vol. II, pp. 299–300; Orme, *History*, Vol. I, pp. 210–12.
25. Madras Records, French Correspondence 1752, letter from a French surgeon.
26. Fort St David Consultations, March 2, 1752.
27. Orme MSS, Vol. 14, pp. 157–66, 'The Sergeant's Diary'.
28. Dupleix to Law, March 14, 1752, quoted in Virginia Thompson, *op. cit.*, p. 307.

29. In a footnote to his translation of Ananda Ranga Pillai's *Diary* (Vol. VIII, p. 120), Dodwell states that Keene deserted to the French at the end of 1750. If this is true, and if Keene had subsequently returned to the English side, it would show his role in yet another light—as a sort of double agent. However, from the records, it seems that Keene did not desert and that the deserter in question was a private or N.C.O. named Kane. Clive's report of Kaveripak as recorded in the Consultations makes no mention of Keene, except to say that he was wounded.
30. Dupleix to Véry, March 22, 1752, quoted in Virginia Thompson, *op. cit.*, p. 309.
31. Lawrence Narrative, quoted in R. O. Cambridge, *op. cit.*, p. 11.
32. Fort St David Consultations, March 9, 1752.
33. There has been some divergence of opinion among historians as to how far this ill-fated monument existed. Malcolm and Macaulay took it that the column was already up: other writers doubt if there was any monument there at all. The version given above, which seems the most likely, comes from Clive's account and Lawrence's Narrative.
34. In the words of Macaulay, '[Clive] cheerfully placed himself under the orders of his old friend'. But there would have been no question of his doing otherwise. He was still the most junior captain; had Lawrence not returned, he would, on reaching Trichinopoly, have come under the command of the ineffective Gingens.
35. One of the younger commanders in the Mysore army was Hyder Ali, who lived to displace the Mysore Rajahs and was to threaten the extinction of English power in India.
36. John Dalton's Journal.
37. Dupleix to Law, quoted in Sir George Forrest, *op. cit.*, Vol. I, p. 171.
38. Lawrence's Narrative, quoted in R. O. Cambridge, *op. cit.*, p. 60.
39. *Ibid.*
40. Orme MSS, Vol. 287, Dalton to Clive, April 14, 1752.
41. Orme gives the credit for this daring plan to Clive; modern historians are undecided as to whether the idea was his, or Lawrence's. Thus S. C. Hill, in the introduction to his catalogue of the Orme MSS, assumes that the idea was Lawrence's. Dodwell, however, quotes a letter written by Dalton to Clive in May as proof that Clive actually did think out this plan. But this letter refers to another plan, later in the campaign. (Henry Dodwell, *Dupleix and Clive*, London, edition of 1967, p. 63 and note.)
42. Dupleix to Law, quoted in Sir George Forrest, *op. cit.*, Vol. I, p. 179.
43. Orme India MSS, Vol. II, Lawrence to Clive, April 13, 1752.
44. John Dalton's Journal.
45. Lawrence Narrative in Palk MSS.
46. Orme India MSS, Vol. II, pp. 302–5.

47. Orme India MSS, Vol. II, Lawrence to Clive, April 16, 1752. Clive later spoke of the hanging of three more of the English deserters, but there is no mention of this in the Consultations, nor is there any complaint about it from Dupleix, who made a major issue of the execution of Kelsey, demanding that Lawrence should be tried for this 'despotic' act. It is typical of Clive's disregard for detail that he persistently referred to Kelsey as Kelsall, this being the name of some highly respectable cousins of the Maskelynes and Walshs with whom he was on friendly terms. Orme makes Kelsey into an Irishman, with no apparent grounds for doing so. No doubt it sounded better to his English readers.
48. *Ibid.*
49. Madras Public Proceedings, April 27, 1752.
50. Orme India MSS, Vol. III, Clive to Lawrence, April 1752.
51. *Ibid.*, Vol. II, Lawrence to Clive, April 20, 1752.
52. To make matters worse for the 'Old Gentleman', he failed to receive the wine and other good things from D'Auteuil's stores which Dalton had promised him.
53. John Dalton's Journal.
54. Orme, *History*, Vol. I, p. 230.
55. Madras Records, French Correspondence, Deposition of Lawrence, August 3, 1752.
56. *Ibid.*, Dupleix to Saunders, May 31, 1752.
57. Orme, *History*, Vol. I, p. 231.
58. Orme MSS, Vol. 287, Madame Duplans to D'Auteuil, May 30, 1752.
59. Madras Records, French Correspondence, Deposition of D'Auteuil, in a letter from Dupleix to Saunders, June 18, 1752; Deposition of Clive, August 21, 1752; Orme India MSS, Vol. II, Lawrence to Clive, May 30, 1752; Madras Public Proceedings, June 8, 1752.
60. Madras Records, French Correspondence, Law to Clive and Repington, August 30, 1752.
61. It was said that he died on the very spot where, sixteen years earlier, he had deceived the widowed Rani of Trichinopoly in an attempt to rob her of her jewels, which, rather than that he should get them, she had ordered to be ground into powder (John Dalton's Journal).
62. Madras Records, French Correspondence, Deposition of Lawrence, August 3, 1752.
63. Ananda Ranga Pillai, *op. cit.*, Vol. VIII, p. 114.
64. *Ibid.*, p. 265.
65. Virginia Thompson, *op. cit.*, pp. 439–41.

CHAPTER V

1. Powis Collection, Box 20, Boddam to Clive, May 30, 1752.
2. Fowke Collection, Vol. 21, Margaret to Mrs Casamajor, December 7, 1775.
3. Powis Collection, Box XVII.
4. *Ibid.*, Dalton to Clive, July 26, 1752.
5. Orme India MSS, Vol. II, Dalton to Clive, July 1, 1752.
6. Powis Collection, Box 20, Robert Sloper to Clive, August 15, 1752. Clive's accounts for the campaign give a good idea of the multitude of servants, coolies and other hangers-on that were necessary for keeping his army in the field – 6 butlers, 6 fowlers, 6 washermen, 6 watermen, 13 coolies for tents, 6 tom-tom coolies, 24 hospital coolies, 18 smiths, 12 bellows-boys and 12 bullock-keepers, not to mention a European butcher. The accounts also give the actual names of the sepoy *subadars* – including that of the famous Cove Nagg – the most outstanding of those Indian soldiers whom Clive trained. These men received 60 rupees a month, something between the pay of an English ensign and an English sergeant. An ordinary sepoy received 6 rupees a month, less than a quarter of the amount paid to an English private. (Orme MSS, Vol. 287, Clive's Account as Steward and Pay of Military Artillery.)
7. Powis Collection, Box 20, Repington to Clive, October 12, 1752.
8. Repington to Clive, quoted in Sir George Forrest, *op. cit.*, Vol. I, pp. 209–10.
9. Ananda Ranga Pillai, *op. cit.*, Vol. VIII, pp. 170–8.
10. Orme, *History*, Vol. I, pp. 263–4.
11. Madras Public Proceedings, Saunders to Lawrence, December 11, 1752.
12. Orme MSS, Vol. 288, Dalton to Clive, October 21, 1752.
13. Powis Collection, Box XV, Clive to Margaret, October 14, 1764.
14. Sutton Court Collection, Box I, Margaret to Carnac, June 8, 1759.
15. Lawrence Narrative in Palk MSS.
16. Orme MSS, Vol. 288, Lawrence to Clive, December 9, 1752.
17. Powis Collection, Box III, Clive to Lawrence, 1753.
18. Powis Collection, Box 21, Maskelyne to Clive, April 19, 1753.

CHAPTER VI

1. Royal Maritime Museum 9956, Clive to Pocock, July 22, 1757.
2. Court Minutes, Vol. 65, October 31, 1753; February 6, 1754.
3. Francis Collection, Vol. 56, Margaret to Francis, November 27, 1777.

4. Powis Collection, Box 27, William Smyth King to Clive, July 13, 1759.
5. Powis Collection, Box 20, Joseph Vere to Clive, December 18, 1752; Powis Collection, Box 21, letters from Benjamin and George Barker.
6. Powis Collection, Box III, Clive to Maskelyne, March 3, 1754 (incorrectly dated 1751 in catalogue); *ibid.*, Clive to Pigot, 1754.
7. Orme MSS, Vol. 288, Clive to Walsh, undated draft.
8. *Ibid.*, Robert James to Clive, December 3, 1754, and memorandum by Clive.
9. Clive to a friend in Madras, quoted in Sir George Forrest, *op. cit.*, Vol. I, pp. 228–9.
10. Powis Collection, Box III, Clive to Pigot, 1754.
11. Clive to a friend in Madras, quoted in Sir George Forrest, *op. cit.*, Vol. I, pp. 228–9.
12. Powis Collection, Box III, Clive to Pigot, 1754.
13. Arnold-Forster MSS, Margaret to Nevill Maskelyne, undated.
14. As a judge, he is remembered for two things, his ruling that a surgeon was an inferior tradesman, and his remark, when someone in his court complained that he was asleep, 'I'm awake enough to hang you.' (Information given by Lady Mary Clive. The story of his remark in court is family tradition.)
15. Namier and Brooke, *History of Parliament, House of Commons, 1754–1790* (London 1964), Vol. I, p. 234.
16. Powis Collection, Vol. 21, Robert James to Clive, March 20, 1755.
17. Powis Collection, Vol. VII, Sandwich to Clive, March 1755.
18. Writing to Clive three years later, John Dalton described himself as living just this sort of life as a small country squire in Yorkshire: 'I have upwards of £700 a year which last affords me two dishes a day, a bottle of port, a post chaise for my wife and three hunters and a pack of beagles for myself. It is now almost three years since I was clapt [*sic*] so that I am grown so fat you'd hardly know me.' (Powis Collection, Box 23, Dalton to Clive, December 5, 1757.)
19. Orme MSS, Vol. 288, undated draft. Clive's father suggested that while he was waiting for the ship to sail he should stand for Parliament at Dover: 'You have a fair opportunity to disappoint the D—— of N—— and after you are elected you may proceed on the voyage.' (Powis Collection, Box 21, Richard Clive to Clive, April 18, 1755.) As the most powerful private 'interest' at Dover was that of Lord Hardwicke, the idea might not have been all that far-fetched. Clive, however, treated it with 'banter'.
20. Powis Collection, Box VII, Richard Clive to Clive, April 29, 1755.

CHAPTER VII

1. Dodwell, *Nabobs of Madras*, p. 109.
2. Clive to Roger Drake, January 31, 1756, quoted in Sir George Forrest, *op. cit.*, Vol. I, p. 259.
3. Ormathwaite Collection, Vol. III, Sarah Mathison to John Walsh, March 28, 1756.
4. *Ibid.*, November 27, 1755.
5. *Ibid.*, March 28, 1756.
6. *Ibid.*
7. The 39th Regiment, which consequently bore the title 'Primus in Indis'.
8. Clive MS. 63, Clive to his father, January 31, 1756.
9. Clive to William Mabbot, quoted in Sir George Forrest, *op. cit.*, Vol. I, pp. 260–2.
10. *Ibid.*
11. Edward Ives, *A Voyage from England to India in the Year 1754* (London 1773), pp. 83–4.
12. *Ibid.*, pp. 87–8.
13. *An Authentic and Faithful History of that Arch Pirate Tulaji Angria* (London 1756), pp. 67–8; R. O. Cambridge, *op. cit.*, p. 161.
14. Edward Ives, *op. cit.*, pp. 86–7.
15. Clive to Bombay Council, April 21, 1756, quoted in Sir George Forrest, *op. cit.*, Vol. I, p. 267.
16. Orme MSS, Vol. 289, Henry Speke to Orme, June 9, 1755.
17. Powis Collection, Box VII, Richard Clive to Clive, December 20, 1755.
18. Letters preserved in Fort St George, Madras: from Clive, July 10, 1756; Clive to Pigot and Council, July 14, 1756; Clive and Pigot to Select Committee, July 6, 1756.

CHAPTER VIII

1. Karam Ali, *Muzaffar-Namah*, in *Bengal Nawabs* (Calcutta, the Asiatic Society, 1952), p. 62.
2. Ghulam Husain Khan, *Seir Mutakherin* (manuscript version), Vol. II, p. 125.
3. In writing to the Directors about these works, the Calcutta Council spoke of their being intended 'for the defence of the place against a country [meaning an Indian] enemy' (C. R. Wilson, *Old Fort William in Bengal* (London 1906), Vol. II, p. 31). In the event, they proved inadequate to this

purpose—the Nawab's spies over-estimated their strength, and even mistook an octagonal summer-house built by one of the Kelsall family for a fort.

4. Karam Ali, *op. cit.*, p. 63.
5. Voltaire, who followed these events with interest, had an interesting theory to explain why Drake was, as he put it, 'a very different man from the famous Admiral Drake', namely, that he was a concealed Quaker. Quoted in S. C. Hill, *Bengal in 1756–7* (London 1905), Vol. III, pp. 241–2.
6. Orme MSS, Vol. 28, Orme to Payne, November 3, 1756.
7. Public Dispatches from England, August 3, 1757, quoted in Henry Dodwell, *Dupleix and Clive*, p. 124n.
8. Hill, *op. cit.*, Vol. I, p. 239.
9. *Ibid.*, p. 242.
10. *Ibid.*, p. 227.
11. Powis Collection, Box 20, John Brown to Clive, February 27, 1751/2.
12. Hill, *op. cit.*, Vol. I, p. 228.
13. Powis Collection, Box I, Orme to Clive, August 25, 1752.
14. Powis Collection, Box III, Clive to William Belchier etc., October 6, 1756.
15. Orme MSS, Vol. 28, Orme to Payne, November 11, 1756.
16. Ghulam Husain, *op. cit.*, p. 48; Karam Ali, *op. cit.*, p. 64.
17. According to Karam Ali, Siraj-ud-daula had wanted to pull down the *liwan* of Manik Chand's house because it spoilt the view from his newly-built palace (*op. cit.*, p. 59). The English were later to speak of him as a friend, causing a modern Indian writer (Ram Gopal, *How the British Occupied Bengal* [London 1963], p. 122) to suggest that he was working for them all along. He was, however, to fight a battle against Clive, and he was regarded by the English as the chief plunderer of the Company's effects.
18. Hill, *op. cit.*, Vol. II, p. 56.
19. Home Miscellaneous Series, Vol. 193, Manik Chand to Clive, December 19, 1756.
20. Hill, *op. cit.*, Vol. II, p. 71.
21. *Ibid.*, p. 74. It is not as abject as Dodwell suggests, when he states that it began by addressing Siraj-ud-daula as 'Sacred and godlike Prince' (*Dupleix and Clive*, p. 125). In fact those epithets apply not to Siraj-ud-daula but to Salabat Jang.
22. Hill, *op. cit.*, Vol. II, p. 76.
23. Powis Collection, Box 21, William Forth to Roger Drake Jr, December 26, 1756.
24. Hill, *op. cit.*, Vol. II, pp. 166–7.
25. Bengal Select Committee Consultations, September 20 and 23, 1756.
26. According to Orme, Manik Chand surprised Clive's troops when they were

asleep, and unguarded by sentries. This seems unlikely, for we know that at the time when he attacked, the English were expecting the garrison from the fort to approach at any moment. Orme here seems deliberately to be finding fault with Clive, for he goes on to say that had Manik Chand attacked with his cavalry as well as with his infantry, the skirmish might well have proved fatal to the English. But as Malcolm points out, it would have been impossible for cavalry to fight in such thickly wooded country. It is significant that this should be in Orme's second volume which he wrote when his relations with Clive were less cordial. Malcolm was himself a soldier with experience of wars in India only a generation after the time of Clive. (Orme, *History*, Vol. I, p. 124; Sir John Malcolm, *op. cit.*, Vol. I, p. 154).

27. Hill, *op. cit.*, Vol. II, p. 97.
28. *Loc. cit.*
29. *Ibid.*, p. 73.
30. Hill, *op. cit.*, Vol. III, pp. 40–1.
31. He was rebuked by Watson for his irregular behaviour, after which he was heard to say: 'If I am flogged for this here action, I will never take another fort by myself as long as I live, by God!'
32. Edward Ives, *op. cit.*, p. 101 and note.
33. *Ibid.*, p. 102.
34. Hill, *op. cit.*, Vol. II, p. 96.
35. *Ibid.*, p. 77.
36. Edward Ives, *op. cit.*, p. 102.
37. Powis Collection, Box 22, Speke to Clive, January 2, 1757.
38. Edward Ives, *op. cit.*, pp. 102–3.
39. Hill, *op. cit.*, Vol. II, p. 96.

CHAPTER IX

1. Hill, *op. cit.*, Vol. III, p. 91.
2. *Ibid.*, Vol. II, pp. 209–10.
3. *Ibid.*, pp. 92–5, 121–2.
4. *Ibid.*, p. 123.
5. *Ibid.*, p. 97.
6. *Ibid.*, p. 132.
7. *Ibid.*, Vol. I, p. 229.
8. Home Miscellaneous Series, Vol. 193, Clive to Manik Chand, January 8, 1757.

9. It has been suggested that he was being deliberately gloomy, so as to encourage Pigot to send reinforcements – a ploy that was to be adopted by Wellington. But Clive knew that Pigot had given him everything he could spare; he was fully conscious of the danger to Madras from Pondicherry. Far from hoping for any more troops from Madras, he expected to be recalled there at any time, or anyhow to be asked to send back part of his force.
10. Hill, *op. cit.*, Vol. II, p. 96.
11. *Ibid.*, p. 97.
12. Edward Ives, *op. cit.*, p. 110n.
13. Clive dressed these troops in a modified version of English military uniform. They were the first Indian soldiers to be dressed in this way and were known as the *Lal Paltan* or 'Red Regiment'; from them originated the Bengal Native Infantry.
14. Home Miscellaneous Series, Vol. 193, Clive to Khwaja Wajid etc., January 8, 1757.
15. Orme India MSS, Vol. XVIII, Scrafton to Clive, December 17, 1757.
16. Hill, *op. cit.*, Vol. II, p. 104.
17. *Ibid.*, p. 110.
18. Hill, *op. cit.*, Vol. II, p. 130.
19. *Ibid.*, p. 133.
20. *Ibid.*, p. 178.
21. *Ibid.*, p. 208.
22. *Ibid.*, pp. 208–9.
23. Home Miscellaneous Series, Vol. 211, Clive's considerations on the former and present state of the East India Company, November 24, 1772.
24. *Ibid.*, Vol. 193, Clive to Siraj-ud-daula, February 3, 1757.
25. Hill, *op. cit.*, Vol. II, p. 176.
26. Luke Scrafton, *Reflections on the Government of Indostan* (London 1763), pp. 63–5.
27. The romantically-minded Jean Law believed that Walsh and Scrafton told Clive of the exact position of the tent in which the Nawab was sleeping, enabling the English army to make straight for it. The eighteenth-century Anglo-Indian use of the word 'garden' or 'gardens' to mean a country house has encouraged later writers to imagine, as Law did, that the Nawab was sleeping under canvas in the grounds of Omichand's house, whereas we have it on good authority that he was staying in the house itself. Clive would have had no need of the cloak-and-dagger methods described by Law to find this out, for Omichand's house was the obvious place in the vicinity of the camp where he would stay, and indeed he had stayed there in the previous June.

    Orme criticizes Clive for going through the camp, instead of approaching from the same side of the Ditch as Omichand's house (*History*, Vol. II, pp. 134–5). But had Clive approached from this side, the Nawab and the troops who were with him could easily have retreated across the Ditch and joined the rest of the army; whereas by coming from the other side, it should have been possible to keep the two sections of the enemy apart. And had he approached from the same side as the house, he would have had to start by throwing himself against the Nawab's best troops–by passing through the camp, he was first able to create a panic among the inferior troops and hangers-on, with good psychological effect.

28. According to Clive's evidence in the report of the 1772 Select Committee of the House of Commons, he himself 'went immediately on board Admiral Watson's ship' to ask for the sailors. But Watson, writing at the time, makes it clear that Clive sent Walsh with this request. This would certainly make more sense than that Clive should have wasted time and energy in going to Watson's flagship and coming back again. Perhaps there was an error in taking down the Select Committee evidence, and 'went' should have read 'sent'–or it may be an instance of Clive's bad memory for details.
29. Hill, *op. cit.*, Vol. II, p. 243.
30. *Ibid.*, pp. 212–13.
31. *Ibid.*, pp. 213–14. The fact that he also condemned Clive's 'conduct yesterday morning' could have been no more than a way of disarming the Nawab's suspicions, knowing that the letter would be read by his spies.
32. Luke Scrafton, *op. cit.*, p. 66.
33. Powis Collection, Box X, Watson to Clive, February 9, 1757.
34. Hill, *op. cit.*, Vol. II, pp. 243–4.
35. *Ibid.*, pp. 243–5.
36. Clive MS. 200, Clive to Stephen Law, February 23, 1757.
37. Hill, *op. cit.*, Vol. II, p. 243.
38. *Ibid.*, pp. 222–3.
39. *Ibid.*, p. 216.
40. *Ibid.*, pp. 222–3.
41. *Ibid.*, p. 240.
42. More correctly Amir Chand or Amin Chand, but I have kept to the eighteenth-century Anglicized version of the name, as being so much better known.
43. His imprisonment is said to have been followed by a ghastly scene when the women and children of his household either butchered themselves or were stabbed to death by his steward. (Hill, *op. cit.*, Vol. I, p. 142; Vol. II, p. 22.)
44. Hill, *op. cit.*, Vol. II, p. 227.

45. More correctly Nand Kumar, but as with Omichand, I prefer to keep to the familiar version of the name.
46. Hill, *op. cit.*, Vol. II, pp. 228–9.
47. *Ibid.*, p. 245.
48. *Ibid.*, p. 230.
49. *Ibid.*, pp. 268–9.
50. *Ibid.*, pp. 271–2.
51. At the same time, he was telling his Madras friends rather vaguely that he would return as soon as possible. (Hill, *op. cit.*, Vol. II, p. 267.)
52. Clive to Select Committee, quoted in Sir John Malcolm, *op. cit.*, Vol. I, p. 199.
53. Watts, *Memoirs of the Revolution in Bengal* (London 1764), p. 34.
54. Hill, *op. cit.*, Vol. II, p. 256.
55. *Ibid.*, p. 273.
56. *Ibid.*, p. 265.
57. Watts, *op. cit.*, p. 29.
58. Hill, *op. cit.*, Vol. III, p. 190.
59. *Ibid.*, Vol. II, p. 232.
60. Mervyn Davies, *op. cit.*, p. 182.
61. Hill, *op. cit.*, Vol. II, pp. 264–5.
62. *Ibid.*, p. 242.
63. *Ibid.*, pp. 263–4.
64. Powis Collection, Box 22, Becher to Clive, March 5, 1757.
65. Hill, *op. cit.*, Vol. II, pp. 270–1.
66. Bengal Select Committee Consultations, March 6, 1757; Hill, *op. cit.*, Vol. III, p. 311.
67. Hill, *op. cit.*, Vol. II, p. 277.
68. *Ibid.*, p. 275. It is notable how, in this letter, Clive makes use of Watson's arguments against the neutrality treaty, even though he apparently disregarded them three days before.
69. Clive MS. 199, Clive to Watts, March 7, 1757.
70. Hill, *op. cit.*, Vol. II, p. 280.
71. *Ibid.*, p. 281.
72. *Ibid.*, p. 279.
73. *Ibid.*, p. 282.
74. *Ibid.*, p. 280.
75. Powis Collection, Vol. X, Watson to Clive, March 10, 1757; Hill, *op. cit.*, Vol. II, p. 281.
76. Hill, *op. cit.*, Vol. II, p. 284.
77. Luke Scrafton, *op. cit.*, p. 71.
78. Clive mentioned this in a speech in the House of Commons sixteen years later; there does not seem to be any earlier record of the transaction.

79. Hill, *op. cit.*, Vol. III, pp. 259–60.
80. According to the translation of Ghulam Husain's *Seir Mutakherin*, Clive's artillery objected to having this French deserter in their corps. We learn, from the same source, that Terraneau later sent some of the money he had made in the English service back to his father, but the old man returned the money saying that he would have nothing to do with a traitor, which caused the son to hang himself.
81. Hill, *op. cit.*, Vol. II, p. 280.
82. *Ibid.*, p. 286; Powis Collection, Box X, Watts to Clive, March 16, 1757.
83. Home Miscellaneous Series, Vol. 193, Clive to Siraj-ud-daula, March 18, 1757.
84. Hill, *op. cit.*, Vol. II, pp. 287–8.
85. *Ibid.*, Vol. III, p. 192.
86. Home Miscellaneous Series, Vol. 193, Clive to Siraj-ud-daula, March 20, 1757.
87. *Ibid.*, Siraj-ud-daula to Clive, March 23, 1757.
88. Powis Collection, Box X, Watts to Clive, March 22, 1757.
89. According to Ghulam Husain, the French had purposely kept this passage clear and it was pointed out to the English by the traitor, Terraneau. But this is not corroborated elsewhere.
90. Hill, *op. cit.*, Vol. III, p. 115.
91. Edward Ives, *op. cit.*, pp. 132–3.
92. Admiral Stavorinus, 1769, quoted in George, Marquess Curzon of Kedleston, *British Government in India* (London 1925), Vol. I, p. 107.
93. Hill, *op. cit.*, Vol. II, p. 307.

CHAPTER X

1. Hill, *op. cit.*, Vol. II, p. 290.
2. *Ibid.*, p. 295.
3. Home Miscellaneous Series, Vol. 193, Siraj-ud-daula to Clive, March 24, 1757.
4. *Ibid.*, April 4, 1757.
5. Hill, *op. cit.*, Vol. II, p. 294.
6. *Ibid.*, p. 314.
7. *Ibid.*, p. 303.
8. Clive to Watts, quoted in Sir George Forrest, *op. cit.*, Vol. I, pp. 399–400.
9. Clive MS. 200, Clive to Payne, April 16, 1757.
10. Hill, *op. cit.*, Vol. II, p. 338.

11. *Ibid.*, pp. 304–5.
12. *Ibid.*, p. 305.
13. *Ibid.*, p. 304.
14. *Ibid.*, p. 319.
15. *Loc. cit.*
16. *Ibid.*, p. 321.
17. *Ibid.*, Vol. III, pp. 203–4.
18. Ghulam Husain, *op. cit.*, pp. 107–8.
19. Home Miscellaneous Series, Vol. 193, Siraj-ud-daula to Nundcomar, undated.
20. Hill, *op. cit.*, Vol. II, p. 318.
21. Powis Collection, Box 22, Watts to Clive, April 16, 1757.
22. Hill, *op. cit.*, Vol. II, pp. 321–2.
23. *Ibid.*, pp. 342–3.
24. Scrafton had himself thought of such a scheme when Watts, so to speak, put him in the picture on his arrival at Cossimbazar. Writing to Walsh on April 9, he compared Siraj-ud-daula's court to that of Ptolemy in Egypt, 'when Pompey fled there after the Battle of Pharsalia. That is, that the head and members are all as corrupt and as treacherous as possible, and the Colonel should be the Caesar to act as Caesar then did, take the kingdom under his protection, depose the old and give them a new king to make his subjects happy.' (Hill, *op. cit.*, Vol. III, pp. 342–3.)
25. *Ibid.*, p. 208.
26. *Ibid.*, Vol. II, p. 330.
27. *Ibid.*, p. 350.
28. *Ibid.*, pp. 349–50.
29. *Ibid.*, pp. 352–3 and 355–7.
30. *Ibid.*, pp. 364–5.
31. *Ibid.*, p. 363.
32. *Ibid.*, p. 369; Vol. III, p. 207.
33. Powis Collection, Box VIII, Watts to Clive, April 29, 1757.
34. Hill, *op. cit.*, Vol. II, p. 367.
35. Bengal Select Committee Consultations, May 1, 1757.
36. Hill, *op. cit.*, Vol. III, p. 304.
37. *Ibid.*, Vol. II, p. 372.
38. *Ibid.*, pp. 376–7.
39. *Ibid.*, p. 303.
40. *Ibid.*, pp. 368–9.
41. Clive MS. 204, Clive to Watts, May 10, 1757.
42. Hill, *op. cit.*, Vol. II, p. 373.
43. *Ibid.*, pp. 379–80.
44. *Ibid.*, pp. 378–9.

45. *Ibid.*, p. 379.
46. *Ibid.*, pp. 392–3.
47. Luke Scrafton, *op. cit.*, p. 79.
48. Hill, *op. cit.*, Vol. II, p. 394.
49. *Ibid.*, pp. 382–3.
50. *Loc. cit.*
51. *Ibid.*, Vol. III, p. 307.
52. Bengal Select Committee Consultations, May 17, 1757.
53. Hill, *op. cit.*, Vol. III, pp. 315–16.
54. Clive had suggested that there should be a clause in the treaty giving compensation to Omichand for his losses in the capture of Calcutta; and also that he should be allowed five per cent on all money received by the English from Mir Jafar. (Hill, *op. cit.*, Vol. II, pp. 377 and 380.)
55. Edward Ives, *op. cit.*, p. 147.
56. Hill, *op. cit.*, Vol. III, p. 320.
57. *Ibid.*, pp. 318–20.
58. Powis Collection, Box 22, Watson to Clive, May 3, 1757, and May 12, 1757.
59. *Ibid.*, June 17, 1757.
60. This was when, towards the end of May, the Nawab asked the English to sign a paper stating that he had fully discharged his obligations under the February Treaty. As part of his policy of 'soothing' the Nawab, Clive considered that it would be as well to promise him such an acquittance; and Watson agreed that this would be a good idea. (Powis Collection, Box 22, Watson to Clive, May 25, 1757.)
61. Hill, *op. cit.*, Vol. II, p. 386.
62. Watts, *op. cit.*, p. 91.
63. Hill, *op. cit.*, Vol. II, p. 394.
64. *Ibid.*, Vol. III, p. 239.
65. *Ibid.*, Vol. II, p. 397.
66. Scrafton had managed to see Mir Jafar on the 31st, before he left for Calcutta, but the meeting was short and achieved nothing.
67. Hill, *op. cit.*, Vol. II, p. 398.
68. *Loc. cit.*

CHAPTER XI

1. The success of the Jameson Raid depended on a rising of the malcontents in the Transvaal, which in the event never took place; just as the success

of Clive's enterprise depended on the so-called 'revolution' against Siraj-ud-daula.

2. Hill, *op. cit.*, Vol. II, p. 399.
3. Certainly when giving evidence before the Select Committee of the House of Commons in 1772, Clive stated in so many words that this was what he expected. 'When the army marched Mir Jafar had promised that he and his son would join them with a large force at Katwa.' (Hill, *op. cit.*, Vol. III, p. 316.)
4. *Loc. cit.*
5. Luke Scrafton, *op. cit.*, pp. 84–5.
6. Hill, *op. cit.*, Vol. II, p. 414.
7. Watts, *op. cit.*, p. 109.
8. Luke Scrafton, *op. cit.*, p. 84.
9. Hill, *op. cit.*, Vol. II, p. 419.
10. *Ibid.*, pp. 417–18, 419–20.
11. *Ibid.*, pp. 421–3; Orme MSS, Vol. V, Select Committee to Clive, June 23, 1757.
12. Hill, *op. cit.*, Vol. II, p. 431.
13. Powis Collection, Box 22, Speke to Clive, June 25, 1757.
14. Hill, *op. cit.*, Vol. III, p. 54.
15. Powis Collection, Box I.
16. Hill, *op. cit.*, Vol. II, p. 419.
17. Orme, *History*, Vol. II, p. 171. This scene is the subject of a relief on the base of Clive's statue in Whitehall, which was erected early this century under the auspices of Lord Curzon.
18. Macaulay, Essay on Clive.
19. Hill, *op. cit.*, Vol. III, pp. 316–17.
20. *Ibid.*, Vol. II, p. 419.
21. *Ibid.*, pp. 420–1.
22. *Ibid.*, p. 420.
23. *Ibid.*, Vol. III, p. 423. Clive made some mistakes in recounting the events of this time to the Select Committee of the House of Commons fifteen years later. He spoke of having to march 150 miles up country after crossing the river, whereas from Katwa to Murshidabad was only about 40 miles, and the whole distance from Calcutta to Murshidabad not much more than 100 miles. He referred to this Council of War as the only one he ever held, whereas in fact he held others; though he could have meant that this was the only Council of War he ever held when it was decided whether or not he should fight. (*Ibid.*, p. 316.)
24. *Ibid.*, Vol. II, p. 433; Vol. III, p. 55.
25. *Ibid.*, Vol. II, p. 457; Luke Scrafton, *op. cit.*, p. 84. Fifteen years later Clive's secretary, Henry Strachey, referred to the discrepancies between Coote's

journal and the other account of the battle, attributing them to the fact that Coote was 'very muddy headed'. Strachey was, of course, strongly prejudiced in favour of Clive; on the other hand he was a man of integrity and sharp intellect. (Powis Collection, Box 65, August 13, 1772.)

26. Hill, *op. cit.*, Vol. III, p. 317.
27. Memorandum in Powis MSS, quoted in Sir George Forrest, *op. cit.*, Vol. I, p. 445.
28. Hill, *op. cit.*, Vol. III, p. 54.
29. K. M. Panikkar, *Asia and Western Dominance* (London 1959), pp. 78–9.
30. Hill, *op. cit.*, Vol. III, p. 317.
31. In the two centuries since the battle, the river here has changed its course, so that the grove, hunting-lodge and other features of the battlefield have disappeared.
32. Luke Scrafton, *op. cit.*, p. 85.
33. Some of these beasts may have been clad in decorated metal plates, for Clive brought home a suit of elephant armour, now at the Tower of London, which is believed to be a trophy of that day.
34. Orme, *History*, Vol. II, pp. 173–4.
35. According to Karam Ali, Mir Jafar was said to have intended to murder Siraj-ud-daula on this occasion, but there were too many loyal troops present. (*Op. cit.*, p. 76.)
36. Ghulam Husain, *op. cit.*, pp. 113–15.
37. Hill, *op. cit.*, Vol. II, pp. 423–4.
38. Hill, *op. cit.*, Vol. III, p. 404.
39. Orme, *History*, Vol. II, p. 175.
40. Carraccioli, *op. cit.*, Vol. I, p. 33.

CHAPTER XII

1. Hill, *op. cit.*, Vol. II, pp. 426–7.
2. Luke Scrafton, *op. cit.*, p. 90.
3. Watts, *op. cit.*, p. 114.
4. Hill, *op. cit.*, Vol. II, p. 431.
5. Powis Collection, Box 22, Walsh to Clive, June 25, 1757.
6. Clive, *Letter to Proprietors of East India Stock* (London 1764), p. 18.
7. By Major John Caillaud (Orme MSS, Vol. 134).
8. Today, Murshidabad has shrunk, so as to give no idea of what it must have been like two centuries ago. The surviving buildings from those times—which include the palace where Mir Jafar lived before becoming Nawab,

with its turreted red brick gateway—are strung out along country lanes shaded by trees and sweet with wild jasmine.

9. Hill, *op. cit.*, Vol. III, p. 314.
10. Powis Collection, Box VI, anonymous testimony of Clive's character. I have found no earlier authority than Macaulay for the better known and more picturesque version of this speech, and suspect it originated from him, and that G. R. Gleig, the first of Clive's biographers to quote it (1848), merely put Macaulay's words into the first person and attributed them to Clive.
11. Clive, *Letter to Proprietors*, p. 23.
12. Ghulam Husain, *op. cit.*, p. 128.
13. Powis Collection, Vol. 23, Latham to Clive, July 5, 1757.
14. Clive MS. 200, Clive to Payne, November 11, 1757.
15. Orme India MSS, Vol. X, Clive and Watts to Committee, July 13, 1757.
16. Luke Scrafton, *op. cit.*, p. 96.
17. He pointed out how unthinkable it would have been for the Duke of Wellington to have accepted a present of £200,000 from Louis XVIII after Waterloo.
18. Watts, and other writers, introduce poetic justice by making the *fakir* into one of Siraj-ud-daula's victims, whose ears had been cut off by his orders. But Ghulam Husain says no more than that the former Nawab had probably 'disobliged or oppressed' the *fakir* in the days of his power; while Karam Ali, who was no less hostile to Siraj-ud-daula, calls the *fakir* a 'dark-hearted man' and makes no mention of his having had any grievances.
19. Luke Scrafton, *op. cit.*, p. 94. According to Karam Ali, Mir Jafar and Miran divided Siraj-ud-daula's wives and concubines between them. They both, 'out of brute passion', wanted Lutf-unnisa, but she said to them: 'Having ridden an elephant before, I cannot now agree to ride an ass.' (*Op. cit.*, p. 78.)
20. Hill, *op. cit.*, Vol. II, p. 444.
21. *Ibid.*, p. 462.
22. *Ibid.*, p. 445.
23. Orme India MSS, Vol. VII, Clive to Coote, July 13, 1757.
24. *Ibid.*, July 24, 1757.
25. Powis Collection, Box V, Coote to Clive, July 18, 1757.
26. Powis Collection, Box 24, Coote to Clive, January 23, 1758.
27. Thus he endeavoured to correct their exaggeration of the part he had played in making up Clive's mind for him before Plassey. (Hill, *op. cit.*, Vol. III, p. 322.)
28. Powis Collection, Box VII, Bussy to Margaret Clive, June 27, 1757.
29. National Maritime Museum 9956, Clive to Pocock, July 22, 1757.
30. Powis Collection, Box 23, Latham to Clive, September 9, 1757.

31. *Loc. cit.*
32. *Ibid.*, August 5, 1757.
33. Clive to Pigot, August 2, 1757, quoted in Sir George Forrest, *op. cit.*, Vol. II, p. 35.
34. Hill, *op. cit.*, Vol. III, p. 361.
35. *Ibid.*, Vol. II, p. 464.
36. Clive MS. 63, Clive to Sir Edward Clive, undated.
37. Hill, *op. cit.*, Vol. III, p. 361.
38. *Loc. cit.*
39. *Ibid.*, Vol. II, p. 464, quoted in Sir George Forrest, *op. cit.*, Vol. II, pp. 34–5.

CHAPTER XIII

1. Clive MS. 200, Clive to Belchier, August 21, 1757.
2. Hill, *op. cit.*, Vol. II, pp. 437–9.
3. *Encyclopaedia Britannica* (1966), article on Clive.
4. Clive MS. 200, Clive to Pigot, February 19, 1758.
5. Hill, *op. cit.*, Vol. II, p. 463.
6. Home Miscellaneous Series, Vol. 193, Clive to Salabat Jang, August 7, 1757.
7. *Ibid.*, Clive to Mohammed Ali, August 4, 1757.
8. *Ibid.*, Vol. 191, pp. 43–52.
9. Powis Collection, Box 23, Scrafton to Clive, October 8, 1757.
10. *Ibid.*, November 7, 1757.
11. Powis Collection, Box 27, Hastings to Clive, August 9, 1759.
12. Luke Scrafton, *op. cit.*, p. 99.
13. Abdul Majed Khan, *The Transition in Bengal* (Cambridge 1969), p. 23.
14. Orme India MSS, Vol. X, Clive to Sumner, June 4, 1758.
15. Hill, *op. cit.*, Vol. II, p. 444.
16. Powis Collection, Box 27, Clive to Hastings, September 21, 1759.
17. Clive to Directors, quoted in A. Mervyn Davies, *op. cit.*, p. 256.
18. A. Mervyn Davies, *op. cit.*, p. 257.
19. Orme India MSS, Vol. XVIII, Scrafton to Clive, December 17, 1757.
20. Powis Collection, Box 23, Scrafton to Clive, October 8, 1757.
21. Home Miscellaneous Series, Vol. 193, Clive to Mir Jafar, September 3, 1757.
22. *Ibid.*, July 15, 1757.
23. Powis Collection, Box XII, March 8, 1758, List of Presents sent by East India Company to Nawab.
24. Powis Collection, Box 24, Scrafton to Clive, March 18, 1758.

25. His supposed candidate, the youthful brother of Siraj-ud-daula, 'almost an idiot' according to Clive, was promptly executed on the Nawab's orders.
26. Third Report, Select Committee of House of Commons, 1772–3.
27. Orme India MSS, Vol. X, Clive to Committee, January 4, 1758.
28. Powis Collection, Box 23, Scrafton to Clive, November 7, 1757.
29. Luke Scrafton, *op. cit.*, pp. 102–3.
30. Orme India MSS, Vol. X, Clive to Scrafton, December 14, 1757.
31. *Ibid.*, Clive to Committee, November 4, 1757.
32. Luke Scrafton, *op. cit.*, p. 102.
33. Clive MS. 295, Clive to a *zemindar*, undated. Abstract of Persian Correspondence, Clive to Raja Tilokchand, February 7, 1759.
34. Clive MS. 261, Raja of Burdwan to Clive, July 10, 1759; *ibid.*, MS. 251, Raja of Burdwan to Clive, undated; *ibid.*, MS. 248, Nundcomar to Clive, September 19, 1758.
35. Clive MS. 261, Clive to Mir Jafar, July 20, 1759.
36. Clive MS. 268, Clive to Mir Jafar, December 5, 1759.
37. Clive MS. 263, Clive to Mir Jafar, December 4, 1759.
38. Microfilm from Pocock Papers, Ames Library of South Asia, Clive to Pocock, December 23, 1757.
39. According to Ghulam Husain, he obtained this protection by means of a trick. His agent prevailed on one of the Nawab's secretaries to draw up a letter confirming him in his office, securing his life and property and releasing him from arrears of revenue. This was shown to the Nawab for his approval after he had dined and, as Scrafton would have put it, 'over-banged himself'. Not very literate at the best of times, Mir Jafar now had no desire to read the letter, so he put his seal to it without ascertaining its contents. The letter was then taken to Clive for his endorsement which he naturally gave, imagining it to represent the Nawab's real intentions; and having thus pledged his word, he insisted that the Nawab should keep the agreement. Whatever truth there may be in this story—which at any rate serves to illustrate the reputation Clive had with the Indians for keeping his word—there was little need for Ramnarayan to go to such lengths, for it was in accordance with Clive's policy to give him his protection.
40. This may have been the occasion when the Nawab rebuked one of his commanders for allowing his troops to quarrel with those of Clive, and the officer replied: 'It would become me very ill indeed to quarrel with the Colonel, I that make every morning three prostrations to his jack-ass [meaning the Nawab], how then could I be daring enough to cope with the rider himself?'
41. Clive MS. 200, Clive to Pigot, February 19, 1758.
42. Ghulam Husain, *op. cit.*, p. 164.

43. Luke Scrafton, *op. cit.*, pp. 110–11.
44. Thus Dodwell (*Dupleix and Clive*, p. 146), who quotes Clive to Watts (Orme India MSS, Vol. X), August 4, 1758: 'I need not hint to you how many good purposes the Nawab's presence will answer.'
45. B.M. 29132, Scrafton to Hastings, August 27, 1758.
46. Orme India MSS, Vol. X, Clive to Watts, June 22, 1758.
47. Orme MSS, Vol. 28, Payne to Orme, February 18, 1758.
48. B.M. 29131, Clive to Hastings, August 31, 1758.
49. *Loc. cit.*
50. *Ibid.*, September 7, 1758.
51. Quoted in Keith Feiling, *Warren Hastings* (London, edition of 1966), p. 31.
52. B.M. 29131, Clive to Hastings, November 28, 1758.
53. Powis Collection, Box 25, Hastings to Clive, October 2, 1758.
54. B.M. 29131, Clive to Hastings, October 6, 1758.
55. *Ibid.*, May 13, 1759; B.M. 29096, Hastings to Clive, April 27 and 29, 1759.
56. B.M. 29132, Scrafton to Hastings, September, 26, 1758.
57. *Ibid.*, January 25, 1759.
58. *Ibid.*, October 12, 1758.
59. *Ibid.*, October 2, 1758.
60. Clive assured Hastings that he intended no slight against him in thus taking the management of the *tuncas* out of his hands; it was just that it seemed more diplomatic for the mortgaged revenues to be paid to the English at their places of origin, away from the resentful eyes of the Nawab and the great men.
61. Keith Feiling, *op. cit.*, p. 33.
62. B.M. 29131, Clive to Hastings, November 28, 1758.
63. B.M. 29132, Scrafton to Hastings, October 2, 1758.

CHAPTER XIV

1. For various reasons, notably labour shortages, the new Fort William was not completed until twenty years later, and in the end it was never called upon to stand a siege, though it still serves its purpose of housing the Calcutta garrison. Its building also necessitated the clearing of the unhealthy, tiger-infested jungle which had hemmed in the southern part of the settlement, and which gave way to the fine open space of the Maidan.
2. Home Miscellaneous Series, Vol. 192, Clive to Madras Committee, August 3, 1757.
3. The son of one of the Irish 'Wild Geese'.

4. Orme MSS, Vol. 292, Forde to Clive, June 25, 1758.
5. Home Miscellaneous Series, Vol. 809, Clive to Forde, June 23, 1758.
6. Clive MS. 63, Clive to Vansittart, August 20, 1759.
7. Powis Collection, Box 23, Sir Edward Clive to Clive, October 27, 1757.
8. *Ibid.*, Box IV, Richard Clive to Clive, November 9, 1757.
9. *Ibid.*, Box 23, William Smyth King to Clive, December 29, 1757.
10. *Ibid.*, Box IV, Richard Clive to Clive, November 9, 1757; India Office, Miscellaneous Letters received, Vol. XL, p. 222, quoted in A. Mervyn Davies, *op. cit.*, p. 277.
11. Powis Collection, Box IV, Richard Clive to Clive, December 6, 1757.
12. *Loc. cit.*
13. *Ibid.*, Box 23, Rev. Robert Clive to Clive, December 27, 1757.
14. *Loc. cit.*
15. B.M. 29132, Scrafton to Hastings, November 30, 1758.
16. H.M.C. Lothian, Champion Branfill to Sir Thomas Drury, February 18, 1758.
17. Powis Collection, Box IV, Richard Clive to Clive, December 23, 1758.
18. *Ibid.*, Box 25, Sarah Clive to Margaret, December 26, 1758.
19. *Ibid.*, Rebecca Clive (sister) to Margaret, undated.
20. *Ibid.*, Sarah Clive to Margaret, December 26, 1758.
21. National Maritime Museum 9956, Clive to Pocock, August 25, 1759. (Draft in Powis Collection, Box IV, dated August 28.)
22. Clive referred to the Shahzada in more suitable terms to Walsh, when he wrote: 'We must now try our hand with the Royal Family.' Ormathwaite MSS, Vol. V, Clive to Walsh, March 14, 1759.
23. Orme India MSS, Vol. X, Clive to John Spencer, April 10, 1759.
24. Clive to Mir Jafar, quoted in Sir George Forrest, *op. cit.*, Vol. II, p. 127.
25. Clive to Shahzada, quoted in *ibid.*, p. 129.
26. Clive to Mir Jafar, quoted *loc. cit.*
27. Bengal Select Committee Proceedings, March 13, 1759.
28. Sutton Court Collection, Box I, notes by Carnac, March 11, 1759.
29. Clive to Ramnarayan, quoted in Sir George Forrest, *op. cit.*, Vol. II, p. 131.
30. Clive MS. 257, Ramnarayan to Clive, April 3, 1759.
31. Clive MS. 261, Ramnarayan to Clive, received July 10, 1759.
32. Orme India MSS, Vol. X, Clive to Manningham, May 8, 1759.
33. Clive MS. 260, Clive to Shuja-ud-daula, May 26, 1759.
34. Orme India MSS, Vol. X, Clive to Manningham, April 24, 1759.
35. Luke Scrafton, *op. cit.*, p. 117.
36. First Report of Select Committee of House of Commons, 1772.
37. Powis Collection, Box IV, Clive to Pocock, draft dated August 28, 1759, of letter in Royal Maritime Museum, 9956, dated August 25.
38. Clive MS. 252, Clive to Seths, January 31, 1759.

39. Clive MS. 295, Seths to Clive, February 9, 1759.
40. Clive MS. 254, Seths to Clive, February 20, 1759.
41. Clive, *Letter to Proprietors*, p. 34.
42. Clive MS. 260, Seths to Clive, received June 4, 1759.
43. Powis Collection, Box IV, Clive to Pocock, draft dated August 28, 1759, of letter in Royal Maritime Museum 9956, dated August 25.
44. First Report of Select Committee of House of Commons, 1772.

CHAPTER XV

1. The house still stands, but in a very sorry state.
2. Later called Tank Square, and then Dalhousie Square. Clive's house would have been close to the site of the present Great Eastern Hotel.
3. Clive MS. 353, sale of sundries by 'outcry', February 20, 1760.
4. Clive MS. 357, Journal of Clive's effects commencing January 1, 1759.
5. Sutton Court Collection, Box I, Margaret to Carnac, May 5, 1763.
6. *Ibid.*, May 19, 1759.
7. *Ibid.*, Margaret to Carnac, March 31, 1759. During the four months he was away, Clive seems to have written Margaret fourteen letters in all. But by the middle of May, Carnac had written her twenty-three. Hers to Carnac are the only ones to survive; though Clive kept almost every other letter, however trivial, he destroyed those from Margaret; or else she herself destroyed them after his death.
8. *Ibid.*, notes by Carnac.
9. *Ibid.*, Margaret to Carnac, March 31, 1759.
10. *Ibid.*, April 1759.
11. *Ibid.*, March 31, 1759.
12. *Loc. cit.*
13. An expression as popular with Indian servants of the present century as it apparently was in Margaret's time.
14. Sutton Court Collection, Box I, Margaret to Carnac, May 30, 1759.
15. *Ibid.*, March 31, 1759.
16. *Ibid.*, April 1759.
17. *Ibid.*, April 16, 1759.
18. *Ibid.*, April 24, 1759.
19. *Ibid.*, June 8, 1759.
20. *Ibid.*, April 16, 1759.
21. *Ibid.*, April 1759.
22. Below the word 'comfort', she has written 'glory'.

23. Sutton Court Collection, Box I, Margaret to Carnac, May 5, 1759.
24. *Ibid.*, April 16, 1759.
25. *Ibid.*, April 7, 1759.
26. *Ibid.*, April 16, 1759.
27. *Ibid.*, June 6, 1759.
28. *Ibid.*, June 8, 1759.
29. *Ibid.*, June 6, 1759.
30. Quoted in Sir John Malcolm, *op. cit.*, Vol. II, p. 99.
31. First Report of the Select Committee of House of Commons, 1772.
32. Dispatches to Bengal, March 23, 1759.
33. B.M. 29131, Clive to Hastings, September 30, 1759.
34. Rev. J. Long, *Selections from Unpublished Records of Government* (Calcutta 1869), pp. 191–4.
35. Powis Collection, Box 27, Hastings to Clive, undated, 'Monday night'.
36. *Ibid.*, Box III, Clive to Captain James Spear, October 23, 1759.
37. He later recovered.
38. Sutton Court Collection, Box III, Narrative of the Dispute subsisting between the English and the Dutch in Bengal in November 1759.
39. It first appeared in the *Biographia Britannica* article.
40. Sutton Court Collection, Box III, Narrative of Dispute.
41. Powis Collection, Box 27, Hastings to Clive, November 25, 1759. Having been deprived by the English of his saltpetre monopoly, Khwaja Wajid would have had a grievance against them; and with his headquarters at Hughli near Cinsura he was likely to have been involved in the intrigues between the Nawab and the Dutch.
42. Clive MS. 269, Clive to Mir Jafar, November 29, 1759.
43. To Hastings, the Nawab expressed the belief that Khwaja Wajid had poisoned himself, adding somewhat callously that he had always been 'a troublesome meddling fellow and had met his deserts'. Powis Collection, Vol. 27, Hastings to Clive, December 26, 1759.
44. Powis Collection, Box III, Clive to Pigot, August 21, 1759.
45. *Ibid.*, Clive to Forde, August 24, 1759.
46. Clive MS. 63, Clive to Vansittart, August 20, 1759.
47. Powis Collection, Box III, Clive to Forde, August 24, 1759.
48. *Ibid.*, Clive to Pigot, August 21, 1759.
49. Quoted in Sir George Forrest, *op. cit.*, Vol. II, p. 168.
50. Thus, at the time of the Shahzada's first invasion, he wrote to Walsh: 'Victory will secure to us our influence another year at least.' (Ormathwaite MSS, Vol. V, Clive to Walsh, March 14, 1759.)
51. Orme India MSS, Vol. X, Clive to John Spencer, April 10, 1759.
52. Powis Collection, Box IV, Clive to Pocock, draft dated August 28, 1759, of letter in National Maritime Museum, 9956, dated August 25.

53. Orme India MSS, Vol. X, Clive to Manningham, etc., April 24, 1759.
54. Powis Collection, Box XV, Clive to Pitt, January 1, 1759.
55. Orme MSS, Vol. 26, John Call to Edmund Maskelyne, October 26, 1759.

CHAPTER XVI

1. Sutton Court Collection, Box III, Carnac to Margaret, 18 June 1760.
2. Powis Collection, Box 27, William Smyth King to Clive, July 13, 1759.
3. Clive MS. 200, Clive to William Smyth King, December 29, 1758.
4. Walpole, Yale Edition (London 1937–), Vol. XXI, Walpole to Mann, March 21, 1758.
5. *Ibid.*, August 1, 1760.
6. *Ibid.*, Vol. VI, Walpole to Mann, July 1, 1762.
7. Annual Register, 1760, p. 120.
8. Clive MS. 357, Clive's Journal commencing January 1, 1759.
9. See G. E. Mingay, *English Landed Society in the Eighteenth Century* (London 1963), p. 19.
10. Walpole, Yale, Vol. XXXI, Walpole to Lady Mary Coke, February 12, 1761.
11. When Margaret was living quietly with her children in England, after Clive's return to India, the household, travelling and family expenses for a year and a half amounted to £7253. (Clive MS. 87.)
12. He also joined with Walsh in providing a fortune of £10,000 for Mun, who had missed sharing in Mir Jafar's bounty, having been obliged, through ill-health, to return to the Coast in March 1757.
13. It seems that Clive's father lost the money on account of the financial difficulties of his seedy banker friend, William Belchier. When Clive was still in India, his father and Belchier tried to help themselves to this sum, out of some of the money which he had remitted home; he was informed of these machinations, but did not allow it to affect his relationship with his father.
14. Sutton Court Collection, Box I, Margaret to Carnac, September 16, 1761.
15. *Loc. cit.*
16. The house, No. 45, is one of the few in Berkeley Square to survive, having continued as the town house of Clive's descendants until 1937. It has been marred by the addition of an extra storey.
17. Carraccioli, *op. cit.*, Vol. I, p. 149.
18. Boswell, *Life of Johnson*, ed. Hill and Powell (Oxford 1964), Vol. III, p. 334.

19. Sutton Court Collection, Box II, Scrafton to Carnac, December 27, 1763.
20. Clive to Carnac, September 26, 1761, in L. B. Bowring, Album II, India Office Library.
21. Sutton Court Collection, Box III, Carnac to Clive, June 15, 1760; Powis Collection, Box 49, Baron de Wüst to Clive, November 3, 1767.
22. Sutton Court Collection, Box I, Margaret to Carnac, May 6, 1761.
23. B.M. 44061, Clive to Orme, July 19, 1762.
24. Sutton Court Collection, Box I, Clive to Carnac, March 4, 1761.
25. Mrs Scott to Elizabeth Montagu, 1762, quoted in Dr Doran, *A Lady of the Last Century* (London 1873).
26. Indeed, Clive was later to oblige him with several loans.
27. Sutton Court Collection, Box II, George Clive to Carnac, April 27, 1761.
28. In theory it was at the disposal of Lord Powis.
29. Clive to Sandwich, May 3, 1761, quoted in Namier, *Structure of Politics* (London 1929), p. 287.
30. He took his title from a small estate near Limerick which he had bought and renamed after his victory. The fact that Plassey in the title refers theoretically to an estate in Ireland rather than to a village in Bengal is taken by certain writers as being somewhat bogus. Actually it was a neat way of commemorating the battle in the territorial designation of his peerage, which had to be a place in Ireland.
31. Powis Collection, Box IV, Clive to Vansittart, February 3, 1762.
32. *Ibid.*, Box VII, Clive to Carnac, February 27, 1762.
33. Even with political power, a rich man might have been excluded from the peerage because he was unpopular, or regarded as too much of an upstart. Thus, Sir Lawrence Dundas, who made a fortune of at least £600,000 as an army contractor during the Seven Years War, built up a Parliamentary interest and worked hard for the rest of his life to get a peerage, but never succeeded in obtaining anything more than a baronetcy. In any case, an Irish barony tended to be the ultimate degree of nobility to which an eighteenth-century tycoon could aspire.
34. Powis Collection, Box VII, Clive to Carnac, February 27, 1762.
35. A. Mervyn Davies, *op. cit.*, p. 287.
36. He thus belongs generically to an important, if frequently overlooked, group of eighteenth-century Irishmen, of whom the most famous is, of course, Edmund Burke.
37. Richard Atkinson, quoted in Namier and Brooke, *op. cit.*, Vol. III, p. 510.
38. *Loc. cit.* Article on Sulivan by Dame Lucy Sutherland.
39. Laurence Sulivan MSS, Bodleian Library, Oxford.
40. Powis Collection, Box 67, Hugh Baillie to Clive, June 6, ?1773.
41. Lucy S. Sutherland, *East India Company in Eighteenth Century Politics* (Oxford, edition of 1962), pp. 68–73.

42. *Ibid.*, pp. 76–7.
43. Clive to Henry Vansittart, November 22, 1762, quoted in Sir John Malcolm, *op. cit.*, Vol. II, p. 197.
44. Powis Collection, Box IV, Clive to John Spencer, April 12, 1762.
45. Sutton Court Collection, Box II, Forde to Carnac, January 27, 1761.
46. Powis Collection, Box VII, Clive to Carnac, February 27, 1762.

CHAPTER XVII

1. Lucy Sutherland, *op. cit.*, p. 89.
2. Powis Collection, Box IV, Clive to Spencer, April 12, 1762.
3. Sutton Court Collection, Box I, Clive to Carnac, March 4, 1761; Powis Collection, Box VII, Clive to Carnac, February 27, 1762.
4. Clive to Pybus, February 27, 1762, quoted in Sir John Malcolm, *op. cit.*, Vol. II, p. 195.
5. Powis Collection, Box IV, Clive to Spencer, April 12, 1762.
6. *Ibid.*, Box VII, Clive to Carnac, February 27, 1762.
7. Sutton Court Collection, Box I, Clive to Carnac, May 6, 1762.
8. Clive invited Orme to help him with the memorandum which he wrote to the new Prime Minister in support of the terms which the Company wished to have incorporated in the treaty. No doubt this was to flatter him, Carnac having reported him as being aggrieved at not having been rewarded for his splendid write-up of Clive in his *History*, soon to be published: 'He had made you the hero of the piece, and had worked up your character to the utmost stretch of fancy.' (Sutton Court Collection, Box III, Carnac to Clive, June 15, 1760.)
9. Powis Collection, Box XIV, Clive to Palk, December 15, 1762.
10. *Loc. cit.*
11. Powis Collection, Box 29, Clive to Vansittart, February 17, 1762.
12. Clive to Carnac, November 25, 1762, quoted in Sir John Malcolm, *op. cit.*, Vol. II, pp. 204–5.
13. Lucy Sutherland, 'East India Company and the Peace of Paris', *English Historical Review*, April 1947.
14. It might be possible to trace an Irish link between Sulivan and Shelburne, who owned vast estates in the part of Ireland from which Sulivan sprang. Shelburne may have patronized Sulivan because he was connected with some of his tenants or dependants.
15. Lucy Sutherland, *op. cit.*, pp. 90–100.
16. Sutton Court Collection, Box I, Clive to Carnac, December 17, 1762.

17. Philip Woodruff, *op. cit.*, pp. 116–18.
18. Sutton Court Collection, Box I, Margaret to Carnac, March 21, 1763.
19. Harry Verelst, *A View of the Rise, Progress and Present State of the English Company in Bengal* (London 1772), p. 48.
20. Powis Collection, Box III, Clive to ——, December 30, 1758.
21. *Ibid.*, Box VII, Clive to Carnac, February 27, 1762.
22. *Ibid.*, Box IV, Clive to Vansittart, February 3, 1762.
23. *Loc. cit.*
24. Clive himself made a substantial part of his fortune available for this purpose, as did the rich Bengal malcontents. His party could also rely, to a greater extent than that of Sulivan, on financial support in the City.
25. Sutton Court Collection, Box III, Colonel Richard Smith to Carnac, March 26, 1763.
26. *Loc. cit.*
27. Clive to Vansittart, April 28, 1763, quoted in Sir John Malcolm, *op. cit.*, Vol. II, p. 225.
28. Sutton Court Collection, Box I, Clive to Carnac, January 1, 1764.
29. Powis Collection, Box VII, Clive to Carnac, February 27, 1762.
30. Sutton Court Collection, Box I, Margaret to Amphlett, January 5, 1764.
31. *Ibid.*, Margaret to Carnac, December 17, 1763.
32. *Ibid.*, Clive to Grenville, November 7, 1763.
33. Grenville Papers (London 1852–3), Vol. II, Clive to Grenville, November 17, 1763.
34. *Ibid.*, December 13, 1763.
35. Walpole, Oxford Edition (Oxford 1903–8 and 1918–25), Vol. V, Walpole to Earl of Hertford, December 29, 1763.
36. Ormathwaite MSS, Vol. V, 'Minutes for a Conversation with Lord Clive' by Walsh, January 20, 1764.
37. *Ibid.*, Clive to Walsh, November 22, 1763.
38. Sutton Court Collection, Box I, Clive to Carnac, January 1, 1764.
39. Ormathwaite MSS, Vol. V, Clive to Walsh, November 22, 1763.
40. Powis Collection, Box IV, Clive to Amyatt, January 1, 1764; *ibid.*, Box 32, Vansittart to Clive, March 4, 1764.
41. Ormathwaite MSS, Vol. V, Clive to Walsh, September 4, 1763.
42. *Gentleman's Magazine*, September 27, 1763.
43. Ormathwaite MSS, Vol. V, Clive to Walsh, September 4, 1763.
44. Bengal Dispatches, February 9, 1764, quoted in Lucy Sutherland, *op. cit.*, p. 116.
45. *London Magazine*, March 12, 1764, quoted in *ibid.*, pp. 125–6.
46. Sutton Court Collection, Box I, Margaret to Carnac, April 14, 1764.
47. Laurence Sulivan MSS, Palk to Sulivan, August 24, 1765.
48. Clive's Memorandum to Directors, 1764, quoted in Sir George Forrest,

op. cit., Vol. II, pp. 202–4; manuscript version in Powis Collection, Box 32, slightly different.

49. Grenville Papers, Vol. II, Jenkinson to Grenville, April 23, 1764.
50. Walpole, Yale VI, Walpole to Mann, June 8, 1764.
51. *Additional Grenville Papers*, ed. John R. G. Tomlinson (Manchester 1962), p. 127.
52. Sutton Court Collection, Box I, Clive to Carnac, May 19, 1764.
53. Powis Collection, Box IV, Clive to Carnac, May 7, 1762.
54. Sutton Court Collection, Box I, Margaret to Carnac, May 19, 1764.
55. Clive to Margaret, June 4, 1764, quoted in Sir George Forrest, *op. cit.*, Vol. II, p. 245.
56. He came of an old but impoverished Somerset family; his ancestral home, Sutton Court, was about to be seized by creditors. Clive saved it by lending him £12,000.
57. Home Miscellaneous Series, Vol. 191.

CHAPTER XVIII

1. Powis Collection, Box VII, Strachey to Margaret, October 14, 1764.
2. Forrest, who prints this letter in full, gives the word as 'charity': either he misread the original, or changed it for reasons of delicacy.
3. Powis Collection, Box XV, Clive to Margaret, October 14, 1764.
4. He was Commodore John Byron, grandfather of the poet, who as a midshipman spent five years on a desert island.
5. Powis Collection, Box XV, Clive to Margaret, October 14, 1764.
6. *Ibid.*, Clive to Grenville, October 14, 1764. Grenville forwarded his report to the Portuguese Government, who acted on it and had the works at Rio repaired.
7. *Ibid.*, Box 32, Clive to Viceroy of Brazil, November 5, 1764.
8. *Ibid.*, Box VII, Strachey to Margaret, January 7, 1765.
9. Clive to Rous, April 17, 1765, quoted in Sir George Forrest, *op. cit.*, Vol. II, pp. 256–8.
10. Ormathwaite MSS, Vol. V, Clive to Walsh, October 14, 1764.
11. Clive's Memorandum to Directors, 1764, quoted in Sir George Forrest, *op. cit.*, Vol. II, pp. 202–4.
12. Curzon, *op. cit.*, Vol. I, p. 12; Sutton Court Collection, Box I, Verelst to Clive, July 20, 1766. The house subsequently became the Council House, and was demolished to make room for the present Government House.
13. Rai Durlabh to Clive, quoted in Sir George Forrest, *op. cit.*, Vol. II, p. 260.

14. Clive to Carnac, May 3, 1765, quoted in Sir John Malcolm, *op. cit.*, Vol. II, pp. 318–20.
15. Clive MS. 218, Clive to Carnac, May 6, 1765.
16. *Loc. cit.*
17. Bengal Select Committee Consultations, May 7, 1765.
18. Sutton Court Collection, Box III, Najm-ud-daula to Carnac, received April 27, 1765.
19. John Johnstone, *Letter to Proprietors of East India Stock* (London 1766), pp. 2–3.
20. Verelst Collection, Clive to Verelst, December 27, 1765.
21. Sutton Court Collection, Box III, Carnac to Clive, May 7, 1765.
22. Clive MS. 224, Clive to Barker, December 20, 1765.
23. Clive MS. 227, Clive to Middleton, May 16, 1766.
24. Orme MSS, Vol. 37, Smith to Orme, March 28, 1767.
25. *Ibid.*, October 2, 1767.
26. Clive MS. 26, Clive to Majendie, June 4, 1765. It speaks of the slovenly methods of his predecessors that this was not already an established practice.

CHAPTER XIX

1. Powis Collection, Box VI, List of Servants belonging to Clive, June 22, 1765.
2. *Ibid.*, Box VII, Clive's Housekeeping, June–July 1765.
3. Mohammed Reza Khan's present-day biographer (Abdul Majed Khan, *The Transition in Bengal* [Cambridge 1969], p. 99) states that 'there is some evidence to suggest that the Khan helped Clive with a sum of six lakhs of rupees during his stay at Calcutta' – the evidence being, apparently, a note by Mohammed Reza Khan himself in the proceedings of the Controlling Council of Revenue, Murshidabad, January 3, 1771. This could be a reason why Clive overcame his prejudice against him. On the other hand, there seems no indication as to the veracity of Mohammed Reza Khan's note; nor is it clear as to whether he implied that the sum in question was an out-and-out bribe, or merely a loan, or, indeed, not for Clive's personal benefit at all, but for the expenses of government. It is possible also that he was referring to the supposed legacy from Mir Jafar which Clive used to start a fund to help impoverished former soldiers and soldiers' widows.
4. Powis Collection, Box III, Clive to Sykes, July 11, 1765.
5. B.M. 29132, Marriott to Hastings, August 16, 1765.

6. As security, he handed over a casket of jewels, which was duly returned to him the following year with its seal unbroken when he had paid all his instalments. But, needless to say, there were stories about Clive keeping the jewels for himself.
7. Letters from Bengal, Clive and Committee to Directors, September 30, 1765.
8. Clive MS. 220, Clive to Call, July 1765.
9. Clive to Barker, March 5, 1769, quoted in Sir John Malcolm, *op. cit.*, Vol. III, p. 252.
10. Abstract of Persian Correspondence, July 24, 1765, Mogul to Clive.
11. With the exception of Philpot, the valet, who was given an 'emolument' of £2196, all Clive's European servants had died by the time he left India.
12. Mrs Kindersley, *Letters from the East Indies* (London 1777), p. 156.
13. Powis Collection, Box III, Clive to Gregory, August 14, 1765.
14. Verelst Collection, Clive to Verelst, August 10 or 16, 1765.
15. Powis Collection, Box V, Mohammed Ali to Clive, undated.
16. Kindersley, *op. cit.*, p. 155.
17. Clive MS. 225, Clive to Smith, May 17, 1766; *ibid.*, 228, Clive to Verelst, June 9, 1766.
18. Powis Collection, Box IV, Clive to Margaret, August 24, 1765, and September 21, 1765.
19. Letters from Bengal, Clive and Committee to Directors, September 30, 1765.
20. Powis Collection, Box III, Clive to Dudley, September 29, 1765.
21. *Ibid.*, Clive to Orme, September 29, 1765.
22. *Ibid.*, Vol. 34, Clive to Walsh, April 17, 1765.
23. Third Report of Select Committee of House of Commons, 1772, evidence of Clive and Walsh.
24. Barwell to his father, January 21, 1766, in *Bengal Past and Present*, Vol. V.
25. In his evidence before the Select Committee of the House of Commons in 1772, he spoke of the benefits of having a high rate of interest in Bengal, which encouraged people to lend their money to the Company, and thus kept private capital in India.
26. Quoted in Sir George Forrest, *op. cit.*, Vol. II, p. 296.
27. In the hope that this would make for better relations with the nominal Government of the Nawab, Clive laid it down that these battalions were not to be officered by Europeans when they performed their primary function of helping wtith the collection of the revenues. Their standard of discipline was in any case lower than that of the regular army, for which they were intended as a 'nursery'.
28. Bengal Select Committee Consultations, July 8, 1769.
29. Clive MS. 220, Clive to Sykes, July 17, 1765.

30. There are those who hold that as Clive was responsible more than anyone for the English takeover in Bengal, he must also be blamed for the economic ills resulting from it—even down to the 1970 flood disaster in East Pakistan. But it is unfair to blame Clive because in 1757 he was not an economist who could see into the future.
31. Dispatches to Bengal, June 1, 1764.
32. Hastings was to make salt a government monopoly again.
33. It grew into the postal system of British India.
34. Unlike Vansittart, whose ancestors had left the Low Countries for Danzig at the end of the sixteenth century, and had been in England for about a hundred years, achieving a certain position.
35. Yet according to Col. Richard Smith, when he became Governor, Verelst was more of a 'martinet' than Clive in his dealing with the army. (Orme MSS, Vol. 37, Smith to Orme, October 2, 1767.)
36. Ducarel Papers, G. G. Ducarel to his mother, December 1, 1769.
37. Clive MS. 220, Clive to Sykes, August 3, 1765.
38. Nubkissen was the son of a *Diwan* of Cuttak who lost his life and fortune at the hands of the Marathas. He became attached to the English at an early age, starting his career as Persian tutor to Warren Hastings.

CHAPTER XX

1. Powis Collection, Box 41, Barker to Clive, August 3, 1766.
2. Clive MS. 228, Clive to Smith, August 31, 1766.
3. Clive MS. 223, Clive to Crommelin, November 28, 1765.
4. Home Miscellaneous Series, Vol. 198, Champion's Journal, February 10, 1766.
5. *Ibid.*, October 27, 1765.
6. Powis Collection, Box III, Clive to Sykes, August 10, 1765.
7. Clive MS. 220, Clive to Sykes, July 15, 1765.
8. Powis Collection, Box 36, Sykes to Clive, October 18, 1765.
9. Bengal Public Consultations, October 14, 1765–March 3, 1766. The fact that he owed money to Verelst made it seem still more suspicious; but Verelst afterwards pointed out that Ramnath deliberately contrived to be in his debt in the hope that he would thus be more speedily released. Clive, moreover, referred to thirty-two precedents of Indians having been confined for months under military guards by previous governors.
10. Ducarel Papers, James Ducarel to his mother, October 6, 1767.

11. Barwell to Beaumont, September 15, 1765; to Hancock, September 21, 1766; to Leycester, September 15, 1766, in *Bengal Past and Present*, Vols. VIII and IX.
12. Clive MS. 231, Clive to Barwell, November 5, 1766.
13. Home Miscellaneous Series, Vol. 765, Rennell to Burrington, March 10, 1767.
14. Vansittart Papers, George Vansittart to Philip Affleck, November 24, 1766.
15. Orme MSS, Vol. 37, Smith to Scrafton, December 4, 1767.
16. Verelst Collection, Clive to Verelst, April 2, 1766.
17. Ducarel Papers, G. G. Ducarel to his mother, December 30, 1765; Home Miscellaneous Series, Vol. 198, Champion's Journal, December 16–20, 1765.
18. Thus Panikkar, *op. cit.*, pp. 118–19.
19. Powis Collection, Box 72, John Brown to ——, 1764.
20. Carraccioli, *op. cit.*, Vol. I, p. 467.
21. *Ibid.*, p. 447.
22. *Ibid.*, Vol. II, p. 34.
23. Ibid., Vol. I, pp. 448–51.
24. Powis Collection, Box 36, Strachey to Margaret, November 7, 1765.
25. *Ibid.*, Box 38, Strachey to Margaret, February 4, 1766.
26. *Ibid.*, Box III, Clive to Margaret, January 31 and March 20, 1766.
27. Clive MS. 224, Clive to Call, March 20, 1766.
28. Powis Collection, Box III, Clive to his son, January 31, 1766.
29. Clive MS. 52, Margaret to Clive, February 27, 1765.
30. Walpole, Yale, Vol. 21, Walpole to Mann, 1766.
31. Powis Collection, Box 40, George Clive to Clive, May 16, 1766.
32. *Ibid.*, Box 80, Accounts.
33. Bengal Select Committee Consultations, November 8, 1765. It was typical of Clive – and also of the eighteenth century as a whole – that in choosing the Madras gentlemen, he should have taken the opportunity of doing a good turn to Margaret's cousin, Thomas Kelsall, who happened to be in dire financial straits, and also to the son of his one-time benefactor, Governor Floyer.
34. *Ibid.*, January 20, 1766.
35. Ormathwaite Collection, Vol. V, Clive to Walsh, February 5, 1766.
36. Clive MS. 224, Clive to Palk, January 27, 1766.
37. Barwell to Leycester, September 15, 1766, in *Bengal Past and Present*, Vol. IX.
38. Clive MS. 228, Clive to Verelst, June 25, 1766.
39. Clive MS. 227, Clive to Verelst, May 21, 1766.
40. Presumably the work of some discontented young gentleman, civil or military. Like many tit-bits from this book, which were supplied by officers returning from India, it rings true. (Carraccioli, *op. cit.*, Vol. III, p. 85).

41. Sutton Court Collection, 'Drafts of Letters, H.S.', Strachey to Rockingham, September 23, 1766.
42. Home Miscellaneous Series, Vol. 198, Champion's Journal, April–May 1766.
43. *Loc. cit.*
44. Powis Collection, Box XIII, Unsigned Account of the Officers' Mutiny.
45. Henry Strachey, *Narrative of the Mutiny of the Officers* (London 1773), pp. 26–33.
46. Powis Collection, Box VI, anonymous testimony of Clive's character.
47. Henry Strachey, *op. cit.*, p. 34.
48. Clive MS. 227, Clive to Smith, May 18, 1766.
49. *Ibid.*, May 16, 1766.
50. Clive MS. 228, Clive to Verelst, April 16, 1766 (misdated 1765).
51. Clive MS. 230, Clive to Palk, October 17, 1766.
52. Home Miscellaneous Series, Vol. 199, Complaints of Duffield and Robertson.
53. *Ibid.*, Vol. 193, Champion's Journal, May 13–14, 1766.
54. Sutton Court Collection, Box I, Fletcher to Clive, September 13, 1766; Henry Strachey, *op. cit.*, pp. 84–128.
55. It showed its impartiality by also cashiering the author of an anonymous letter containing the false allegation that Fletcher had accused Clive of intending to reduce the army 'to contempt and beggary'.

CHAPTER XXI

1. Dispatches to Bengal, February 19, 1766.
2. Ormathwaite Collection, Vol. V, Clive to Walsh, September 8, 1766.
3. Orme MSS, Vol. 37, Smith to Orme, August 31, 1767.
4. Clive MS. 228, Clive to Verelst, July 15, 1766.
5. Sutton Court Collection, Box I, Strachey to Walsh, December 13, 1766; Powis Collection, Box 43, Carnac to Margaret, December 4, 1766; *ibid.* Box III, Clive to Margaret, January 1, 1767.
6. Dispatches to Bengal, May 17, 1766.
7. Powis Collection, Box 40, Walsh to Clive, Scrafton to Clive, May 17, 1766.
8. Vansittart Papers, George to Henry Vansittart, November 27, 1766.
9. Powis Collection, Box VIII, Clive's Emoluments as Governor.
10. Rumbold was originally in Bengal, where he was commended by Clive as one of the best of the junior servants. Though Bengal made him a rich

man, he became very much richer—and by dubious means—after his appointment as Governor of Madras in 1777.

11. Vansittart Papers, George to Henry Vansittart, November 27, 1766.
12. Powis Collection, Box 44, Nubkissen to ——, February 17, 1767.
13. Clive MS. 231, Clive to Call, December 30, 1766.
14. Sutton Court Collection, 'Drafts of Letters, H.S.', Strachey to D'Oyly and Quarme, January 1, 1767.

CHAPTER XXII

1. Powis Collection, Box 40, Walsh to Clive, May 16, 1766.
2. Clive MS. 26, Clive to Gosling, August 17, 1767.
3. Clive to Verelst, 9 February 1768, quoted in Sir John Malcolm, *op. cit.*, Vol. III, p. 221.
4. Clive MS. 261, Clive to Verelst, December 7, 1767.
5. Walpole, Yale, Vol. 21, Mann to Walpole, August 8, 1767.
6. *Ibid.*, Vol. 22, Walpole to Mann, July 20, 1767.
7. Johnstone Papers, 622, John Johnstone to his brother, undated.
8. *A Letter to Lord Clive on . . . promoting the interests of Agriculture by forming an Experimental Farm* (London 1767).
9. Powis Collection, Box 45, Rous to Clive, July 28, 1767.
10. *Debates in the Asiatic Assembly* (London 1767), p. 27.
11. Powis Collection, Box 44, Walsh to Clive, March 26, 1767.
12. Grenville Papers, Vol. III, Wedderburn to Grenville, September 25, 1766.
13. Powis Collection, Box 43, Walsh to Clive, December 21, 1766.
14. Clive MS. 56, Strachey to Robert Mackintosh, undated.
15. Clive MS. 230, Clive to Palk, October 17, 1766.
16. Clive to Verelst, February 9, 1768, quoted in Sir John Malcolm, *op. cit.*, Vol III, pp. 221–2.
17. Sir James Porter to Edward Weston, January 30, 1768, in H.M.C. Report on Charles Fleetwood Weston Underwood MSS.
18. Sutton Court Collection, Box V, Margaret to Strachey, September 22, 1767.
19. Clive MS. 56, Clive to Sir James Hedges, November 28, 1767.
20. Powis Collection, Box XIV, undated fragment from Clive.
21. Clive to Verelst, November 7, 1767, quoted in Sir John Malcolm, *op. cit.*, Vol. III, pp. 216–17.
22. Laurence Sulivan MSS, Sulivan to Vansittart, May 28, 1770.

23. Clive to Verelst, November 7, 1767, quoted in Sir John Malcolm, *op. cit.*, Vol. III, pp. 216–17.
24. Powis Collection, Box 47, Walsh to Clive, September 1767.
25. *Ibid.*, Box 48, Scrafton to Clive, October 1767.
26. Clive to Scrafton, October 6, 1767, quoted in Sir John Malcolm, *op. cit.*, Vol. III, pp. 208–9.
27. Powis Collection, Box 48, Scrafton to Clive, October 1767.
28. Clive to Scrafton, October 2, 1767, quoted in Sir John Malcolm, *op. cit.*, Vol. III, pp. 205–6.
29. This was not, as is generally supposed, on account of his extravagance, for we have it on the authority of Walsh that he lived quietly; but because his fortune was far smaller than most people imagined it to be.
30. Palk succeeded the disreputable Fordyce as Chaplain at Fort St David. He later transferred to the secular service of the Company, becoming Governor of Madras in 1763 and returning to England with a sizeable fortune in 1767.
31. Powis Collection, Box 50, Walsh to Clive and Scrafton to Clive, December 23, 1767.
32. Verelst Collection, Clive to Verelst, March 9, 1768.
33. Clive also had a similar functionary named Crisp.
34. 5th Earl of Carlisle to George Selwyn, February 3, 1768, in John Heneage Jesse, *Selwyn* (London 1843), Vol. II, pp. 249–50.
35. Diary of Jane Latham, in possession of Lord Strachie, from which much of the information on this tour is derived.
36. Clive to Verelst, February 9, 1768, quoted in Sir John Malcolm, *op. cit.*, Vol. III, p. 221.
37. Sutton Court Collection, Box V, Margaret to Strachey, March 3, 1768.
38. *Ibid.*, March 21, 1768.
39. *Ibid.*, Clive to Strachey, May 10, 1768.
40. *Ibid.*, undated, received June 7, 1768.
41. *Ibid.*, Margaret to Strachey, April 27, 1768.
42. *Ibid.*, March 21, 1768.
43. Jane Latham's Diary.
44. Sutton Court Collection, Box V, Clive to Strachey, July 5, 1768.
45. *Ibid.*, April 22, 1768.
46. Clive had insisted that Mun's supporters should be paid only if he was successful.
47. John, Lord Campbell, *Lives of the Lord Chancellors* (London 1847), Vol. VI, pp. 83–8.
48. *North Briton*, January 7, 1769.
49. Clive to Verelst, February 9, 1768, quoted in Sir John Malcolm, *op. cit.*, Vol. III, p. 221.

50. Powis Collection, Box 52, Walsh to Clive, April 8, 1768.
51. Clive to Russell, February 10, 1769, quoted in Sir John Malcolm, *op. cit.*, Vol. III, p. 241.

CHAPTER XXIII

1. Powis Collection, Box 57, Grenville to Clive, May 28, 1769.
2. Sutton Court Collection, Box V, Clive to Strachey, June 28, 1769.
3. This figure was exclusive of a mortgage which Clive already held on the property, having obliged the Duke of Newcastle with a loan.
4. Clive MS. 61, Clive to Verelst, December 7, 1767.
5. Dorothy Stroud, *Henry Holland* (London 1966), p. 32.
6. This would have been for the sake of dryness, and also perhaps to please Margaret, who did not regard basements of the normal kind as good enough for the servants.
7. Christopher Hussey, letter to the author.
8. Sutton Court Collection, Box V, Clive to Strachey, July 5, 1771.
9. *Ibid.*, Box I, Lovett to Strachey, April 9, 1767.
10. Orme MSS, Vol. J, Speech of George Johnstone in General Court, undated.
11. Powis Collection, Box 52, Nubkissen to Clive, March 18, 1768.
12. *Ibid.*, Box 72, Colebrooke to Clive, undated (1769).
13. B.M. 29132, Palk to Hastings, June 23, 1769.
14. Powis Collection, Box 57, George Clive to Clive, June 16, 1769.
15. *Ibid.*, Box 58, Coote to Clive, November 15, 1769.
16. *Gentleman's Magazine*, May 1769.
17. Laurence Sulivan MSS, Sulivan to Vansittart, January 24, 1770.
18. Orme MSS, Vol. 38, Smith to Scrafton, September 1768.
19. Powis Collection, Box 59, Mark Guido to Clive, April 31 [*sic*] and May 14, 1770.
20. *Ibid.*, Box 72, undated fragment by Clive.
21. Orme MSS, Vol. 222, Orme to Smith, November 18, 1767.
22. Quoted in Brady and Pottle, *Boswell, in Search of a Wife* (London 1957), p. 288.
23. It is possible that Clive alienated Dalton by taking too much credit in the account of the Trichinopoly campaign which he wrote for Orme's *History*.
24. From this marriage were descended a number of distinguished nineteenth-century Indian administrators; and in more recent years, Lytton Strachey.
25. Sutton Court Collection, Box V, Clive to Strachey, September 1, 1771.
26. Ormathwaite Collection, Vol. VIII, Margaret to Walsh, October 3, 1770.
27. *Ibid.*, Margaret to Walsh and Strachey, undated 1770.

28. *Ibid.*, Margaret to Walsh, October 3, 1770.
29. *Ibid.*, Margaret to Walsh and Strachey, undated 1770.
30. Powis Collection, Box 70, Earl of Powis to Clive, October 1770.
31. Ormathwaite Collection, Vol. VIII, Margaret to Walsh, undated.
32. *Ibid.*, Strachey to Walsh, October 12, 1770.
33. Powis Collection, Box 60, Walsh to Clive, October 9, 1770.
34. He was a Fellow of the Royal Society and was particularly noted for his enquiries into the properties of electric eels.
35. Ormathwaite Collection, Vol. VIII, Margaret to Walsh, September 8, 1770.
36. Clive to Wedderburn, November 18, 1770, quoted in Sir John Malcolm, *op. cit.*, Vol. III, p. 232; Wedderburn to Clive, November 14, 1770, quoted *ibid.*, pp. 230–1.
37. Campbell, *op. cit.*, Vol. VI, p. 88.
38. Barwell to Mary Barwell, July 25, 1776, in *Bengal Past and Present*, Vol. XV.
39. B.M. 29132, Clive to Hastings, August 1, 1771.
40. Clive MS. 61, Clive to Sykes, November 12, 1768.
41. B.M. 29132, Clive to Hastings, August 1, 1771.
42. Sutton Court Collection, Box V, Clive to Strachey, September 1, 1771.
43. Clive MS. 61, Clive to Kelsall, February 15, 1770.
44. Powis MSS, Shrewsbury. As though to satisfy himself that this was not really excessive, he drew up a list of what he believed each of his contemporaries had brought back from India, putting his own fortune second to Pigot's £600,000. But his figures were not very reliable; he estimated Vansittart's fortune at £200,000, about four times what it really was, and rated both Stringer Lawrence and Sykes at £70,000, making the first far richer and the second far poorer than was actually the case. Sutton Court Collection, Vol. II, note in Clive's hand.
45. *Morning Chronicle*, January 6, 1773.
46. Sutton Court Collection, Box V, Clive to Strachey, May 1771.
47. Powis Collection, Box 61, Strachey to Clive, May 22, 1771.
48. Sutton Court Collection, Box V, Clive to Strachey, May 15, 1771.
49. Walpole, Yale, Vol. 32, Walpole to Lady Upper Ossory, December 14, 1771.
50. Now in the Barber Institute, Birmingham.
51. Sutton Court Collection, Box V, Clive to Strachey, October 6, 1771.
52. *Ibid.*, Clive to Strachey, September 1, 1771.

CHAPTER XXIV

1. Egerton MSS, Vol. 239, pp. 177–273.
2. Walpole, Oxford Edition, Vol. VIII, p. 153.
3. Boswell, *Johnson*, ed. Hill and Powell (Oxford 1964), Vol. III, pp. 400–1.
4. Powis Collection, Box XIII, Johnstone's Declaration to Committee of Correspondence, December 20, 1771.
5. B.M. 29133, Leycester to Hastings, March 12, 1772.
6. Walpole, *Last Journals* (London 1910), Vol. I, pp. 72–3.
7. B.M. 29133, Leycester to Hastings, March 12, 1772.
8. *Public Advertiser*, March 3, 1772.
9. Clive MS. 58, Clive to Palk, October 12, 1767.
10. Sir George Forrest, *op. cit.*, Vol. II, p. 383; A. Mervyn Davies, *op. cit.*, p. 476.
11. Laurence Sulivan MSS, Sulivan to Vansittart, May 28, 1770.
12. Powis Collection, Box 63, Clive to Directors, January 12, 1772.
13. *Middlesex Journal*, October 6–8, 1774.
14. B.M. 35375, J. Yorke to Hardwicke, pp. 81–2.
15. Clive's Speech, March 30, 1772 (printed).
16. Powis Collection, Box VI, anonymous testimony to Clive.
17. *General Evening Post*, April 2–4, 1772.
18. *Public Advertiser*, April 11, 1772.
19. *Loc. cit.*
20. Powis Collection, Box 63, Cawthorne to Clive, April 21, 1772; *ibid.*, Box 64, Cawthorne to Clive, June 23, 1772. In the following year, when he was about to be imprisoned for debt, Cawthorne tried a little veiled blackmail, suggesting that the material which Clive had given him when he employed him a few years before might now be harmful to his cause. Having failed to get any response from Clive himself, Cawthorne tried to blackmail his family after his death, in collusion with Clive's former valet, Isaac Talboys, who had, incidentally, benefited from his Will to the extent of £30 a year. They did not, however, specify what they would reveal. Strachey, on behalf of the family, ignored their threats, which came to nothing; it later turned out that Talboys was mentally deranged. Sutton Court Collection, 'Drafts of Letters, H.S.', Strachey to Lord Lansdowne, September 15, 1785.
21. *Boswell for the Defence*, ed. Wimsatt and Pottle (London 1960), pp. 93–4.
22. *Public Advertiser*, April 15, 1772.
23. First Report, Select Committee of House of Commons, 1772.
24. Powis Collection, Box VI, anonymous testimony to Clive.

25. After the Committee had heard his evidence, the Directors sent Munro his two lakhs.
26. Clive Papers, 820, Clive to Strachey, September 20, 1772.
27. Powis Collection, Box 64, North to Wedderburn, September 18, 1772.
28. *Craftsman*, October 3, 1772.
29. Quoted in Sir John Malcolm, *op. cit.*, Vol. III, p. 313.
30. One of them, Elijah Impey, was soon to become the first Chief Justice of Bengal.
31. B.M. 35631, p. 116.
32. John Debrett, *History, Debates and Proceedings of both Houses of Parliament* (London 1754–74), Vol. VI, pp. 410–19; Walpole, *Last Journals*, Vol. I, pp. 162–4.
33. Powis Collection, Box XV, Clive to Strachey, November 7, 1772.
34. A. Mervyn Davies, *op. cit.*, p. 481.
35. Lucy Sutherland, *op. cit.*, p. 261.
36. Thus, Letters from Bengal, Clive and Committee to the Directors, September 30, 1765.

CHAPTER XXV

1. Powis Collection, Box XVII, undated memorandum; *ibid.*, Box 66, Hoole to Sulivan, May 6, 1773.
2. *Ibid.*, draft by Clive, January 2, 1773.
3. B.M. 29133, Palk to Hastings, February 8, 1773.
4. *Lloyd's Evening Post*, January 6–8, 1773.
5. *Ibid.*, March 29–31, 1773.
6. Walpole, *Last Journals*, Vol. I, pp. 197–203.
7. Egerton MSS, Vol. 246, p. 62.
8. B.M. 35375, J. Yorke to Hardwicke, pp. 79–80.
9. Walpole, *Last Journals*, Vol. I, pp. 197–203.
10. Egerton MSS, Vol. 246, pp. 62–71; *Craftsman*, May 8, 1773.
11. Egerton MSS, Vol. 246, p. 73.
12. *Ibid.*, Vol. 246, p. 87.
13. Before he sat down, Clive told the House of Sulivan's expressed determination to 'mark' him, of which he had heard second-hand. This caused Sulivan to protest that he had never wished to be malevolent to him, and that if he had, he would long ago have revealed how Clive had deliberately suppressed his Indian correspondence relating to the granting of his *jagir:* the Directors had repeatedly asked him for it, to no avail. Clive replied to

this unpleasant insinuation by saying, quite truthfully, that he had lent the correspondence in question more than ten years ago to a certain author named Dr John Campbell, who had never returned it; and that in any case it contained nothing that he would wish to suppress. (*Craftsman*, May 8, 1773.) When Campbell read in the newspapers of this exchange, he unearthed the missing correspondence and sent it back to Clive, who forwarded it to the Company. (Powis Collection, Box 66, Campbell to Clive, May 5, 1773.) Regarding the *jagir*, it contained nothing more than the letters between Clive and the Seths which Clive had made public nine years before in his *Letter to the Proprietors of the East India Stock*.

14. *Public Advertiser*, May 11, 1773.
15. Thus, a letter in the *Public Advertiser* of June 2, 1773, speaks of Burgoyne's boasted friendship with George Johnstone.
16. B.M. 35375, pp. 79–80.
17. W. B. Pemberton, *Lord North* (London 1938), pp. 177–8.
18. Walpole, *Last Journals*, Vol. I, p. 198.
19. *Loc. cit.*
20. *Public Advertiser*, May 20, 1773.
21. Sir John Fortescue, *Correspondence of George III* (London 1927), Vol. II, No. 1237.
22. Burke, *Correspondence* (Cambridge 1958), Vol. II, p. 433n.
23. *Morning Advertiser*, May 12, 1773.
24. Lucy Sutherland, *op. cit.*, p. 256.
25. Walpole, *Last Journals*, Vol. I, p. 199.
26. Egerton MSS, Vol. 246, p. 205.
27. Walpole, *Last Journals*, Vol. I, p. 200.
28. Powis Collection, Box 66, Wedderburn to Clive, May 10, 1773.
29. Egerton MSS, Vol. 246, pp. 180–6.
30. Walpole, *Last Journals*, Vol. I, p. 201.
31. Walpole, Yale, Vol. 28, Walpole to Rev. William Mason, May 15, 1773.
32. Kenyon MSS, Lloyd Kenyon to his father, May 11, 1773.
33. Fortescue, *op. cit.*, Vol. II, No. 1243.
34. *Morning Advertiser*, May 12, 1773.
35. *Gibbon Letters*, ed. Norton (London 1956), No. 221.
36. B.M. 35375, pp. 87–8.
37. Egerton MSS, Vol. 247, pp. 1–19.
38. B.M. 35375, pp. 87–8.
39. Fortescue, *op. cit.*, Vol. II, Lord North to King, May 19, 1773.
40. B.M. 35611, p. 91.
41. Egerton MSS, Vol. 247, pp. 49–87.
42. *Ibid.*, p. 109.
43. *Morning Advertiser*, May 11, 1773.

44. Powis Collection, Box VIII, 'An Independent Englishman'.
45. *Lloyd's Evening Post*, May 21–24, 1773.
46. Walpole, *Last Journals*, Vol. I, p. 231.
47. B.M. 29134, Sykes to Hastings, November 8, 1773.
48. *Ibid.*, Caillaud to Hastings, January 21, 1774.
49. Egerton MSS, Vol. 248, pp. 128–34.
50. B.M. 29134, Sykes to Hastings, November 8, 1773.
51. *Ibid.*, Caillaud to Hastings, January 21, 1774.
52. *Loc. cit.*; Walpole, *Last Journals*, Vol. I, p. 234.
53. *London Chronicle*, May 22, 1773.
54. Quoted in Alan Chester Valentine, *Lord North* (Oklahoma 1967), Vol. I, p. 288.
55. Walpole, *Last Journals*, Vol. I, p. 232.
56. Quoted in Valentine, *op. cit.*, Vol. I, p. 288.
57. Walpole, *Last Journals*, Vol. I, p. 232.
58. Burke, *Correspondence*, Vol. II, p. 434.
59. Kenyon MSS, Lloyd Kenyon to his father, May 25, 1773.
60. *Craftsman*, May 29, 1773.
61. Walpole, *Last Journals*, Vol. I, pp. 232–4.
62. Fortescue, *op. cit.*, Vol. II, No. 1255.
63. Christopher D'Oyly, who was Strachey's colleague in the War Office. Fuller could only be prevailed upon to second the amendment after he had convinced himself of the justice of Clive's case by taking a Counsel's opinion.
64. Walpole, *Last Journals*, Vol. I, p. 198.
65. *Morning Chronicle*, May 26, 1773.
66. Quoted in Sir John Malcolm, *op. cit.*, Vol. III, p. 329n.
67. *General Evening Post*, May 20–22, 1773.
68. A. Mervyn Davies, *op. cit.*, pp. 485–6.
69. B.M. 35504, pp. 268–70, Thomas Bradshaw to Sir Robert Murray Keith, undated.

CHAPTER XXVI

1. Carraccioli, *op. cit.*, Vol. IV, p. 544.
2. Sutton Court Collection, Box V, Clive to Strachey, April 30, 1774.
3. Johnstone Papers, 654, John Johnstone to his brother, October 16, 1773.
4. H.M.C. Palk, No. 196. His futile efforts in Parliament were followed by the indignity of being sued by one of the confraternity of scribblers, from

whom he had commissioned a libel on Clive which he did not publish—and consequently failed to pay for—having secured his reappointment to Madras. On arriving back there, he exceeded even himself; he led a conspiracy against Pigot, who, owing to financial troubles, had been obliged to return to his old post as Governor, kidnapped him and kept him in confinement. This caused Pigot's death; but by that time Fletcher was also dead, so he escaped retribution.

5. Powis Collection, Box 67, Andrew Ligoe to Clive, June 29, 1773; John Philips to Clive.
6. *Morning Chronicle*, May 27 and October 14, 1773; Powis Collection, Box 67, Secker to Clive, August 17, 1773.
7. *Public Advertiser*, June 8, 1773.
8. Namier and Brooke, *op. cit.*, Vol. II, p. 228.
9. The son of a Church of Ireland clergyman who translated Horace and pamphleteered for Henry Fox, Francis inherited his father's literary and pamphleteering abilities, and has since been regarded as a likely candidate for the authorship of the letters of 'Junius'. After Strachey had left the War Office, he kept in touch with him through their mutual friend Christopher D'Oyly. There is no evidence, however, that Francis came into Clive's life before the summer of 1773, or that Clive used his influence to get him appointed to the Supreme Council.
10. Feiling, *op. cit.*, p. 129.
11. Francis was genuinely fond of cats.
12. Francis Collection, Vol. 46, Francis to Margaret, September 6, 1773.
13. *Ibid.*, Vol. 49, Margaret to Francis, May 5, 1774.
14. *Ibid.*, Vol. 47, Francis to Strachey, April 5, 1774.
15. See Lucy Sutherland, *op. cit.*, p. 292n.
16. Powis MSS, Shrewsbury.
17. Fowke Collection, Vol. 21, Jane Latham to Margaret Fowke, August 28, 1774.
18. Sutton Court Collection, Box V, Margaret to Clive, February 25, 1774.
19. Clive MS. 69, Minutes of executors' meetings.
20. Quoted in W. T. Whitley, *Artists and their Friends in England* (London and Boston 1928), Vol. I, p. 296.
21. Arundell MSS, Fr. John Thorpe to 8th Lord Arundell, January 12, 1774.
22. *Loc. cit.*
23. P.R.O., S.P.F. 93/29, Sir W. Hamilton to Earl of Rochford, February 23, 1774. Hamilton, at this time, had already been in Naples for ten years; though his Emma was still an unknown child of eight.
24. Arundell MSS, Thorpe to Arundell, January 12, 1774.
25. *Ibid.*, January 15, 1774.
26. *Ibid.*, February 26, 1774.

27. *Ibid.*, June 4, 1774.
28. *Ibid.*, March 19, 1774.
29. Sutton Court Collection, Box V, Strachey to Clive, March 15, 1774.
30. In *Biographia Britannica.*
31. Home Miscellaneous Series, Vol. 211, Considerations on the East India Company, November 24, 1772.
32. Sutton Court Collection, Box V, Strachey to Clive, January 25, 1774.
33. *Ibid.*, Strachey to Clive, February 25, 1774.
34. *Ibid.*, Clive to Strachey, April 30, 1774.
35. *Ibid.*, Margaret to Clive, January 14 and March 1, 1774.
36. *Ibid.*, February 25, 1774.
37. Francis Collection, Vol. 49, Maria Ducarel to Francis, December 17, 1774.
38. *Ibid.*, Vol. 58, Betsy Francis to Francis, June 17 and 21, 1774.
39. For this reason, after Clive's death, Leighton was unseated in favour of Pulteney.
40. In addition to Walsh, Rous and Clive himself, the party consisted of George Clive, Strachey, Wedderburn and Ned, who though under age was returned unopposed for Ludlow, the borough at the gates of Oakly. Carnac had retired from politics, since he was in financial difficulties and about to return to India.
41. Sutton Court Collection, Box V, Strachey to Clive, February 8, 1774.
42. *Ibid.*, April 30, 1774.
43. Powis Collection, Box 68, Clive to Lord North, September 27, 1774.
44. T. Falconer to Charles Gray, September 3, 1774, in H.M.C. Report on Round MSS.
45. Ingham had died some years before.
46. He obviously dressed that morning, for his executors speak of gold buckles, a pocket book containing £30 and other articles being on his person at the time of his death.
47. Francis Collection, Vol. 49, Maria Ducarel to Francis, December 17, 1774.
48. Maria Ducarel, writing to Francis, attributed his death to this cause: 'He was taken with an epileptic fit after the operation of a medicine, and expired immediately.' Like Clive himself, Maria clearly used the word 'epileptic' in a vague sense to denote a convulsive spasm. Her letter gives a detailed account of Clive's illness which one imagines to be true, apart from the suppression of the real cause of his death. Francis Collection, Vol. 49, Maria Ducarel to Francis, December 17, 1774.
49. The *Middlesex Journal* suggests that the thought of the impending petition by Pulteney against the Shrewsbury election proved too much for Clive. One cannot, however, believe that a matter of this sort would have caused his death, still less driven him to suicide. It is true that the petition, which was heard early in 1775, resulted in the unseating of Leighton; but it did not

harm his reputation, and he regained the seat at the next general election.

50. This is what Walpole told Lady Upper Ossory on November 23 (Walpole, Yale, Vol. 32) and what a lawyer named Pardoe reported from London to a friend in Shropshire on the 26th (*Transactions of Shropshire Archaeological Society*, Series IV, Volume V).
51. Thus, Coke, *op. cit.*, Vol. IV, pp. 447–8.
52. B.M. 29135, Sykes to Hastings, December 20, 1774.
53. Sir John Malcolm, *op. cit.*, Vol. III, p. 372.
54. *Spectator*, November 4, 1893, Account of Clive's Death by Sir Edward Strachey. Jane also 'remembered having seen Lord Clive, when at her house some days before, take up a penknife from the inkstand, feel its edge, and then lay it down again'. Clive could hardly have gone to the Stracheys' house 'some days' before his death, as he would then have been still at Bath. The incident may have happened, but not later than June 1774, unless of course it took place somewhere other than at the Stracheys' house. In any case, it need not necessarily have denoted suicidal tendencies. This memory of Jane's was probably the basis of a more elaborate and almost certainly apocryphal story recounted by the early Victorian biographer of Clive, G. R. Gleig (London 1848), of how, a short while before his death, 'a female friend' (presumably Jane herself) asked him to sharpen a pen for her, which he did, and then used the knife to destroy himself. Jane was heavily pregnant at the time of Clive's death; the child was born with a red mark on his forehead which she attributed to having seen Clive covered with blood just before his birth.
55. Coke, *op. cit.*, Vol. IV, pp. 447–8.
56. Clive MS. 69.
57. Arnold-Forster MSS, Margaret to Nevill Maskelyne, May 28, 1775.
58. Fowke Collection, Vol. 21, Margaret to Mrs Casamajor, December 7, 1775.
59. *Loc. cit.*
60. Francis Collection, Vol. 47, Jane Strachey to Francis, December 13, 1775.
61. Clive Papers, 480, Margaret to her son, April 2, 1803.
62. The fact that he changed his name to Herbert on inheriting the estates is taken by one of Clive's biographers (R. J. Minney, *Clive of India*) as having been a sad slight on Clive's memory. But he had to take the name under the Will of his uncle; Clive would have been the first to appreciate the necessity for commemorating the name of so great a family as the Herberts of Powis who in their day were Marquesses and even Jacobite Dukes.
63. He took as his second title Viscount Clive.
64. Clive Papers, 1658.

Manuscript and Printed Primary Sources

Ananda Ranga Pillai. *Diary*. English translation, Madras, 1904–22.
Arnold-Forster MSS, in the possession of Nigel Arnold-Forster, Esq.
Arundell MSS, in the possession of John Arundell, Esq.
B.M. MSS in the British Museum (now known as the British Library), London; notably the Warren Hastings Collection.
Bengal Past and Present. Journal of the Calcutta Historical Society, in which the letters of Richard Barwell, and other documents, are printed.
Clive, Robert, Lord. Speech of March 30, 1772. (Printed.)
Clive MS.; Clive Papers. Clive Collection on loan to the National Library of Wales, Aberystwyth. (The numbers after 'Clive MS.' refer to a series of manuscript volumes; the numbers after 'Clive Papers' refer to a series of individual papers.)
Coke, Lady Mary. *Journal*. Edinburgh 1896.
Dalton, John. *Journal*. Manuscript version in the Howard-Vyse Papers on loan to the East Riding of Yorkshire County Record Office, Beverley, Yorkshire.
Debrett, John. *History, Debates and Proceedings of both Houses of Parliament*, London 1754–74.
Ducarel Papers in Gloucestershire Records Office (D 2091).
Egerton MSS, in the British Museum (now known as the British Library), London.
Fortescue, Hon. Sir John (editor). *Correspondence of King George III*. London 1927.
Fowke Collection, in the India Office Library, London.
Francis Collection, in the India Office Library, London.
Ghulam Husain Khan. *Seir Mutakherin*. Manuscript version in the India Office Library, London.
Grenville Papers. London 1852–3. *Additional Grenville Papers*, ed. John R. G. Tomlinson. Manchester 1962.
H.M.C. Reports of the Royal Commission on Historical Manuscripts; volume according to name.
Hill, S. C. (editor). *Bengal in 1756–7*. (Documents published in the Indian Records Series) London 1905.
Home Miscellaneous Series, in the India Office Library, London.

House of Commons, Select Committee of, 1772. First Report.
Johnstone Papers. The Pulteney (Johnstone) Papers in the Henry E. Huntington Library and Art Gallery, San Marino, California, U.S.A.
Kenyon MSS, in the possession of Lord Kenyon.
Latham, Jane. *Diary*. Manuscript in the possession of Lord Strachie.
Lawrence, Stringer. *Narrative*. Printed version in R. O. Cambridge, *Account of the War in India*, Dublin 1761, to which the page numbers refer. Occasional references to manuscript version in Palk Collection, Exeter City Library, which differs in some places from the above. There is another manuscript version in the British Museum (now known as the British Library), King's Library, No. 195.
Long, Rev. J. (editor) *Selections from Unpublished Records of Government for the years 1748 to 1767 inclusive*. Calcutta 1869.
National Maritime Museum. Letters of Admiral Sir George Pocock in the National Maritime Museum, Greenwich.
Ormathwaite Collection, on loan to the India Office Library, London.
Orme MSS; Orme India MSS. The two series of volumes of manuscripts that constitute the Orme Collection in the India Office Library, London.
P.R.O. MSS in the Public Record Office, London.
Pocock Papers, in Ames Library of South Asia, Minnesota, U.S.A.
Powis Collection, on loan to the India Office Library, London.
Powis MSS, Shrewsbury. Powis MSS on loan to the Shropshire County Archives, Shrewsbury.
Sulivan, Laurence, MSS, in the Bodleian Library, Oxford.
Sutton Court Collection, in the India Office Library, London.
Vansittart Papers. Letters of George Vansittart on loan to the Bodleian Library, Oxford.
Verelst MSS. Collection of manuscript letters from Clive to Harry Verelst in the India Office Library, London.
Walpole, Horace. *Letters*; Oxford Edition, ed. Mrs Paget Toynbee and Paget Toynbee, Oxford, 1903–8 and 1918–25; Yale Edition, ed. W. S. Lewis, London 1937– . *Last Journals*, ed. A. F. Steuart, London 1910.

EAST INDIA COMPANY RECORDS IN THE INDIA OFFICE RECORDS, LONDON

Fort St David. Consultations.
Madras. Public Proceedings; Dispatches to England; Letters to Fort St George; Country Correspondence; French Correspondence.

Bengal. Public Consultations; Select Committee Consultations; Letters from Bengal; Persian Correspondence.

East India House. Court Minutes; Dispatches to Bengal.

(*Note:* In the case of some of the above Records, there are printed versions in the India Office Records, and the originals are in India.)

Select Bibliography

ABDUL MAJED KHAN. *The Transition in Bengal.* Cambridge 1969.

BOLTS, WILLIAM. *Considerations on India Affairs.* London 1772.

CAMBRIDGE, R. O. *Account of the War in India.* Dublin 1761.

Cambridge History of India. Volume V, edited by Henry Dodwell. Cambridge, 1909.

CARRACCIOLI, CHARLES. *Life of Robert, Lord Clive.* London *c.* 1777.

CHATTERJI, NANDALAL. *Clive as an Administrator.* Allahabad 1955.

CLIVE, ROBERT, LORD. *Letter to the Proprietors of the East India Stock.* London 1764.

CULTRU, PROSPER. *Dupleix, ses plans politiques, sa disgrace.* Paris 1901.

CURZON OF KEDLESTON, GEORGE, MARQUESS. *British Government in India.* London 1925.

DAVIES, A. MERVYN. *Clive of Plassey.* London 1939.

DODWELL, HENRY. *Dupleix and Clive.* London 1920.

DODWELL, HENRY. *Nabobs of Madras.* London 1926.

DOW, ALEXANDER. *An Enquiry into the State of Bengal, with a Plan for restoring that Province to its former Prosperity and Splendour, a Prefix to the History of Hindostan.* London 1772.

EDWARDES, MICHAEL. *The Battle of Plassey.* London 1963.

FEILING, KEITH. *Warren Hastings.* London 1954.

FORDE, LIONEL. *Lord Clive's Right Hand Man.* A memoir of Colonel Francis Forde. London 1910.

FORREST, SIR GEORGE. *Life of Lord Clive.* London 1918.

GAEBELÉ, YVONNE ROBERT. *Créole et Grande Dame.* Pondicherry 1956.

GHOSE, N. N. *Memoirs of Maharaja Nubkissen.* Calcutta 1901.

GUPTA, BRIJEN K. *Siraj-ud-daula and the East India Company, 1756–1757.* Leiden 1966.

HALLWARD, N. L. *William Bolts.* Cambridge 1920.

IVES, EDWARD. *A Voyage from England to India in the Year 1754.* London 1773.

JOHNSTONE, JOHN. *A Letter to the Proprietors of East India Stock.* London 1766.

KARAM ALI. *Muzaffar-Namah.* (In *Bengal Nawabs,* publication of the Asiatic Society) Calcutta 1952.

MACAULAY, THOMAS BABINGTON, LORD. *Essay on Clive.* (First published January 1840.)

MALCOLM, SIR JOHN. *Life of Robert, Lord Clive.* London 1836.

MARTINEAU, ALFRED. *Dupleix*. Paris 1931.

MINNEY, R. J. *Clive of India*. London 1931.

NAMIER, SIR LEWIS and BROOKE, JOHN. *History of Parliament, House of Commons, 1754–1790*. London 1964.

ORME, ROBERT. *History of the Military Transactions of the British Nation in Indostan*. London 1763–78.

PANIKKAR, K. M. *Asia and Western Dominance*. London 1959.

RAM GOPAL. *How the British Occupied Bengal*. London 1963.

SCRAFTON, LUKE. *Reflections on the Government of Indostan*. London 1763.

SINHA, N. K. *Economic History of Bengal*. Calcutta 1956.

SPEAR, PERCIVAL. *The Nabobs*. London 1932.

STRACHEY, HENRY. *Narrative of the Mutiny of the Officers*. London 1773.

SUTHERLAND, LUCY S. *East India Company in Eighteenth Century Politics*. Oxford 1952.

THOMPSON, VIRGINIA. *Dupleix*. New York 1933.

VANSITTART, HENRY. *Narrative of the Transactions in Bengal from 1760 to 1764*. London 1766.

VERELST, HARRY. *A View of the Rise, Progress and Present State of the English Company in Bengal*. London 1772.

WATTS, WILLIAM. *Memoirs of the Revolution in Bengal*. London 1764.

WOODRUFF, PHILIP (Philip Mason). *The Men Who Ruled India. Volume I, The Founders*. London 1953.

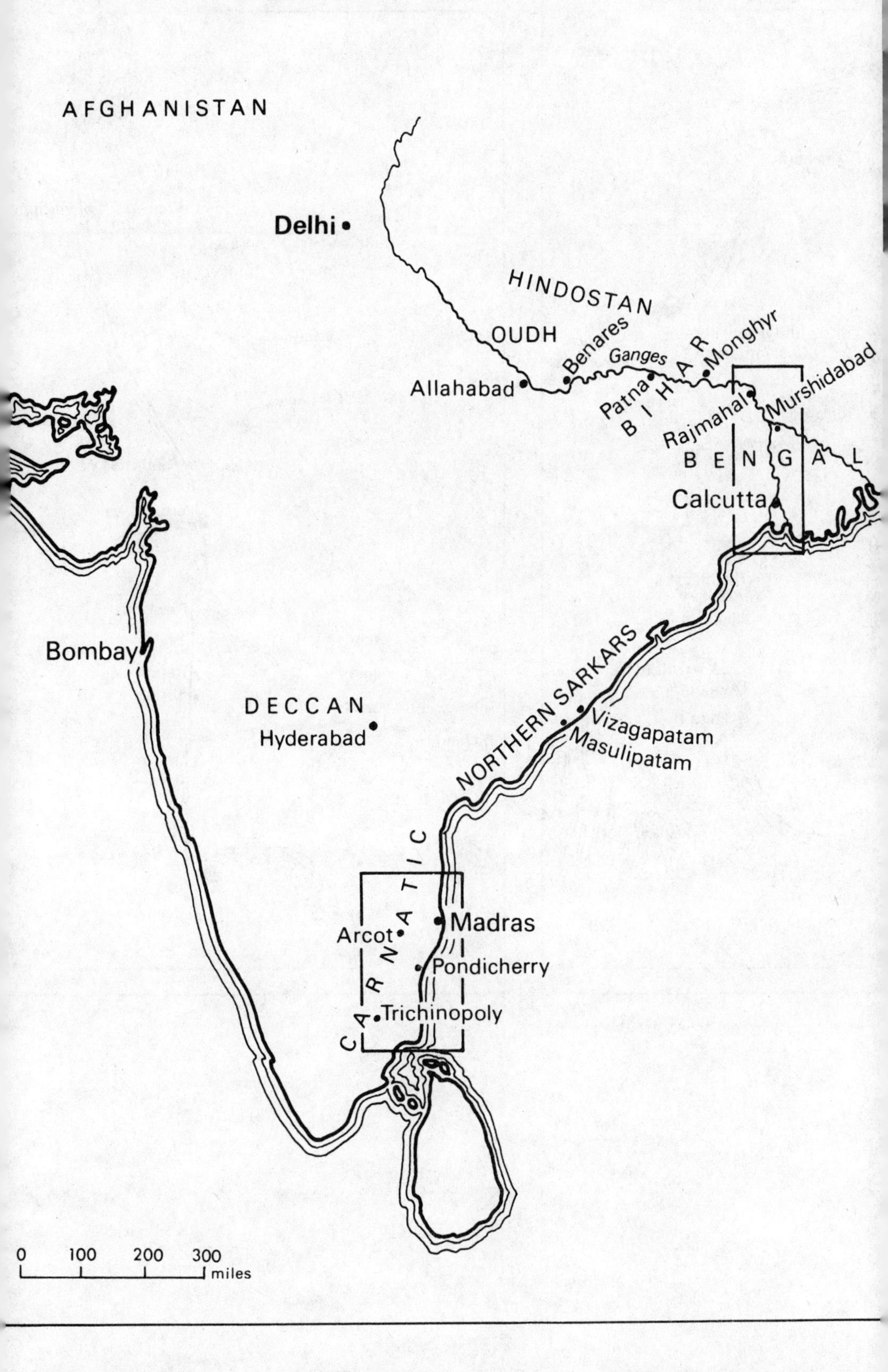
AFGHANISTAN
Delhi
HINDOSTAN
OUDH
Benares
Ganges
Allahabad
Patna
B I H A R
Monghyr
Rajmahal
Murshidabad
B E N G A L
Calcutta
Bombay
DECCAN
Hyderabad
NORTHERN SARKARS
Vizagapatam
Masulipatam
C A R N A T I C
Madras
Arcot
Pondicherry
Trichinopoly
0
100
200
300
miles

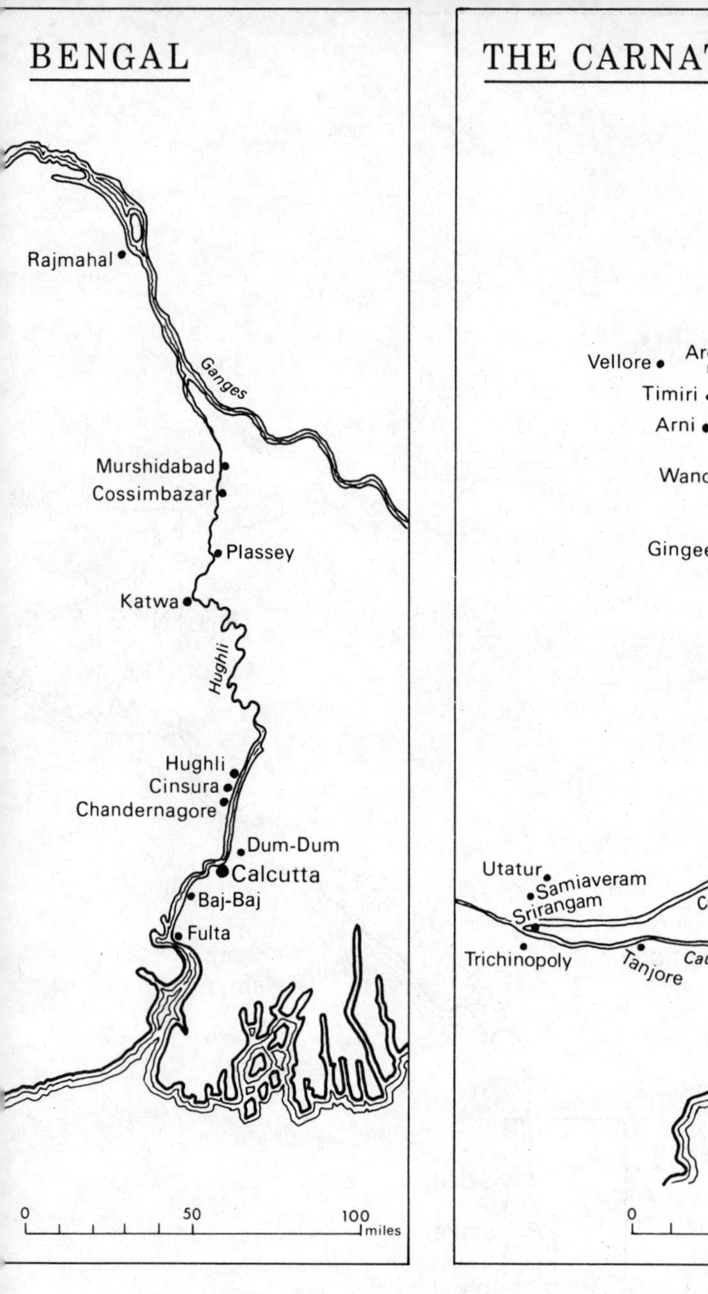
BENGAL
Rajmahal
Ganges
Murshidabad
Cossimbazar
Plassey
Katwa
Hughli
Hughli
Cinsura
Chandernagore
Dum-Dum
Calcutta
Baj-Baj
Fulta
0
50
100
miles

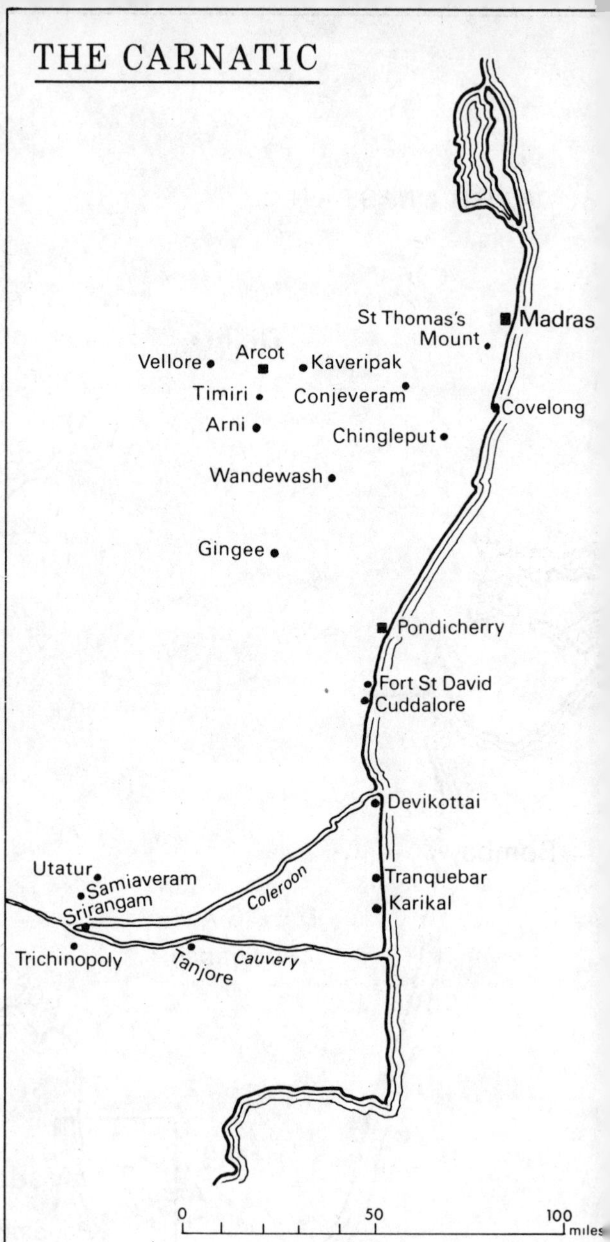
THE CARNATIC
St Thomas's Mount
Madras
Vellore
Arcot
Kaveripak
Timiri
Conjeveram
Covelong
Arni
Chingleput
Wandewash
Gingee
Pondicherry
Fort St David
Cuddalore
Devikottai
Utatur
Samiaveram
Srirangam
Coleroon
Tranquebar
Karikal
Trichinopoly
Tanjore
Cauvery
0
50
100
miles

Index